...nesseth That William Edward Jones by and with the consent of his Father William Jones of Carmarthen in the County of Carmarthen Gentleman Doth put himself ...nd County of Bristol Surgeon and Apothecary to learn his Art and with him after the ...nto the full end and term of Five years from thence next ensuing to be fully complete... shall serve his secrets keep his lawful commands everywhere gladly do he shall do no... ...ll tell or forthwith give warning to his said Master of the same he shall not waste ...not play at cards or dice tables or any other unlawful games whereby his said Master ...without license of his said Master he shall neither buy nor sell he shall not haunt ...nlawfully but in all things as a faithful Apprentice he shall behave himself towards his ...plain in consideration of the faithful services of the said Apprentice his said Apprentice ...that he can shall teach and instruct or cause to be taught and instructed sufficient... ...g found and provided for the said Apprentice by the said Apprentice or his said ...nts and agreements either of the said parties bindeth himself unto the other by these ...ntures interchangeably have put their hands and seals the Twenty fifth day of ...dy Victoria by the Grace of God of the United Kingdom of Great Britain and Ireland Queen ...ndred and Eighty Eight

William Edward Jones

William Jones

Harry ....

A History of the Society of Apothecaries

The Society's armorial bearings feature Apollo, the sun god and god of healing, overpowering the dragon of disease. The unicorn supporters refer to the ancient belief in the healing power of the unicorn's horn, and echo the unicorns introduced into the royal arms by King James I, who granted the Society its charter in 1617. The crest is a rhinoceros, whose powdered horn was believed to have medical properties. The motto, *opiferque per orbem dicor*, from Ovid's *Metamorphoses* translates "I am called throughout the world the bringer of aid".

A History of the Society of Apothecaries

Penelope Hunting

1998

© The Society of Apothecaries,
Apothecaries' Hall
Black Friars Lane
London EC4V 6EJ

All rights reserved. No part of this publication
may be reproduced, stored in a retrieval system, or
transmitted in any form or by any means, electronic,
mechanical, photocopying, recording or otherwise
without the prior permission of the publisher
in writing.

ISBN 0 9504 9874 2

Endpapers: Indenture of William Edward
Jones who with the consent of his father,
a gentleman of Carmarthen, was apprenticed
to Henry Desplan, a surgeon and apothecary
of Bristol, for five years from 25 June 1858.

Filmset in Garamond
and printed in England by
BAS Printers Limited
Over Wallop, Hants

List of illustrations

Frontispiece: the Society's armorial bearings	page 2
Roman glass phial	12
Roman oculist's stamp	13
Roman mortar	14
Sopers Lane and Bucklersbury in the mid-sixteenth century	16
King Henry VIII, his Physicians and Royal Apothecary, 1540	19
Portrait of King James I, 1676	28
Joliffe Lownes's account, 1622	31
Letters Patent granted by King James I, 1617	33
Letters Patent of arms, 1617	36
Gideon de Laune's mortar, 1625	37
The Court Minutes, 1617	39
Portrait of John Parkinson, 1629	42
Portrait of Gideon de Laune, 1640	44
Advertisement for de Laune's pills, *circa* 1680	46
A seventeenth-century apothecary's shop	48
Warrant of appointment of John Chase, Royal Apothecary, 1666	53
Apothecary's drug jar, 1647	56
John Battersby's pestle and mortar, 1662	64
William Boghurst's manuscript on the plague, 1666	65
James Gover's drug jars	66
Apothecaries' Hall and Black Friars, 1676	68
John Smithies' pill tile, 1686	71
William of Orange at Exeter, 1688	72/73
Plan of Black Friars, *circa* 1538	74
Map view of Black Friars *circa* 1553–59	78
Plan of the east side of Apothecaries' Hall, *circa* 1740	87
Ground plan, Apothecaries' Hall, 1771	88
Ward map, 1720	89
The Society's property at Chatham Place, 1799	91
Chatham Place, 1838	92
Elevations for new houses, Water Lane, 1782	94/95
Apothecaries' Hall, 1787	96
Courtyard, Apothecaries' Hall, 1814	98
Ground plan, Apothecaries' Hall, *circa* 1874	100
Ground plan, Apothecaries' Hall, *circa* 1911–16	103
Apothecaries' Hall, 1947	106/107
A burial in the Dominican church	109
Redevelopment of Apothecaries' Hall, 1981	110
West elevation, Apothecaries' Hall, 1985	111
The Society's ceremonial barge, 1732	112
Plaque from the Society's barge, 1691	112
The barge-houses, Chelsea Physic Garden *circa* 1859	117
Map marking the Apothecaries' Garden, Chelsea, 1664–1717	121
Isaac Rand F.R.S., 1732	127

Contents

List of illustrations	6
Acknowledgements	8
Foreword	9
Chapter 1. The emergence of the apothecary	11
Pepperers, spicers and apothecaries	14
Apothecaries to Court and convent	18
Apothecaries and Grocers	22
The physician's cook	24
Chapter 2. The seventeenth-century Society	29
An organized Society	36
Apothecaries versus Physicians	47
Chapter 3. War, plague, fire and surrender	57
Civil war	57
The Great Plague	62
The Great Fire	67
The surrender of the charter	69
Chapter 4. Apothecaries' Hall	75
The Hall rebuilt 1668–70	83
Late-eighteenth-century developments	88
Acquisitions and survival	97
Redevelopment in the 1980s	105
Chapter 5. The barges and the Physic Garden	113
The ceremonial barges	113
Establishing the Physic Garden	116
Sloane and Miller	125
Gardeners, patrons and Demonstrators	135
The Garden as a charity	148
Chapter 6. The trade	153
The Elaboratory	154
The Operators	160
The Laboratory Stock and the Navy Stock	164
From Black Friars to Bombay	173
The expansion of trade	174
Medicines to America and Australia	177
The United Stock	183
Decline and closure	187
Chapter 7. The age of reform	193
The Apothecaries' Act 1815	196
Examinations and examiners	198
Unlicensed practitioners	216
Towards reform	220
Chapter 8. The twentieth century	227
Dispeners of medicines	229
Diplomas	235
The Faculty	241
Charity	245
Prizes and awards	248
The Society, the profession, the City	254
Abbreviations and Notes	263
Sources and Bibliography	297
List of Masters of the Society 1617–1998	301
Index	306

Plans for new greenhouse, Chelsea Physic Garden, 1732	128
The greenhouse and improvements, Chelsea Physic Garden, 1732	129
Samuel Dale, *circa* 1730	131
Survey of the Physic Garden, 1751	133
Plan of Chelsea Physic Garden, 1772	137
William Curtis memorial window	139
Thomas Wheeler F.L.S., *circa* 1790	140
Admission ticket to the Physic Garden	141
N. Bagshaw Ward F.R.S., F.L.S., 1867	143
Looking south, Chelsea Physic Garden, *circa* 1845	144
Survey of the Physic Garden, 1871	147
Statue of Sir Hans Sloane, Chelsea Physic Garden, 1895	149
Nineteenth-century medicine chest from Apothecaries' Hall	152
Late-seventeenth-century laboratory equipment	155
Ambrose Godfrey Hanckwitz F.R.S., 1718	162
Hanckwitz's laboratory, Covent Garden, *circa* 1728	164/165
Seal or trade mark of the Navy Stock	169
Chemical glassware used in the laboratory	175
Drawings of the laboratory equipment	177–179
Ground plan of the manufactory at the Hall, 1823	185
Drug manufacturing at the Hall, 1915	188
Trade premises at the Hall, 1922	189
The retail shop, Apothecaries' Hall *circa* 1920	191
View over the Great Laboratory, *circa* 1920	192
"The Quack Doctor", 1814	194
Friendly Medical Society invitation, 1800	195
L.S.A. certificate, 1822	199
Portrait of George Man Burrows, 1851	201
Portrait of John Keats, *circa* 1816	203
John Keats's examination entry, 1816	204
Portrait of Elizabeth Garrett, 1870	208
L.S.A. examination paper, 1865	209
Scientific conversazione, Apothecaries' Hall, 1855	212
Court of Examiners, 1880	213
West elevation of Apothecaries' Hall, 1855	219
Court of Assistants, 1899–1900	226
Sir Thomas Boor Crosby, Lord Mayor 1911–12	228
The Society's fire brigade, 1913	232
Entrance to Apothecaries' Hall, 1998	236
The courtyard, Apothecaries' Hall, 1998	237
Dr W. S. C. Copeman, *circa* 1960	242
Bookplate for prize	249
The Galen medal	250/251
Honorary freedom certificate of Sir Ronald Ross, 1915	253
The entrance hall and staircase, Apothecaries' Hall, 1998	257
The Great Hall, 1998	258
Portrait of Alderman Sir John Chalstrey, 1996	261
Lord Mayor's Day procession, 1995	262

Acknowledgements

I am grateful to the members, officers and staff of the Society of Apothecaries for the help, hospitality and kindness extended to me. I would particularly like to thank Dr Paul Knapman, the Clerk Lt Colonel R. Stringer, the Bedel Mr Dai Walters, the Registrar Lt Commander A.M. Wallington-Smith and the Archivist Ms Dee Cook, who faced a daunting task as more and more material came to light at Apothecaries' Hall.

Dennis Barrie, Major J.C. O'Leary, Colonel K.W. Nicholls Palmer, and Ruth Stungo, historical researcher at Chelsea Physic Garden, were generous with their time in discussing various subjects. Robin Price, until recently Deputy Librarian of the Wellcome Institute for the History of Medicine Library and Honorary Secretary of the Faculty, arranged for access to the Library and gave an interview. Dr Ellen Jordan allowed copies to be made from her research, and Geoff Miller corresponded from Australia. J. Sampson Lloyd of Lloyd Leroy Architects and R.P.J. Jackson, Curator of Prehistoric and Romano-British Antiquities at the British Museum, gave advice. Bruce Watson of the Museum of London Archaeology Service contributed passages on archaeological discoveries to Chapter 4. Professor Michael Biddiss, Dr J. Fisher, Major J.C. O'Leary, Alan Robson, the Clerk, the Registrar and the Archivist read the text and offered suggestions and corrections, and the Index was compiled by J.D. Lee.

The staff of Guildhall Library and the Wellcome Institute for the History of Medicine Library were always helpful and sympathetic, for which I thank them.

The majority of the illustrations are reproduced by permission of the Society of Apothecaries, new photography is by Geremy Butler.

The remainder are reproduced by permission of the following: pages 12, 219 copyright The British Museum; pages 112 top, 129, 133, 137 Chelsea Physic Garden; pages 106, 107 Country Life Picture Library; pages 16, 39, 68, 78, 89, 91, 92 Guildhall Library, Corporation of London; page 13 copyright the Museum of London; pages 74 and 109 were provided by the Museum of London Archaeology Service, the plan on page 74 was drawn by Jane Sandoe using material supplied by Farebrother (chartered surveyors), page 109 photography by Maggie Cox; pages 56, 194 Museum of the Royal Pharmaceutical Society; page 162 by courtesy of the National Portrait Gallery, London; page 117 Royal Borough of Kensington and Chelsea Libraries and Arts Service; page 208 Royal College of Surgeons of England; pages 110, 111 J. Sampson Lloyd; page 14 Science Museum London/Science & Society Picture Library; page 203 V & A Picture Library; pages 37, 46, 48, 155 Wellcome Institute Library, London; pages 164, 165 Westminster City Archives; page 19 by kind permission of the Worshipful Company of Barbers.

Penelope Hunting 1998

Foreword

This history supersedes three previous publications. The first, C.R.B. Barrett's tome of 1905, begins in 1617, ends in 1864 and is no longer available. The second, *A History of the Worshipful Society of Apothecaries of London* volume i, originated with the Society's archivist, Dr Cecil Wall, was edited after his death by Dr H.C. Cameron, then revised and annotated after the death of Cameron by Dr E.A. Underwood and was published in 1963. It is limited to the years 1617 to 1815 and only a few copies are to be found. A second volume was planned but was unfinished at the time of Dr Underwood's death in 1980. A third, brief history of the Society from 1617 to 1967 was written by Dr W.S.C. Copeman to commemorate the 350th anniversary of the grant of the royal charter by King James I.

This work stretches further back in time than the previous histories, to the roots of the Society among the pepperers, spicers and apothecaries of medieval London and it extends to the mayoralty of Sir John Chalstrey at the end of the twentieth century. It examines evidence for the existence of the mistery of apothecaries in 1328, the position of apothecaries within the Grocers' Company and those who were influential in securing the royal charter of 1617. The book follows a broadly chronological sequence, although Chapters 4, 5 and 6 pursue their subjects – Apothecaries' Hall, the Chelsea Physic Garden and the trading activities of the stock companies – through three centuries. Plague, war, fire, conflict with the College of Physicians, medical reform and education are among the subjects explored in a comprehensive history of the Society of Apothecaries of London from the thirteenth to the twentieth centuries.

Michael Pugh
Master 1997–98.

Chapter 1

The emergence of the apothecary

The apothecary of the medieval City of London kept a store of spices, herbs and drugs which he compounded, dispensed and sold from his shop or stall. His shop was probably in the Spicery of Westcheap from whence he supplied wealthy households – perhaps even the king's Court or the monks of Westminster – and the local community. Initially described as a spicer, the apothecary came to be known as such towards the end of the thirteenth century; in modern terms the medieval spicer-apothecary was a pharmacist.

The skill of the apothecary originated in the preparation of substances used in the treatment of disease and injury. In earliest recorded history this function was usually carried out by a physician, priest or magician. Ancient Egyptians used a large number of drugs and expected the physician to prepare medicines. There was no equivalent to the pharmacist or apothecary at that time, although the activities of Pa-hery-pedjet during the reign of Ramses II (1279–1213 B.C.) might qualify him for the title of the first recorded pharmacist.[1]

The Ancient Egyptian contribution to the early development of medicine was in due course superseded by the critical approach of the Greeks, and the influence of Hippocrates, Aristotle and Galen endures. In the first century A.D. the physician Dioscorides compiled *De Materia Medica*, a compendium of some 600 remedies which was still a standard work of reference for the apothecaries of sixteenth-century London. Likewise, the work of Celsus and Galen influenced physicians and apothecaries for many centuries.

Roman medicine was dominated by Greeks and the Greek tradition, and Roman medical texts continued to recommend that the physician should be responsible for pharmaceutical remedies, their storage and preparation. There was still no equivalent to the medieval apothecary-pharmacist – the druggists, spice-dealers and ointment-sellers of the Roman market place were infamous and the wise physician obtained his raw materials directly.

The Roman invasion of Britain in 43 A.D. brought the military physician Scribonius Largus to Londinium, along with his book of prescriptions, some of which required imported drugs. The medicines used by Roman Londoners have perished but containers and equipment used in their preparation have survived – glass phials, flasks, probes, scoops and ointment pots have been discovered during archaeological excavations in the City. A Roman version of the vessel traditionally associated with the apothecary, the mortar, was found at Cheapside and is illustrated on page 14. A stone pallet used by Romans to prepare medicaments, a bronze weighing balance, and the stamps with which Roman oculists engraved their names and preparations onto cakes or sticks of eye ointment can be seen at the British Museum and the Museum of London.

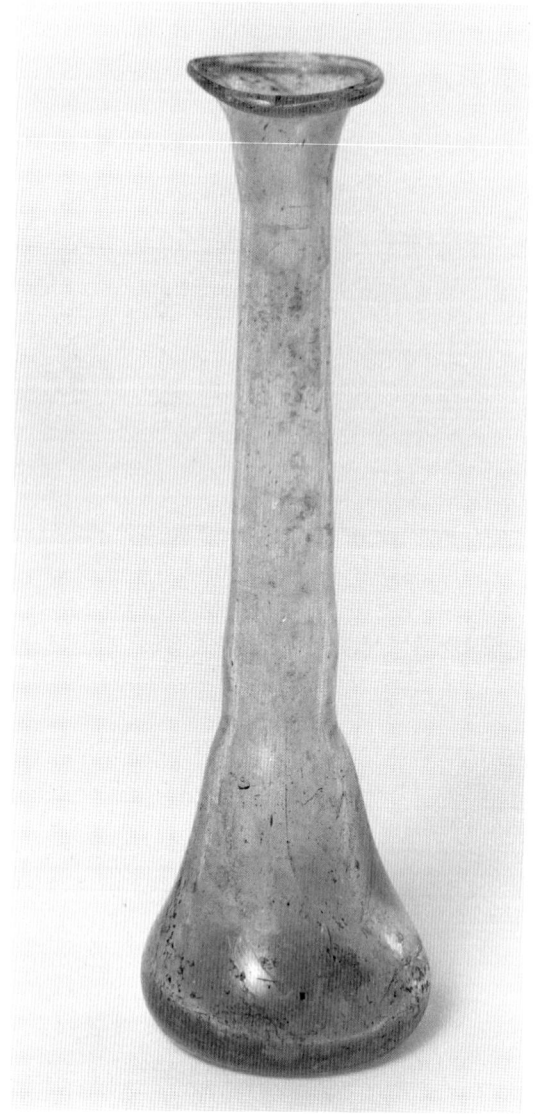

Height 10 cms.

A Roman glass phial or *unguentarium* of the 1st to 3rd century A.D., used for unguents, cosmetics or medicaments, which could be scooped out with a slender probe. This example was found in the Fleet Ditch, near Apothecaries' Hall, by a Liveryman of the Society, John Conyers. Conyers owned a shop in Fleet Street where he practised throughout the Great Plague of 1665. Apothecary, author, inventor and archaeologist, Conyers probably discovered the Roman phial during the transformation of the Fleet Ditch into the New Canal under the direction of Wren (1670–74).

Following the official Roman withdrawal from Londinium in 410 A.D. the epitaph Dark Ages, not accurate in all spheres, can justly be applied to medicine and certainly to the lack of archaeological or documentary evidence relating to pharmacy and apothecaries. From what can be gleaned it appears

A Roman oculist's stamp of the 2nd or 3rd century A.D., excavated in the City. The lettering on the stamp gives the name of the oculist or *pharmacopolus*, Caius Silvius Tetricus, and the names of the preparations he supplied, which were stamped onto them.

that the Anglo-Saxons relied on plant lore, folk medicine and remedies derived from indigenous herbs, plants and animals which were prescribed and prepared by the medicus or leech (from the Anglo-Saxon word *laece* to heal). The rare medical manuscripts that survive from this period show the continuing influence of classical texts, combined with a reliance on herbal preparations and superstitious beliefs.

By the eleventh century Arabic works relating to medicine and pharmacy were becoming accessible, and some of the monks who came to this country with the Norman kings had trained at the medical school of Salerno where the *Antidotarium Nicolai* originated, a collection of prescriptions deriving largely from Arabic sources that remained in use for several centuries. England's first notable medical writer was Gilbertus Anglicus who probably trained at Salerno – his compendium of *circa* 1240 contained medicinal recipes based on the contemporary belief that all diseases were either hot, cold, moist or dry.

Some important Greek medical texts survived in Arabia and with the spread of medical and pharmaceutical knowledge from the Arab world through Spain and Sicily to Salerno, Montpellier and thence to northern Europe, came the development of the trade in spicery from Asia and Africa to the Mediterranean and London. The Crusades (1096–1272), followed by a series of French queens of England with their relatives and retinues, and the expeditions to France by the Norman, Angevin and Plantagenet kings had

A Roman mortar *circa* 1st century A.D. This earthenware mortar, with a rim and pouring spout, was found in Cheapside.

the effect of stimulating imports of sugar, spices and drugs from which the pepperers, spicers and apothecaries were to profit. Thus in thirteenth-century London the flourishing trade in spicery went hand-in-hand with the development of pharmacy and the emergence of the spicer-apothecary.

Pepperers, spicers and apothecaries

The Grocers and Apothecaries of London evolved from an association of Pepperers called the *Gilda Piperariorum* in the Pipe Roll of 1180. The Grocers' Company and the Society of Apothecaries celebrated the octocentenary of the Pepperers' Guild in 1980, yet the existence of this guild was brief and fleeting – it surfaced from and returned to obscurity in 1180, having been fined for associating without royal licence. The amount of the fine imposed upon the Pepperers was 16 marks and by comparison with the eighteen other guilds fined contemporaneously this was a large amount, suggesting that the Pepperers were either wealthier, more powerful or more contentious than the Clothworkers' or Butchers' Guilds which were fined only 1 mark.[2]

The late-twelfth-century *Gilda Piperariorum* disappeared from record but individual pepperers, spicers and apothecaries were active in thirteenth-century London. In 1316 pepperers of Sopers Lane drew up ordinances aimed at eliminating fraud in their trade which was chiefly concerned with the import, weighing and distribution of spices such as pepper, ginger, cloves, saffron, alum, wax, sugar, dyes and dried fruit. The association of those dealing in pepper advanced further in 1345 when the Pepperers of Sopers Lane founded a religious fraternity to the honour of God, the Virgin Mary, St Anthony and

All Saints. Twenty-two founder members met on St Anthony's day (9 May) and in little more than a month agreed on regulations for the government of the Fraternity of St Anthony. Fees, social occasions and religious rites were all itemized in ordinances defining an impressive organization. Among the founder members stood one spicer-apothecary – Vivian Roger or Rogeroni, from Lucca.

The Pepperers made it clear in their ordinances that ropers and spicers were eligible to join the Fraternity provided they were men of good condition. Ropers (retailers of imports such as wax, dyes, iron and tin), spicers (this group included spicer-apothecaries) and pepperers were accustomed to co-operating in matters of mutual concern such as choosing brokers, electing the Weigher of the City's Great Beam and appointing representatives to the Court of Common Council (1351), so it was to be expected that they might also associate in a religious fraternity.

The spicer-apothecaries were at first reluctant to join the Fraternity of St Anthony, dominated as it was by Pepperers. However, following Rogeroni's example some apothecaries became members – notably Adam de Carlisle (later an Alderman), Thomas de Walden (apothecary to the Abbot and convent of Westminster and a City Chamberlain) and John de Bovingdon, a property-owner of Honey Lane and Cheapside. In 1373 one of the Wardens of the Fraternity was a spicer-apothecary, John Maryns, and there were by then another half-dozen apothecaries among the membership of 124.[3] At this time Pepperers were known as Grocers and their Fraternity had evolved into the Grocers' Company, a powerful trading organization whose members' interests lay in the wool and wine trades and the import and export of a wide variety of heavy goods – it was from the weighing of heavy goods by the *peso grosso* or hundredweight of 112 pounds that they took the name grosser or grocer.

The spicer-apothecaries, meanwhile, had retained a measure of independence. As yet described as spicers, their service to king and Court has been traced from the early thirteenth century. The names of the apothecaries who attended the monks at Westminster from 1350 to 1540 are known, while the City records reveal scattered information about spicer-apothecaries who lived, worked and died in mid-thirteenth-century London.[4] Details can be found relating to their property, families, official appointments, even their quarrels, and there is good evidence that the apothecaries of the City constituted a mistery or craft guild in 1328 (see page 17).

For convenience and to implement fair trading, those who followed the same occupation congregated in the same neighbourhood or quarter of the medieval City. Hence pepperers inhabited Sopers Lane, described as a new street in the early thirteenth century, and since replaced by the north end of Queen Street.[5] The canvas dealers, corders and ropers were to be found in the Ropery (part of Thames Street near All Hallows church), while the spicers and

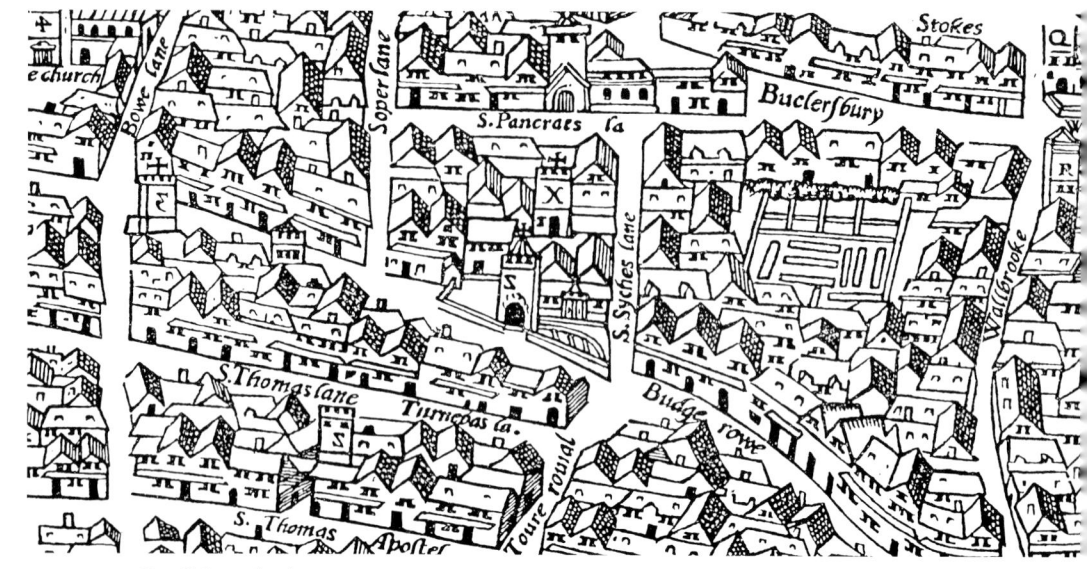

Detail from the Agas map view of London in the 1550s showing Sopers Lane where pepperers congregated in the fourteenth century, and Bucklersbury, a street dominated by spicers and apothecaries.

spicer-apothecaries had their shops and stalls in the Spicery of Westcheap, the main market place of medieval London (Cheapside). Spicers, apothecaries and grocers also favoured Bucklersbury, a street they were to dominate by the close of the sixteenth century.

Records relating to the royal household reveal the names of the spicers who supplied the king in the first half of the thirteenth century: the king's spicer in 1207 was known as William; Joseph the Spicer of London supplied the king's physician in 1236, Richard Derkyn was the king's spicer in 1238, and Bartholomew Spicer owned a house in Bread Street near the Spicery of Cheapside in 1249.[6] The picture fills out with the grant to Robert de Montpellier of "the seld with shops in the Chepe of London"[7] – the City's first pharmacy (1246). As spicer-apothecary to King Henry III, Robert de Montpellier supplied spiced wine, electuaries (powdered spices mixed with syrup or sugar), spices, medicines and confections to the Court. Montpellier's will of 1279 confirms that his principal shop was in the Spicery of Westcheap, while he lived nearby in Milk Street.

Two of Robert de Montpellier's sons, Richard and Henry, followed the same path as their father, probably by apprenticeship to him, and they are described in the records as ypothecaries or apothecaries. The word apothecary, deriving from *apotheca* meaning the place where wine, spices and herbs were stored, came into use in this country during the thirteenth century and was applied to the Montpelliers and their fellow-apothecaries Nicholas Russel and Hugh de Freningham. As his name indicates, Robert de Montpellier came from the prosperous Mediterranean town renowned for its medical school and as a centre of the spice trade. De Montpellier first attended King Henry III in Bordeaux in 1243 and his family were among the spicers, pepperers and apothecaries to benefit from the expansion of London's trade and economy – the last decades of the thirteenth century saw an increase in the number of recorded pepperers and spicers of London from twenty-three in the 1270s to fifty-four in the 1290s.[8]

With the increasing imports of spices and drugs came the regulation and supervision of the trade. Before the end of the thirteenth century four trusted apothecaries were elected and sworn in before the Mayor as brokers. They were responsible for bringing together the buyers and sellers of spices and ensuring that regulations were observed. Among these apothecary-brokers was Silvester de Farnham who in 1294 was appointed Weigher of the Great Beam – a prestigious office controlled by the Grocers from 1365 (apothecaries also used the Small Beam, as did the Mercers under whose control it came).

One wealthy apothecary, John de Selling, was elected to represent the City in Parliament in 1312, likewise Thomas de Walden, a Member of Parliament in 1346 and later City Chamberlain. The number of fourteenth-century apothecary Aldermen might be put at five, and three apothecaries occupied the post of City Chamberlain (the chief financial officer), given that the same man can be described variously as spicer, grocer or apothecary.[9] Apothecaries were thus taking part in the commercial and political life of the fourteenth-century City, although their contribution pales beside the succession of Pepperers and Grocers in positions of power – in 1383 over half the total number of Aldermen of the City were members of the Grocers' Company.

Before the Grocers' Company became recognized as such (*circa* 1373) and prior to the foundation of the Fraternity of St Anthony in 1345, there is reference to Apothecaries as a mistery or craft in 1328. This was at a time of recession and disorder in London. King Edward III had been crowned the previous year, aged fourteen, and his mother's favourite had taken it upon himself to remove the Court of the King's Bench and the Exchequer to York. As political factions jostled for power in the capital, the Mayor endeavoured to stabilize the situation by calling upon men from twenty-five misteries, who were elected by the others of their craft, to govern and instruct the same. Thus the Fishmongers were to be supervised by twenty-one men of that mistery, the Goldsmiths by eight, the Grocers chose two of their number, and the Apothecaries elected seven men of their mistery: John de Essex, Thomas de Walden, Thomas de Maryns, William Gras, William de Hodesdone, David de Tillebery, and John atte Pole.[10] It therefore appears that the mistery of Apothecaries existed in 1328 when it was sufficiently organized to elect leaders and its status was acknowledged by the Mayor. Apothecaries are referred to again in 1365, apparently amalgamated within the mistery of Pepperers of

Sopers Lane. On this occasion twelve surveyors were elected in a move towards closer supervision of the spicery trade in the face of competition from Italian spice merchants.

Curiously, a mayoral order of 1370 gives instructions to the Apothecaries to act jointly with the Mercers, with no reference to the Pepperers or Grocers. In response to a rumour that London was in danger of invasion by a multitude of armed men sighted in ships off North Foreland, the Mayor ordered that men of seventeen trades must keep a night watch. The Apothecaries and Mercers joined forces to provide forty men-at-arms and sixty archers to watch and guard the City every Wednesday night until the alarm subsided.[11]

Apothecaries to Court and convent
Spices, drugs, sugar and other luxuries of the thirteenth-century apothecaries' shops were much in demand at Court. Trade with France through Montpellier, Bordeaux and Gascony brought an increasing supply of these luxury goods to the London market and when overland trade routes were interrupted by war, improvements in shipping allowed goods to be imported directly from Italy. Accounts (bills) surviving from the reign of King John detail the commodities supplied by the king's spicer: medicines, plasters, ointments, spiced wine for festivals, sweetmeats, perfumes and cosmetics.[12] To a lesser extent other wealthy households generated a similar demand; by 1315 over fifty spices were in common use and the following century saw a 155 per cent rise in imports of spicery. The spicer also supplied imported sugar in various forms, drugs such as camphor, rhubarb, senna, tournesol (from the sunflower), mirobolains (berries from India), mastic and aloes, perfumed waters, conserves, plasters and applications, oils and electuaries, honey, comfits, also wax and nuts if required.[13]

The king's spicer-apothecary was distinct from the royal physician who diagnosed the problem and prescribed the remedies. The spicer-apothecary to the medieval Court was essentially a pharmacist responsible for supplying and preparing drugs, spices, confectionery and spiced wines. He might also be required to provide medicines and wax for the king's army, he might double as a ship-owner and importer of wine, or prepare gunpowder at the Tower of London.[14] The king's apothecary could expect gifts and perquisites in addition to a salary and profits from the items he supplied – a suit of clothes, food, drink and lodging, trading privileges, even a grant of property might be forthcoming. If the king or queen was ill the Royal Apothecary stood to gain substantial sums – King Edward I's malaise during a few weeks of 1306 elicited a bill for £159 11s 10d from his apothecary for over 2,196 pounds of electuaries, among other items. Edward IV's apothecary assumed some medical duties when the surgeon or barber was absent and was obliged to fumigate the king's clothes and sheets; at this time the "yeoman potycary" ranked below the surgeon and above the barber in the king's household. He was soon to be dignified with the title of Serjeant Confectioner, hinting at the popularity of sweets and confections among members of the royal household.

William Burton, apothecary to Kings Henry IV and V, was a Master Warden of the Grocers' Company and was twice elected M.P. for the City (in 1414 and 1421). He owned a shop in London, two in Cambridge, traded in wool, and his will of 1438 left his chattels and large mortar to his son John. Richard Hakedy, apothecary to Henry VI, was also a Warden of the Company and joint Garbeller of Spices (the Garbeller ensured that goods were not weighed or sold before being inspected for quality); his will of 1456 testified to his wealth. A successor, John Grice, apothecary to Henry VII and Elizabeth of York, was granted no less than seven City properties by a grateful monarch.[15]

King Henry VIII took an interest in pharmacy and several prescriptions are attributed to him personally.[16] He appointed a succession of apothecaries, amongst them Thomas Alsop who is shown in the painting below. It fell to Alsop to supply and prepare the remedies required by the portly king at the end of his life when his corpulence, fever, varicose ulcerations, piles, dropsy and ill-temper were treated with plasters, pills, lozenges, a continuous supply of *manus Christi* (translated literally as the hand of Christ, this was a cordial of sugar boiled with rose-water, violets or cinnamon and was prescribed for general weakness), injectives, waters, gargles and perfumes. Alsop also provided

Thomas Alsop, Royal Apothecary to King Henry VIII, Edward VI and Queen Mary, is shown on the far left in the group portrait of Henry VIII and the Barber-Surgeons, painted by Hans Holbein in 1540.

medicines for the king's hounds, rhubarb pills for the hawks, more delicate medicaments for the women of the household and urinals for the Councillors. Described as "gentleman poticary", Alsop lived at the sign of The Angel in Bucklersbury, and he and his fellow-apothecary Patrick Reynold were rewarded with 100 marks each, left to them in the king's will.[17]

By the Tudor period the position of Royal Apothecary was one of the most sought after in the kingdom, endowing the holder with wealth and influence. One of Queen Elizabeth I's apothecaries, Hugh Morgan, was distinguished by the special title of Pharmocopolus to Her Majesty. He was a respected member of the Grocers' Company prior to his royal appointment, being entrusted with the inspection of apothecaries' wares and the auditing of accounts; he was a Warden in 1574 but requested to be excused the Master Wardenship in 1584 on account of his recent royal appointment.[18] The careers of the Royal Apothecaries from 1200 to 1952 have been traced, as members first of the Grocers' Company and after 1617 as leading figures of the Society of Apothecaries, and from 1687 the Royal Apothecary was given a place of honour at meetings of the Court of Assistants. The monarch continues to appoint an apothecary and the present Royal Apothecary, Dr Jonathan Holliday, is a Liveryman of the Society.

Like the royal household, large ecclesiastical households were served by spicer-apothecaries. The Archbishop of Canterbury's household was supplied by Roger the Spicer in the 1140s, and when the Bishop of Exeter died in 1307 large quantities of almonds, rice, wax, sugar, pepper, cloves, liquorice, mace and saffron (the most expensive spice) were found in his spicery.[19]

Similarly, medieval monastic communities usually included an *apothecarius*, meaning one of the monks who kept the store of spices. After 1215, when it was forbidden for priests and monks to perform any treatment involving the shedding of blood, religious communities used a surgeon or barber (to treat external injuries and fractures and to let blood), a physician (to diagnose and prescribe) and an apothecary to dispense the recipes or bills, as prescriptions were called. The Benedictine monks at Westminster were attended by a physician and an apothecary who, with the infirmarer, inspected the annual bill for medicines. The infirmarer (one of the monks) was in charge of the infirmary and its garden where herbs and medicinal plants were cultivated. He probably prepared some remedies himself, the apothecary being summoned to devise more complex prescriptions such as *theriaca* (treacle, which sometimes contained fifty ingredients and was used to counter the effects of poison) and to supply lozenges and golden pills (a popular stand-by composed of aloes, rose petals, saffron, fennel and anise). Among the apothecaries appointed by the Abbot and convent of Westminster from the beginning of the fourteenth century until its surrender in 1540 were several figures whose names reappear in the records of the City and of the Grocers' Company – for example John de Bovingdon who belonged to the Fraternity of St Anthony, Thomas de Walden, who attended to the monks during the Black Death when about half the community died, and John de Hoo, an Alderman of the City (1425–26).[20]

There were some thirty-four hospitals and almshouses in late medieval London. These were religious institutions offering hospitality to travellers and sometimes education to children, as well as accommodation to the infirm, poor, and needy sick. The sick were cared for by brethren or sisters, and a barber or surgeon would be called when necessary. The first hospital to make provision for the regular attendance of a surgeon, a physician and an apothecary was the Savoy in 1505. The closure of the monastic hospitals at the Dissolution threw the system into disarray and it was not until after the refoundations of the second half of the sixteenth century that hospitals began to be staffed by physicians, surgeons and apothecaries. St Thomas' reopened in 1551 and the first official Apothecary to the hospital, Thomas Coliffe, was appointed in 1566; the first recorded Apothecary to St Bartholomew's Hospital (Bart's) was William Weston (1571–85), later a Royal Apothecary. Roger Gwynn, Apothecary to both St Thomas' and Bart's between 1581 and 1620, also practised medicine and was Master of the Grocers' Company in 1620.

Clearly, medieval and Tudor apothecaries showed considerable versatility, whether as merchants, confectioners, City officials, or shop-owners; some specialized as pharmacists and others acquired medical skills. Nor was it unknown for an apothecary to fulfil the surgeon's role as did John le Spicer in 1354. He was reprimanded for treating Thomas de Shene's wound – "a certain enormous and horrible hurt on the right side of the jaw". The apothecary was rebuked for his lack of skill which rendered Shene's jaw incurable.[21] As a spicer-apothecary might turn his hand to surgical cases, so a surgeon sometimes trespassed on the apothecary's ground. At least one fourteenth-century surgeon, John Arderne, gathered his own herbs from which he concocted medicinal preparations. His treatises of 1376 contain prescriptions for medicines and ointments in addition to directions for surgical operations – ultimately his fame as a pharmacist outlasted his reputation as a surgeon.[22]

Ideally, the physician and the apothecary were interdependent and co-operative – if Chaucer is to be believed they worked to mutual advantage to line each other's pockets. The Doctor of Physic in *The Canterbury Tales* is described as having apothecaries to hand

"To send drogges and his letuaries
For ech of hem made oother for to wynne".[23]

The co-operation of the physician and the apothecary is further illustrated by the amicable arrangement between the physician William Goldwyne and the apothecary John Byrell in the late-fifteenth century. Goldwyne attended

Lady Stonor, for whom he prescribed four recipes – the concoctions included *manus Christi*, wild figs, syrup, myrtle, endive, compot of berberis and absinthe. He forwarded the prescriptions to the apothecary John Byrell of Bucklersbury for dispensing, with a friendly covering note requesting him to make haste.[24]

Apothecaries and Grocers
The power and influence of the wealthy merchant Grocers reached a peak in the last quarter of the fourteenth century when the Company's control extended not only over the wholesale grocery trade but also over the retail trade of spicers and apothecaries of London.

During the political rivalry of the last decades of the fourteenth century the power of the merchant Grocers, Fishmongers, Butchers, Vintners and other victuallers was challenged by John of Northampton leading the Drapers, Taylors and Goldsmiths in a revolt against the high prices for which the Grocers and their allies were blamed. Antagonism between the two parties mirrored the schism at Court between King Richard II and his uncle John of Gaunt, Duke of Lancaster. In the City the party supporting the king, led by the Grocer Nicholas Brembre, reigned supreme between 1377 and 1381, interrupted by the Peasants' Revolt after which John of Northampton was elected Mayor, succeeded by Brembre for a second term. It was claimed that in the election campaign the Grocer, now Sir Nicholas Brembre, and his armed supporters (doubtless apprentice grocers and apothecaries) stormed Cheapside and terrorized the City. Further confrontations and three days of rioting resulted in Brembre's re-election and the triumph of the Grocers in City politics – at least until the execution of their leader at Tyburn in 1388.

The Grocers' power in City politics was mirrored within the Company. Members, including spicer-apothecaries, were not permitted to attend provincial fairs unless their wares had first been inspected; regulations relating to the weighing of powdered drugs further enforced the Grocers' control over apothecaries, and from 1400 the Company's tentacles reached beyond trading standards to the fixing of rents and restrictions on credit. These measures, aimed primarily at foreign competitors during a time of economic recession, made it difficult for apothecaries to be successful unless they belonged to the Grocers' Company and submitted to its regulations, discipline and the searching and inspection of their shops and wares by the Wardens. Many did join the Company and were pre-eminent, such as John Aubrey, one of the wealthiest Grocers of the fourteenth century, who kept an apothecary's shop, as did John Chichele, a Warden in 1417 and later City Chamberlain. The Royal Apothecaries were by definition successful and would normally have belonged to the Grocers' Company: ten of them were Wardens between 1404 and 1612.

Apothecaries and their wares were in heavy demand during epidemics, especially in the recurrent outbreaks of the bubonic plague. It has been estimated that the plague may have killed 30,000 Londoners in 1407 and there were less severe bouts in the 1420s and 1430s, two outbreaks between 1450 and 1470, topped by a dangerous disease called the styche, not to mention the flux, and the sweating sickness in 1485. The nature of these and other diseases not being properly understood, remedies were manifold and an astute apothecary could both profit from and serve the community. Moreover, the fifteenth-century apothecary, like his contemporary grocer, mercer or haberdasher, was at liberty to stock a range of goods in his shop and thus augment his profits. In addition to spices, herbs, remedies and medicaments he might supply sponges, leather bags, silver spoons, canvas, flax, thread and wine.[25] Other apothecaries specialized as pharmacists, notably the unfortunate John Hexham, who was hanged in 1415 for counterfeiting coin as a sideline. An inventory of his shop listed ninety-two separate items, all of them pharmaceutical – twenty-five different vegetable drugs, a few animal drugs, one chemical, fifteen oils, twelve syrups, twenty phials, eighty glass bottles of waters and one still, but his weights had vanished or been confiscated.[26]

The Master and Wardens of the Grocers' Company did not hesitate to assert their right to search the apothecaries' shops for faulty wares which were then confiscated. John Ashfield, for instance, was fined 6s 8d in 1456 for making "untrue" powder of ginger, cinnamon and saunders.[27] From 1447 the Grocers were granted the exclusive privilege of garbelling (cleansing and inspecting) drugs and spices, including electuaries, plasters, syrups, ointments and powders appertaining to the apothecary. Further restrictions enforced by the Company forbade its members to sell powders unless ground in their own shops or bought from fellow-members; brokers were appointed to inform the Wardens about anyone outside the Company trading in groceries and spices, and the Company also attempted to fix selling prices. Apothecary members were thus controlled and disciplined; they were also subject to the usual fines and fees of membership, bound to observe the Company's regulations and to appear at church services (attendance at the burial of a member was compulsory). They were expected to contribute to loans required by the monarch, to pay corn money, to subscribe towards the building of Grocers' Hall, and to take part in the muster at Greenwich in 1559. There were, of course, certain advantages in belonging to the Company that was ranked second of "The Great Twelve" – not least social status and participation in the entertainments at Grocers' Hall, and the use of the bowling alley and garden there with its beds of herbs, roses and vines which yielded bunches of grapes for the members. Royal receptions, City ceremonies such as the barge procession on Lord Mayor's Day, pageants, the annual election dinner and St Anthony's feast day were opportunities for enjoyment, and when all else failed a member of the Company was assured of charity and a decent burial.

Apothecaries were a minority group within a major City livery company, yet they were not swallowed up. Their skills were recognized, sometimes publicly as in 1424 when two apothecaries were appointed to inspect drugs and medicines exposed for sale. Similarly in 1472 the Grocer Lord Mayor, William Edward, summoned seventeen apothecaries to give judgement on some confiscated treacle – this was declared unwholesome and was burned in Cheapside.

Hugh Morgan, later appointed apothecary to Queen Elizabeth I, was one of the Grocers responsible for inspecting the drugs and wares seized from dishonest members in the searches of 1563–64. Rhubarb, a box of pepper dust, a bag of wormseed, boxes of golden pills and "naughty turbitt" were some of the items judged to be faulty, so were cast onto the parlour fire at Grocers' Hall.[28] Apothecaries' wares were particularly susceptible to adulteration – the physician could not always oversee the apothecary while he made up the prescription and the patient was not qualified to judge the quality of the ingredients or their correct measurement. Fraudulent practice was detrimental to the public good and to the reputation of apothecaries, hence there were repeated calls for the correction of abuses. From 1585 the College of Physicians cogitated the publication of the first English *Pharmacopoeia* to counteract the fraud and deceit of those who sold "filthy concoctions and even mud under the name and title of medicaments for the sake of profit".[29] The Grocers' Company reacted with a show of diligence: searches of shops for faulty goods were increased to three times a year in 1587, while the apothecary members of the Company pressed for the "reformation of divers abuses" and the resolution of their "griefes and complaintes".[30]

Threatened by the restrictions of the proposed *Pharmacopoeia* and suspicious that the College of Physicians intended to encroach upon their interests by establishing a physic garden, leading apothecaries of the Grocers' Company petitioned for a monopoly of compounding and selling medicines in 1588. The Grocers' Court of Assistants supported the petition on the understanding that the monopoly would be enjoyed by apothecaries within that Company. The College of Physicians opposed the petition. Monopolies in general were unpopular, the country was at war with Spain and when Parliament was prorogued in 1589 the apothecaries' petition failed.[31]

The physician's cook
At the opening of Henry VIII's reign the medical care of Londoners was in the hands of a small number of graduate physicians, apothecaries, surgeons, barbers, empirics and a host of quacks (so-called because of the quacking, noisy patter they used to hawk their wares), charlatans, mountebanks, midwives and unqualified fraudsters. The situation was unregulated, open to abuse and dangerous to public health, particularly in view of the outbreaks of bubonic plague, sweating sickness, smallpox, syphilis, tuberculosis, typhoid,

dysentery and cholera to which the population of the crowded City was prone. The king's physician, Thomas Linacre, is usually credited with promoting reform by an Act of Parliament (1511) and by the incorporation of the College of Physicians in 1518, of which he was the first President.

The Act of 1511 aimed to eliminate the illicit practice of medicine by placing the licensing of London physicians (other than graduates of Oxford and Cambridge, who were assumed to be competent) in the hands of the Bishop of London or the Dean of St Paul's assisted by four physicians or surgeons. The foundation of the College of Physicians in 1518, ratified by Parliament in 1523, carried the concept of a licensed body of physicians a step further by giving the College licensing powers and a hold over apothecaries, who were instructed to dispense prescriptions for Physicians of the College only. The College went on to subjugate apothecaries to searches of their shops conducted by Censors of the College with or without the assistance of Wardens of the Grocers' Company, and it secured power to fine or have imprisoned any apothecary found guilty of selling faulty wares. These measures, enacted by Parliament in 1553, gave the College of Physicians unrivalled authority over medical practice in England. Ten years later the College sought to enforce its authority by a Bill in Parliament affirming its right to the "rule, correction and punishment" of apothecaries and proposing that every apothecary should be examined by the College before being permitted to set up shop. At this point the Grocers rose to the defence of their apothecary members, declaring that the Physicians' Bill was contrary to the charter of the City and would make apothecaries mere servants of the Physicians.[32] Confrontation was avoided when Parliament was dismissed on account of the plague and the Bill lapsed.

Legislation, the founding of the College of Physicians, the uniting of the Barbers and Surgeons under a royal charter with rules and ordinances relating to their practice, and the "Quacks Charter" of 1542–43 can be seen as the beginning of a governmental public health policy. This worthy intent was frustrated by the practicalities of life in Tudor London where there were insufficient licensed Physicians (between twenty and twenty-four in 1576) to meet the medical needs of the multiplying population (about 50,000 at the beginning of the sixteenth century, 200,000 at the end).[33] Yet if, in response to public demand for medical care, a Barber-Surgeon, an apothecary or empiric indulged in medical practice he was liable to prosecution by the College.

Thus the seeds were sown for a contest between the august and exclusive College of Physicians exercising a monopoly of medical practice, and the apothecaries, surgeons, and other individuals who might administer medical care. Tensions between Physicians and apothecaries can be detected as early as the reign of Queen Elizabeth I when a contemporary observer criticized the tendency of Physicians to play the apothecaries' part and *vice versa*, "as though a Physician and an Apothecary were all one".[34] Another commentator, William Bullein, an apothecary-surgeon of Cripplegate, composed "The Apothecaries' Rules" (1562) which drew attention to the versatility of the Elizabethan apothecary. He should read Dioscorides, possess knowledge of plants and herbs and be able to invent medicines. He should remember that his role was "to be ye Physician's Cook", yet he was also expected to know how to open a vein in order to treat a patient for pleurisy and he was advised to keep a special place in his shop for surgical equipment.[35]

The useful role of the apothecary was underlined when the Elizabethan poor laws came into operation, establishing Overseers of the Poor in each parish. With limited funds at their disposal the Overseers tended to rely on the apothecary or surgeon when necessary, rather than pay for a consultation with one of the few qualified Physicians in the capital. For the same reason plague victims, whether in their homes or in the City Pest House, were usually served by an apothecary. Other ailing inhabitants of the Elizabethan City who could not afford a Physician's fee resorted to the apothecaries' shops in Bucklersbury for advice and remedies. The street was "on both sides throughout . . . possessed by Grocers and apothecaries",[36] a place "replete with physic, drugs and spicery and perfumed by the pounding of spices, the melting of gum and making of perfumes".[37]

In the apothecaries' shops could be found strange and rare spices, fragrant herbs and twisted roots, coloured waters, poisons and possibly the remains of a tortoise, if Shakespeare's apothecary of Mantua (who sold poison to Romeo) was true to type:

> "I do remember an apothecary,
> And hereabouts he dwells, which late I noted
> In tatter'd weeds, with overwhelming brows,
> Culling of simples; meagre were his looks,
> Sharp misery had worn him to the bones;
> And in his needy shop a tortoise hung,
> An alligator stuff'd, and other skins
> Of ill-shap'd fishes; and about his shelves
> A beggarly account of empty boxes,
> Green earthen pots, bladders and musty seeds
> Remnants of packthread, and old cakes of roses".[38]

Shakespeare describes a wretched man of meagre means, yet opportunities for advancement, even access to medical practice, lay open to the resourceful and adept apothecary. With a seven- or eight-year apprenticeship behind him, followed by a working relationship with both Physicians and patients, a keen apothecary could acquire medical skills in addition to trading acumen and pharmaceutical expertise. By the close of the sixteenth century printed medical works in the vernacular and popular tracts on disease were becoming more readily available to apothecaries, surgeons and the reading public. This tended to undermine the Physicians' position and the College determined to quell any form of competition and to enforce its authority by reprimanding unlicensed practitioners whether apothecaries, quacks, surgeons, or physicians with degrees from foreign universities, such as William de Laune, whose son Gideon was instrumental in founding the Society that was to cause the College of Physicians so much trouble.

King James VI of Scotland and I of England. This portrait was commissioned by the Society in 1676 from an artist named Snelling. He copied an earlier portrait by Mytens.

Chapter 2

The seventeenth-century Society

By the nature of their occupation apothecaries were never wholly integrated within the Company of merchant Grocers. Their dilemma had a parallel in other City livery companies – the Haberdashers, for instance, included feltmakers until 1604, and the Leathersellers' Company embraced glovers prior to 1638. In the late sixteenth century apothecary members of the Grocers' Company made an unsuccessful bid for a monopoly of compounding and selling drugs and medicines, and pleaded for "a reformation" of abuses and the resolution of their "griefes and complaintes" – to no avail.

The accession to the throne of King James I, who was known to be sympathetic to new incorporations (he was credited with promoting the Faculty of Physicians and Surgeons of Glasgow in 1599), the conclusion of war with Spain and the increasing volume of new and exotic drugs being imported from the East Indies and South America created fresh and encouraging prospects for the apothecaries of London. Between 1567 and 1609 the volume of imported drugs more than doubled and astute apothecaries must have been aware of the profits to be reaped from obtaining a monopoly of the trade for themselves, and of the advantages of economic independence from the Grocers' Company.

The apothecaries' desire for the monopoly and control of their own trade by secession from the Grocers' Company and the creation of a new incorporation found support at Court through the influence of Dr Theodore Mayerne, Dr Henry Atkins, Gideon de Laune and his brother-in-law, Peter Chamberlen. Mayerne and Atkins were the king's well-beloved and trusted Physicians; de Laune was apothecary to the king and queen, Peter Chamberlen was the queen's surgeon/accoucheur. All but Atkins were French Protestants: Dr Mayerne settled in England in 1611 welcomed by pensions and gifts from both king and queen; Dr Atkins enjoyed the confidence of the College of Physicians of which he was President seven times; Gideon de Laune, a wealthy apothecary of Black Friars, was favoured by the queen, as was Peter Chamberlen.[1] It was de Laune who was identified as the leader of the separatists who in 1610 sought an Act of Parliament for the creation of a new incorporation of apothecaries. Doctors Mayerne and Atkins recommended the apothecaries' petition to the king and to the College of Physicians, and as the newly appointed Lord Keeper, Francis Bacon was instrumental in advancing the final document of 1617.

The Grocers' Company had secured a confirmation of privileges by a charter of April 1606 in which the apothecaries were acknowledged as part of the Company and subservient to its government.[2] This may have rankled with the apothecary members, prompting their Bill for separation from the Grocers the following month. When the Court of the Grocers' Company was presented with a copy of the apothecaries' Bill, reaction was adverse. The Court Minutes, usually stilted and pedestrian, suddenly come alive with expressions of surprise and outrage. Gideon de Laune was identified as the ring-leader of the separatists and was summoned with eleven other apothecaries to appear before the Grocers' Court to explain their desire "to divide the Corporation of this ancient Company by procuring to themselves a new corporation of Apothecaries only".[3] Described as "a stranger born", de Laune was perceived as an outsider, being of French descent and not a member of the Worshipful Company of Grocers. Among his companions, however, stood some of the most respected members of that Company: Edmond Phillipps "an ancient brother", Roger Gwynn who was Apothecary to St Thomas' and St Bartholomew's Hospitals, William Besse, an expert on the preparation of treacle, the botanist William Quick, Thomas Fones Master of the Apothecaries (1624–26), Anthony de Soda and Robert Morer who were acknowledged to be two of the "most sufficient and skilful apothecaries of this Company and Assistants of the Court".[4] These men were neither radicals nor conspirators. Their aim in seeking independence from the Grocers' Company was not to undermine the *status quo* but to secure the government and regulation of apothecaries by apothecaries and thereby the elimination of fraud and incompetence.

The Court of the Grocers' Company was not persuaded. It saw the apothecaries' proposed Bill as divisive and a threat to the Company's position and income; the Assistants were not even prepared to listen to de Laune who was sent out of the room. After conferring with the remaining eleven apothecaries, the Court recalled de Laune. His feathers ruffled by the treatment he had received, he expressed "great indignation" and used "threatening terms against the Court and Company", then departed. Without a leader, the deputation lost its fire and de Laune's companions denied complicity, pleading only for the reformation of the abuses of their trade.[5] Of the dozen apothecaries present during this confrontation all but four were to be founder members of the Society of Apothecaries in 1617. For the present, however, the failure of the apothecaries' bid for independence was ensured by the opposition of the Grocers' Company and the dissolution of Parliament.

By 1614 the apothecaries had secured the support of Dr Mayerne, the king's favourite Physician; receipt of a grant of arms had improved de Laune's standing and both men ranked high in the estimation of King James and Queen Anne. Possibly Mayerne and de Laune collaborated in drafting the apothecaries' petition to the king, for it displayed familiarity with the position of apothecaries in other countries and a sensitivity to the king's vanity. The

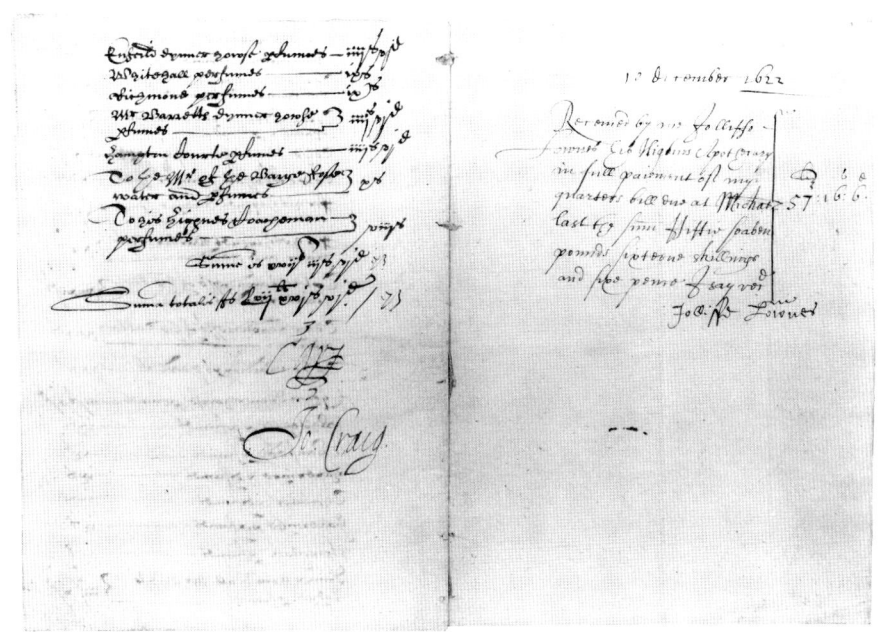

The final pages of an account submitted by Joliffe Lownes, Royal Apothecary and one of the founder members of the Society, for perfumes, waters and powders supplied to Charles, Prince of Wales (later King Charles I) at Whitehall, Havering, Hampton Court and Theobalds between July and September 1622. Lownes also supplied the Prince's grooms, pages of the bedchamber, the Master of the barge and oarsmen with perfumes and waters (left hand page). On the opposite page he acknowledged receipt of payment of £57 16s 6d, December 1622.

Court of the Apothecaries' Society later acknowledged that de Laune had been "a principal means for the procuring of the said Company to be made a corporation",[5] and the Society's royal charter recorded that the apothecaries' cause had been promoted by Mayerne and Atkins, who wanted to see apothecaries severed from the control of the Grocers but subservient to the College of Physicians.

The apothecaries' petition stressed the confusion that had arisen through the lack of government of their profession, the incompetence of Grocers to oversee apothecaries, the great benefit to the life and health of all men and women that would result from the control of the preparation and sale of wholesome, standardized medicines and from the suppression of empirics. Comparison was made with the privileges of the Physicians and Surgeons, and with apothecaries on the continent (Paris apothecaries had long been separated from spicers).[6]

As Lord Keeper, Francis Bacon signified his approval in principle and advised consultation with the College of Physicians and with the Company of Grocers.[7] The latter continued to protest, fearing a loss of income from the secession of apothecary members, inflated prices of apothecaries' wares and a possible challenge to the order of precedence of the livery companies. The Grocers denounced the petition, claiming it was the result of the plotting of a few disgruntled apothecaries, empirics and sundry tobacco-sellers – no more than twenty-eight in all.[8] Crucially, the king took the advice of Francis Bacon, Dr Mayerne and Dr Atkins and signified his approval of the apothecaries' petition for a royal charter. On the basis of an early draft, Atkins had convinced the College of Physicians that the independent apothecaries would be subordinate to the College which therefore concurred with the apothecaries' separation from the Grocers. Redrafting, hesitation on the part of Lord Chancellor Ellesmere (who resigned in March 1617), and the possiblity of a settlement with the Grocers delayed the issue of Letters Patent until December 1617.

Meanwhile, a public scandal surrounding the death of Sir Thomas Overbury focused attention on apothecaries and their culpability in cases of poisoning. Overbury had died in the Tower of London allegedly poisoned at the instigation of the ruthless Frances Howard who had married firstly the Earl of Essex and secondly the king's favourite, Robert Carr, Earl of Somerset. Several apothecaries were implicated in the murder enquiries, including Paul Lobel (a founder member of the Society, Dr Mayerne's brother-in-law and the son of the king's botanist) and J.W. Rumler (Royal Apothecary and later Master of the Society). Lobel, Mayerne and Rumler were cleared of guilt – indeed the episode served to enhance Mayerne's reputation as "the only physician in England worth anything" – but an apothecary was executed, among others.[9]

The apothecary members of the Grocers' Company were growing impatient: Compton was fined for disobedience, three others refused a summons to the Livery in 1614 and Stephen Higgins declined to act as Steward in 1615. Another, Michael Eason, caused embarrassment when he was found guilty of supplying defective wares to Prince Charles's apothecary, Joliffe Lownes, and was imprisoned.[10] Between the apothecaries' petition to the king for a royal charter in April 1614 and the sealing of the final document in December 1617 lay hurdles, negotiations and drafts, the Grocers' Company and the Common Council of the City being formidable objectors to the new incorporation. Initial drafts of the charter list 115 seceders, later supplemented by five foreigners and two troublesome apothecaries (William Quick and Michael Eason), suggesting that the inclusion of foreigners ("aliens" as they were called), of Quick (alleged to have been a chief instigator of the separation) and of Eason (guilty of supplying defective wares) was contentious.[11]

With the appointment of Francis Bacon as Lord Keeper in March 1617 the apothecaries came a step closer to achieving their aim. Encouraged, perhaps, by the bribes he received,[12] Bacon ensured that the proposed charter to "the Master, Wardens and Society of the Art and Mystery of Apothecaries of the City of London" advanced.

The Letters Patent or charter granted by King James I to the founder members of the Society, 6 December 1617. The original seal (centre) is broken; replicas on either side show the two faces of a complete seal.

The royal charter or Letters Patent of 6 December gives the names of 122 founder members of the new Society – the five foreigners (three Royal Apothecaries among them), Michael Eason and William Quick were now included. The aggrieved Grocers claimed that "almost a fourth part" of their Company had departed and, a few years later, a Court Minute referred to the separation of 200 apothecaries.[13]

The charter named Edmond Phillipps as the first Master, Stephen Higgins and Thomas Fones as the first Wardens,[14] and listed twenty-one Assistants. Among the founder members were six Royal Apothecaries and two who were to succeed them.[15] The Royal Apothecaries could be sure of the king's favour, especially Gideon de Laune who had the ear of the queen, and J.W. Rumler who was granted a monopoly for the manufacture of calomel (mercury sublimate), who gave the king a box of Indian plums at New Year and was present at his last illness. Another Royal Apothecary named in the royal charter, Lewis Le Mire, was related by marriage to both Rumler and Lobel. Although not officially a Royal Apothecary, Edmond Phillipps, the first Master of the Society, accompanied Dr Atkins in attendance on Prince Charles in 1604 and he belonged to a group appointed by the king to garbel tobacco. Clearly there were strong links, personal and professional, between founder members of the Society of Apothecaries and the royal Court.

Among other founder members were two Apothecaries who were later to become Aldermen – Edmond Phillipps and William Bell, the latter having been M.P. for Westminster from 1640 to 1648. The Society's first Bedel or Beadle, Tobias Wyncke, was Apothecary to St Bartholomew's Hospital (1616–19), as were John Evans and Richard Glover; their contemporary, Ralph Yardley, was to be Apothecary to Bethlehem Hospital. Another founder member, John Parkinson, the botanist/horticulturalist and author, shared an interest in botany with Thomas Hicks, William Quick and Paul Lobel, while the wealthy Edward Cooke, who practised physic as a sideline, represented the manufacturing and trading apothecary. He exported his wares to the Russian Court including, no doubt, Cooke's Pills and Cooke's Golden Eggs (see page 158).

The charter gave the new incorporation its framework and objectives: the Apothecaries were to be governed on the lines of other City livery companies, to have a common seal, the right to own property and make ordinances. The wording was intended to reassure the City and the College of Physicians that the Society of Apothecaries posed no threat. It was claimed that the separation of the Apothecaries from the Grocers' Company was for the public good – the king's intention was to inaugurate a reputable corporation of Apothecaries to protect his subjects from unskilful and ignorant empirics who compounded "unwholesome, hurtful, deceitful, corrupt and dangerous medicines". The Master, Wardens and Assistants were given responsibility for restraining and punishing fraudulent practice and for burning adulterated medicines, drugs, oils, etc. Standards were to be maintained by searches of Apothecaries' shops by the Master and Wardens in conjunction with delegates from the College of Physicians, and by the training of apprentices, who were to be examined and approved by the Master and Wardens and by Physicians of the College before being permitted to keep a shop. The king and his advisers anticipated that the College of Physicians and the Society of Apothecaries would enjoy a satisfactory, productive working relationship. The College expected that the new Society of Apothecaries would be subservient and, with this in mind, plans for the publication of the *Pharmacopoeia Londinensis* accelerated. However, in the rambling prose of the Apothecaries' royal charter there was nothing to restrain them from prescribing remedies *and* attending patients –

that is to say, from practising medicine. This left the door open to controversy and led to interminable disputes between the Society and the College of Physicians.

The City and the Grocers' Company remained opposed to the foundation of the Society of Apothecaries. The City authorities showed disapproval by refusing to enrol the Society's charter until instructed to do so by the king.[16] The Grocers reacted by compiling a list of the goods they claimed were their monopoly, from alum to prunes, and including wares that now fell within the Apothecaries' domain such as perfumes, rose-water and all distilled waters, arsenic, treacle and liquorice.[17] The Apothecaries' list embraced drugs, perfumes and tobacco. The document allocating the various commodities to the separate bodies was of little worth until the king intervened in support of the Apothecaries, confirming that the compounding and selling of all medicines in the City and suburbs belonged to the Apothecaries alone and ordering that the differences between Apothecaries and Grocers, recently investigated by Royal Commissioners, should cease (1620).[18]

A year later distillers, druggists and confectioners of the City joined the Grocers in complaining about the impeachments of the Apothecaries. The Grocers then attempted to cripple the Apothecaries financially by claiming that they owed £200 towards the fund for the Elector Palatine (the king's son-in-law). Furthermore, they claimed that the Apothecaries' charter was void and must be revoked for the simple reason that it had been obtained without their consent.[19] Francis Bacon, who had been created Viscount St Albans in 1621, was no longer in a position to support the Apothecaries, and a restless House of Commons took up the Grocers' cause, presenting complaints against the Society of Apothecaries in a list of grievances laid before King James in 1624. The king, in defiant mood, replied: "I myself did devise that corporation and do allow it. The grocers, who complain of it, are but merchants; the mystery of these apothecaries were belonging to apothecaries, wherein the grocers are unskilful; and therefore I think it is fitting they should be a corporation of themselves".[20]

The Apothecaries did not remain passive in the face of opposition. On the contrary, the fledgeling Society defended its position aggressively by launching an action against eleven individuals for contempt of its charter. Battle had commenced with allegations that the offenders met illegally at the Mercers' Chapel and that they were undermining the Society's authority by their wilful and contemptuous refusal to take the Apothecary's oath. Among the defendants stood Roger Gwynn, Apothecary to St Thomas' and Bart's who remained firmly within the Grocers' Company, becoming Master in 1620, and George Shiers, a Royal Apothecary. Seven of the group had been or were members of the Grocers' Company so were presumably antagonistic to the separation of the Apothecaries: three were founder members of the Society, evidently now discontented or disillusioned in some respect. The interrogations extended to the point of absurdity, developing into a contest between the Grocers' Company and the Society of Apothecaries in the Court of the Star Chamber in 1622 and becoming an issue between king and Parliament in 1624 (see page 35).[21]

The Society was also fighting in another field, against the infringements of distillers, for the charter of 1617 specifically gave Apothecaries a monopoly of distilled waters. Encouraged by Dr Mayerne, the distillers petitioned for their own charter in 1621 which was eventually enrolled in 1658, despite the opposition of the Apothecaries', Vintners' and Barber-Surgeons' Companies.

An organized Society

Once King James's charter had been issued the Society was quick to confirm its status and to commence business. The Grant of Arms was procured on 12 December, just six days after the charter, and four days after that the Court of Assistants assembled for the first time. The first page of the first Court Book

Letters Patent of arms to the "Master, Wardens and Societie of the Apothecaries of the Cittie of London" 12 December 1617, signed by William Camden, Clarenceux King of Arms. Viewed and approved by Henry St George, Richmond Herald, in 1634. The motto, *opiferque per orbem dicor* is from Ovid and translates "I am called throughout the world the bringer of aid".

records a meeting of the Master, Wardens and sixteen Assistants at Gray's Inn to take their oaths before the Attorney General, Dr Mayerne and Dr Atkins. On the same day, 16 December 1617, Robert Metcalfe was chosen "Clerke of ye Company", whereupon the Court adjourned until March of the next year.[22]

Thereafter new members were enrolled at a steady rate, apprentices were bound and examined, Tobias Wincke was engaged as Bedel, ordinances were compiled, ratified and sealed, and searches for defective drugs and medicines were conducted in London, Westminster and Southwark, resulting in the fining of offenders.[23] Edmond Phillipps, Stephen Higgins and Thomas Fones continued to serve as Master and Wardens for the next year and responsiblity for drawing up a schedule of all the medicines of the Apothecary was allocated to Gideon de Laune, Daniel Darnelly, John Parkinson and Adrian Barton.

The charter authorized the Master and Wardens to purchase a Hall or Counsel-House in the City but as yet this was beyond the resources of the Society. For the meanwhile the Society's treasures – documents, the seal, plate and pewter, cushions, a table carpet, weights, a chamber pot and a brush were

A mortar made for Gideon de Laune and inscribed "Thomas Bartlett made me for Gideon de Laune 1625". Bartlett was a bell-founder of Whitechapel.

kept in a chest under lock and key, probably at the Master's house or with de Laune until 1621 when the Society rented Painter-Stainers' Hall in Little Trinity Lane for Court meetings.[24] The chest soon contained a collection of silver spoons for it had been decreed in 1620 that on attaining his freedom a member should present a piece of plate to the value of 13s 4d at least. This amount or less was sufficient to purchase a silver spoon, and by 1627 the Society possessed sixty-seven spoons, together with three standing cups and covers.[25] Gideon de Laune added to the collection by giving a silver college cup "out of his love to the Company" and to thank Liverymen for accompanying him to his wife's funeral.[26]

The Society soon accumulated items of value but liquid assets were harder to come by, and it was not until 1626 that regular Wardens' Accounts commenced with the Account of Israel Wolf beginning on 2 September 1626 and concluding on 21 August 1627 with a balance of £55 15s 3d. The Society's finances improved once a scale of fees was established, providing a regular income: 7s 2d was due from each member on being granted the freedom, and the fee due on election to the Court of Assistants was a substantial £22 in the 1620s. Payments of 4s 8d for binding an apprentice, and quarterage (a subscription) were collected regularly from members. Fines were exacted from Apothecaries discovered to be in possession of inferior drugs, for keeping a foreigner or more apprentices than the charter allowed, for being disputatious and for failing to appear before the Court when summoned.[27] In addition to these sources of income the Society relied on loans and gifts from wealthy members, whether towards corn money, the purchase of property or hogsheads of claret for the Lord Mayor.[28] Remarkably, within eleven years of its foundation and without any major endowment the Society was in a position to begin repaying loans and by 1631 was out of debt – for the time being.

Legal costs were a principal expense in the early years of the Society's history. The Apothecaries had taken legal advice regarding their separation from the Grocers' Company, the prolonged suit in the Star Chamber had proved expensive, and a decade later £87 had to be raised to defend the Society in the face of a writ of *Quo Warranto* instigated by the College of Physicians.[29]

In the ordinary course of events the wages of the Clerk and Bedel had to be paid (£10 and £5 per annum respectively in 1636), and the annual rent for the use of Painter-Stainers' Hall (£10). Searches of Apothecaries' shops necessitated boat hire, sustenance and possibly the transportation of bad or old drugs, herbs or medicines for burning. Dinners and refreshment at various taverns and charitable gifts were among other regular expenses – a poor box was set up even before the Society owned a Hall, a pension was awarded to the Bedel's widow, and donations were made to the poor of Ludgate.[30]

The Court of Aldermen had been reluctant to enrol the Apothecaries' charter and was equally reluctant to grant the Society a Livery, for this posed

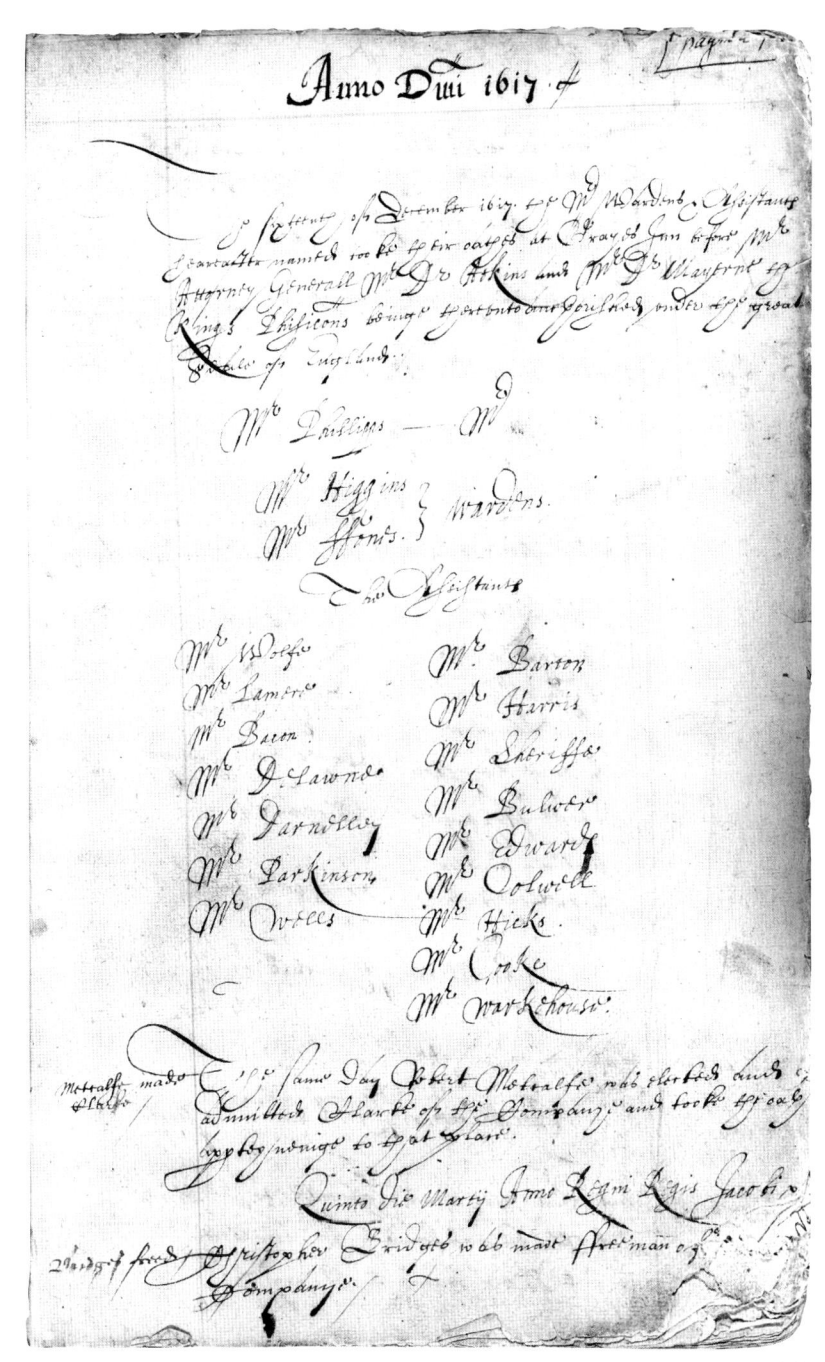

The first page of the first volume of Court Minutes records the meeting of the Court of Assistants, 16 December 1617. The first Master, Wardens and Assistants took their oaths at Gray's Inn in the presence of the Attorney General, Dr Atkins and Dr Mayerne. The election of the Society's first Clerk, Robert Metcalfe, is noted. Guildhall Library Ms 8200 vol i.

the thorny question of precedence – there had been a flood of new incorporations since the beginning of the seventeenth century, causing resentment among the older livery companies. Some members of the Apothecaries' Society had been Liverymen of the Grocers' Company and therefore wore gowns, but it was not until 1630 that the Apothecaries' own Livery was officially sanctioned. Two hogsheads of wine presented to the Lord Mayor may have been instrumental, for three months later patterns were ordered for the gowns and Livery fines of £15 boosted the Society's finances (twenty-eight Liverymen paid immediately, four paid to be excused).

With the investiture of the Livery came the first Livery dinner held on 28 October 1630 at a cost of £6 6s 4d.[31] The venue is not disclosed although the Apothecaries' favourite haunts at this time were The Star in Cheapside, The Three Tonnes in Newgate Market and The Mitre in Bread Street. Audit day in August or September was followed by a dinner with venison to eat and tobacco to smoke from 1655 (tobacco was believed to be medicinal). Search days provided another opportunity for dinners and in the 1620s meetings of the Court on quarter days called for the provision of ten dozen cakes, two gallons of claret, beer and candles; from 1633 dinners were usually held in the recently acquired Apothecaries' Hall.[32] After the destruction of the Hall in the Great Fire of 1666 the Society resorted to The King's Head in Fleet Street or Cooks' Hall, with the more serious business being conducted at St Andrew's Quest House.

The civil war of the 1640s and the Interregnum brought financial demands on all City livery companies. The Society of Apothecaries escaped comparatively lightly and individual members shouldered much of the burden. There were also repeated demands from the Lord Mayor for corn money (individuals subscribed £1 each to the purchase of corn which was stored against possible shortages). Economies were necessary: the simpling day (as the botanical excursion was called – see pages 41–43) was cancelled in 1642 and gratuities and payments were suspended. To augment corporate funds seventy-eight freemen were called to the Livery in 1645 – only thirteen took up the offer, nevertheless the fines imposed on those who refused served the purpose. By the middle years of the seventeenth century rents from tenants of portions of the Black Friars estate eased the Society's finances by an average of some £70 per annum, but this shrank to a pittance after the Great Fire destroyed the buildings. However, income could be secured by letting parts of the Hall – to Lady Darcy (1640), to Liverymen for the storage of drugs (1657), to the Feltmakers' Company from 1650 and, after some debate in 1681, to a dancing master called Richardson for the instruction of young ladies.

The Society survived the financial strains of the seventeenth century through the generosity of its members. The purchase and repair of Apothecaries' Hall, its rebuilding after the Great Fire, the foundation of the

Laboratory, the purchase of a barge and the expense of the Physic Garden at Chelsea were only possible through the contributions of individual Apothecaries, which reflected their pride in their Company.

The grant of a Livery brought new dignity to the Apothecaries and a steady flow of income; it also gave the Apothecaries a place in the hierarchy of the City as fifty-eighth in the list of eighty-four seventeenth-century livery companies.[33] For the first time, at Christmas 1630, Liverymen of the Society were summoned to worship with the Lord Mayor and the other livery companies at St Paul's Cathedral. Torches were purchased and at this service the Apothecaries occupied the seats of the Merchant Taylors' Company.[34] The Apothecaries were also included in the procession of the Lord Mayor and City companies to Westminster on Lord Mayor's Day 1631. This required the hire of a barge for the Liverymen, a boat for the "younger brethren" and the purchase of ribbons, herbs, rushes, cushions, a barge cloth, three banners and two long streamers decorated by the herald painter Taylor at a cost of £38.[35] Participation in the procession of barges on Lord Mayor's Day became an annual event, prompting the building of a barge in 1673, with the provision of a barge-house on the waterfront of the Apothecaries' Physic Garden at Chelsea (see Chapter 5).

Another event enjoyed by the Apothecaries was simpling day. Following the lead of a group of late-sixteenth-century apothecaries, notably Hugh Morgan, John Riche, Thomas Gray and James Garrett, and stimulated by the work of John Gerard, William Bullein, the Tradescants and Dr William Turner, the study of botany – fundamental to the training of an apothecary – was gaining ground. Several early-seventeenth-century Apothecaries were famous botanists, notably John Parkinson who was *Botanicus Regius Primarius* to King Charles I, Job Weale, John Buggs, John Sotherton, William Broad, William Quick, Roger Young, Thomas Hicks and his friend Thomas Johnson.

The identification and study of plants was essential to the education of an Apothecary and, at this time, uncatalogued and rare plants were to be found growing on the open spaces within reach of the City. Therefore, expeditions were mounted in order to collect and study plants with medicinal qualities. These expeditions, to Hampstead Heath or Greenwich for example, were originally known as simpling days (a simple being a plant or herb employed for medical purposes). The Society's first recorded simpling was held on "the Thursday after Whitsunweek" (14 June) 1620 when the group assembled at St Paul's at 5 a.m. Simpling days, later known as herbarizings, were a means of instructing apprentices and stimulating an interest in botany among the next generation, who were to enjoy the facilities of the Society's Physic Garden from 1675. The simplings or private herbarizings for the apprentices were organized by leaders, until the appointment of a Botanical Demonstrator in 1724 gave him the duty of leading and instructing the expedition. The general

John Parkinson, botanist, author, founder member of the Society of Apothecaries in 1617 and a Warden (1620–21). The portrait formed the frontispiece to his work *Paradisi in sole Paradisus Terrestris* (1629), which was prefaced with a poem by his fellow-Apothecary Thomas Johnson.

herbarizing was for members and honoured guests such as Sir Hans Sloane, and required the appointment of Stewards, who became largely responsible for the dinner. The day always started early and beer and cakes were supplied for the expedition to Kentish Town in 1629. The Society was soon contributing £1 towards the excursion and the refreshments became more substantial, taking the form of a venison dinner in the early nineteenth century.[36]

Herbarizing expeditions led by Thomas Johnson, a freeman of the Society with a shop and a physic garden in Snow Hill, became very popular after 1629. Johnson guided his friends and fellow-Apothecaries William Broad (and his apprentice Edward Brown), Job Weale, John Buggs, Leonard Buckner (Master in 1656), Robert Lorkin, Thomas Crosse and Thomas Wallis on a herbarizing to Kent which he recorded in Latin, complete with a catalogue of the plants found (1629). Johnson's second herbarizing in Kent (1632) was attended entirely by Apothecaries and his account of the expedition was dedicated to the Master, Wardens and Assistants. Again, on a longer excursion to Bath, Bristol and the Isle of Wight in 1634 Johnson was accompanied by the Master (Richard Edwards), Cooke, Hicks, Young, Broad, Lorkin and Clarke, with three apprentices. There was evidently a band of keen botanists in the Society as early as the 1620s and 1630s – "loving friends and fellow travellers in this study and of the same profession", as Johnson described them.[37]

Several important publications were written by this generation of botanist-Apothecaries – John Parkinson, who was elected a Warden in 1620, was the author of *Paradisi in Sole Paradisus Terrestris* (1629) and *Theatrum Botanicum* (1640). Parkinson and Stephen Chase, both founder members of the Society and Apothecaries to King Charles I, acquired a plot of land for a garden for plants next to the king's tennis court in St James's Fields – possibly fellow-Apothecaries had access to this before the Society's Physic Garden was established. Nicholas Culpeper, the famous herbalist/physician/astrologer, trained as an apothecary and his *Herbal* (1653) became the manual of country gentlewomen. Thomas Johnson wrote *Iter Plantarum in agrum Cantianum* (1629) – the first English local plant catalogue – followed by further works emanating from his herbarizing expeditions, and an expanded version of Gerard's *Herbal* (editions of 1633 and 1636). The latter was dedicated to the Society of Apothecaries and the author presented a copy to the Court; in return he was admitted to the Livery and given a gown and hood.[38] Johnson later distinguished himself with the Royalist army at Basing House (see page 59); his other claim to fame was the introduction of bananas to London. His friend, Dr Argent, President of the College of Physicians and a relation of Gideon de Laune by marriage, sent Johnson a stalk of bananas from Bermuda. Johnson hung the novelty in his shop from April to June in 1633, by which time the fruit was somewhat soft.

The Society's general herbarizing was cancelled in 1642 for reasons of economy, and was suspended in the summer of the Great Plague. Otherwise the tradition was upheld well into the nineteenth century, with a record of eight herbarizings in the summer of 1672, although more usually there were six. The tradition was upheld for over two hundred years until the sprawling extension of the nineteenth-century capital rendered regular herbarizings impractical (see page 142).

The Society's earliest records testify to its rapid organization and with the grant of a Livery in 1630 the Society was fully fledged in the City hierarchy. As early as 1617 the Society had obtained a grant of arms featuring Apollo (the God of healing) killing the dragon of disease, supported by two unicorns (from King James's coat of arms) and with a miniature rhinoceros as the crest (the powdered horn was believed to be medicinal). The search for a Hall began in 1621, resuming a decade later when various premises were viewed, resulting in the purchase of Cobham House at Black Friars late in 1632. With the Hall

The Society's benefactor, Gideon de Laune (1565–1659). In 1642 de Laune presented the Society with this portrait, painted in 1640 in the style of Cornelis Jonson van Ceulen. It was removed from the Hall at the time of the Great Fire and returned in 1751.

established at Black Friars, Liverymen transferred their allegiance from St Mary-le-Bow in Cheapside to St Ann's church, where they reserved a pew and attended a special service on Confirmation Day (Master's Day), as they still do at St Andrew-by-the-Wardrobe.

King James signified his continued approval of the Society and de Laune in particular by obtaining the freedom of the City for him on the grounds of his "faithful service to the late Queen".[39] Queen Anne had died in 1619 having relied on her Physician and the Royal Apothecary, de Laune, to ease the pain of a long illness. She was adept at bringing her favourites to the king's notice and de Laune fell into this category. With the grant of the freedom of the City he was eligible for election as an Alderman; this he achieved in 1626, only to be discharged immediately, being a foreigner. Nevertheless, he was successful in the contested election for the Mastership of the Society in 1628, and was to serve as Master again (1637–38). De Laune was the Society's founder and chief benefactor, "a principal means for the procuring of the said Company to be made a corporation and for the purchasing of the capital messuage now belonging to the said Company called Apothecaries' Hall". He gave two cups to the Society, presented his portrait in 1642 "for the better ornament of ye Companies' rooms" (illustrated opposite) and he is commemorated in a bust.[40]

The charter of 1617 had been obtained with the intention of securing self-government for Apothecaries in order to raise standards and eradicate fraud and malpractice. In this the Society was successful: it was governed by a Court of experienced elders of the trade; searches of Apothecaries' shops were conducted regularly, resulting in confiscations of bad oil of mace, treacle, rhubarb and other items of poor quality, disputes between members or between members and their apprentices were settled and the unruly were disciplined. Most importantly, a thorough system of training and education was established for apprentices. It was incumbent upon the Society by the words of its charter to ensure that its members were trained and examined in the required skills and in 1623 the Book of Ordinances formalized rules for apprentices.[41]

Aspiring apprentices, usually aged fourteen, were examined in general knowledge and Latin before they were bound to a master; those who were found to have insufficient learning were eliminated at this stage. Successful applicants paid a fine to be bound, agreed on a fee to cover the eight years' apprenticeship which included accommodation and apparel (Nicholas Culpeper's apprenticeship in the 1630s cost £50) and took an oath. The apprentice would then be trained in pharmacy, to recognize drugs, and to compound, make, dispense and administer medicines and remedies. He would assist in and clean his master's shop, and accompany him on visits to patients and physicians when he might be asked to assist with blood-letting and enemas, to help with embalming or a post-mortem. He was obliged to attend the private herbarizings and, before the end of the seventeenth century, he

Delaun Reviv'd,

Viz.

A Plain and short discourse of that *Famous*

DOCTOR'S PILLS,

Their Use and Virtues.

VVith Choice Receipts for the Cure of the *Scurvy, Dropsy, Jaundies, Venereal* and other Diseases.

Before I speak to this Famous *Medicine*, I will declare who Delaun was; Then, the Price of *his* Pill *and how to take it*, and *of its several* Virtues *in order, in such* Plain *words, as the weakest capacity may understand*:

And I intreat those who hope for help hereby, would throughly *Read* this short book, and observe my Directions for their own good and the Authors's Credit.

His *Famous* Author was not like any the *Quacks* of this Age, whom the Honourable *London Colleagues* could comptrol, as they did *Bromfield of Fetter Lane* most deservedly, and compell'd him to pay *Forty marks*; for that, that he, though the chief of the *Pill-sellers*, was never bred to Physick, or had Learning enough to understand his *Accedence*; Mr. *Scott* in *Grubstreet* Attorney for the Colledge, who prosecuted many others, will averr this truth: which, if *Bromfield* (or

who Delaun *was*

any

A

Advertisement of *circa* 1680 for de Laune's pills. They were originally manufactured by de Laune at Black Friars and were said to contain colocynth (bitter apple, a plant of the gourd family producing a purgative drug) and scammony (a gum resin obtained from the roots of convolvulus, also used as a purgative). The author of this advertisement, "N.L.", recommended the pills for scurvy, gout, worms, the stomach, headache, etc. He claimed that Dr William Harvey had commended them.

could further his botanical studies at the Chelsea Physic Garden and gain some knowledge of chemistry in the Laboratory at Apothecaries' Hall. An assiduous apprentice with an encouraging master might have access to educational books, to lectures in surgery and anatomy and dissections at Barber-Surgeons'

Hall, to private anatomy and chemistry classes and instruction at Gresham College. At the expiry of his apprenticeship he appeared before the Court of Assistants and the President of the College of Physicians (the Physicians' attendance lapsed at times) for oral examination. If approved, he gave a silver spoon to the Society, paid his fine, was sworn in and granted his freedom, enabling him to open a shop in London or the suburbs.

As a freeman the practising Apothecary was still under the surveillance of the Master and Wardens, and his shop was liable to be inspected. If dirty, bad-quality or corrupt wares were found they were confiscated, the offender fined and possibly his shop shut. The rigorous training of apprentices, the better regulation of the trade and the increasing volume of drugs available on the London market combined to make the Apothecary's occupation profitable and popular – indeed, one of the grievances of the College of Physicians was the proliferation of Apothecaries' shops. The Society itself was well aware that large numbers of freemen Apothecaries could lead to a loss of control over the trade or art, therefore the number of apprentices was restricted and a committee was appointed in 1643 to see what could be done about the less reputable druggists.[42]

Unqualified druggists, empirics, apothecaries who were not free of the Society or who were members of the Grocers' Company, unlicensed surgeons, physicians, midwives and charlatans proved insuppressible. The Society of Apothecaries could exert authority over its members but possessed no wider brief. The College of Physicians, on the other hand, possessed power to regulate medical practice generally by prosecuting illicit practitioners. Between 1626 and 1640 more than twenty members of the Society of Apothecaries were reprimanded by the College, adding fuel to an uneasy relationship.

Apothecaries versus Physicians
Opposition to the authority of the College of Physicians had been voiced by the Grocers, including the apothecaries within that Company, in the 1560s. The proposed extension of the College's powers by a Bill in Parliament was vehemently rejected by the Grocers' Company, its apothecary members and the City on the grounds that it would make apothecaries mere servants of Physicians, and subject to the rule and correction of the College. The Bill failed and relations between Physicians and apothecaries became increasingly antagonistic.

With the accession of King James I, the Grocers' charter confirmed that apothecaries were a section within that Company and controlled by it. Dissatisfied apothecaries agitated for independence in 1610 and four years later petitioned the king for a royal charter. The College of Physicians concurred to a draft of the apothecaries' charter on the understanding that apothecaries of the proposed incorporation would be subservient and

Engraving of an apothecary's shop attributed to William Faithorne, who lived in Playhouse Yard *circa* 1680–91. Published as a frontispiece to Peter Morellus, *The Expert Doctor's Dispensatory* (1657).

restricted to dispensing prescriptions for Physicians of the College. As it materialized, the charter confirmed the Apothecaries' traditional freedom to trade, prepare and sell drugs and medicines, but it contained no restriction confining Apothecaries to the prescriptions of Physicians of the College. This allowed for sales from an Apothecary's shop without a Physician's prescription, and for the copying and repeating of prescriptions without reference to a Physician – giving Apothecaries the opportunity to deal directly with the sick or injured, particularly in an emergency. The Physician could thus be deprived of his fee while the Apothecary profited – there was an element of economic rivalry in the contest between Physicians and Apothecaries as well as professional jealousy.

In promoting the first English *Pharmacopoeia Londinensis* King James required Apothecaries to compound their medicines in accordance with it. The *Pharmacopoeia* was an important document, long in gestation, and it was intended to be *the* standard authority containing recipes and instructions for compounding current medicines. Its compilation was potentially a subject for co-operation between the College of Physicians and the Society of Apothecaries, and six Apothecaries were consulted about the publication, at the eleventh hour. John Parkinson claimed that the Physicians did not take the advice proffered by the Apothecaries,[43] and when the *Pharmacopoeia* finally appeared in May 1618 it contained many errors and was rapidly re-issued in an enlarged, corrected version.

For the next few years the Apothecaries and Physicians maintained a *modus vivendi* until in the 1620s the College reprimanded several Apothecaries for illicitly practising medicine. The charge was justified: John Reeve (medical attendant to the Earl of Exeter), Thomas Johnson the botanist, and John Buggs, to name but a few, made no secret of their medical practice. This was unpalatable to the College of Physicians which fixed on discommuning as an appropriate punishment – this meant depriving the offending Apothecary of business from Physicians of the College. The reprimands and punishments meted out by the College were directed in particular at Apothecaries who manufactured their own medicines and drugs such as Edwards, Cooke, Haughton and Weale. From 1629 this group was in the ascendant at Apothecaries' Hall as Wardens and Masters, representing the Society's opposition to the College of Physicians.

In the 1630s the contest focused on several incidents which combined to heighten the tension and led to legal proceedings in the Star Chamber (1635–40). Firstly, the Apothecary Brookes was found in possession of an unclassified powder he had invented. His stock was seized and the President of the College of Physicians took the opportunity to propose that the "defective" oath taken by freemen Apothecaries should be amended. The Master and Wardens were unreceptive to this proposal but took a conciliatory stance by inviting Physicians to dine with them at The Mitre in Bread Street.[44]

A second case concerned John Buggs, erstwhile tobacco-seller and actor, and one of the group of botanist-Apothecaries. He was held responsible for three deaths and for illicitly practising medicine. Having pursued Buggs for two years, the College of Physicians succeeded in having him committed to the Fleet Prison. When released, the incorrigible Buggs obtained an M.D. from Leiden (1633), followed by a licence to practise medicine from Cambridge and later from Oxford, thereby dealing a snub to the College of Physicians. Buggs declared that his training in an Apothecary's shop was sufficient to make him a physician; nevertheless, he also acquired the academic qualifications to practise as a physician and was one of a handful of Apothecaries to do so in the 1630s – forerunners of many.

The third case to exacerbate relations between the College of Physicians and Apothecaries related to the death of Joseph Lane in 1632. The College alleged that Lane had died of mercurial poisoning as the result of an Apothecary's carelessness in providing a prescription without consulting a Physician (an autopsy later proved inconclusive as to the cause of death). The College seized the opportunity to demand that the Apothecaries' oath be altered to harness them to Physicians. The Apothecaries protested, Sir

Theodore Mayerne and Dr William Harvey entered the fray and the matter was referred to the Privy Council, to no effect.

Another incident concerned the faulty preparation of milk of sulphur, *lac sulphuris*, a medicine that was not in the *Pharmacopoeia* and therefore not officially sanctioned even though it was prescribed by Mayerne and was used to treat a host of complaints from asthma to ulcers. The Apothecaries' Court was itself taking disciplinary action over the preparation of the medicine when the Censors of the College intervened. The situation became violent during a search of Job Weale's shop in July 1634 (he was known to make *lac sulphuris*). The Censors threw some apparently bad drugs into the street, whereupon Weale became abusive and threatened to call a constable to evict the Physicians.

On another search in July 1634 a quantity of *lac sulphuris* was found in George Haughton's shop; the Physicians declared it was faulty and Haughton found himself in Newgate Prison. Coincidentally the Physicians endeavoured to reassert their right to examine candidates for the freedom of the Society of Apothecaries and this was refused. The College then resorted to the Attorney General, obtaining a writ of *Quo Warranto* (1634) naming twelve Apothecaries including Buggs, Weale and three Masters of the Society. In the course of the proceedings which traced the disputes from 1625, eighty-five witnesses were called and the evidence was colourful. Dr William Harvey, who had published his treatise on the circulation of the blood in 1628, appeared, and he cited the example of the continent, where apothecaries were subservient to physicians.

Cooke, Hicks and Edwards – all of them successful traders and at different times Masters of the Society – were accused of scandalous speeches inciting their fellow-Apothecaries against the College. They were quoted as having said they esteemed their worst brother Apothecary more than the best Physician, and of having spoken libellous words: "from small beere and the tyranny of Physicians . . . Good Lord deliver us".[45]

The College claimed that Buggs, Cooke, Haughton, Edwards and Holland practised physic. The Society retorted that the College treated Apothecaries like slaves and that Haughton had been falsely imprisoned. It was left to judicial referees to find a settlement but before this could be agreed the king was forced to call Parliament – the Short Parliament of the spring of 1640, followed by the revolutionary Long Parliament which had more serious matters to consider than the quarrel between Physicians and Apothecaries.

The abolition of the Court of the Star Chamber and the outbreak of civil war brought a cessation in the strife between the College and the Society. During the lull, national events and the climate of opinion were to work in favour of Apothecaries rather than the Physicians. The new doctrines of religious liberty, political equality and individual freedom promulgated during the 1640s and 1650s were not congenial to the *status quo* of the College of

Physicians. Republican sympathies and the Puritan ethic assailed the privileged position of the College, and the dearth of Physicians during the Great Plague of 1665 drew attention to the flaws in the existing system of medical care.

After the Restoration of the monarchy the College obtained a new royal charter re-establishing it as the "King's College of Physicians" (1663). The number of Fellows was raised to forty and their authority over Apothecaries, druggists and members of the Distillers' Company was asserted. However, the Barber-Surgeons and Apothecaries combined to oppose the ratification of the charter by Parliament, successfully.

For a brief period in the 1660s it seemed that Physicians and Apothecaries might reach an "amiable understanding":[46] an agreement was drawn up proposing that Apothecaries should not practise physic, nor should Physicians prepare or compound medicines, and Apothecaries were to give assurances of the faithful preparation of their medicines according to the Physicians' prescriptions.[47] At this point the most virulent attack of the plague began to rage through London. Those who could left the capital – the Physicians were noted for their absence while Apothecaries distinguished themselves by their stalwart attendance on victims, gaining thereby the confidence and gratitude of the public (see Chapter 3).

The Great Fire of 1666 destroyed both Apothecaries' Hall in Black Friars Lane and the College of Physicians near St Paul's, and it was not until 1669 that the controversy between the Physicians and Apothecaries re-surfaced with the publication of Dr Christopher Merrett's pamphlet, *Short View of the Frauds and Abuses committed by Apothecaries*. The title speaks for itself and the Apothecaries found the attack particularly offensive in view of the fact that Merrett had been made an Honorary Freeman of the Society in 1659. When the pamphlet was read to the Court it was ordered that the Master and Wardens should go to the College forthwith to ascertain responsibility. John Chase and Lt Colonel Rosewell, Royal Apothecaries, opened negotiations and a meeting took place with the Physicians at The Queen's Head in Paternoster Row.[48] Merrett's pamphlet, however, sparked a propaganda war between the Physicians of the College and the Apothecaries, in the course of which both sides were ridiculed and criticized – broadly, the Physicians for their conservatism and incompetence, the Apothecaries for their greed and ignorance.[49]

Apart from the flurry of insults they contained, the pamphlets acknowledged that the Apothecaries had assumed the duties of Physicians during the Great Plague and that Physicians had compounded medicines. As the dust settled, the Apothecaries established a Laboratory at their Hall and the Physicians concentrated on the purchase of a site for the rebuilding of the College.

Relations between the College and the Society remained unresolved when the College came forward with a new venture. In August 1675 the Court of the

Apothecaries learned that the College intended to establish a dispensary for the sick poor. This laudable plan was revealed to the Court with the request that the Society would co-operate by providing medicines at reduced rates for the poor. A meeting was arranged to discuss the proposition and the Apothecaries agreed to dispense prescriptions for the poor at "the lowest and most reasonable rate".[50] A prototype dispensary was duly established but it lasted no longer than a decade.

In 1677 the Royal College of Physicians revived its complaint about Apothecaries practising physic without licence. The Apothecaries replied with appeasement, ordering that "due and constant care be taken to admonish every member of this Company not to practise physick whereby to give any offence to the College"; on all occasions patients were to be advised to consult a Physician.[51] It seemed that Apothecaries had been put in their place, when, to the chagrin of the College, an apothecary from Cambridge called Talbor or Tabor achieved royal acclaim. Talbor's fame rested on his mastery of the safe administration of quinine, the so-called "Jesuit's bark", as a cure for fever. His method cured the king's ague (an acute fever), whereupon he was promptly appointed Physician in Ordinary to His Majesty and knighted (1678), the College of Physicians being commanded by royal authority to turn a blind eye to the fact that Talbor was not a licentiate of the College.

In normal circumstances the College refused adamantly to recognize the Apothecary as a medical practitioner, as in the case of John Badger, an "Apothecaryite". Badger served an apprenticeship of eight years, gained the freedom of the Society in 1675, and on his graduation from Cambridge six years later he applied to the College of Physicians for recognition. This was refused unless he disfranchised himself from the Society of Apothecaries. Despite Badger's relentless overtures, the College blocked his attempt to gain legal recognition for the medically qualified Apothecary. Undeterred by the fact that he had fallen foul of both the College and the Society, Badger styled himself Doctor of Physic and did well from the manufacture and sale of "Badger's Cordial".[52]

Apothecaries and Physicians alike were threatened in the last years of Charles II's reign by the king's exercise of absolute power in issuing writs of *Quo Warranto* forfeiting the charters and privileges of corporations. While the Society was ordered to surrender its charter (see pages 69–70), the College of Physicians escaped the purge but was preoccupied instead with formulating new statutes aimed at curbing Apothecaries. The placatory James St Amand, Alderman, M.P. and Master (1687–88), sought an agreement with the College, as did the notorious Judge Jeffreys, but in vain. The Apothecaries lost patience when it was revealed that some files of prescriptions had been searched by Physicians; this was a violation that could not be countenanced, whatever the motive. The Master, James Chase, explained to "a great appearance at

Warrant dated 22 February 1666 appointing John Chase Royal Apothecary to King Charles II, with the reversion of the office to his son, James. John Chase was Master from 1664 to 1666; his son was Master from 1688 to 1689 and later a Member of Parliament.

Common Hall" how the Physicians "take to ruin the Company by searching the files of bills and other things".[53]

It was to be expected that the Society of Apothecaries would ally with the Barber-Surgeons in opposing the Physicians' Bill in Parliament (1689–90); more surprising was the Apothecaries' temporary alliance with the Physicians against the Surgeons' Bill proposing that surgeons should be allowed to administer internal medicines in surgical cases. Neither Bill met with success.

From April 1690 a mood of conciliation pervaded Apothecaries' Hall as the Society made a serious attempt to achieve a settlement with the College of Physicians. A joint committee was appointed to secure fair practice between the two professions and conferences were held, ending in deadlock. The Society's representatives in the negotiations included its most influential Past Masters (Alderman St Amand and John Chase M.P.), and the current Master,

Thomas Warren, and Wardens (1689–90). Thomas Warren lived at the sign of The Heart and Anchor in St Lawrence Lane, Cheapside, where he claimed to have perfected, "after a great deal of cost and trouble . . . a most curious way of preserving Dead Bodies from Putrification or change of colour" without disembowelling, mangling or cutting any part thereof, by the use of a special powder.[54]

The next bone of contention between Apothecaries and Physicians centred on dispensaries. Much publicity had been given to the excessive consultation fees charged by Physicians, well beyond the means of most Londoners who relied instead on Apothecaries. The College of Physicians found a means of averting criticism while cutting a thrust at Apothecaries by establishing dispensaries for the sick poor. The Physicians' first dispensary had been shortlived and a second attempt took shape in the 1690s. The project raised questions about the supply of free medicines, the supervision of prescriptions and the respective roles of Apothecary and Physician on which agreement was elusive. Therefore the Physicians proceeded independently, founding a dispensary for the sick poor in the stables and coach-house next to the College in Warwick Lane, another one in Suffolk Street near Charing Cross and more were to follow. The Court of the Apothecaries registered displeasure, not only because the College had encroached upon the Apothecaries' trade by opening "a public shop for the making and vending of all sorts of medicines and compositions" but also because foreigners were employed there, and because the Physicians sent their patients directly to these dispensaries rather than to Apothecaries' shops.[55]

The saga was recounted by Sir Samuel Garth (a Physician) in his poem *The Dispensary* (1699) describing a mock-Homeric battle between Physicians and Apothecaries in which the protagonists were thinly disguised and the Apothecaries blatantly ridiculed. Garth's poem achieved astonishing popularity, running to ten editions, to the detriment of the reputation of Apothecaries. Garth's friend John Dryden also took up the theme:

> "The Apothecary tribe is wholly blind,
> From files a random recipe they take,
> And many deaths from one prescription make".[56]

The Apothecaries were unconvinced of any altruistic motive of the Physicians in opening dispensaries. By way of a riposte the Society undertook to provide free medicines for the poor children and servants of the Bishopsgate Workhouse for four years, a philanthropic gesture that cost the Society £357 in 1706.[57]

If the opening of dispensaries was a weapon wielded by the College of Physicians against Apothecaries, the Society found a tool to use against the Physicians in the Apothecaries' Act of 1695. The Society had first petitioned for exemption from civic duties in 1684, unsuccessfully.[58] In the more stable atmosphere of 1694 the Society again sought official recognition for the status of its members by claiming exemption from civic offices and duties such as jury service, to put them on an equal footing with Physicians and Surgeons. In the debate the argument swung in favour of the Apothecaries who, it was claimed, had nineteen-twentieths of all medical practice and gave valuable service to the poor.[59] The College of Physicians was in decline and failed to mount an effective retaliation: its members had been discredited during the Great Plague, they disagreed among themselves, its academic reputation had been challenged by the Royal Society and its position weakened by the brief emergence of the Society of Chemical Physicians in 1665. The Apothecaries won the round, as they were ultimately to do in the Rose case of 1704.

This important episode in the history of the Society revolved around William Rose, an Apothecary of St Nicholas Lane who had prescribed, compounded and administered medicines to a butcher named Seale during the winter of 1699–1700. For whatever reason, Seale's health did not improve but deteriorated and he resented Rose's charges. Seale took his case to the College of Physicians whereupon Rose was promptly prosecuted for practising medicine, arrested and found guilty.

Rose, a Liveryman, appealed to the Society of Apothecaries for support. On his behalf the Society consulted the Attorney General and obtained a writ of error enabling the judgement against Rose to be considered by the House of Lords. In March 1704 their Lordships judged in favour of Rose – it was decreed that he had not acted illegally in his treatment of Seale.[60] This settled the longstanding issue between the College of Physicians and the Society of Apothecaries by giving legal sanction to the right of an Apothecary to practise medicine.

A display drug jar bearing the arms and motto of the Society of Apothecaries (the word *opiferque* appears as two words, incorrectly). This is the earliest known dated example (1647).

Chapter 3

War, plague, fire and surrender

King James I's public reception into London was delayed until March 1604 due to an outbreak of the plague and there were serious recurrences of the epidemic in 1609, 1625, 1636, 1647 and 1665 – the year of the Great Plague of London which killed at least 68,596 people. The Apothecaries who stayed in the City during the summer of 1665 in order to serve the sick were brave and dutiful, as the personal experiences of one of them, William Boghurst, testifies.[1] The plague enhanced the reputation of Apothecaries generally and individuals accumulated wealth as a result of the great demand for remedies, yet the corporate finances of the Society were insecure and its very existence was to be threatened by King Charles II's writ of *Quo Warranto* and the subsequent surrender of the Society's charter in 1684. The financial demands placed upon the Society by king and Parliament, civil war, the destruction of Apothecaries' Hall in the Great Fire of 1666 followed by the rebuilding, the cost of the ceremonial barge and the Physic Garden, not to mention the contest with the College of Physicians and the surrender of the royal charter of 1617, were major challenges faced by the seventeenth-century Society of Apothecaries.

Ironically, the disasters suffered during the course of the seventeenth century were of some benefit to the Apothecaries. The civil war and Interregnum had the effect of reducing the pre-eminence of the College of Physicians; the Great Plague allowed Apothecaries to shine in the absence of Physicians, and although both the College building in Warwick Lane and Apothecaries' Hall were destroyed by the Great Fire of 1666, the Apothecaries recovered comparatively quickly to establish themselves in a position of strength.

Civil war

National events such as the outbreak of war or the execution of the king were apparently too grave to warrant recording in the Society's Court Minute Books. Nevertheless, the seriousness of the situation is indicated by the extraordinary expenses listed in the Wardens' Accounts – sums spent on gunpowder and muskets, the fortification of the Hall, and desperate references to debts and taxations which necessitated repeated appeals for subscriptions from members and the imposition of economies. Whilst King James was on the throne, the Society of Apothecaries could be confident of royal favour. His successor, Charles I, was immediately unpopular on account of his demand for a loan from the City, and further financial demands took the form of taxes, notably tonnage and poundage (aimed at wealthy merchants) and ship money (a tax on property to pay for the Fleet). The Apothecaries submitted reluctantly to the payment of ship money but drew the line at Bishop Laud's request for a contribution towards rebuilding St Paul's Cathedral.[2]

The eleven years' tyranny of Charles I's rule without Parliament (1629–40) aroused discontent, exacerbated by the king's determination to pursue war with Scotland which required "loans" to finance it. The Apothecaries were evidently concerned about the situation when Parliament was at last called in 1640. Representatives from the Society went to the "Parliament House", spending 6s 3d at the tavern afterwards[3] and they undertook several more journeys by water to Westminster before the Short Parliament dispersed. Concern centred on the king's attempt to force a loan of £100,000 from the City; this met with resistance and four Aldermen were imprisoned. The fury of Londoners then focused on Archbishop Laud and the Earl of Strafford (the former was impeached, the latter executed). The wealthier livery and trading companies of the City bore the brunt of the king's financial demands – the Apothecaries pleaded penury and paid just half of the £600 required of them in 1640.

Even the peace with Scotland had its price, for the disbanded troops caused tumult in the City during the autumn of 1641. The Lord Mayor commanded that the streets be well lit at night and the soldiers were ordered home. At Apothecaries' Hall ammunition, gunpowder, muskets and bandoleers, pikes and doublets, swords and belts were amassed in a small armoury and corn was purchased and stored in the gallery.[4]

The king's triumphant return from Scotland was the occasion for an ostentatious display of loyalty by the Lord Mayor, Aldermen and City companies in November 1641. The Apothecaries were invited to attend the procession, each Assistant and Liveryman contributing to the expense.[5] The celebrations in London did not disguise the fact that the Great Rebellion had broken out in Ireland. The City raised £100,000 towards the speedy supression of the Roman Catholic "rebels", of which the Apothecaries' share was £600. The alacrity with which members came forward with contributions – within twelve days – suggested strong feelings of repugnance at the massacre of Protestants.

At Westminster, the king's invasion of the House of Commons with the intention of arresting five Members on the charge of high treason made civil war inevitable. The five took sanctuary in the City where the citizens shut up shop and took up arms.

London was a Parliamentarian stronghold throughout the civil war, defended from Royalist attack by eleven miles of fortifications which members of the livery companies helped to construct. However, there were some wealthy citizens, Apothecaries among them, who were Royalists. The king's apothecary, J.W. Rumler, a prominent member of the Society who was elected Master three times, supplied the king with medicines during the war, personally carrying packages to him at Oxford. The Royal Apothecaries Adrian and Francis Metcalf were likewise loyal supporters of Charles I: Adrian accompanied the king and his physician William Harvey to Scotland in 1641, and Francis claimed to have lost a waggon of supplies at the battle of Naseby when the Royalist army was put to rout. The Apothecary Thomas Crosse attended the Lord General of the Army in the North (the Earl of Northumberland), but his cures failed and the Lord General resigned on account of his sickness in 1641. The botanist-Apothecary, Thomas Johnson of Snow Hill, joined the Royalists at the outbreak of the war, serving as a Lt Colonel under Sir Marmaduke Rawdon at the siege of Basing House (1643–44). During a skirmish with Sir William Waller's troops he was wounded and died shortly thereafter, eulogized as "the best herbalist of his age in England ... no less eminent in the garrison for his valour and conduct as a soldier".[6]

The Apothecary William Rosewell had the king's ear by 1639 when he was personally recommended by Charles I for the post of Apothecary to St Thomas' Hospital. The hospital Governors were not sympathetic to the king's will at the time and Rosewell was passed over until 1660. During the intervening twenty years he gave the king faithful service, for which he forfeited his estate during the Commonwealth. King Charles II was to put in a special plea for Rosewell in 1661, easing his passage onto the Court of Assistants without a fine, followed by his rapid promotion to the Mastership of the Society of Apothecaries (1661–62).[7] Thereafter, Major (Lt Colonel from 1667) Rosewell regularly acted as spokesman for the Society and was apothecary to Queen Catherine of Braganza from 1665.

One member of the Society was directly involved with the Restoration of the king in 1660 – Thomas Clarges, variously described as apothecary, doctor, a medical man, politician and envoy. He was a freeman of the Merchant Taylors' Company (1641), later paying £20 to be admitted to the freedom of the Apothecaries' Society by redemption (1646) and becoming a Liveryman in 1652. His political career was launched soon after the marriage of his sister Anne to General George Monck – as Monck's "seamstress" Anne Clarges had attended to his every need during his sojourn in the Tower of London. They married and she duly became the Duchess of Albemarle. As a result of Anne's influence over her husband, Clarges was entrusted with despatches from Richard Cromwell (Lord Protector) to General Monck in Scotland, where Clarges held a Parliamentary seat. These communications between Cromwell, Monck, army officers and Parliamentarians were to culminate in the Restoration of Charles II. Clarges personally journeyed to Breda in the spring of 1660 with Parliament's invitation to the exile to return and the king knighted him on the spot. Few men trusted Clarges – the diarist Samuel Pepys had little time for him ("a man of small entendimiento") or his sister, "a plain homely dowdy ... a damned ill-looked woman" but there was no denying they were both instrumental in the Restoration of King Charles II. Their family name is remembered in Clarges Street on the north side of Piccadilly, where Sir Thomas owned ten houses at the time of his death. The site was developed *circa* 1717–18 into a street of fashionable West End houses, named after Sir Thomas's son, Walter, a Baronet.[8]

Apart from these few notable Royalists, the trading Apothecaries were inclined to follow the Parliamentarian/Puritan tenor of the City generally, exemplified through the leadership of the Master (1639–41), Edward Cooke, who expressed his allegiance to the Parliamentarians by a legacy of £14,000, and through the example of their benefactor Gideon de Laune. The Protestant de Laune and Chamberlen families, related by marriage and religion, lived within the Black Friars precinct and Gideon de Laune was buried at the parish church of St Ann. De Laune's brother, Paul, served as physician/apothecary with the Parliamentary army of the Earl of Essex, and later as Physician General to Admiral Blake's Fleet in the West Indies; Gideon's nephew, Peter Chamberlen, was a fervent Anabaptist and eccentric pamphleteer.

Apothecaries' Hall was situated in one of three pre-eminently Puritan parishes in the City. The neighbourhood was peopled by Protestants, printers, actors, artists and Puritan feather-dressers, and large crowds were attracted to Black Friars to listen to the sermons given by William Gouge, the Presbyterian minister of St Ann's who read fifteen chapters of *The Bible* daily. The Society of Apothecaries signalled its warm support for Gouge by granting him the Honorary Freedom of the Society in 1633 and in 1649 he was awarded a gratuity of £40.[9]

At the outset of civil war Parliament voted a daily rate for medical officers – 5s for physicians, 4s for surgeons and 2s 6d for apothecaries to serve the force of 10,000 men enlisted under the Earl of Essex. Edward Odling, a freeman of the Society from 1624, served as physician with the Earl of Essex's troops, and Nicholas Culpeper, who had been an apprentice and journeyman apothecary, left his practice in Spitalfields to fight with General Sir Thomas Fairfax at the Battle of Newbury in 1643. There were other less conspicuous apothecaries supplying the New Model Army and the casualties of war who were cared for at Bart's, St Thomas', the Savoy, Bethlehem, Bridewell and Ely House. With the formation of the regular standing army in the reign of Charles II, the apothecary Robert Miller was appointed to the hospital for wounded soldiers in Ireland (1662), becoming Apothecary General there in 1671. Richard Whittle was Apothecary General to the Army (1666–89), succeeded by Charles Angibaud (Master of the Society 1728–29) and Isaac Teale, who served with Marlborough in Flanders (1702–10); other apothecaries were with the British forces in the West Indies and Portugal (1692–1712).

Shortly before Oliver Cromwell took the title of Lord Protector, two members of the Society of Apothecaries were elected Aldermen of the City of London – William Bell and John Lorrimer. Bell, Master (1641–42), sat in the Commons between 1640 and 1648, representing Westminster. He was one of the M.P.s excluded in "Pride's Purge" of December 1648 leaving the sectarian Rump Parliament which was determined to bring the king to trial. The election of Bell and Lorrimer as Aldermen came at a time of tension in City politics when many elected to office preferred to pay a fine to be discharged rather than serve – as did Lorrimer, who paid the large sum of £400 to avoid taking office, whereas Bell served one year.

By 1643 the Parliamentary Puritans controlled the City and financial demands were no longer for the king but to support the Parliamentary army. The Society of Apothecaries complained of "the great and extraordinary taxations and payments laid upon this Company", its debts and disability, forcing the suspension of all gratuities and payments.[10] When the next financial demand was received it was met by the personal generosity of two Assistants, Young (Apothecary to St Thomas' Hospital 1621–55) and de Laune, thus precluding the sale of the Society's plate.

General Fairfax, commander of the New Model Army, obtained weekly assessments levied on the City to support his soldiers – again, the Apothecaries' quota was subsidized by de Laune. When Fairfax's troops descended on London in December 1648 soldiers were billetted at Apothecaries' Hall once the windows had been removed, and the plate, documents and precious possessions placed in a trunk and entrusted to Abraham Webb, a Past Master. Some silver spoons were sold to pay debts and any remaining were distributed to Assistants for safekeeping[11] – a wise precaution in view of Fairfax's orders to seize the treasuries at Goldsmiths' and Weavers' Halls. In such turbulent times the Society hired soldiers of the trained bands to safeguard the Hall and during the crisis of the winter of 1648–49 dinners were held at Cooks' Hall in Aldersgate Street.[12]

The execution of King Charles I on 30 January 1649 went unrecorded by the Clerk, the only hint of regicide being the order for the replacement of the king's arms at the Hall by those of the Commonwealth.[13] With the end of the civil war a measure of normality was restored – the beds occupied by the soldiers were counted and cleaned and the Hall was repaired, then inspected by Mr Mills (Peter Mills, the City bricklayer and later one of the surveyors overseeing the rebuilding after the Great Fire).[14] The new Lord Protector, Oliver Cromwell, made peace with the Dutch in 1654 and the City settled into a period of Puritan military government.

The apprentices rioted in December 1655, generating widespread concern for the peace and safety of the City. The alliance of the City authorities with General Monck averted further disruption and in February 1660 Monck's army was well-received in London. Church bells rang, the troops were fêted and bonfires lit from Cheapside to Temple Bar – there was a spit for roasting rumps on the bonfire at Ludgate Hill (a reference to the approaching dismissal of the Rump Parliament). The king arrived in the capital in May welcomed by the gift of £12,000 from the City, to which Apothecaries contributed £72, with an additional £18 "for entertaining His Majesty". The expenses were met by the sale of plate, and gifts from members who gladly contributed to the levy for "His most excellent Majesty as a testimony of this Court and the whole City". The Lord Mayor planned a suitable reception for the monarch towards which the Society of Apothecaries was ordered to provide twelve of the "most grave, tall and comely personages . . . well horsed and in the best array or furniture of velvet, plush or satin and chains of gold", attended by footmen. Banners, streamers and ornaments of triumph were required; the footmen were each given 5s 6d for a new pair of shoes, and the king's arms went up in the Hall once again. The contingent of "comely" Apothecaries in the procession to welcome the king was headed by John Lorrimer and no cost was spared at the celebration dinner on coronation day.[15]

The euphoria was marred by the extent of the king's debts, reduced by the imposition of customs on beer, ale, tea and coffee and the unpopular hearth tax. Worse was to follow in the resumption of the Dutch War, the Great Plague and the Great Fire.

The Great Plague
The playwright Thomas Dekker observed that during the plague of 1625 "none thrive but apothecaries, butchers, cooks and coffin-makers".[16] The same applied during the epidemic of 1665. Even Dr Christopher Merrett, who berated the frauds and abuses of Apothecaries, admitted that "In the plague time (most physicians being out of town) they [Apothecaries] took upon them the whole practice of physic".[17] This was not to say that the College of Physicians was totally negligent for in June 1665, once the gravity of the epidemic was apparent, the College appointed eight "plague" Physicians. These men did their duty and survived – one of their number, Nathaniel Hodges, wrote an account of the year. He thought the origin of the bubonic plague lay in "an Aura that is poisonous"; he went on to explore the merits of powder of toads, tobacco and ground unicorn's horn as antidotes – personally he relied on lozenges and sack (white wine) to ward off infection.[18] Other Physicians besides the appointed eight could be found in the capital – Dr Thomas Wharton for instance, who was an Honorary Freeman of the Society of Apothecaries, and some two dozen colleagues.[19] The rest fled, including the famous Dr Thomas Sydenham and Dr Micklethwaite, Physician to Bart's. The absent Physicians incurred a good deal of criticism, as did the quacks who sold "cures" to the gullible public. By contrast, the reputations of the Apothecaries who stayed in the City and coped with the emergency were enhanced.

The Society's records only hint at the severity of the Great Plague: the summer herbarizing was cancelled due to "the sickness" and the Bedel was given £7 in recognition of his long service and poverty in the contagion.[20] The number of deaths multiplied as the summer progressed and the inhabitants of the City deserted it if they could. Infected houses were boarded up and shops closed, although Apothecaries' shops were busy for there were profits to be made. Social gatherings were discouraged for fear of spreading the infection and taverns were shut to all but travellers. As with previous outbreaks, the crowded parishes close to the City walls and the riverside recorded the greatest number of deaths. Disease, and especially the plague, spread rapidly in the neighbourhood of the insanitary River Fleet, at Bridewell and Black Friars. Deaths in the parish of St Ann totalled 652 for the plague year, 476 of them being attributed to the epidemic. Undeterred by the increase in deaths as the summer went on, the Apothecaries held a Livery dinner in June, followed by dinners at The Swan in Fish Street on the search day in August and on Election Day.

Samuel Pepys was one of those who remained in London and his Diary reveals that his Physician, Dr Burnett, died of the plague in August. Pepys's friend John Battersby, an Apothecary with a shop at the sign of The Great Helmet in Fenchurch Street, survived to be Master of the Society (1674–75). Pepys found the City strangely deserted during the summer of the Great Plague, and "in Westminster there is never a physician and but one apothecary left, all being dead".[21]

Pepys consulted Apothecaries on matters of health and counted several members of the Society among his drinking companions: Valentine Fage (nominated Master in 1669) treated a symptom Pepys referred to as a cancer in his mouth; Battersby treated both Mr and Mrs Pepys; Ludwig Fowler, a freeman Apothecary, was a kinsman of the diarist; Walter Pelling (Master 1671–72) was a close friend of Pepys, who was himself Master of the Clothworkers' Company (1677–78). He was influential in the Navy Office and later at the Admiralty, in which capacity he forwarded to the king a memo from one of his staff, Richard Gibson, recommending that naval surgeons should be supplied with medicine chests from Apothecaries' Hall – thus sowing the seed from which the Navy Stock germinated (see page 166).[21]

An analysis of Apothecaries during the Great Plague reaches the conclusion that "probably as many as three-quarters of the Apothecaries and their apprentices remained in London" and that about fifty Apothecaries or members of their families died at that time.[22] The Royal Apothecary Stephen Chase died of the plague, so did Henry Best, Apothecary to Charterhouse, and William Johnson, the Apothecary/chemist to the College of Physicians who had helped distribute medicines for the poor and who devised his own antidote to the sickness. When the epidemic had subsided the depleted

Pestle and mortar dated 1662 and belonging to the Apothecary John Battersby whose shop was at the sign of The Great Helmet, Fenchurch Street. Battersby was Master of the Society (1674–75) and was a friend of Mr and Mrs Samuel Pepys.

number of the Society of Apothecaries was indicated by the call of 111 to the Livery – only twenty-five accepted.[23]

Nathaniel Upton, an Apothecary who was Master of the Pest House for plague victims in Finsbury Fields, survived, despite having to inspect the dead in the City. His apprentice, John Houghton, recalled that his master was very busy at the time, even though London was "so thin that I saw before Drapers' Hall behind the Exchange grass growing of a considerable length". Houghton later established a shop and meeting place where coffee, chocolate and sago could be purchased as well as the regular remedies. He was a member of the Court of Assistants and was proposed for Fellowship of the Royal Society by Robert Hooke in 1680. Nothing if not versatile, Houghton collected specimens for the Royal Society's Museum, published his advanced theory of free trade in *England's Greatest Happiness*, and another publication earned him a reputation as the father of English advertising.[24]

One of the acknowledged heroes of the Great Plague was Francis Bernard, Apothecary to Bart's, who worked indefatigably in the absence of the hospital's Physicians, Micklethwaite and Tearne. His medical skills were to be recognized in his appointment as a Physician to Bart's, and to King James II, also through a Fellowship of the Royal College of Physicians. He was the friend of Dr William Harvey and Sir Hans Sloane, who acquired part of Bernard's library. Elevated as he was, he retained a soft spot for the Society of Apothecaries, shown by his gift of £20 in 1689. James James, Apothecary at Bethlehem Hospital, remained at his post during the plague and the efforts of an Apothecary named Slade were saluted by the king's gift of a piece of plate. Perhaps the best known Apothecary in the City during the plague was William Boghurst, whose shop was at the sign of The White Hart, St Giles-in-the-Fields. He attended forty to sixty patients a

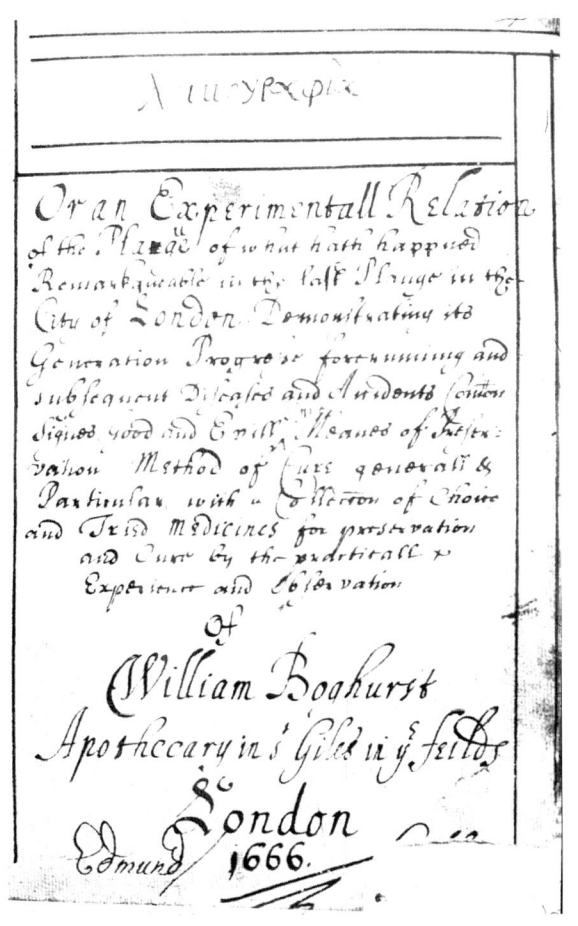

Title page of William Boghurst's manuscript "Loimographia", his account of the Great Plague of 1665. Boghurst was a freeman of the Society with a shop called The White Horse in the parish of St Giles-in-the-Fields.

day during the summer of 1665, "with wonderful success". Experience taught him that those who caught the plague usually died within six days. His remedies were manifold and he attributed the cause of the disease to a poison in the soil. Boghurst lamented the absence of Physicians whose duty was to watch over people's lives and he complained of the upstart empirics who sold useless medicines at extortionate rates. He was in no doubt that Apothecaries who lived by their own practice were duty-bound to attend to the needs of the plague victims. He personally dressed sores, let blood, sat at the bedsides of the dying and laid out the corpses.[25]

Another Apothecary who remained in London during the epidemic was John Conyers, who could be found at the sign of The Unicorn in Fleet Street. Like Boghurst, he wrote a pamphlet on the prevention and cure of the plague. Conyers was also an inventor, a maker of instruments, the author of papers in *Philosophical Transactions* and has been cited as London's first archaeologist (the Roman phial illustrated on page 12 came from his collection).[26]

The Great Plague reached a peak in September with 26,230 recorded deaths in the City, giving an official total of 68,596 deaths attributed to this bout of the epidemic.[27] One year later the capital was struck by a second disaster.

Display drug jars that belonged to James Gover (Master 1690–91), inscribed with his initials and the name of the contents: c. anthos (conserve of rosemary, said to be beneficial for nerves); s. melissoph (syrup of bastard balm, a stimulant); c. absynth (confection of wormwood, an antispasmodic).

The Great Fire

The Great Fire of London swept westwards for two days before reaching Black Friars on 4 September 1666. The inhabitants of the City packed their belongings into carts and boats and sought refuge outside the City walls. As the flames approached Apothecaries' Hall, the Society's records, some portraits, leather chairs, plate and pewter were rescued but most of the furnishings perished. The Renter Warden, John Battersby, looked after a trunk of treasures and pewter, Hinton and Johnson stored pewter and plate and John Lorrimer's widow took care of her husband's portrait.[28] When Gideon de Laune's portrait (on page 44) was eventually recovered and returned to its rightful place in 1751, it was said to have been charred by the Great Fire – the legend lives on.

On Tuesday 4 September the fire reached Baynard's Castle on the Thames waterfront, then approached the Black Friars precinct, the parish church of St Ann and Apothecaries' Hall. Another arm of flames approached St Paul's Cathedral from Cheapside – John Evelyn saw the stones of the Cathedral flying like grenades and "the lead melting down the streets in a stream".[29] Another spectator told how the flames "rushed like a torrent down Ludgate Hill"[30] leaving a layer of charcoal and burnt debris some 3 inches thick on the road surface. It was hoped that the Fleet Ditch (which then flowed sluggishly into the Thames along the line of the present New Bridge Street) would act as a firebreak and to assist this the houses on both sides of the Ditch were demolished. The strategy failed, for the wind blew burning flakes over the Ditch to Salisbury Court and Bridewell Dock, the fire advancing along Fleet Street and proceeding as far as the Temple before it abated as the wind fell.

Apothecaries' Hall was one of fifty-two livery company halls destroyed. Many members of the Society must also have suffered the loss of their shops and homes. Apparently unperturbed, the Court met on 2 October at an undisclosed rendezvous and resumed normal business.[31] The City presented a sad prospect during the winter of 1666–67, for some 13,200 houses, eighty-seven churches and the Cathedral, six chapels, Guildhall, the Royal Exchange, Custom House, Sessions House, over fifty company halls, Blackwell Hall, Bridewell, Newgate Gaol, the Wood Street and Poultry Compters, three City gates and four bridges had been destroyed or severely damaged. Rebuilding could not commence until a workable plan had been authorized – Wren's first, unexecuted plan allocated the site of Apothecaries' Hall for the City's wood market. In February 1667 a more practical master-plan was sanctioned, so the surveying and staking out of the streets and sites began. The Apothecaries made arrangements to use Cooks' Hall on the north side of the City while their own Hall was rebuilt under the supervision of a committee. The rebuilding of Apothecaries' Hall is described in Chapter 4, it suffices to say that the Court acted swiftly and positively by negotiating to acquire additional land next to the Hall from Lady de Laune, by securing a wharf and by organizing a supply of

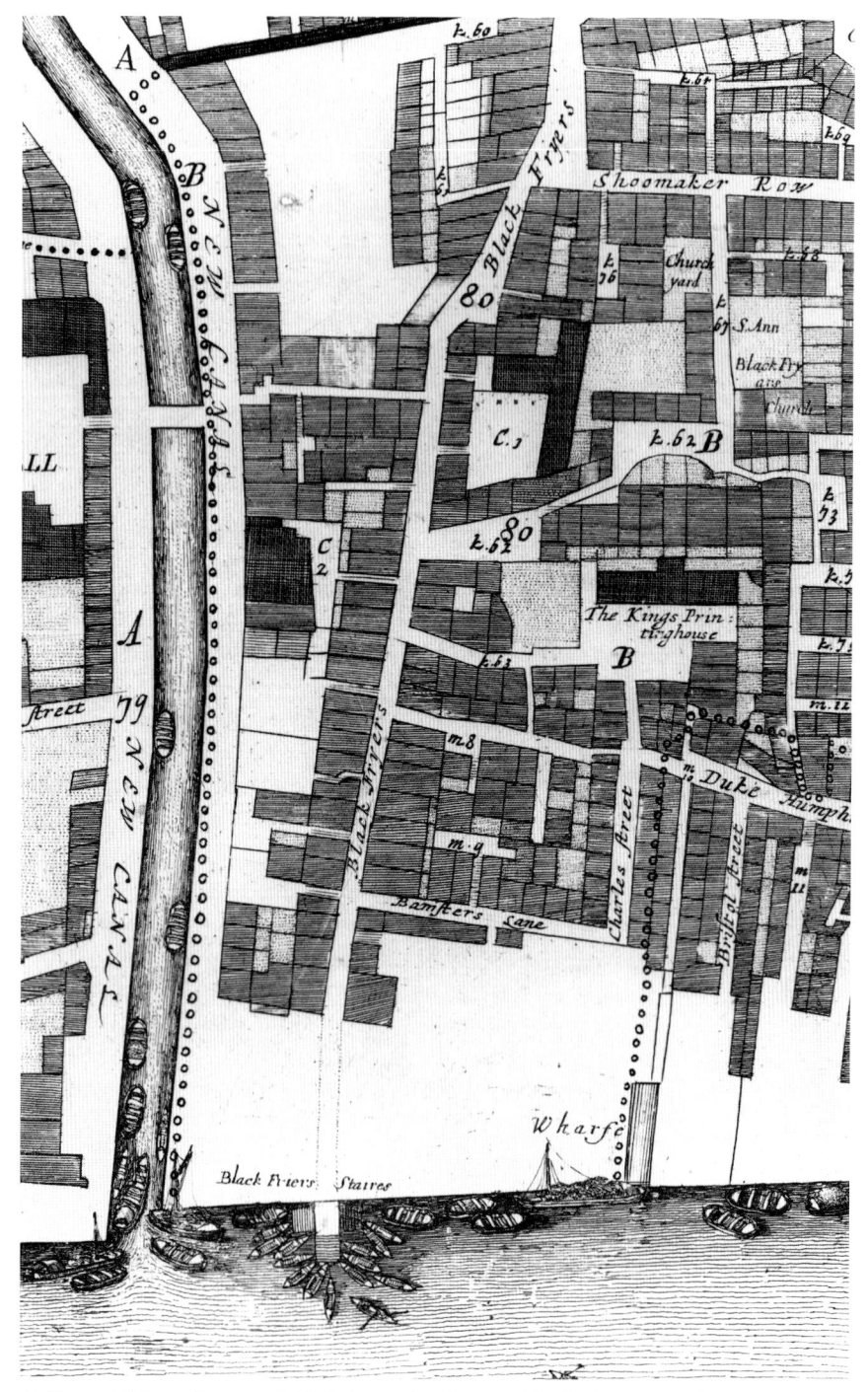

Ogilby and Morgan's map of 1676 shows Apothecaries' Hall, the courtyard (C3) and Black Friars ten years after the Great Fire.

New River Water (fresh water from the New River Company). Further determination was shown by the decision to apply money that would have paid for an Election Day dinner to the rebuilding fund and to sell all the Society's plate except the gifts of benefactors.[32]

The Hall had not been completely razed to the ground by the fire: at least one chimney and some walls remained standing.[33] To the east, walls of the late-thirteenth-century Dominican Priory were revealed once the fire debris was cleared; to the west along the Fleet Ditch a major building programme was soon underway with the construction of the New Canal (1670–74). The project for this new waterway, 40 feet wide and lined by wide wharfs, was under the direction of Sir Christopher Wren leading a workforce of 200 men. The rebuilding of Apothecaries' Hall proceeded at the same time, creating a confusing scene for some years. Ogilby and Morgan's map of 1676 (opposite) shows Black Friars ten years after the Great Fire – mostly rebuilt with the exception of the church of St Ann which had disappeared forever, and the strip along the riverside reserved for the proposed Thames Quay.

The surrender of the charter

The rebuilding of the Hall and the provision of the Laboratory there, the acquisition of a ceremonial barge and the Physic Garden engrossed the Society during the 1670s. The burnt-out City was being reconstructed, the New Canal was dug and the foundation stone for the new St Paul's Cathedral was laid in 1675. The third Dutch War was afoot from 1672, bringing unwelcome taxes, and the scandal of the conversion of the king's brother to Roman Catholicism amid rumours that the king would soon follow, rocked the country. The fiercely anti-Catholic Parliament passed the Test Act in 1673 obliging office-holders to take the sacrament according to the rites of the Church of England. A precept from the Lord Mayor required the Master, Wardens, Assistants and Clerk of the Society of Apothecaries to do so and there were no objections.[34]

The king's reaction to growing opposition in Parliament and in the City was to bring both to heel. He reduced the City to submission by demanding the surrender of its charter, and removing the Lord Mayor, some Aldermen and Sheriffs. He then turned to the livery companies, recalling their charters and replacing office-holders and Liverymen by his own nominees. The Master of the Apothecaries, Peter Sambrooke, revealed to the Court that a writ of *Quo Warranto* had been issued against the Society's charter in April 1684. The Society immediately petitioned its objection to this arbitrary act, only to be informed by the Attorney General that it was His Majesty's pleasure that "the Company do surrender into His Majesty's hands the power of electing Master, Wardens, Assistants and Clerk".[35] The same treatment was being dealt to other livery companies, the aim being to achieve the compliance of the City and Parliament to the king's autocratic will.

There was no realistic option but to surrender, as the Society did, thereby transferring to the king the power to elect the Master, Wardens and Assistants. Accordingly, the Master and the Upper Warden were removed from office and a list of forty-one eligible Apothecaries was submitted to the Attorney General to enable him to select acceptable Assistants. The Society was then reconstituted in February 1685 with a new charter (conserved among the Hall archives but in a fragile state), a new Master and a new governing body of men willing to take the oath of Supremacy and Allegiance to the king.

The Clerk, John Meres, who had served the Society since 1673, was evidently not pleasing to the king, so was dismissed from his post and evicted from his house at Apothecaries' Hall in favour of a royal nominee, the hitherto unknown Edward Fleetwood. Another new face was that of Sir John Clarke who decided that "according to his honour and quality" he was entitled to a prominent place on the Court of Assistants, causing some resentment.[36]

King Charles II achieved his objective in packing the City with his supporters, but he died soon thereafter, on 6 February 1685, ten days before the new charter was read to the Apothecaries' Court.

His successor and brother, James II, adopted a similar policy of interference in City politics. A mayoral precept informed the Society of Apothecaries that the king would be pleased to grant a new Livery, and suitable men were chosen and sworn in.[37] The Society then settled down to its domestic affairs, administering the Laboratory and adopting measures against fraudulent sellers of medicines.

Tranquillity was shortlived, for in 1687 King James took further measures. Following his Declaration of Indulgence suspending laws against Roman Catholics and Dissenters, he removed hardened Tories from civic offices and livery companies. Many City Aldermen were dismissed or resigned, allowing the king's apothecary, James St Amand (Master for the same year) to fill one vacancy (he had been apothecary to the king before his accession to the throne, so his loyalty was assured).

The livery companies of the City were then purged. By an Order in Council twenty-five named Assistants and twenty-six Liverymen were removed from their positions in the Society of Apothecaries with the instruction that their places were to be filled by men who would elect the king's supporters as Members of Parliament. Sir John Clarke (to be Master 1694–95), Dr Francis Bernard, Dr John Jones (formerly apothecary to Charles II's household) and John Chase (Master 1664–66 and the apothecary to Charles II) were among those removed. Evidently the Apothecaries who had served Charles II were no longer to be relied upon, but James Chase (son of John above), described as "belonging to the person of the King" and Dr Robert Lightfoot, "belonging"

Pharmaceutical tile dated 1686 and belonging to the Apothecary John Smithies, who was made free of the Society that year. Tiles were sometimes used for rolling pills, more usually they were hung in apothecaries' shops. The arms and motto indicated affiliation to the Society.

to the Queen Dowager, were reinstated. Similarly, the Master of the Society, St Amand, was apothecary to the king and queen, and was therefore acceptable. The subservience of the Court of Assistants to the king's will was underlined by seating the Royal Apothecaries Chase and Lightfoot in places next to the Master and Wardens at the table, an honour that had been accorded to J.W. Rumler in 1633 and was henceforward a tradition. The obsequious Assistants went further by sending an Address of Thanks to the king for his Declaration of Indulgence (the Apothecaries' was one of the first to be received).[38] Another change of personnel took place in the spring of 1688 when the removal of thirteen Assistants and twenty-two Liverymen was ordered, restoring some old faces to the Court.[39]

With the king's second Declaration of Indulgence in April 1688 his unpopularity reached a peak. Archbishop Sancroft and six bishops took a stand and found themselves committed to the Tower, assured of the support of London's populace. By the end of June an invitation to invade had been sent to William of Orange as the prelude to the Glorious Revolution. Prince William landed with his supporters at Torbay on 5 November 1688 and entered London in December. Reassured by the advent of a new monarchy, the Court of the Society of Apothecaries met on 28 November to cancel the surrender of 1684 and restore the charter of 1617. The Assistants installed by James II "dissolved themselves and departed", James Chase was elected Master (he was soon to enter Parliament as M.P. for Marlow) and the Clerk John Meres was recalled.[40] The Glorious Revolution was completed by the Convention Parliament of 1689 which proclaimed William III joint sovereign in conjunction with his wife, Mary.

The vicissitudes of the 1680s had no long-term effect on the Society of Apothecaries. At the earliest opportunity the Society reverted to the authority of its original charter, which remains valid, and resumed its habitual contest with the College of Physicians.

The entry of William of Orange into Exeter, November 1688, attributed to Jan Wijck and presented to the Society by Reuben Melmoth (Master 1749–50).

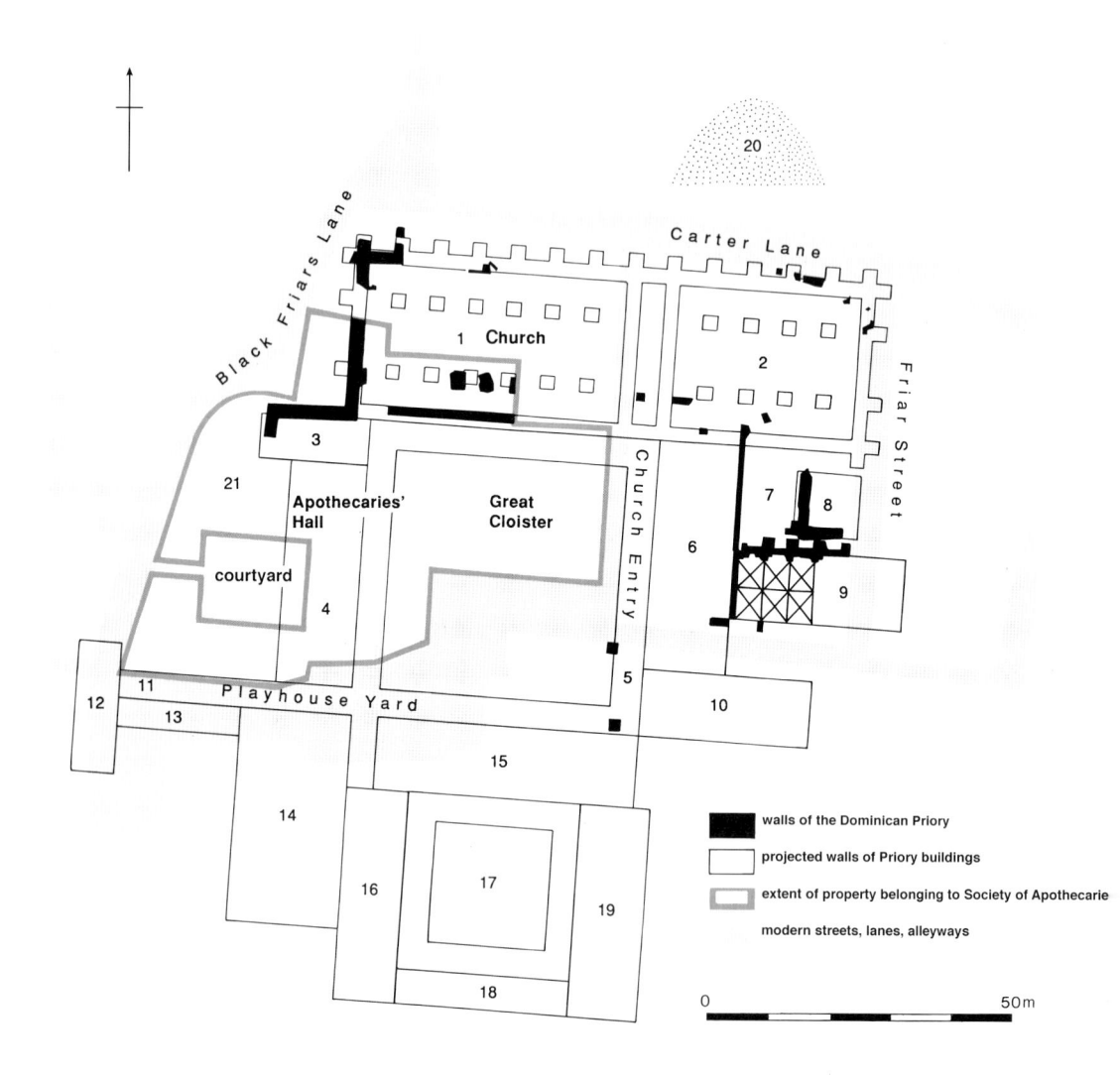

A plan of the buildings of London Black Friars *circa* 1538, based on archaeological work and documentary research. The layout of some buildings is projected from a survey of 1550 and other documents.

KEY. 1. Nave. 2. Choir. 3. Porter's Lodge. 4. Guest-house, kitchens, pantry and buttery. 5. Passageway around the Great Cloister. 6. Chapter-house. 7. Garden. 8. Prior's Lodgings. 9. Provincial's Hall. 10. Dorter. 11. Passageway. 12. Portinary's House – former gatehouse? 13. Duchy Chamber. 14. Parliament Chamber or hall. 15. Frater. 16. Infirmary. 17. Infirmary Cloister. 18. Bake and brewhouses. 19. Library. 20. Cemetery. 21. Gallery to Bridewell Palace.

Chapter 4

Apothecaries' Hall

The royal charter of 1617 endowed the Society of Apothecaries with the right to possess property and specifically to "have, purchase, retain and appoint a certain Hall, or Counsel-House" in the City. Yet it was not until 1632 that the Society purchased its first Hall, a property known as Cobham House that had been the guest-house of Black Friars Priory. With Cobham House the Society acquired a coach-house and stables, outbuildings, a garden and ground extending south to the River Thames. This chapter traces the history of Cobham House, which became Apothecaries' Hall in 1632, and that of the adjoining premises and other properties at Black Friars belonging to the Society.

For reasons unspecified but probably because subscriptions towards the proposed purchase were disappointingly low, the Society's attempt to acquire a house in Foster Lane proved abortive in 1621. Discouraged and mindful of its precarious financial position, the Society made no further attempts to purchase a Hall for ten years. Meanwhile, meetings of the Court were held at Painter-Stainers' Hall and possibly at Scriveners' Hall.[1] By 1631 the Society was out of debt and thoughts turned to the acquisition of property for a Hall. Premises at Bucklersbury and St Peter's Hill were viewed and finally "a house in the Blackfriars", after which members adjourned to The Greyhound for serious discussion. The house at Black Friars was Cobham House, and in October 1632 the Court agreed to buy it "to make a hall for ye Company".[2] Once the decision was taken, negotiations with the vendor proceeded swiftly; the purchase price of £1,800 was agreed in November and on 3 December the Clerk took possession of Cobham House on behalf of the Society of Apothecaries.[3]

Thus the Society acquired the site of the guest-house within the precinct of the former Priory. The Dominicans who gave their name to the area (on account of the black hooded cloaks they wore) had moved there in 1278, at which time part of the Roman city wall was demolished and stone by stone a new wall was built further west, along the east bank of the Fleet Ditch to give a precinct of some 5 acres – part of this late-thirteenth-century wall survives beneath Pilgrim Street.

The Priory of the Black Friars was dominated by a large church built between 1279 and 1288 with a twin-aisled nave and choir, separated by a passage-way and topped by a spire. To the south of the church was the Great Cloister, surrounded by domestic buildings – the guest-house, kitchens, frater, dorter and chapter-house. Further south was a smaller cloister around which were grouped the infirmary, bake and brew-houses – the location of all these buildings can be seen on the plan opposite. To the north of the church was the Priory cemetery, laid out over the infilled southern ditch of a Norman castle known as Montfichet's Tower. As the entire site of the Priory sloped from north to south, the buildings would have been constructed on various levels or terraces. The whole complex was palatial and is described in the late-fourteenth-century poem *Piers Ploughman* as having a "wonderously-built minster", alabaster tombs, buildings "all walled with strong stone standing on high", with leaded roofs, tiled floors and glazed windows, orchards and gardens, "pillared and painted cloisters", "the chapter-house wrought like a great church" and the frater had a hall fit for a king. Black Friars was the most important Priory of medieval London, patronized by royalty, used for meetings of Parliaments and Councils, for trials and for the accommodation of dignitaries.

Since 1981 the Museum of London archaeologists have undertaken a number of investigations on sites within the Black Friars precinct which have located fragments of the east and west ends of the church, the Prior's Lodgings, the Provincial's Hall, and a large portion of the Priory cemetery has been excavated. This has allowed earlier archaeological work and documentary evidence to be reassessed to produce the new plan of the precinct buildings (page 74).

The Priory was an appropriate place to accommodate Emperor Charles V during his visit to London in June 1522. The visit was of national importance, marking the recent alliance of King Henry VIII and the Emperor against France; it was a triumphant public occasion and the opportunity for ostentation. The Emperor arrived with 2,000 courtiers, staying first at Greenwich Palace, and going thence to Black Friars, where he lodged in the Priory guest-house. To facilitate communications between the king at Bridewell and the Emperor at Black Friars a new gallery was built connecting the Palace and the Priory – a timber-framed structure, hung with tapestries and with a resting place mid-way. It crossed the Fleet immediately south of Bridewell Bridge and traced the line now taken by Apothecary Street, entering the Priory guest-house at first floor level – the position of the present Library at Apothecaries' Hall. It provided private access between the two establishments and proved particularly convenient during King Henry VIII's divorce proceedings of 1529 when the tribunal assembled in the Parliament Chamber at Black Friars to hear the case against Queen Catherine. Both king and queen lodged in apartments at Bridewell Palace in early June, consulting their respective advisers about the impending trial while cardinals, archbishops, bishops and their attendants descended on Black Friars Priory. When the time came for the queen to appear before the tribunal, she was residing at Baynard's Castle, and travelled the short distance to the Parliament Chamber at Black Friars. The crucial episode was immortalized by Shakespeare in *King Henry VIII* Act II Scene 4 when Queen Catherine kneels before her husband and pleads for mercy as "a most poor woman" and "a true and humble wife". The queen then escaped to Greenwich, leaving the king to witness the unsatisfactory termination of the trial in July, after which the ecclesiastics dispersed from Black Friars because the case was referred to Rome.

The gallery between Bridewell Palace and Black Friars Priory, paced by King Henry VIII during the summer of 1529, was repaired and plastered for the benefit of the French Ambassador in 1534 but had decayed by 1548[4] – the Priory was by then dissolved and Bridewell was no longer used as a royal palace. At ground level the gallery was replaced by a row of tenements, rebuilt as six messuages by a goldsmith named Hardrett in the 1630s, passing as houses, shops and yards to Edward Corbett (possibly the same Corbett who was the Society's cook) in 1662. Where it crossed the Fleet Ditch the gallery was replaced by the wooden Bridewell Bridge, and after the Great Fire by a stone equivalent until this stretch of the Fleet was filled in to form New Bridge Street (1764). At its eastern end the sixteenth-century gallery survived to be re-tiled by Peter Mills as part of the renovations undertaken by the Apothecaries soon after the acquisition of Cobham House for their Hall in 1632. The room continued to be known as the gallery until it was converted into a repository for books in 1682 – the Library.[5]

During the reign of King Edward II (1307–27) seventy-five friars lived and worshipped at the Priory; at its dissolution in 1538 the Prior and just fifteen friars surrendered. The friars had augmented their income by letting some of the buildings to laity – Lord Cobham, Sir Henry Wyatt and Lord Zouche were among the residents in 1522. After the dissolution major grants of property in the precinct went to Sir Thomas Cawarden, and to George Brooke, Lord Cobham, who in 1546 secured his foothold by obtaining a mansion there with "le Closett Wyndowe" giving a view into the church, and confirming that his mansion abutted onto the south-west end of the nave.[6] Cobham added to his property by purchasing "a nether room" and a hall adjoining Cobham House from Cawarden, giving him the substantial range of buildings that had once formed the guest-house on the west side of the Priory's Great Cloister. A survey of *circa* 1556 described Cobham House as "a house and gardens with many fair edifices ... certain lands and tenements", including the old convent kitchen marked by the remains of a medieval well under the courtyard of Apothecaries' Hall, and chambers to the south used by the first Black Friars Playhouse in 1576.[7]

It is likely that Lord Cobham carried out major repairs to convert the guest-house for his own use, incorporating some of the sturdy foundations and walls of the medieval Priory, which have since been traced. In 1915 when part of the Society's premises was redeveloped, work revealed two substantial wall foundations. The first was the west wall of the nave of the Dominican church

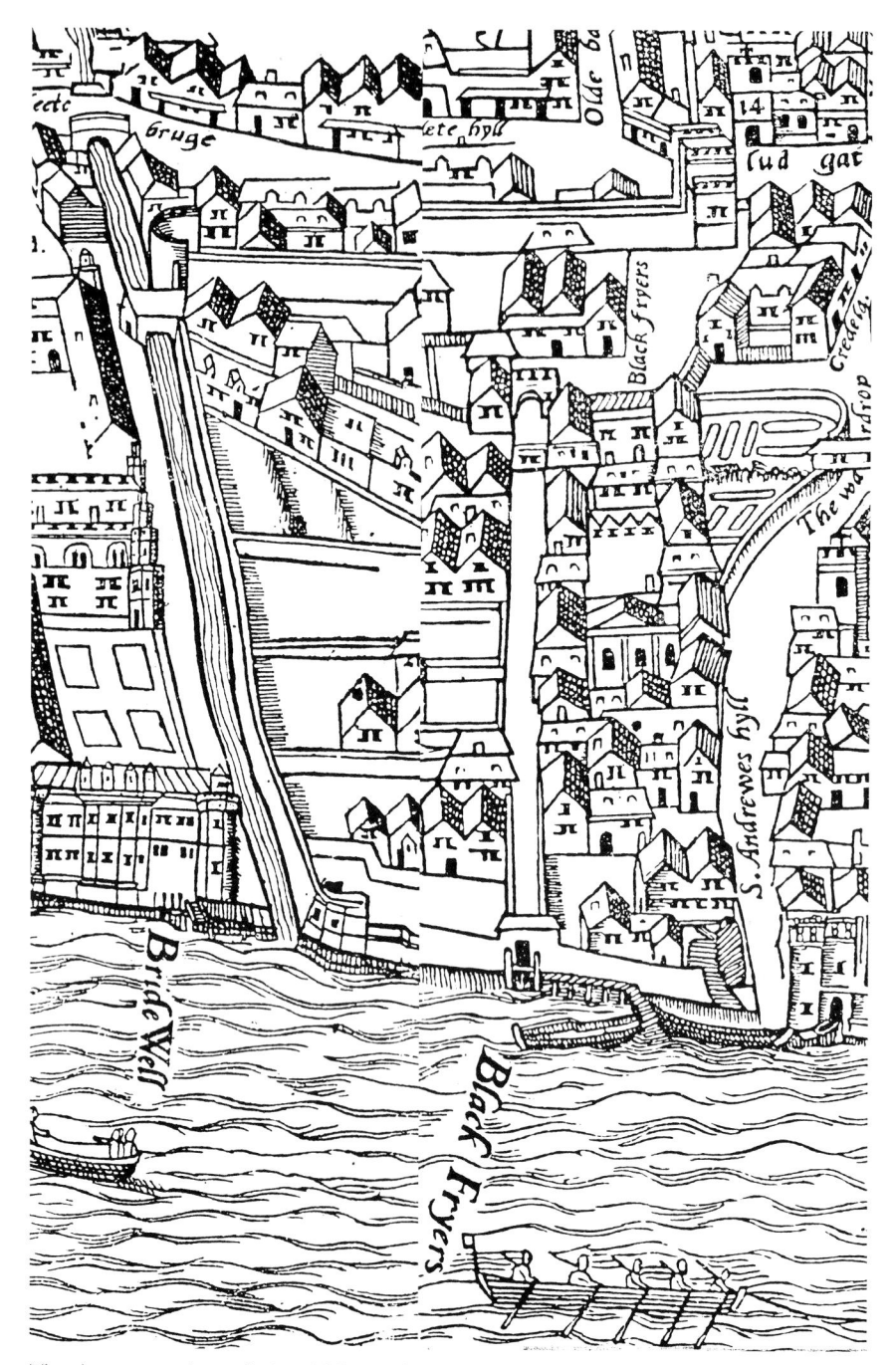

The Agas map view of *circa* 1553–59 shows the river stairs at Black Friars. The former Priory buildings on the east side of Water Lane were in lay ownership at this time. The gallery that had linked the Priory guest-house with Bridewell Palace has been replaced by a row of cottages leading to Bridewell Bridge.

and the second was the north wall of the Porter's Lodge adjoining the guest-house. Part of the latter and three pier bases for the arcade of the church's south aisle were examined in the redevelopment of 20–26 Black Friars by the Society in 1983.

Although the Priory buildings no longer stand above ground level, echoes of their plan can still be seen in the modern streetscape – a number of alleys and property boundaries follow the lines of the medieval Priory buildings. Carter Lane marks the northern side of the church, Friar Street is on the line of the east wall of the choir, while Church Entry was formerly the passage between the nave and the choir, and further south, it approximates to the eastern arm of the Great Cloister. Sadly, there are only two fragments of the Priory walls standing above ground level: in the garden in Ireland Yard a short length of the south wall of the Provincial's Hall is visible and nearby at 10 Friar Street part of the north wall including a complete ground storey window is preserved within a new building.[8] Stonework from the Priory buildings was found recently in a sixteenth-century well south of Apothecary Street and medieval carved stone fragments have been preserved in the courtyard of Apothecaries' Hall.

When the Society of Apothecaries made its home at Black Friars the precinct was outside the jurisdiction of the City authorities and for this reason it attracted residents who wished to avoid close surveillance such as actors, foreigners and conspirators. Sir Thomas Cawarden, the chief beneficiary of ecclesiastical property at Black Friars, rejoiced in the title of Master of the Revels, being responsible for royal entertainments. A more serious side to his nature, his Protestant faith, made him a prime suspect during the reign of the Catholic Queen Mary. He was suspected of involvement in Wyatt's rebellion of 1554 when the rebel forces reached Ludgate before they were repulsed. Cawarden was arrested, imprisoned in The Clink and when his mansion at Black Friars was searched an arsenal of weapons and arms was discovered, sufficient to equip a small army. Despite being indicted for heresy five times, Cawarden retained his freedom and his Black Friars property, which passed on his death to Sir William More of Loseley House near Guildford, whose tenant at Black Friars was Dr William de Laune. Cawarden left a memento of his occupation in the form of a seal from a bottle bearing the initials TC, which came to light during excavations at the Hall in 1983.

George Brooke, ninth Baron Cobham of Cobham House, Black Friars, was also arrested for complicity in Wyatt's rebellion, and on the accession of King James his descendants, the eleventh Baron Cobham and his brother, were responsible for the Cobham Plot "to kill the King and his cubs" and place Arabella Stuart in the throne. Lord Cobham's loyalty to Queen Elizabeth, however, had never been questioned. He was made a Knight of the Garter in 1599 and the following year he entertained the queen at Black Friars as part of the marriage celebrations for Lord Herbert and Anne, daughter of Lord Russell. Sir Robert Sidney reported that the entertainment was great and plentiful – Cobham House was evidently grand enough to receive the queen who dined with Lord Cobham and was entertained by a masque; she was even persuaded to dance, at the age of sixty-seven.[9]

With the discovery of the Cobham Plot in 1603, Lord Cobham and his brother were accused of treason and imprisoned in the Tower with Sir Walter Raleigh. Lady Cobham, daughter of Lord Howard of Effingham (Earl of Nottingham and Lord High Admiral at the time of the Spanish Armada), abandoned her disgraced husband and retreated to Cobham Hall in Kent. She gave Cobham House at Black Friars to her brother and sister-in-law, William and Lady Anne Howard, as a wedding present in 1609 and it was the trustees of Lady Anne who sold Cobham House to the Society of Apothecaries in 1632.

In the 1630s the precinct of Black Friars was no longer a haven for courtiers and conspirators; it had become populous and at times riotous. The decline of the neighbourhood was attributed to the Playhouse, first established in chambers vacated by Lord Cobham (1576). By the early seventeenth century this had been superseded by the Burbages' Playhouse in the former Parliament Chamber of the Priory, a popular resort but a source of irritation and inconvenience to local residents. The inhabitants petitioned regularly, complaining about the "common playhouse" which attracted "vagrant and lewd persons". A second petition prompted an order for the suppression of the Playhouse on the grounds that it generated unruly behaviour in the precinct where the great multitude of coaches caused chaos in the narrow lanes, leading to "quarrels and effusion of blood".[10] Proximity to the Playhouse induced actors to take lodgings at Black Friars – William Shakespeare and Ben Jonson, no less, in the early seventeenth century, when artists, printers, Huguenots and Puritans dominated the neighbourhood. In the year that the Apothecaries established their Hall here, Anthony van Dyck arrived from Flanders to take up residence in order to paint the portraits of King Charles and Queen Henrietta Maria: the king was a regular visitor to van Dyck's studio at Black Friars, while the queen favoured the Playhouse. An order of Parliament forced the closure of the Playhouse in 1647 and the building was demolished in 1655 to make way for tenements but its site is immortalized in Playhouse Yard, larger since it absorbed Glasshouse Yard to the east where glass was made in the late sixteenth century. Undeterred by the official prohibition of playhouses, the cavalier poet laureate Sir William Davenant organized surreptitious performances wherever he could find suitable premises, such as at Apothecaries' Hall where the dais in the Great Hall formed a stage. Davenant's entrée to the Hall may have been engineered by Gideon de Laune, for the two were firm friends; the poet also had connections with the Society through his marriage to an Apothecary's widow

– one of her sons became Davenant's secretary, another was a freeman of the Society in 1667. A contemporary ballad refers to Davenant's masques at "Pothecaries Hall" (*circa* 1654–56) and with the resurgence of drama after 1660 Davenant's Company rehearsed "The Siege of Rhodes" (the first English opera) at the Hall, also a comedy called "The Wits". Both opened at Davenant's new theatre at Lincoln's Inn Fields in the summer of 1661, to the delight of Samuel Pepys.[11]

Londoners with a more serious intent came to Black Friars to hear the sermons given by the Presbyterian ministers of St Ann's – the congregation reinforced residents' complaints about the Playhouse, claiming that the music disturbed their worship. At the opposite end of the religious spectrum, a Roman Catholic assembly attending "the fatal vespers" in a building adjoining the French Ambassador's house at Black Friars on a Sunday in October 1623 met with disaster when the floor collapsed. Some perished, others were dismembered, some were wounded and some survived. Ninety-five bodies were dug out of the ruins to be taken away by relatives or buried in a mass grave nearby.[12]

Although the precinct was not the fashionable place it had been and traffic congestion caused problems, Black Friars was a convenient location for the Apothecaries. There was easy access to the river at Black Friars Stairs, the Apothecaries' shops of Bucklersbury were a short walk away, the College of Physicians was within reach, as were the City taverns. The residence at Black Friars of the Society's principal benefactor, Gideon de Laune, may well have influenced the decision to purchase Cobham House – the fact that de Laune kept the deeds relating to the purchase until June 1633 when they were delivered to the Hall, suggests that he was involved with the legal transactions, at least.[13]

The question of payment for Cobham House was answered by gifts and interest-free loans from members. The total contributed to the purchase price was £1,166 13s and a separate fund for "reparations and beautifying" the Hall raised £304 14s 10d – donors to the latter fund liked to specify how their money was to be used, whether towards the gallery, wainscoting, carving or the canopy for the Hall door. The first instalment of the purchase price was paid on 23 November 1632, the remainder in April 1633. In addition to the total purchase price of £1,800 there were legal expenses and a licence in mortmain cost £52. The deficit between members' loans and gifts and the overall price was made up by loans at 6 per cent interest. When in 1634 the Treasurer reviewed his accounts for the purchase and restoration of the property he concluded that payments had totalled £3,192, receipts £3,141 – a commendable balance.[14]

The pride attached to the possession of a Hall was reflected in the first meeting of the Society held there on 11 December 1632. The occasion was marked by the reading of the Ordinances and the collection of quarterage, the formalities being eased by ample supplies of wine and beer. The first purchases for the new Hall were bellows and a large padlock to secure the premises until repairs commenced in the spring, when Peter Mills tiled three roofs and the gallery, re-pointed brickwork and repaired chimneys, receiving payment of £166 10s 9d for that and for work "about ye Hall and gable ends". Clues such as this reveal that the Hall had a pitched roof and a battlement constructed by Mills along the west front with two "outwindows" (oriel windows?).[15] The yard was paved, the Great Hall was painted by Mr Garlick and the forecourt walls were given a coat of ochre (a pigment the colour of pale brownish yellow). Kingston did carpentry work, Woodward was the joiner, Glendenning the mason, Pendrid the plasterer; Garland carved the Society's arms on the chimneypiece and Sutton supplied stained glass. New stairs and a house of office were essential and the great table in the parlour was mended. Members paid for the wainscoting and benches in the Great Hall (204 yards cost £68) and the Parlour (£24). Bundles of rushes went on the floors and the grass plot in the garden was mowed and protected by rails.[16]

The Apothecaries' property stretched south of the Hall to the River Thames (being wider than at present, the river bank was then on the line now followed by Queen Victoria Street), where stairs gave access to the many small boats that plied the Thames. John Lidford, who made hats of beaver fur, held the tenancy of the riverside property in 1633, succeeded by the stonemason John Young from 1642. Proceeding north up Water Lane, as Black Friars Lane was called, a passage on the east led to the Playhouse, and a few steps further a painted sign indicated The Three Blackbirds tavern. In the immediate vicinity of Apothecaries' Hall lay stables, grounds and tenements, with the de Laune family property to the east and north. With improvements being carried out at the Hall and a new landlord replacing an absentee owner, tenants were quick to apply for leases – Lord Hertford for the stables and Dr Argent for a cellar.[17]

The 1640s saw the consolidation of the Apothecaries' Black Friars estate with the purchase of the yard where the coaches of theatre-goers turned, and the gift from Gideon de Laune of a messuage, appurtenances and void ground adjoining the Hall. At the Hall the ground floor of the gallery was enclosed and the Master, John Lorrimer, paid for the Parlour to be painted and gilded (1655) – it was to be known as the White Painted Room. At the riverside the tenant John Young was obliged to build a new brick wall to secure the property.[18]

The payment of 9 shillings in tax on fortifications at the Hall hints at the insecurity of the Interregnum, when soldiers of the trained bands were employed to guard the place. General Fairfax's troops were billeted there in December 1648 and by 1651 repairs were necessary. The workmanship was inspected by Mills, who was to return to the site to survey the destruction wrought by the Great Fire and to keep an eye on the Society's carpenter (1667–68).[19]

The Hall rebuilt 1668–70

The Apothecaries' first Hall burned in the Great Fire of London on 4 September 1666. With two days' notice of the approaching inferno it was possible to remove some of the Society's possessions (see page 67) but the building was gutted. Vestiges of the most substantial walls on the north, east and west sides of the Hall, some chimneys and the foundations remained, sufficient to allow the new Hall to be rebuilt according to the old ground plan. While London and its inhabitants waited upon the deliberations of the Commissioners for the Rebuilding of the City (Christopher Wren, Robert Hooke, Hugh May, Roger Pratt, Edward Jerman and Peter Mills), there was little that could be done during the winter of 1666–67. The Apothecaries' Court instructed two of its members to safeguard any remaining iron and lead that could be salvaged from the ruins of the Hall, arranged to hold meetings at Cooks' Hall for the immediate future, then continued with the customary business of binding apprentices, searching Apothecaries' shops and swearing in freemen.[20]

Once the Rebuilding Act was passed in February 1667 property-owners could formulate plans within the prescribed framework of building regulations which encouraged the redevelopment of the City on the lines of the former street plan but with wider streets and more substantial, safer buildings than previously. The staking out of streets and foundations by the surveyors began in the spring with the clearance of fire debris and the planning of the first wave of redevelopment.

The Apothecaries entrusted the rebuilding of the Hall to a committee of seventeen, an unwieldy body later reduced to seven. Peter Sambrooke (Master 1683–84) took a keen, practical interest, probably because he owned property near the Hall. Otherwise, the Master and Wardens with Messrs Chase, Hinton, Johnson and Hollingsworth oversaw the building work.[21] In the summer of 1667, ten months after the Fire, Mr Jerman and Mr Ryder were appointed "for surveying ye ground where ye hall stood" so that "we may have ye survey ready against ye next Court of Assistants". For their part, members of the rebuilding committee viewed other halls, seeking inspiration, and held conferences at coffee-houses and taverns – there was an Apothecaries' Arms in St Paul's churchyard and another in the Strand, but The Sun Tavern was the preferred rendezvous for meetings with the surveyor Jerman.[22]

In consulting Ryder and Jerman the Society set its sights high. Richard Ryder was soon to be appointed the king's Master Carpenter and Edward Jerman was responsible for designs for the new Royal Exchange and several company halls; he was also one of the Commissioners for the rebuilding of the City generally. Jerman's commission for the Royal Exchange dated from April 1667 and over the next eighteen months he worked on that building and on designs for the Halls of the Fishmongers, Haberdashers, Mercers,

Wax Chandlers, Drapers, Weavers, possibly the Vintners, and for repairs to Goldsmiths' and Barber-Surgeons' Halls – a formidable workload. A survey, design or model for Apothecaries' Hall might well be added to this list, although nothing so tangible has come to light. Jerman was asked to survey the ruins of Apothecaries' Hall in July 1667; he was sufficiently committed to view the site in August accompanied by a carpenter called Clisbie or Clisby; he was entertained to dinner at Mr Corbett's (the Society's cook) the following January, and he kept another appointment with the Apothecaries in March.[23]

There is no reference to Jerman thereafter and he died in November 1668. Already, in the previous April, Thomas Lock had been appointed the Society's surveyor, in preference to Mr Kirbie, and George Clisbie took the post of carpenter. On the very day of his appointment, Lock produced a model for the new Hall mentioned in the Rough Court Minutes as "Mr Lock's model"[24] but he can hardly have had time to prepare it himself; it may therefore have been the work of Jerman, inherited by Lock.

Thomas Lock, a carpenter and a member of the Fishmongers' Company, was working with Jerman at Fishmongers' Hall and had previously worked at Horseheath Hall in Cambridgeshire under Sir Roger Pratt, a leading exponent of the new style of country house architecture and a Commissioner for rebuilding the City. This is not as impressive as it might appear – Pratt complained of Lock's mistakes and the Fishmongers' Company vowed never to employ Lock again.[25] His chief contribution to the design of Apothecaries' Hall seems to have been to give it a flat roof (contrary to the model), an unspecified "other part" was finished as he proposed, then in 1669 he measured the ground where four new tenements were to be built on the south side of the forecourt at the Hall.[26] The limited extent of Lock's involvement at Apothecaries' Hall can be judged by his modest remuneration: in January 1670 he claimed £50 as payment for his services since April 1668 – a span of nearly two years during which his name appears in the records only occasionally. The Court of Assistants offered Lock £30 and a compromise was reached at £40.[27] This compares unfavourably with £1,318 paid to the carpenter George Clisbie for his work between 1668 and 1671, and the mason's bill of £30 for just one doorcase.[28]

Lock's successor at Apothecaries' Hall was Leonard Sowersby, surveyor and measurer of works for Wren at several City churches and at the Sheldonian Theatre, Oxford in 1669. Structural work at Apothecaries' Hall was complete at the time of Lock's departure, although there was still work to be done on the houses to the west, south and east. However, with the payment of £40 Lock's employment by the Apothecaries ceased and by August Sowersby was checking the craftsmen's work at the Hall, including the bill submitted by the plasterer for "the fret ceiling" of the Great Hall (fretwork was an ornamental pattern sometimes called key pattern). Sowersby was still working for the

Society in 1673, supervising joiners' work in the Court Room and at the Chelsea Physic Garden.[29]

The rebuilding of Apothecaries' Hall had begun in earnest in August 1668 when 22,000 bricks stacked at the waterside were carried to the site in wheelbarrows and baskets for the attention of the bricklayer, Edward Salter. Salter, Clisbie the carpenter and John Young the mason worked together on the new Hall for the next two years. Little is known of Salter, whereas George Clisbie was one of the carpenters at Wren's church of St Edmund the King in Lombard Street (1670–74). He was the principal carpenter at Apothecaries' Hall, responsible for structural work, floors and the oval ceiling of the Great Hall. The mason at the Hall and at the Chelsea Physic Garden, John Young, was renowned for his work at Greenwich Palace and at Mercers' Hall (in particular the ornate porch which now adorns Swanage Town Hall). Young's design for the doorcase at Apothecaries' Hall probably echoed his design for the Mercers on a modest scale – he presented two designs and the Society chose the cheaper. He built the stone staircase and balustrade in the courtyard of Apothecaries' Hall in lieu of four years' rent that he owed; he paved the courtyard for £47 10s in 1673; and in 1676 he was paid £4 for carving the bust of Gideon de Laune, which can still be seen in the Great Hall.[30]

Two other skilled craftsmen, Robert Burges and Roger Davis or Davies, carved the wainscot and the screen in the Great Hall in 1671, later completing the panelling and making a cedar table for the Court Room.[31] Davis is known to have worked under Wren at three City churches, also at St Paul's, at Whitehall Palace, and at Chelsea and Greenwich Hospitals. The more sophisticated carving of the Society's coat of arms to surmount the screen in the Great Hall was executed by Henry Phillips. He was the first to hold the appointment of Master Sculptor and Carver in Wood to the king, and he worked at St James's Palace, Hampton Court, Somerset House and Windsor Castle.[32] Plasterwork was by Blunt (perhaps the same Blunt or Blount employed at St Sepulchre's church), the glazier's name was Tipping (presumably he was responsible for the stained glass panels in the staircase, 1670–71) and there was a band of secondary craftsmen – additional bricklayers, painters, another carpenter and a team of labourers paid 20d a day (2d more than was being offered at the Royal Exchange).

As the Hall approached completion members gave their attention to furnishings, and the pewter and plate that had been rescued as the Great Fire approached was recalled. Anthony Hinton and Mr Pelling gave tables and chairs, additional "Spanish" tables and six leather chairs were purchased and William Clarke's chest dated 1668 found a home. A copy of a portrait of King James I was commissioned from Snelling (illustrated on page 28), and John Jones, Royal Apothecary, presented the Society with a portrait of King Charles

l. The arrangements "below stairs" in the kitchen were left to Mr Corbett to do as he thought fit.[33]

The Society took the opportunity to extend its Black Friars estate after the Great Fire at a time when land was readily available and new housing was in demand. Negotiations with the de Laune family for the ground contiguous to the Hall opened in 1667, the Society obtaining a long lease and eventually the freehold of properties known as The Bacchanalian and The Blue Ball and Crown.[34] Smaller portions of land were acquired from Thomas Russell and Simon Bartram, compensating for the sacrifice of a thin wedge which the surveyors had claimed after the fire, probably for the widening of Water Lane.[35] A bricklayer called Braithwaite, and Clisbie the carpenter, built new dwellings facing the Lane with another four on the south side of the forecourt replacing The Three Blackbirds Tavern. The houses were ready for occupation in May 1670 on condition that tallow chandlers and blacksmiths were prohibited because of the offensive nature of their crafts. The Apothecary John Pelling took the lease of the four houses facing Water Lane – he was appointed Apothecary to Bethlehem Hospital (Bedlam) in 1685 and was a relation of Walter Pelling, Master (1671–72), the friend of Samuel Pepys.[36]

A third set of new tenements went up on the toft of ground that had been de Laune's property and was now the north side of Playhouse Yard. The Society obtained a lease from Sir Edward Dering, de Laune's son-in-law, and promptly built "four substantial brick messuages" each with a shop on the ground floor. The Society imposed strict conditions regarding the progress of work on the builder who was also instructed to level and wall the void ground "designed for a garden to their said hall".[37]

The decision taken in September 1671 to establish a Laboratory at the Hall had its roots in 1623, and in Edward Cooke's gift of £500 for building a laboratory on waste ground at the waterside (1641).[38] The 1640s were not conducive to building projects, and the Apothecaries' Laboratory did not materialize for thirty years when the large vault under the Great Hall was adapted and equipped as the Society's Laboratory (see Chapter 6). The chimneys, constructed under Lock's supervision, were insufficient for their purpose and overheated, causing damage to the wainscot of the Great Hall. Following complaints from neighbours about sulphurous fumes which "suffocate them and make them so sick", they had to be rebuilt.[39]

With the Apothecaries' property at Black Friars enlarged and rebuilt there remained some doubt about the ownership of a plot reclaimed from the Thames by the Society's tenant, John Young the stonemason, in 1673. Young had acted on his own initiative in contravention of official plans for the Thames Quay, a project intended to give the City a uniform waterfront from London Bridge to the Temple. It proved impossible to fulfil this ambitious plan; Young escaped prosecution and the Apothecaries gained the land he had

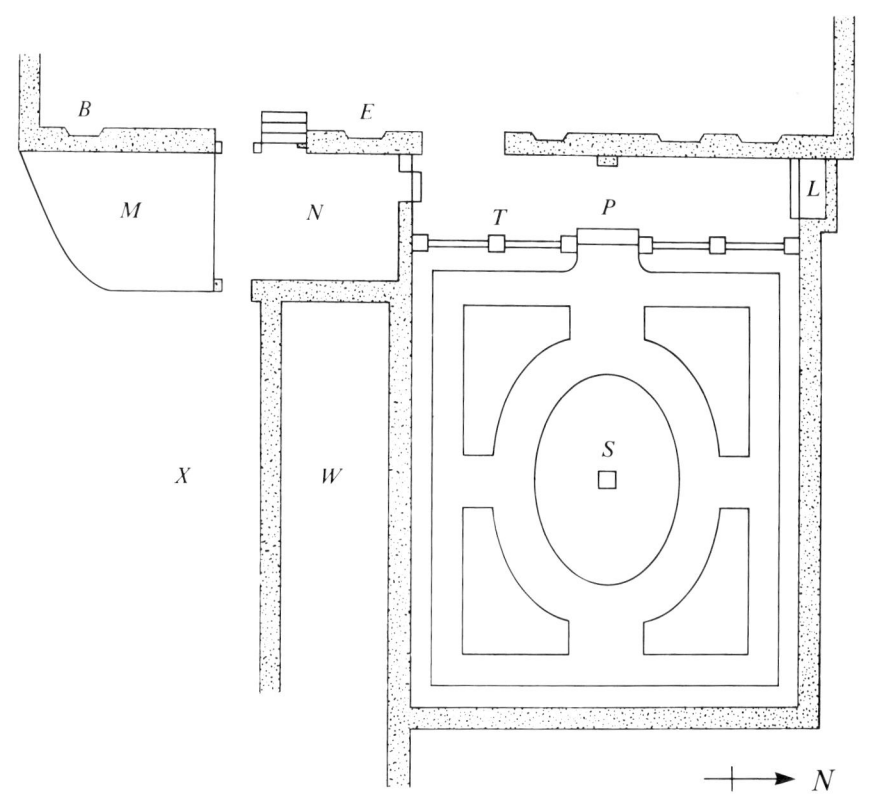

Reconstruction of a plan of "the back frunt" of Apothecaries' Hall and ground adjoining, including the garden east of the Hall. The original plan (Guildhall Library Ms 8267) was made between 1726 and 1756.

KEY: B – The window looking out of the Laboratory near the sulphur furnace.
    E – The window looking out of Mr Dutch's office into the back yard (Cornelius Dutch was Clerk to the Society 1726–56).
    L – The alcove in the garden pavement.
    M – The extent of the ground which an old house stands on.
    N – The back yard where the stills belonging to the Laboratory stand.
    P – The pavement.
    S – The garden.
    T – The dwarf wall between the pavement and garden.
    W – Mr Lavin the bedstead-maker's and the continuance of that building.
    X – Glasshouse Yard.

reclaimed for a peppercorn rent. A small plan of the site in question survives, signed by the surveyor John Oliver, who was paid 2 guineas for his trouble.[40]

The appearance of the late-seventeenth-century Hall was not as imposing as at present, being obscured by the small houses lining Water Lane. Nevertheless, early-eighteenth-century descriptions award it merit. Edward Hatton, writing in 1708, found Apothecaries' Hall "a handsome tho' not very large Building adorned with columns of the Tuscan order". He gave the date

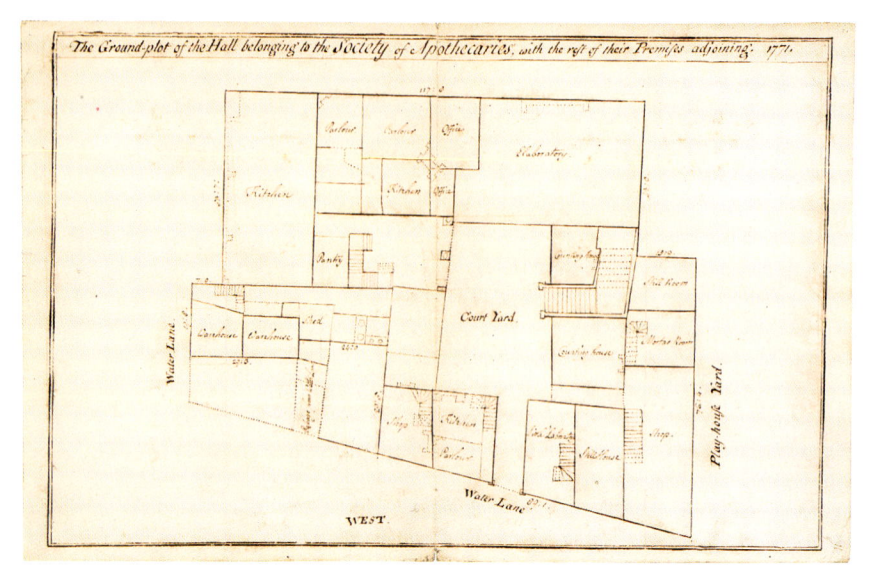

Ground plan of Apothecaries' Hall in 1771 showing the location of the Laboratory (under the Great Hall) and other premises used by the stock companies.

of the post-Fire rebuilding correctly and confirmed that the ceilings of the Great Hall and Court Room were decorated with fretwork.[41] A decade later Strype described the Hall as "a good Building, with a fair pair of Gates that leads into an open Court handsomely paved with broad stone; at the upper end of which is the Hall and other apartments".[42]

Late-eighteenth-century developments

By 1730 the Great Hall was "in great want of repair" and the subsequent renovations gave it casement windows. Two dozen leather chairs were purchased, also two new stoves for the Court Room and Parlour and a "portable feeding Engine with proper pipes". This described the Society's fire engine which was equipped with two dozen leather buckets emblazoned with "Apothecaries' Hall 1734" – a fire in the Laboratory under the Great Hall had alerted the Court to the need for precautions and insurance. The Society was later to appoint an Engine Keeper, John Kirby, who was instructed "that the engine be brought out and played four times a year".[43] After an explosion at the Hall in 1842, the Society's employees formed a fire brigade and in 1908 the Master presented the team with brass helmets (one of them can be seen in the Library). Members of the Apothecaries' fire brigade remained active until the closure of the trade operations at the Hall in 1922, competing for prizes in an annual demonstration and parading on Lord Mayor's Day (a photograph of the team, taken in 1913, is illustrated on page 232).

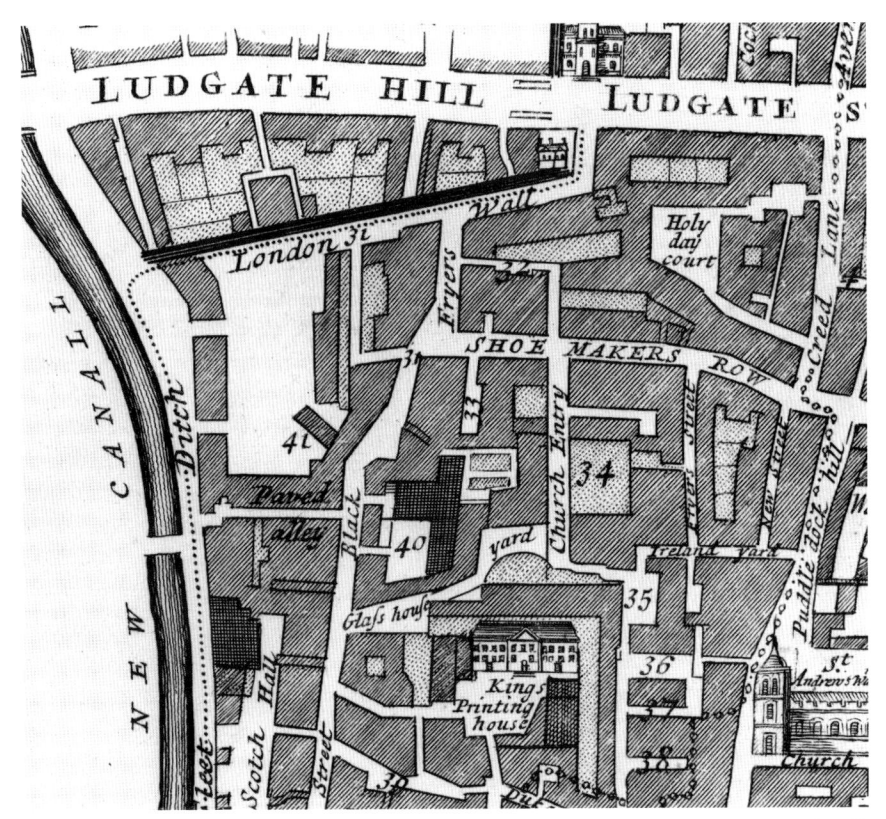

A detail from a map of Farringdon Ward Within, 1720. Number 40 marks Apothecaries' Hall, with the garden to the east.

With the completion of improvements both to the appearance and the safety of the Hall, Sir Benjamin Rawling, Sheriff and Master (1736–37), presented the twenty-four-light chandelier for the Great Hall, later giving the Renter Warden £50 to ensure that it was provided with candles evermore.

The mid-eighteenth century was a period of decline in the Society's membership, to the distress of the Livery and Yeomanry who in December 1746 addressed a remonstrance to the Master, Wardens and Court. They pointed out that "the Company had considerably declined" and was in danger of annihilation, pointing a finger at the encroachers and invaders of the Company's liberties – men who practised as apothecaries but were not members of the Company, were untrained and uncontrolled.[44] A Bill in Parliament was drafted in an attempt to extend the Company's charter – this failed, whereupon the Society tried another tactic by lowering the redemption fee in the hope of attracting a wider membership. The decline in membership had resulted in the diminution of income from fees and fines, giving cause for concern about the Society's finances and the adoption of economy measures

– no cakes on Common Hall or Quarter days, restrictions on dinner expenses and the deferment of building work on the houses at Black Friars Stairs and on the south side of the Hall courtyard.[45] As luck would have it, the houses by the Thames at Black Friars Stairs were destroyed by a fire in 1757, yielding £1,050 in compensation.[46]

The Apothecaries' Thames-side property was part of the original purchase from Lady Anne Howard in 1632 when it comprised a house and garden, void ground, stables and a coach-house. After the Great Fire the Society's tenant and mason, John Young, had reclaimed land there for a wharf.[47] Following the less serious fire of 1757 there was barely time to rebuild before the City opened negotiations to acquire land as a prelude to the construction of the first Black Friars Bridge. At the time (1760–69), this was the third bridge to span the Thames at London, and was a masterpiece of engineering design by a Scotsman as yet unknown in London, Robert Mylne. He was awarded the commission for the new bridge at Black Friars in competition with sixty-nine entries, defeating George Dance senior and William Chambers, the leading architects of the day. Mylne was announced the winner in February 1760, and as the plans for the bridge and its approaches took shape, the City's Bridge House Estates Committee approached the Society of Apothecaries with a view to purchasing 28 feet of the waterside, and hinterland stretching nearly 130 feet north. The land was surveyed and valued by George Wyatt at £1,400 but the Society accepted £1,100.[48]

There remained a larger portion of the Society's property to the east of the new bridge. This was embanked and developed soon after the completion of Black Friars Bridge, according to proposals provided by Robert Mylne and in association with Edward Barlow, who proved an unworthy partner. The agreement of October 1770 gave Barlow (described as a wine merchant of Tower Hill) a ninety-nine year lease of the Society's wharf and premises at Black Friars Bridge where the east side of a new square called Chatham Place was to be built. Like Albion Place at the south end of the bridge, Chatham Place was to add dignity to the new approach to the City from Southwark. An elevation of the Apothecaries' development shows a terrace of three-storey houses rising above an eighteen-bay arcade and topped by a parapet – an essay in restraint characteristic of Mylne.[49]

Barlow undertook to spend £5,000 on building eight or more substantial brick houses to form the east side of Chatham Place, and other buildings on the south side of Earl Street, within two years. He would pay the Society a rent of £150 per annum for the first two years, and £300 per annum once the houses were complete. He agreed to construct regular, uniform houses according to the elevation provided by Mylne for Chatham Place, and went on to build warehouses, stables, a hotel and a coffee-house known as Barlow's Buildings, on the south side of Earl Street (Earl Street was later Upper Thames

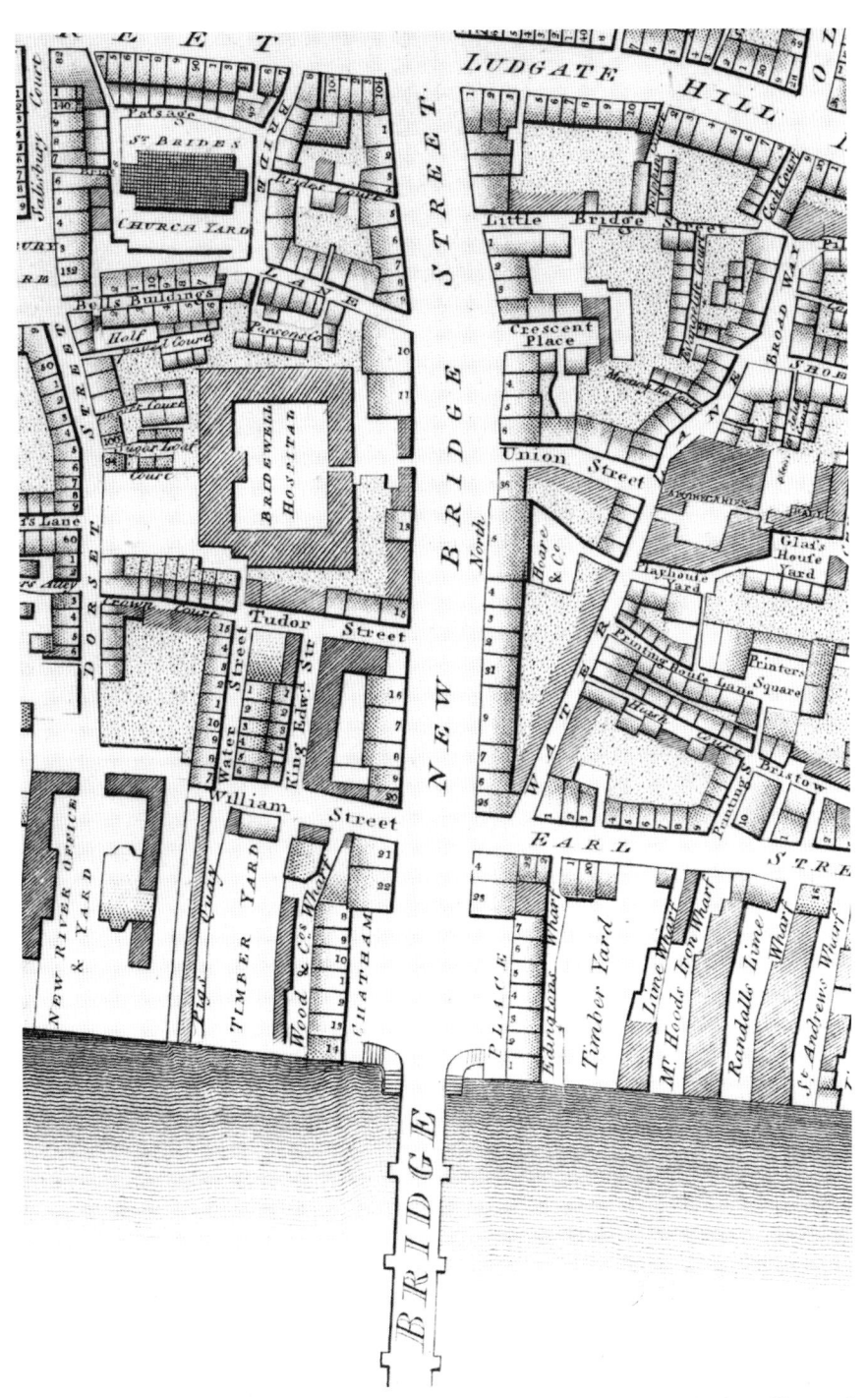

Detail from Horwood's map of 1799 showing the Society's property at Chatham Place and Edington's Wharf.

The drawing by John Tallis (1838) shows the terrace of houses on the east side of Chatham Place built to designs by Robert Mylne (1770). Earl Street was later Upper Thames Street.

Street). Barlow's Buildings were no credit to him – the surveyor Samuel Burchett reported that they had damp cellars, defective brickwork and needed underpinning.[50]

Barlow failed to complete the development within the two years allowed, blaming "the distresses of the times". The Society obligingly granted him a mortgage of £5,000 and arranged for separate leases of the various houses in Chatham Place, the wharf, houses, stables and coach-house. Notwithstanding these concessions, Barlow was in arrears with the ground rent. Having taken legal advice, the Society obtained permission to distrain his goods and auction the properties. Barlow then determined to glean what he could for himself and minimize any profit to the Apothecaries by removing tiles, stoves and iron, by pulling down doorcases and generally wreaking havoc in the half-completed buildings.[51] With the departure of Barlow in 1778 the houses in Chatham Place and secondary premises to the east were let. John Nash was one of a group using the wharf and adjoining buildings from 1778, becoming the sole tenant. A later occupant, a coal merchant called Edington, gave his name to the wharf (see Horwood's map on page 91).[52]

The development of Chatham Place had been prompted by the construction of a new bridge to serve the City; its demise came a hundred years later with the construction of a new railway into the City and a new road from Black Friars Bridge to the Mansion House to be called Queen Victoria Street. In 1859 the London, Chatham and Dover Railway Company informed the Society of Apothecaries that some of its property in Chatham Place and Earl Street was required to build a railway-line from Black Friars to Ludgate. Over the next four years the Society received a stream of notices for the compulsory purchase of four houses and stables in Earl Street, 38 New Bridge Street and numbers 1–3 Chatham Place. In between, missives from the Metropolitan Board of Works were received, requiring the compulsory purchase of numbers 5, 6 and 7 Chatham Place in order to construct Queen Victoria Street. Thus the Society was obliged to offer up its riverside estate on the altar of Victorian metropolitan improvements, pocketing some £20,000 in compensation.[53]

The building of Black Friars Bridge and its approaches improved the vicinity of Apothecaries' Hall, the main advantage being the disappearance of the Fleet Ditch underneath New Bridge Street. A century later, the construction of the railway reduced the Society's property-holding to make way for the obtrusive viaduct and Ludgate Hill Station to the west of Apothecaries' Hall (demolished in 1990).

The second half of the eighteenth century was a period of prosperity for the two stock companies operating under the wing of the Society (see Chapter 6). By 1777 both companies had outgrown their premises adjoining Apothecaries' Hall and were looking for expansion. A committee was appointed to investigate how accommodation for the stock companies could be extended, as a result of which it was determined to secure the premises behind the Hall known as Cloister Garth belonging to Mrs Thornicroft and previously held on a lease. A plan made in conjunction with the purchase of Mrs Thornicroft's estate shows that there was once a skittle ground in Church Entry, while directly behind the Hall a formal garden was approached from the Hall by a raised terrace.[54] The committee's first task was the reconstruction of the four old houses, a stable, wash-house and long shed in Glasshouse Yard for the use of the Laboratory Stock. Two houses in Water Lane on the south side of the entrance to the Apothecaries' courtyard needed rebuilding and at the same time the Clerk suggested that his apartments facing Water Lane could be used by the stock companies if the Society would agree to erect a new house for him and his family. The piecemeal rebuilding of small, late-seventeenth-century dwellings surrounding the Hall soon escalated into the creation of a new west and south range to the courtyard. In the process the Bedel's house, the house next door to it and the house on the corner were demolished, prior to the erection of a uniform street front along Water Lane.

The Society's usual surveyor at the time, Samuel Burchett, and the more sophisticated surveyor Richard Norris, reported on the state of the Society's premises prior to the submission of estimates for rebuilding by Norris and George Dance. Norris's estimate was then accepted, being the cheaper. He was surveyor to Christ's Hospital, the Clothworkers' Company and to the Charterhouse estates; George Dance the younger was Clerk of the City Works. Norris's survey of Apothecaries' Hall had revealed two defective girders (timber beams) – one in the Parlour and one in the Great Hall (a sad reflection on Thomas Lock's rebuilding of 1668–70) and he reported that the basement

ELEVATION.

Elevations for the new houses on Water Lane (Black Friars Lane) by Richard Norris (1782). The left hand drawing shows the street front and arch leading to the courtyard of Apothecaries' Hall; on the right is the courtyard elevation.

piers were erroneous and very defective in 1780 – they were probably of medieval origin, re-used by Lock.[55]

The rebuilding began with the premises for the stock companies and during

the disruption their business was conducted in the Library, Great Hall, Kitchen, garret and Clerk's rooms. Richard Norris provided the design and supervised the contractors, John Priest (the carpenter) and John Severn (the bricklayer). With large new buildings for the trade being erected, the Society was shamed into rebuilding two old houses on Water Lane to improve the street frontage. The committee pronounced that it was "very disgraceful to the Company that the front of their Hall should appear so long in its present ruinous state" and members of the Court were asked to subscribe towards its improvement. Articles of Agreement were signed in July 1782 authorizing the clearing of the site and the construction of a new building on the north side of the archway to designs by Norris (illustrated on pages 94, 95).[56] By the summer of 1783 these houses were ready for occupation. The one nearer the entrance provided an office and dwelling for the Bedel, and the other was to be occupied by the Society's Chemical Operator.[57]

Meanwhile, the parapets on the Hall roof had been "ramped" and the balustrades repaired. The courtyard was then stuccoed by George Wyatt at a cost of £79 15s (1783). Two further houses on Water Lane were rebuilt in 1784 when Norris was replaced by Mr Carr as surveyor. When building work was finished in the spring of 1785 Messrs Adam were called upon to stucco the front of the Hall where the Society's arms were erected.[58]

The rebuilding programme of 1780 to 1786 transformed the western range of Apothecaries' Hall from a row of motley late-seventeenth-century dwellings into a well-balanced block with tall bays at either end giving the distinct appearance of warehouses (see below). Despite the fact that the industrial appearance of the street front was subsequently modified, a recent appraisal finds that the west front of the Hall "struggles hard to harmonize domestic, industrial and ceremonial features and functions".[59]

In the centre of the new street front was the archway leading into the courtyard, where an inscription above the inner face of the arch testifies that the Hall was indeed *multum ampliata et ornata* by 1786. The completion of the

Apothecaries' Hall showing the newly built western range. Drawn by John Carter and published in the Stationers' London Almanack for 1787.

building was marked by the plaque with its Latin inscription and by the grant of leases to the trustees of the Laboratory and Navy Stocks (see Chapter 6).

The Laboratory Stock now occupied the larger part of the space under the Great Hall for use as its Chemical Laboratory, and a chemical warehouse under the Library. The head warehouseman had a house and warehouse on the north side of the courtyard where there was another house and yard adjoining, and the Chemical Operator lodged in the house on Water Lane next to the Bedel's dwelling. In Playhouse Yard the Laboratory Stock also used the Still House, the Magnesia Laboratory, a laboratory for salts, a committee room and cellar – all at a rent of £2 per annum paid to the Society. The Navy Stock occupied part of the area under the Great Hall as a Galenical Laboratory as well as other premises on the south and west sides of the courtyard allocated for a committee room, a counting house and the wholesale and retail warehouses – rented for the princely sum of £3 per annum.[60]

The eastern range comprising the Great Hall, Parlour, Court Room, Library, Kitchen and offices of Apothecaries' Hall retained its late-seventeenth-century form except for the alteration to the skyline by the "ramping" of the parapet or battlements in the 1780s. The Hall had been surveyed by Norris prior to the rebuilding of the 1780s, yet he had failed to investigate the roof of the Great Hall thoroughly. Just ten years after his survey, its roof needed renewing and covering with lead. The opportunity was taken in 1793 to make the room "more commodious" by placing the Assistants' table at the south end and moving the carved screen back against the wall. A new raised floor instead of a dais, the musicians' gallery and repairs to the wainscot completed the late-eighteenth-century alterations to the Hall.[61]

Apart from a separate entrance to the retail shop (1823), new entrances for tenants (1882) and the enclosure of the colonnade in the courtyard in 1929, the external appearance of the quadrangular Hall has altered little since the late eighteenth century, while the arrangement of Great Hall, Parlour and Court Room remains as rebuilt between 1668 and 1670. However, the location of some rooms of the late-eighteenth-century Hall remains a puzzle: inventories dating from 1783 to 1811 record the existence of a strong room called Newgate (a reference to Newgate Gaol), a stone repository with an iron chest, and a museum where specimens were stored in cabinets of drawers.[62]

Acquisitions and survival

The prosperity of the stock companies prompted the acquisition of several properties adjoining the Society's premises in the last decades of the eighteenth century: Mr Chillingworth's house in Water Lane was purchased in 1772, and a long lease was taken on the ground and appurtenances east of the Hall. Messuages in Paved Alley and at 38 New Bridge Street were acquired between 1777 and 1778, allowing the alley to be widened to form Union Street

The courtyard of Apothecaries' Hall by George Shepherd (1814).

(now Apothecary Street), and giving easier access for large quantities of goods delivered to and carted from the trade premises at the Hall.[63] After long negotiation, Mrs Thornicroft's small estate in Glasshouse Yard was purchased in 1778, and a dwelling on the corner with Little Broadway occupied by Mr Hammett and belonging to Raines Charity, was acquired in 1783. The freehold of seven cottages in Fleur de Luce Court was purchased (1794–95) and the policy of acquisition to accommodate the trade continued with the purchase in 1801 of a small estate in Glasshouse Yard, formerly The Blue Ball and Crown and The Bacchanalian, a lease of premises in Saffron Place, the purchase of the site for the Mill House and engine house in Water Lane, and a brick messuage and warehouse at the east end of Playhouse Yard on the south side of Glasshouse Yard in 1808. The last property negotiations before a reversal of fortune and policy, gave the Society a new lease and use of premises in Glasshouse Yard including the iron foundry in 1822 (immediately converted into a chemical laboratory known as the Great Laboratory) and Mr Morgan's house nearby (1841).[64]

The rebuilding of the 1780s eradicated the assortment of inadequate old buildings on Water Lane, providing the Society and the stock companies with more efficient, larger premises and a more elegant façade onto Water Lane. The last of the seventeenth-century buildings in Playhouse Yard survived until 1813 when they were demolished to provide an additional warehouse for the "very extensive concerns" of the Navy Stock. The surveyor to the Society, William Jupp, condemned the old buildings as dangerous and recommended new premises be erected at an estimated cost of £4,000 (he had provided a cheaper scheme which was rejected). The builder miscalculated and made a loss of £300 on the project, receiving £150 to compensate.[65]

With the amalgamation in 1823 of the two stock companies to form the United Stock, came the re-organization of the retail and prescription departments at the Hall to form a more economical unit. This entailed alterations to the north side of the courtyard where the retail drug department and shop were given enlarged premises, taking in the passage to the housekeeper's apartments and about 3 feet of the colonnade. The shop entrance in Water Lane, still in evidence, was made at this time and, in anticipation of a rosy future for the trade, the chemical warehouse was enlarged.[66]

The vicissitudes of the trade dictated the architectural changes to the Society's property, and the trading activities sometimes endangered the fabric of the Hall – furnaces, stills, heavy equipment and chemicals were hazardous and an explosion in 1842 damaged a wall, windows and paving. More serious was the fate of the Society's Chemical Operator, Henry Hennell, who lost his life in the accident (see pages 184, 186).

A survey of 1846 reveals the extent of the drug manufacturing and retail business at the Hall where a new "capital well with five pumps" capable of supplying 30 gallons of water a minute to the boiler house and Mill House had been sunk. Entered from Water Lane was the retail shop with a dwelling house above it, the prescription room, a laboratory and another dwelling behind. The heart of the business of the United Stock was carried on in the Chemical Laboratory, sometimes called the Great Laboratory, around which clustered the Still House, mortar room, boiler house, spirit room and cellar. The counting house, Magnesia Room, the retail and wholesale warehouses, more

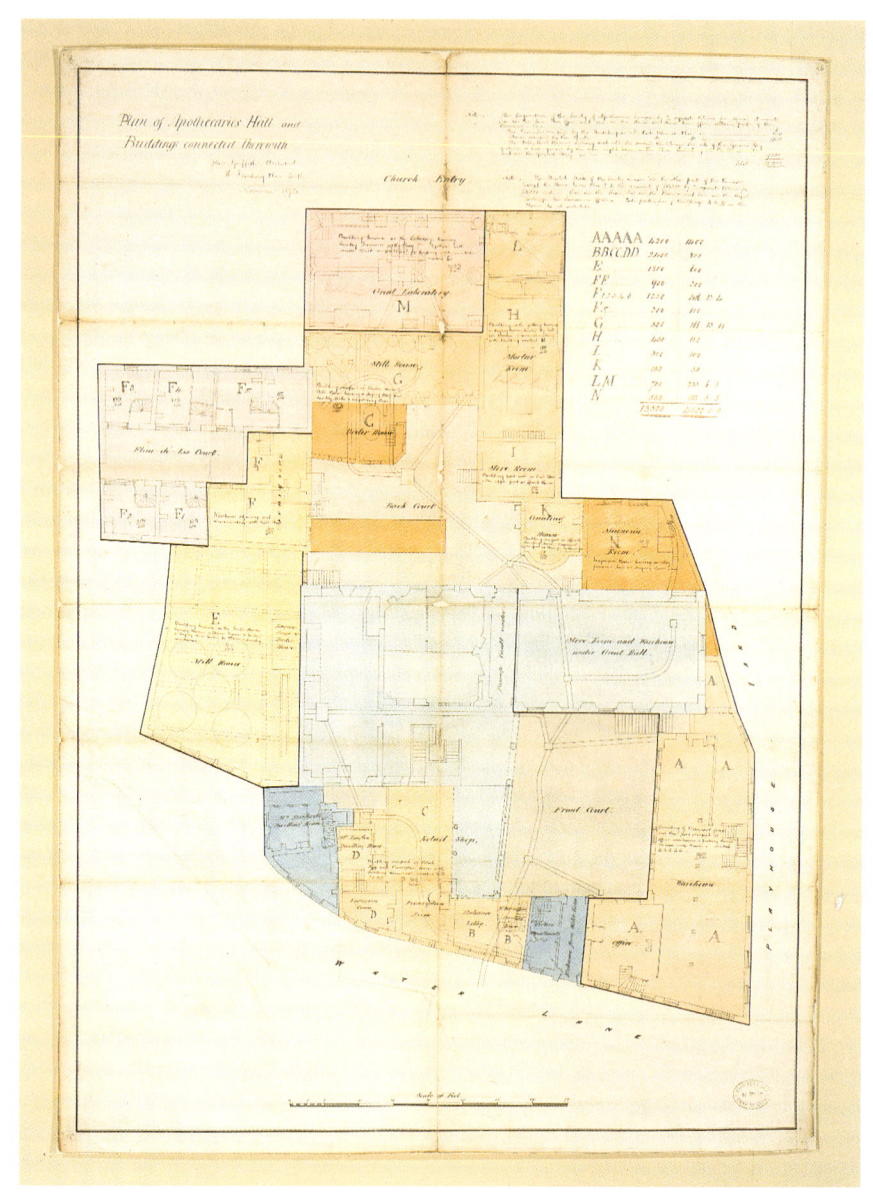

Ground plan of Apothecaries' Hall and buildings connected with it, stamped by the Hand in Hand Fire and Life (Insurance) Office, July 1874 and signed by John Griffith, architect, November 1874. The premises were insured for £23,900, an increase of 60 per cent on the previous amount. Mrs Danford, the Society's housekeeper from August 1870 to August 1874, lived in one of the houses on Water Lane. Mr Thomas Tingle, Accountant to the Trade Department, and from 1874 Head of the Retail Department, occupied another dwelling. Warington's house indicates the accommodation provided for the Society's Chemical Operator from 1842 to 1866, Robert Warington, and his son and successor, George Warington, who departed at Easter 1869. Possibly Warington's house continued to be known as such after the departure of the family; alternatively Griffith may have based this plan on an earlier one.

warehouses with a cellar, the attendant's room, lofts and more cellars formed extensive premises along the north side of Playhouse Yard east as far as Church Entry, and extending west around the corner into Water Lane. Charles Baldwin, printer of *The Standard* in the Society's premises at 38 New Bridge Street, was also the tenant of property in Glasshouse Yard from 1827; six tenements in Fleur de Luce Court were also let, others were being used as warehouses while the four-storey warehouse on the south side of Glasshouse Yard was for storage and the accommodation of employees.[67]

Two years after this survey the large building on the south side of Glasshouse Yard was sold for £2,700 to John Walter of *The Times*, who in 1859 took the lease of the dwelling on the corner of Church Entry. The first (1785) and subsequent issues of the *Daily Universal Times* (soon abbreviated to *The Times*) bore the address of Printing House Square, near Apothecaries' Hall, Black Friars, and by the mid-nineteenth century the "thunderer" was in its prime, its noisy printing works and offices dominating the site where headless bodies, victims of a battle in 1066, have recently been discovered.[68]

The disposal of property was an indication of things to come as the business of the United Stock declined, leading to its dissolution at the end of 1880. Shortly afterwards the trade premises on the corner of Water Lane and Playhouse Yard were let to Messrs Miller and Richard (typefounders of Edinburgh) and the architect John Johnson designed two new entrances to give the tenants private access.[69]

At the close of the nineteenth century the Society's chief preoccupation was with the examination of students and this gave rise to the building of examination halls to designs by the Society's surveyor N.W. Robinson (1892). The new building replaced a warehouse which in turn had replaced three small cottages in Fleur de Luce Court. It consisted chiefly of a large examination hall on the first floor (the Brande room) and a well-lit anatomical hall on the second, with facilities for dissections (the Wheeler room). The Brande Block, as it was to be known, was completed in 1893, and the remaining cottages in Fleur de Luce Court were eventually sold to the Trustees of the London Parochial Charities in 1896.[70]

The Brande Block was named after W.T. Brande, D.C.L., F.R.S., Master (1851–52), Professor of Chemistry at the Royal Institution and for many years Superintending Chemical Operator and Professor/lecturer to the Society (see pages 163, 184). The Wheeler room was a reference to the Society's Botanical Demonstrator from 1778 to 1820, Thomas Wheeler F.L.S. (see pages 138, 140). The new building was erected on the strength of the Society's survival as a medical licensing body after the rigours of the 1880s when it had to struggle to secure a seat on the General Medical Council and had instituted the new qualification in Medicine, Midwifery and Surgery to conform with the Medical Act of 1886.

The Brande room was still being used for practical exams in the 1960s but the Wheeler room was let and the whole was demolished in the redevelopment of the 1980s, to the disappointment of one journalist, who lamented the loss of "an architectural gem with the most delicate of roof structures".[71]

The changing nature of the Society's interests dictated the alterations at the Hall in the early years of the twentieth century. With the loss of contracts to supply drugs and medicines to the British army and the Admiralty, and growing competition from large pharmaceutical manufacturing firms and pharmacies, the trade department at Apothecaries' Hall became less profitable. Accommodation for manufacturing and trading activities at the Hall was limited and the Society could not compete on a commercial basis with the large, commercial companies. As the realization dawned, ideas for the better use and/or development of the trade premises were aired in the first decade of the twentieth century, beginning with the radical proposal to demolish all the existing buildings including the Hall, and ending with the decision to let the surplus buildings.[72] The war years were hardly conducive to property development, nevertheless the Society persisted. Efforts to let the warehouses and trade premises in Playhouse Yard proving unsuccessful, attention turned to the Mill House and housekeeper's accommodation north of the Hall. Allegedly the oldest Mill House in London, it contained an old beam engine, a boiler installed in 1854, three stone mills for drug-grinding and various pieces of antiquated machinery.[73]

With the decision to redevelop the site most of the equipment was broken up or sold with the exception of one mill and some machinery transported to a small mill house behind the Great Hall. Fortunately the lead cistern formerly belonging to the Laboratory Stock and bearing the date 1786 was rescued from the housekeeper's accommodation and placed in the Hall courtyard. During the demolition of the Mill House, wall foundations of the medieval Dominican church and other stonework from Black Friars Priory were discovered and removed.

Martin Saunders, the Society's architect, negotiated with the London County Council for the widening of Water Lane and drew up plans for the new building to be called Cobham House, built by Higgs and Hill (1915–16). Overtures had been made to ascertain if Messrs Lyons (of tea-house fame and neighbours in Water Lane) were interested in the site, but as it was the greater part of Cobham House was occupied by a firm of blouse manufacturers and a newspaper exporter. Also, a Mr Fox took a shop, and the Hall caretaker and his wife were installed in rooms overlooking Water Lane.[74]

There remained the former trade premises on the north side of Playhouse Yard, still unlet. The proposition that the site should be sold was put to the ballot – only the Master's casting vote prevented this. On the advice of Sir

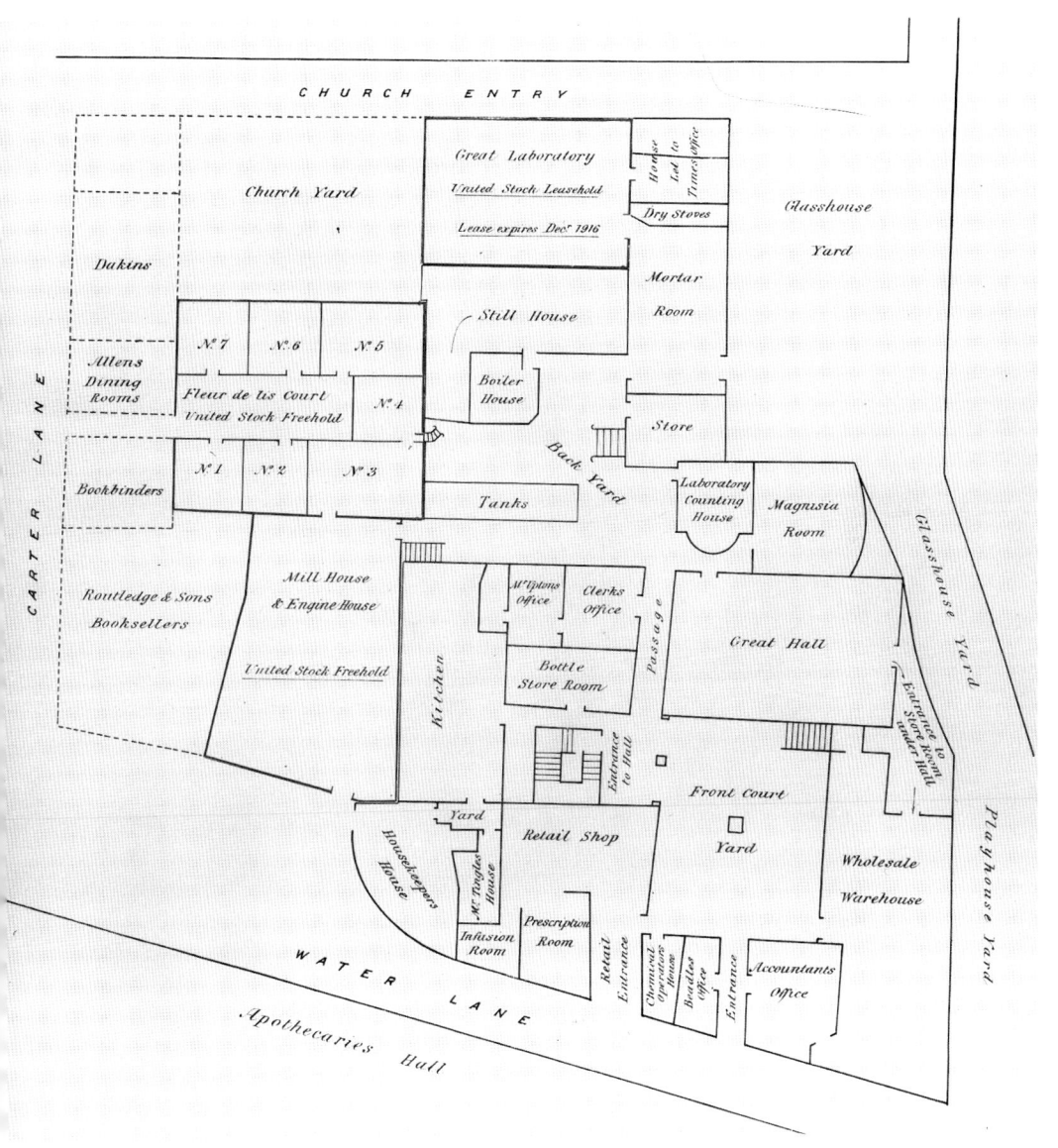

Ground plan of the Hall and trade premises at the Hall *circa* 1911–16. The darker lines show the United Stock property.

William Wells, senior partner of Messrs Chestertons, the buildings (excluding Magnesia House) were advertised in 1921 but it was several years before an agreement was reached with Messrs E.D. Winn, on the basis of a building lease, which resulted in Nestor House (1929).[75]

Apothecaries' Hall, meanwhile, had been slightly damaged in an air-raid on the night of 19 May 1918 when a window and skylight were smashed by shrapnel. Some ten years later what began as the comparatively minor improvement of facilities escalated into the restoration of the staircase and the creation of a new entrance hall at a cost of around £20,000. Sir William Wells and his surveyors discovered that the Death Watch Beetle had been at work in roof timbers and floor joists to the extent that the Hall was on the verge of collapse. Licentiates in all parts of the world were invited to contribute to a restoration fund, and in the long run the discovery of the destructive beetle proved fortunate because as a result the Hall gained new structural bones. A more hospitable entrance was created by enclosing the colonnade, and a brighter stairwell was achieved by sacrificing one end of the Library.[76]

Before the outbreak of the Second World War the appearance of the Great Hall was improved by a new oak floor, and the custom of inserting Past Masters' coats of arms in the windows was initiated. The national emergency of 1939 dictated that four air-raid shelters be provided and the Master and Assistant Bedel were found temporary sleeping quarters under the Great Hall. Sand-bags were ordered, entertainments were curtailed and the Society's stock of cigars lay untouched at the Army and Navy Stores. With the country at war the London County Council changed the name of Water Lane to Black Friars Lane to avoid confusion with Water Lane in E15; Union Street was renamed Apothecary Street, and the Hall gained a William Kent mantelpiece presented by Dr Reginald Hayes for the Court Room.[77]

The City boasted thirty-six livery Halls in 1939. At the end of the war twenty had been destroyed by bombing or wrecked beyond repair and fourteen others incurred serious damage, leaving Vintners' Hall and Apothecaries' Hall the oldest Halls intact. Not that the latter was inviolate. As the Master reported, in the early morning of 12 October 1940 a 500 pound bomb was dropped by an enemy aeroplane, penetrating the roof of Cobham House and falling through the floors to the basement. The party wall with the Parlour was damaged and a chimney breast was blown out, but with just £238 of damage the Hall escaped lightly.[78]

Another bomb falling on the west side of New Bridge Street during the night of 8–9 December damaged the pitched roof and broke windows and doors of the Society's property including one of the bull's-eye windows of the Great Hall. Again on 10–11 May 1941 incendiary bombs fell on the roof of the Wheeler room and premises to the rear of the Hall but no damage was done due to the vigilance of the firewatchers (see pages 236–37).[79] Other less fortunate livery companies were homeless and were offered accommodation at Apothecaries' Hall. Sir Stanley Woodwark (Master 1941–44) was also Master of the Turners (1943–44), and that Company took up the offer, as did the Spectacle Makers in 1946. Both Companies continue to enjoy the use of the Hall.

With no end to the war in sight, the Master negotiated for the storage of the

Society's treasure chest stuffed with silver, and for the safe-keeping of the portraits of John Hunter, James I and Mary Queen of Scots, and banners from the Society's barge. Along with the Jacobean table, the cedar chairs and some archives, these were hidden in the basement of County Hall while the contents of the Library found refuge in the crypt of the Foundling Hospital Chapel at Berkhamsted.[80]

When peace was restored, the future role of the Society of Apothecaries came under scrutiny. Its position as an examining body was insecure and the question of finance and the upkeep of the Hall came under discussion. Enquiries were made with a view to other City companies "establishing their Halls in our buildings thus forming a Guildry", and one such company was reported to be prepared to spend £156,000 on reconstruction. Professor Sir Charles Dodds Bt. F.R.S.(Master 1947–49) went so far as to suggest the Hall might be sold to the Pharmaceutical Society for their headquarters, an idea that was not at all popular.[81]

The survival of Apothecaries' Hall was marked soon after the war by an article on its history in *Country Life*.[82] The illustrations of the post-war Hall, however, showed the need for repairs and redecoration. The dilapidations were soon rectified (1950–51) under the direction of Leslie T. Moore, followed by the re-roofing of the south and western ranges (1953–57). There was another flurry of activity in 1967 when the Society celebrated the 350th anniversary of King James's charter. Two stained glass windows displaying the coats of arms of the Society and the Stuart royal arms were installed in the Court Room, the courtyard was re-paved and Dr W.S.C. Copeman's book on the history of the Society was published.

Redevelopment in the 1980s

While other livery companies rebuilt their bombed halls and the City generally embarked upon the lengthy process of reconstruction, Apothecaries' Hall awaited major redevelopment. Various suggestions were floated in the 1960s for the formation of a charity or for the improvement of the Society's properties to give higher rents, and in 1973 the City published official guidelines for the redevelopment of the area. Reports from the Society's advisers confirmed that the redevelopment or upgrading of the Society's premises in Black Friars Lane and Playhouse Yard was overdue.

The 1980s was a decade of redevelopment in the City and the Society of Apothecaries chose to take this path at a propitious moment. Office space was in demand, building sites obstructed the streets and property values soared. The Society's properties at Black Friars enjoyed an ideal location but several were in need of modernization or redevelopment and were occupied by tenants paying unrealistic rents. Among them was Carl Edwards, a designer and glazier whose work can be seen in the Court Room, Liverpool Cathedral

Apothecaries' Hall escaped serious damage in the Second World War, although as the photographs taken in 1947 show, it was in need of repair.

and Temple church, and who had occupied part of the Brande Block for several years; other such tenants included printers and photographers. It was clear that more beneficial use could be made of the premises in economic as well as environmental terms.

There was no question of demolishing the late-seventeenth-century Hall or

the late-eighteenth-century street front, for these were buildings of historic and architectural importance. However, some improvement of domestic arrangements at the Hall was required. Architects were invited to submit proposals and with the appointment of Green, Lloyd and Adams – specifically J. Sampson (Sam) Lloyd – in May 1980, working in conjunction with Richard Timmis of Messrs Farebrother, Ellis and Co (chartered surveyors), the redevelopment was launched.[83] Initially the scheme focused on the restoration and redevelopment of the Society's premises in Black Friars Lane and Playhouse Yard, the rehabilitation of the Library and the provision of a new wine dispense. Within this plan the most radical proposal was for the demolition of Cobham House and the Brande Block, to be replaced by a new office building at an estimated cost of £1,960,000.

Before any plans were submitted to the authorities, consultations were held with the City architect, the Royal Fine Art Commission, the Greater London Council's historic buildings committee, the Georgian Group, the Society for the Preservation of Ancient Buildings and the Department of the Environment. Even so, the plans drawn up by Green, Lloyd and Adams did not please everyone. A report in the *Sunday Observer* announced "the threat to a vital fragment of the City" by the building of the new Cobham House – "far too neat and careful in its reproduction of Georgian architecture to be pleasant or comfortable". This correspondent urged the City planners to throw out the scheme on the grounds that the "huge edifice" of Cobham House, "a bizarre pastiche of Georgian architecture" would dwarf its neighbours and raise local rents.[84] The Society's architect responded in measured tones, pointing out that the new office building comprised 38,000 sq.ft., not 75,000 as the reporter supposed. The idea behind the Black Friars Lane façade was to echo the gentle curve of the Mill House formerly on the site, using "the Georgian vernacular in our palette". The tower, a reference to the Priory church, was within the height regulations, nor had the architect overstepped the acceptable plot ratio. It soon became clear that the City authorities were in sympathy with the proposals: planning permission was granted in the summer of 1981 with the proviso that the seventh floor of the proposed Cobham House be omitted. Before the close of the year archaeological work in the basement at 22–26 Black Friars Lane revealed three burials inserted under the floor of the aisle of the nave of the medieval Priory church. One of these was an adult, one an adolescent and the third a child. More below-floor burials and two brick-lined burial vaults were found on the site of the choir in 1989. Many of these burials are probably patrons who paid handsomely for the privilege. For instance in June 1437 Hugh Russel, citizen and vintner, paid 40 shillings for his burial in the church and for the friars to pray for his soul.[85]

Once planning permission had been obtained, there followed six years of intense activity in Black Friars Lane, Playhouse Yard and at the Hall itself. The Society's Honorary architect and a Liveryman, Dr S.E.T. Cusdin, had drawn up a memorandum on the development and was closely involved. The restoration of the Library was inspired by Sir Ronald Gibson; Sir Brian Windeyer gave advice and the whole was under the supervision of a redevelopment committee, chaired first by Professor J.A. Dudgeon (Master 1985–86) and latterly by Colonel F.G. Neild (Master 1988–89). A project officer was appointed in Major Canning, while Major O'Leary, the Clerk, endeavoured to

One of the adult burials excavated in the choir of the former Dominican church in 1989. The base of the coffin is marked by a line of nails.

conduct the usual activities of the Society. The main contractors working under the instruction of Green, Lloyd and Adams were Harry Neal and Sons Ltd, with R. Mansell (City) Ltd responsible for the Library and wine dispense. The property developers, St Anselm Development Company Ltd (a subsidiary of Harry Neal), entered the arena in 1983 taking a ground lease of Cobham House for 125 years. Even before the Society had exchanged agreements with the developers, two firms of solicitors had expressed interest in the proposed offices on the site of Cobham House – Messrs Rowe & Maw were to be successful.

Early in 1981 Mansell began work on the Library at the Hall; it was completed in little over a year and opened in July 1982 by H.R.H. The Duke of Kent, the Society's first royal Honorary Freeman. Work proceeded at Cobham House and Magnesia House, a Grade I listed building that had deteriorated badly. Originally furnished with vats and boilers for the preparation of magnesia and manufacture of saline preparations, Magnesia House had since been used as a drug store where dangerous and toxic powders were kept. Behind it was the eighteenth-century counting-house with the original pine panelling and a double-faced clock, all retained in the sensitive restoration of 1982–85 which gained a City Heritage Award. A firm called Messrs Euromoney, neighbours at Nestor House, took the lease of Magnesia House in October 1984, promptly changing the name to Euromoney House. The rent of £42,500 per annum was subject to rent reviews every five years and the rentals of Cobham House at 20 Black Friars Lane, and the western

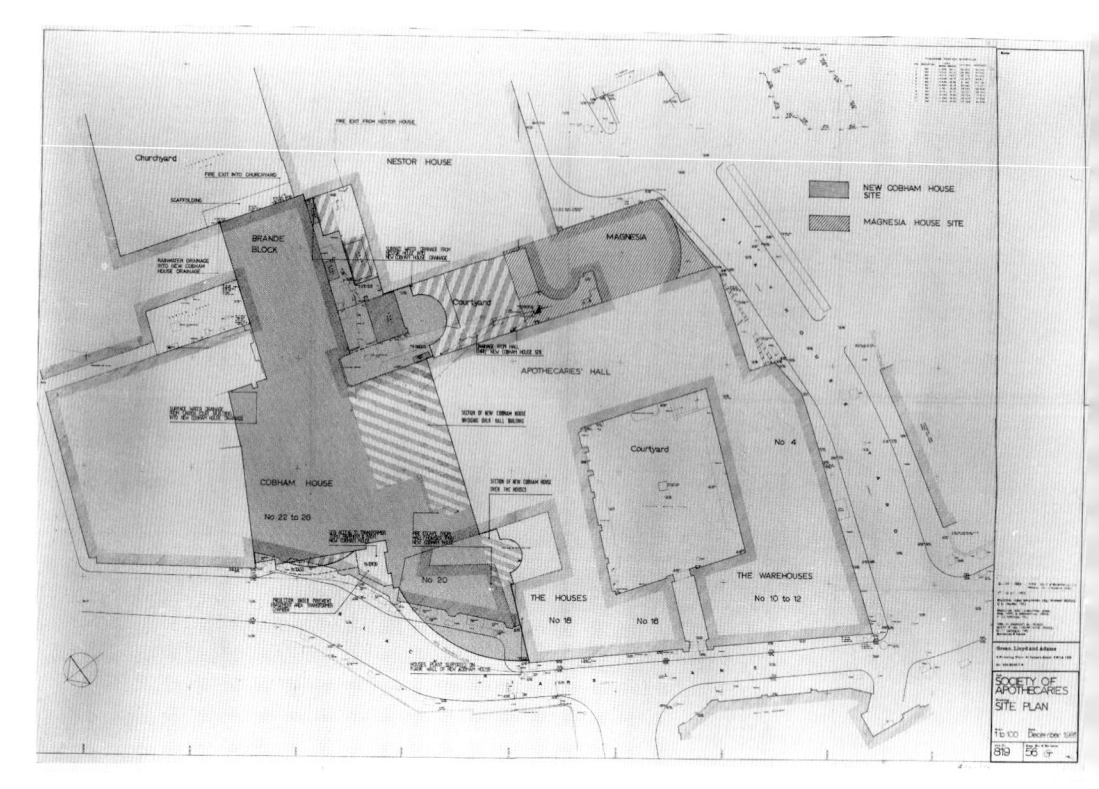

Ground plan for the redevelopment of the Society's property by the architects Green Lloyd and Adams, December 1981.

and south sides of the courtyard formerly known as "the Houses" and "the Warehouses" were likewise arranged to the advantage of the Society, for at that time rents could only be adjusted upwards. The topping-out ceremony for Cobham House took place on 15 October 1984 when the Master, Professor N.H. Ashton, laid a commemorative plaque. A year later Rowe & Maw moved in and the same firm was soon to occupy the refurbished "Houses" and "Warehouses" on the west and south sides of the Apothecaries' courtyard.

The Society's Hall was not forgotten: its modernization and redecoration was to complete the redevelopment programme. Beginning with the restoration of the Library, the relocation of the wine dispense, the adjustment and renovation of the stone staircase in the courtyard, improvements continued with the installation of a new kitchen on the first floor. Accommodation for the Master, Clerk and caretaker was upgraded, a laboratory for examinees and a workshop were established on the ground floor (the laboratory was to be converted into the comfortable Brande room in 1993). Cracks in the ceiling of the Great Hall aroused great consternation because they were indicative of structural movement, which was soon remedied by the insertion of steel rods and anchors into end walls.

The redevelopment of the Society's properties, with the exception of Nestor House which awaits the expiry of its lease in the early years of the twenty-first century, was completed in 1987. The Lord Mayor, Alderman Sir Greville Spratt, visited Apothecaries' Hall in December of that year to unveil a plaque in the courtyard recording the completion of a redevelopment from which the Society emerged with architectural and financial credit.

West elevation showing the redevelopment of Apothecaries' Hall by Green Lloyd and Adams, September 1985.

A detail from Edward Oakley's plan of Chelsea Physic Garden (1732), depicting the Apothecaries' ceremonial barge.

A wooden cartouche from the stern of the Society's first barge bears the date 1691 and the initials of James Gover (Master 1690–91). The inscription *altissimi de coelo creavit medicinam* (the Lord has created remedies from the earth) is from the *Apocrypha*, Ecclesiasticus 38 v.4.

Chapter 5

The barges and the Physic Garden

The Apothecaries' Physic Garden at Chelsea was established in conjunction with the possession of the Society's first state barge. The ceremonial barge was a mark of civic dignity, a source of pride and pleasure to the Society; the Physic Garden was primarily an educational enterprise. The two interests merged in 1673 when the Society purchased land at Chelsea where the barge could be housed and a Physic Garden cultivated. The Apothecaries' Physic Garden should also be seen in the context of the establishment of the Laboratory at the Hall and in relation to the Society's rivalry with the College of Physicians. In the wider scheme of things the Physic Garden was a manifestation of the intellectual endeavour of the late seventeenth century, epitomized by the Royal Society, to which several Apothecaries belonged and to which the Garden was linked from 1722.

The ceremonial barges

The Apothecaries first hired a barge to take part in the river procession on Lord Mayor's Day in 1631. Proud of the recent grant of a Livery, the Society bedecked the barge with its own banners and streamers, barge cloth and cushions. Musicians were hired to serenade the Liverymen – possibly as many as fifty enjoyed the expedition and partook of a dinner to complete the festivities. The day marked the arrival of the Society as a fully-fledged livery company with a recognized place in the pageantry of the City.[1]

Not all livery companies possessed their own barges. "The Great Twelve" usually did and lesser companies aspired to do so, finances permitting. The subject had been broached at Apothecaries' Hall in 1658 when enquiries were made to see if members would make voluntary contributions to the expense of the Society's own barge. The response was negative – this was the period of the Interregnum when republicanism, sobriety and stringency were the order of the day. The Restoration of the monarchy in 1660 brought the revival of pageantry, drama and ceremonies such as the elaborate river procession to celebrate the king's marriage in 1662. The Apothecaries were swept up in the prevailing mood, and with an eye to commissioning a barge, negotiated with the Barber-Surgeons to share a barge-house. The imposition of a forced loan to the king dispelled such thoughts.[2]

In 1673 the subject was raised again, the immediate impetus being complaints about the unsatisfactory vessel hired the previous year: members disliked the "inconveniency" and "unhandsomeness" of the hired barge and were in an expansive mood.[3] The post-Fire Hall had recently been completed and it was time to acquire the added prestige of a ceremonial barge. The Court therefore agreed that members should subscribe to the expense of acquiring the Society's own barge and barge-house. The committee charged with the task of securing the same made rapid headway. At a meeting of the Court in July 1673 it was reported that a contract for building a barge had been signed and no better place could be found for a barge-house than Chelsea. The Court immediately resolved to take a lease of a site there "att ye cheapest rent ye can get".[4] This was to provide the site for the barge-house and for the Physic Garden.

The riverside at Lambeth or Southwark was the usual location for livery company barge-houses, Chelsea being rather out of the way. Possibly because there was no suitable site available at Lambeth, the Assistants fixed on Chelsea, where land was cheaper. The Tallow Chandlers' Company was quick to apply to build its own barge-house alongside that of the Apothecaries. Negotiations between Past Master Lt Colonel Rosewell and Sir Joseph Sheldon (Master of the Tallow Chandlers 1667–68, Lord Mayor 1675–76) led to an agreement whereby that Company erected a double barge-house in 1675, next to the Apothecaries' single one which was built by the carpenter George Clisbie or Clisby and the bricklayer Allansby.[5] The double barge-house harboured at various times the vessels belonging to the Tallow Chandlers', Weavers', Vintners', Goldsmiths' and Skinners' Companies.

In July 1673 the bargewright Nicholas Wheatley was commissioned to build the Apothecaries' first barge for £110 – £10 less than he had charged the Mercers' Company for a similar commission two years before. The Articles of Agreement specified that the Apothecaries' ceremonial barge must be built of "well seasoned oak ... as large and good in all respects whatsoever as the barge built for the Company of Mercers". The Mercers' carver, Cleere, was engaged to execute wooden carvings of unicorns on either side of the entrance to the cabin, a rhinoceros over the door and the Apothecaries' coat of arms on the stern. The vessel was to be finished in a workmanlike manner by 20 September, in good time for Lord Mayor's Day in November 1673.[6]

With the acquisition of a barge came the building of the barge-house, the employment of Barge Master Thomas Lambkin (whose family held onto the post for seventy-eight years), his mate and eighteen watermen dressed in coats, caps, breeches, waistcoats, shoes, stockings, sashes, ribbons and cravats provided by the Society in the appropriate colours.[7]

Apart from its ceremonial function the Apothecaries' barge was put to good use on summer herbarizing expeditions when members were rowed to the chosen spot – Fulham, Putney or Greenwich, returning later that day. Otherwise, the barge was used during the alarm surrounding the Popish Plot of 1678 when it was commandeered to take soldiers to ships moored down-river, and on at least one occasion it was rented by the Salters' Company. Barge Master Lambkin was paid for a full repair in 1688 and three years later a wooden cartouche was made for the stern, commemorating James Gover's year as Master (1690–91). Forty years was a fair life-span for a seventeenth-century state barge – the Apothecaries' first vessel was old and decayed by 1713. It was then offered for sale at £5 but, with no bidders, the materials were salvaged.[8] A new barge was not commissioned until 1727 when members subscribed £361 to the cost. A further call on members' generosity was made the following year when £1,000 was needed to build a new wharf at Chelsea.

John Hall built the Society's second barge assisted by the carpenter, Hillyard, and the painter and decorator, Goodyer. The latter's description of his work details a flamboyant decorative scheme for which he was paid £47. A major feature was the Society's great shield, painted and gilded. Carved foliage, an ogee-shaped cornice around the cabin, fluted Corinthian pilasters, carved and gilded figures of the four seasons, Apollo (god of the healing arts), Aesculapius (Apollo's son and the god of healing), Hercules, Industry, Neptune and Thetis in a chariot drawn by sea-lions, and a dolphin painted on the rudder completed the décor.[9] Those who subscribed to the barge fund were acknowledged on a list at the Hall and were given the privilege of using the craft once or twice a year. For all its ornamental carving, the Society's second barge was not as robust as its predecessor. Repaired in 1737 and again in 1753, it was useless on Lord Mayor's Day of that year. Once riverworthy its appearance was revived with new banners and streamers of crimson and blue silk made in 1761.[10]

The Society's third and last barge was built by Charles Cownden "with proper images and ornaments" in 1765 at a cost of £640 excluding the plate glass for the cabin. The Apothecaries' surveyor, George Bowman, was asked to supervise the building and decoration of Cownden's barge, presenting a drawing of the finished product to the Society – since lost.[11] The barge was patched up by Cownden in 1786 and provided with a new set of colours in 1797, now displayed in the Great Hall. By 1802 the barge was unsafe, so could not be used for the herbarizing expedition to Greenwich, and the following year it was damaged by spring tides at Chelsea.[12] Although the barge was over forty years old and much repaired, the Society was proud to be able to use it as part of the funeral procession for the nation's hero, Admiral Lord Nelson, on his last journey in January 1806.

Thereafter, references to the barge are sparse. It was used on the general herbarizing in July 1811, for which the watermen were voted an allowance of 9 shillings each for the day and 1s 6d for dinner.[13] The barge was still in good repair, yet the Court declined the Lord Mayor's invitations to State Water Parties on the river, claiming that members' professional duties precluded attendance. The last order for the preparation of the barge for Lord Mayor's Day was issued in 1815 – a memorable year for the Society and for the nation. The barge was reported to be in good condition in October 1815 but seems to have deteriorated rapidly, possibly due to neglect – the Society was engrossed with the consequences of the Apothecaries' Act at the time.

By January 1817 the barge was ruinous and full of water. The bargewright Roberts was summoned and he was confident that the vessel could be repaired and beautified for £329. There was no discussion: Roberts was instructed to sell the vessel at the best price he could get and in March orders were issued for the dismissal of the Barge Master and the clearance of the barge-house, which was to be let. John Lyall of the neighbouring Swan Brewery took the lease in 1818, shutting out the river and repairing the structure in order to store casks there, and his successor used it as a boat-house. The Curator of the Physic Garden in the 1860s constantly drew attention to the need for repairs to the building, not least because it was haunted by ragamuffins who lurked along the riverside – one lad was caught stripping lead from the gutter of the barge-house for which he was condemned to a fortnight's imprisonment with hard labour.[14] The Goldsmiths' Company continued to use the westernmost barge-house and in 1836 that Company's surveyor, Philip Hardwick, applied for permission to lengthen the building, involving alterations to the Physic Garden wall. The Goldsmiths' last barge was sold in 1846 but the Skinners' Company, who had shared the double barge-house with the Goldsmiths, used the building until 1858 (the last river procession of state barges on Lord Mayor's Day was in 1856). The future of the Garden then being uncertain, the barge-houses deteriorated. Following the construction of the Chelsea Embankment in the early 1870s all three were demolished, although some seventeenth-century bricks were incorporated into the store-yard wall.[15]

The final destiny of the Apothecaries' last barge is not recorded: sold, sunk or demolished? The lease to Lyall obliged him to clear, repair and paint the barge-house, implying the building was devoid of its barge, possibly removed to bargewright Roberts's yard by August 1818. As a final indignity, the barge was denuded of its glass in November (for sale), suggesting that it was being dismantled.[16] A wooden coat of arms and the cartouche from the stern of the Apothecaries' first barge, eighteenth-century banners and streamers and an incidental but not necessarily accurate illustration (on page 112) survive as tokens of the Society's participation in the pageantry of the City's barge processions on the River Thames.

Establishing the Physic Garden
As the City of London rose from the ashes after the Great Fire, the Society displayed new strength and vitality in rebuilding Apothecaries' Hall, establishing a Laboratory, commissioning a state barge and founding a Physic Garden for the study and teaching of botany. The Apothecaries' Physic Garden followed the example of gardens first established in the sixteenth century at Pisa (1543), Leiden (1587) and Montpellier (1593), followed by

those at Oxford (1621) and Edinburgh (1670). In London, John Gerard had cultivated a late-sixteenth-century garden where he grew plants to maintain life and recover health; the Tradescants of Lambeth introduced many species from overseas in the early seventeenth century and there were other gardens belonging to the great houses of the aristocracy and ecclesiastics, to livery halls and individual apothecaries, physicians and botanists, where medicinal and culinary plants were grown. The Apothecaries' Garden at Chelsea, however, was in the tradition of the physic gardens attached to the medical faculties of universities, being used for teaching and as a source of *materia medica*, and was the second such garden to be established in England after Oxford.

From the time that the Society's herbarizings commenced in 1620, the study of botany had been promoted by a core of dedicated botanist-Apothecaries led by Thomas Johnson and John Parkinson (see pages 42–43). Most medicines then being derived from herbs, plants and vegetables, it was essential that apprentice Apothecaries should be instructed in the identification, properties and uses of the *materia medica*. The Chelsea Physic Garden served this purpose and more, becoming a centre of botanical and scientific interest and a garden of international renown.

Charles II's reign, sometimes dubbed "the age of experiment", was an era of intellectual advances, not least in medicine, botany and other subjects of interest to Apothecaries. The Royal Society took the leading part in the

The barge-houses at Chelsea Physic Garden from a painting by G. Lambert *circa* 1859.

movement and its influence was felt at Apothecaries' Hall and the Physic Garden. The king himself showed the way by appointing a Botanic Professor and a Chemical Physician; he took a keen interest in the Royal Society, granting its royal charter in 1662 and becoming its patron, even if he did laugh at some of the experiments. Fellows of the Royal Society were learned men from all spheres: names such as Boyle, Wren, Newton and Locke spring to mind. Several of them were closely associated with apothecaries in Oxford, with whom they lodged and shared an interest in experiments. Once the Royal Society was formally constituted in London, some members of the Society of Apothecaries became Fellows and, with other Fellows, actively supported the Chelsea Physic Garden. The most conspicuous of the group was Sir Hans Sloane, Secretary and later President of the Royal Society, who as Lord of the Manor of Chelsea from 1713 was the chief benefactor of the Apothecaries' Physic Garden.

The Apothecaries John Houghton (known as the father of English advertising, see page 64), Samuel Doody (a friend of Sloane) and James Petiver (a natural scientist whose collection was the envy of Sloane) were early Fellows of the Royal Society. Dr Christopher Merrett, one of the first to be awarded the Honorary Freedom of the Society of Apothecaries, Ambrose Hanckwitz/Godfrey (the Apothecaries' Chemical Operator), James Sherard, Isaac Rand, John Meres junior (the Clerk), Silvanus Bevan (founder of the Plough Court pharmacy that evolved into Allen & Hanburys) and Philip Miller (the Gardener) were likewise Fellows.[17] They and many other Apothecary-Fellows of succeeding generations sustained the Garden and made their influence felt at Apothecaries' Hall. John Conyers, an Apothecary of Fleet Street, Samuel Dale who bequeathed his library, portrait and herbarium to the Society, Miller, Petiver, Sherard, Doody, Houghton and Bacon – all of them Apothecaries – contributed papers to the Royal Society's *Philosophical Transactions*, which from 1722 published the list of specimens received from the Physic Garden.

At a less formal level than the Royal Society, Apothecaries were among the coterie of botanists of the Temple Coffee-house Club, meeting every Friday evening to share their botanical discoveries. This club was well-established by 1691 with forty members and many more guests. Sloane was the leading light, and the members included Petiver, Doody, Watts and Dale, also William Sherard (brother of the Apothecary James and cousin of Petiver), Henry Compton the Bishop of London, the botanists Rev Adam Buddle (of Buddleia fame) and Leonard Plukenet (Superintendent of the Gardens at Hampton Court). When meetings of the Royal Society were suspended during the summer, members of the Temple Coffee-house Club arranged excursions on the lines of the Apothecaries' herbarizings until the demise or old age of members brought a halt to the activities of this "unofficial appendage to the

Royal Society at one of its periods of greatest renown".[18]

Its successor, John Martyn's Botanical Society, was founded in 1721 and it too "was clearly very much an offshoot of the Apothecaries' excursions". Martyn's Botanical Society was a more organized assembly than the Temple Coffee-house Club, with rules, and a Demonstrator in attendance at meetings at the Rainbow Coffee-house, Watling Street, or in members' houses. Of the twenty-three identified members about one-third were Apothecaries and most of the remainder were physicians, surgeons or surgeon-apothecaries. When John Martyn was enticed to Cambridge, his London Society dwindled and ceased. However, as Professor of Botany at the University, Martyn pressed for the establishment of the Cambridge Physic Garden, achieved some thirty years later under the Curatorship of Philip Miller's son. Thus in the course of time, "Cambridge botany became doubly the offspring of Chelsea".[19]

The Society of Apothecaries was also well represented in the Linnean Society, founded in 1788 and the first specialist scientific grouping after the Royal Society. William Hudson, *Praefectus Horti* at Chelsea (1765–71) and his successor William Curtis, Thomas Wheeler the Botanical Demonstrator for forty-two years, John Fairbairn the Gardener from 1784 to 1814 and his successor William Anderson, Professor John Lindley the Botanical Demonstrator, and Nathaniel B. Ward all boasted F.L.S. after their names.

The tradition of the Society of Apothecaries' herbarizings and the prominence of its members in learned societies and botanical circles demonstrated the Apothecaries' enthusiasm for botany, professionally, intellectually and socially. In practical terms it fell to Past Master Lt Colonel Rosewell to further these interests in his role as chief negotiator for the land at Chelsea where the Physic Garden was to be established.

There was already a garden behind Apothecaries' Hall with a grass plot and possibly herbs and plants, in addition to which some Apothecaries cultivated their own botanic or "medical" gardens. The Laboratory at the Hall, operating from 1672, brought a new demand for herbs and medicinal plants which the Physic Garden was to supply – the managers of the Laboratory contributed to the cost of building the wall around the Garden on condition that a section of it was devoted to herbs for the Laboratory. Nicholas Staphorst, the Society's Operator at the Laboratory and the friend and instructor of Sloane, recorded his appreciation for 150 pounds of mint harvested from the Chelsea Garden (used to make mint oil), and a good crop of sage, rue, pennyroyal and sweet marjoram was expected from the same source.[20]

There were obvious advantages to the Society in cultivating its own Physic Garden and its riverside position had the advantages of a ready supply of water and a berth for the barge. The historian John Bowack, writing in 1705, thought the learned botanist-Apothecaries favoured Chelsea because the soil there was conducive to the cultivation of curious plants. The Court Minutes fail to explain the virtues of Chelsea: Richard Tomlinson reported to the Court that he could not find anywhere better to build a barge-house and the Assistants concurred.[21] Contacts between Apothecaries and the Royal Society may have focused attention on the area around Chelsea College (granted by the king to the Society in 1667) and there were some notable private gardens beside the Thames at Chelsea, such as as the Great Garden of the Manor House. Between Chelsea College (later the Royal Hospital) and Chelsea Manor House lay part of the east field described in 1647 as "several parcels of arable land . . . abutting south on the Thames . . . containing by estimate four acres more or less". This has been identified as the land the Society of Apothecaries leased from the Lord of the Manor, William Cheyne, later Lord Cheyne and Viscount Newhaven, for sixty-one years from 1673 at £5 per annum. The lease of that year describes the potential garden as arable pasture ground with a messuage called The White Swan to the east.[22]

William Gape (Master 1672–73 and Apothecary to the Duke of York) was the first to promote "walling in ye ground at Chelsea taken for a garden" in October 1673 with a donation of £50, although the decision to build the Garden wall was not formally agreed by the Court until January 1675 when subscriptions were raised and the work put in hand.[23] The wall built by Munden was 10 feet high above the ground and 76 rods in length (418 yards). Sixty-five individual members of the Society contributed to the cost of building it (£394), the committee managing the Laboratory gave £50, and £150 came from corporate funds. The wall was broken at the riverside by a watergate, and the garden gates were the work of the stonemason Young, who had worked at the Hall.[24] The botanist Edward Morgan was consulted and he presented plants from his "medical" garden at Westminster to help establish the Chelsea Garden (Morgan was considered for the keepership of the latter but his age was against him), and more plants came from William Gapes's Westminster garden.[25]

The Society's first Gardener at Chelsea, a freeman called Spencer Piggot (later Master), put the Society to "great and unnecessary expenses in doing things very improperly", and was therefore replaced in January 1678 by Richard Pratt who was to receive a salary of £30 per annum and accommodation in a house built for him (Assistants volunteered to subscribe to the cost).[26] At the instigation of Robert Phelps, a Warden, the Garden was planted with fruit trees in the winter of 1678 – "Nectarines of all sortes, Peaches, Apricocks, Cherryes and plumes",[27] and there was a pond in the Garden by 1679. Phelps (Master briefly in 1681 on the death of Skinner) was a man of vision, venturing to suggest that a greenhouse would be convenient. This was duly erected in the middle of the Garden facing the river gate, and equipped with stoves (1681) – by all accounts the first heated greenhouse in England.[28]

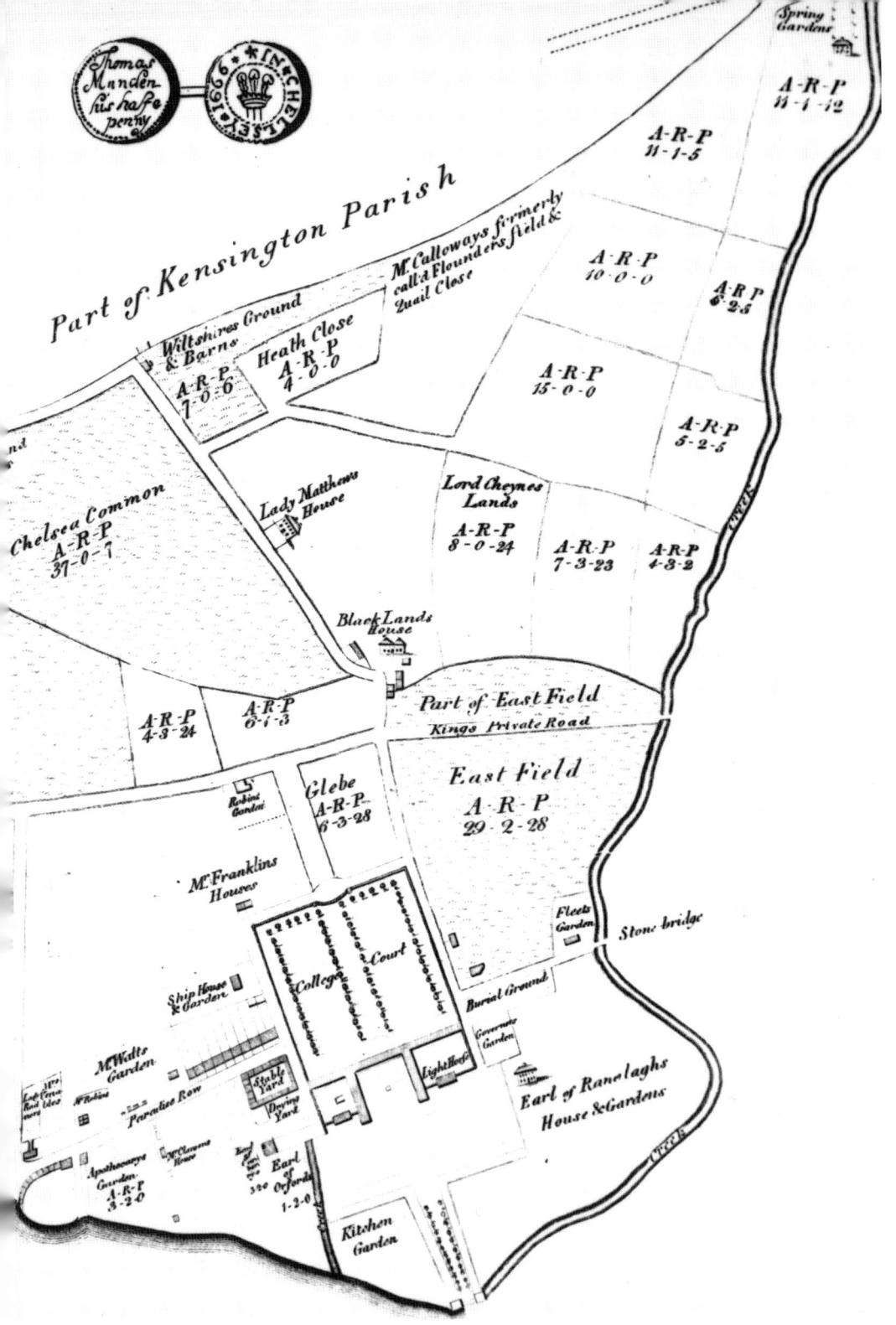

Detail from James Hamilton's map of Chelsea (1664–1717), published in T. Faulkner's *Historical and Topographical Description of Chelsea* (1810). The Apothecaries' Physic Garden is marked as containing 3 acres 2 rods (lower left). On the opposite side of Paradise Row is the garden of Mr Watts who was appointed Gardener at the Physic Garden in 1680. The token (top left) bears the name of Thomas Munden who built the wall around the Physic Garden (1676–77).

Pratt proved as unsatisfactory as his predecessor: he was not the sort of gardener most members of the Court wanted. Despite the fact that he had laboured to transform the land from a heap of gravel and rubbish into a garden and had compiled a list of 1,200 plants, leading members on the Court wanted to see the care of the Garden entrusted to the botanist John Watts, a member of the Society. In January 1680 Watts put his proposals to the Court: for a salary of £50 a year he promised "to husband things to the Company's best advantage" and to make the Garden equal to any other within a few years. George Johnson opened the debate by questioning the advantage of Watts over the present Gardener, Pratt. Herne and Phelps were adamant that Pratt was incapable of making the Garden "answer the end the Company designed it for", whereas Watts's "genius leads him that way". Chase credited Pratt with bringing the Garden to its present maturity, Barrow argued against, and the final decision was taken by John Battersby, deputizing for the Master, who ordered that Watts should undertake the care and management of the "Botanick Garden".[29]

Under Watts the Physic Garden became established as a source of botanical knowledge, scientific interest and visual delight, stocked with plants both native and foreign, including seventy orange trees besides the fruit trees planted between 1678 and 1679. Shells lined the paths and seats were installed in anticipation of the queen's visit in 1685.[30] Watts initiated an exchange of seeds and plants with the botanic garden at Leiden from whence he obtained four 3-feet-high cedar trees, among the first to be planted in England. These were a major feature of the Garden and their demise was much lamented: two were felled in 1771, one in the middle years of the nineteenth century and the last during the winter of 1903–04.[31] Wood from broken branches of the cedars was used to make chairs for the Master and Wardens in 1812 and 1847, since when a writing-case, boxes, another chair and a gate-legged table made from the Physic Garden cedars have come to light.

The Society's apprentices studied botany at the Physic Garden, as did a promising young student called Sloane, then lodging with the Society's Chemical Operator at Apothecaries' Hall. Sloane took advantage of the Laboratory at the Hall to study chemistry and went to the Apothecaries' Physic Garden to study botany. Following a period of study in France he returned to London in 1684, visiting the Physic Garden shortly afterwards. He commented on the recently acquired cedar trees and Watts's ingenious heating system which enabled delicate plants to survive a severe English winter (the Thames was frozen from December to February 1683–84). Sloane's interest may have influenced his decision to live at Chelsea – the Manor House he purchased in 1713 was a short walk from the Apothecaries' Garden.

Dr Paul Hermann, Professor of Botany at Leiden, came to inspect the Physic Garden in 1682; the botanist-author Dr Leonard Plukenet, who was assisting John Ray ("the Father of English Botany") to arrange *Historia Plantarum*, studied there; and in 1685 the diarist John Evelyn, himself the owner of a remarkable garden at Sayes Court, came to see the Garden. Like Sloane, he was intrigued by the subterranean heating of the greenhouse – he described the Apothecaries' Garden as the "garden of simples at Chelsey: where there is a collection of innumerable varieties of that sort: Particularly, besids (*sic*) many rare annuals the Tree bearing the Jesuit's bark". This was the Cinchona tree from Peru, the bark of which was the source of quinine used to cure fever and the ague.[32]

The expense of the Physic Garden proved hard for the Society to bear. Watts's enthusiasm led him to overspend – he employed six labourers and complained that the garden consumed all his salary. There was also the maintenance of the buildings, wall and river stairs, the cost of seeds, plants and barge-loads of dung. Under a new contract of 1685 Watts, who had recently been admitted to the Livery without fine, obtained a rise in salary and was allowed to sell plants and fruit from the Garden.[33]

For the next few years all went well. The Society placed a stone plaque on the Garden wall inscribed in gold letters *Hortus Botanicus Societatis Pharmaceuticae Lond 1686* (still in evidence, but no longer gold) and members of the Court were given keys to the garden door so that they might bring their wives and friends there between sunrise and sunset. Watts undertook to bring plants from the Physic Garden to decorate Apothecaries' Hall on Master's Day. Fruit from the Garden graced the dinner table and herbs went to the Laboratory. Watts's expertise extended to the garden behind the Hall in 1688, when he was given carte-blanche to stock and arrange it as he thought fit.[34]

Watts was a wealthy merchant and, having devoted himself to the Apothecaries' Physic Garden for several years, his attention seems to have been diverted to the creation of his own garden at Enfield, or possibly it was the Apothecaries' demand for a catalogue of the plants in the Chelsea Garden that defeated him. For whatever reason, Watts went missing and the Garden was neglected. The Apothecary James Petiver reported that the Garden was "slenderly stocked" and at a low ebb in March 1690. The following year Dr Hamilton found there was a "great variety of plants, both in and out of greenhouses; their perennial green hedges and rows of different coloured herbs, are very pretty and so are the banks set with shades of herbs in the Irish stitch-way; but many plants of the garden were not in so good order as might be expected".[35] Another commentator, William King, was bemused by the curious, not necessarily beautiful, plants at Chelsea. He poked fun at the rarities – "the stinking nettle of Japan . . . the Armenian gooseberry bush that bears no fruit . . . the Blooming Bramble of Lapland, with a hundred other Curious plants as a particular Collection of Briars and Thorns".[36]

The disappearance of Watts and the consequent deterioration of the

Chelsea Garden raised the question of whether the Society should continue to maintain it. Some 1,000 plants were missing, leaving nothing fit for the instruction of apprentices and the ground lay uncultivated for three years, although one improvement was the rebuilding of the walls of the pond in 1701.

Jacob Bobart, who had succeeded his father as *Hortulanus* of the Oxford Physic Garden, was reported to be tired of Oxford by 1691 and interested in replacing Watts at Chelsea. However, the Society preferred to accept the offer of one of its members, Samuel Doody, to care for the Garden *gratis* for a year from August 1692. Doody was supported by fellow-enthusiasts – Petiver, Dare, Broomwich and Jones, assisted by George Wilson, described as a servant of the Society at the Garden. As Watts had failed to produce a catalogue, Dare and Doody assumed responsibility for this, compiling a list of plants growing there in November 1706: there were still over thirty orange trees in the greenhouse while, outside, the quarters of the Garden were dominated by scores of yews in various forms, box, holly and juniper.[37] Having supervised the Garden for a year free of charge, Doody had his term of office extended at a salary of £100 per annum, and at his death the Court voted £5 towards his burial.[38]

In 1707 a committee under the capable leadership of James Petiver took responsibility for the Garden, promising to invest in it for seven years from 1708.[39] Even so, it was necessary to subsidize the Garden from increases in quarterage, fines and new fees, a step that received legal sanction in 1717.

James Petiver, Apothecary to Charterhouse, succeeded as Botanical Demonstrator at the Garden in 1709. He was a keen naturalist, entomologist and collector, yet he failed to make a good impression on Von Uffenbach, a young German traveller who found him "quite deficient . . . For he appeared to be wretched both in looks and actions . . . speaking very poor and deficient Latin and scarce able to string a few words together". The herb garden, as Von Uffenbach described the Physic Garden, was also disappointing in some respects:

> "It is fairly large and made vastly pleasant by the fine chopped hedges and all manner of figures of yew. But they were not able to show us many curious and rare plants. The green-house also is small and wretched, with few plants. In the garden itself are one or two tolerably high and well-grown cedars of Lebanon, which are more or less similar to our fir trees, but thicker and with closer needles. We saw, moreover, a cucumber tree whose bark forms the cucumbers that are used as stoppers. It resembled a lime tree with three knots or crowns".

This "cucumber tree" is most likely to have been a cork tree.[40]

Petiver was the friend and correspondent of Sloane, whom he invited to one of the Apothecaries' herbarizings at Putney Heath with a lecture and dinner afterwards at The Bowling Green. The Society entertained Sloane in 1707 and invited him to dine at the Hall on Confirmation Day in 1731 – there may have been other less formal occasions attended by Sloane. At his request Petiver travelled to Leiden in 1711 to purchase Dr Hermann's collection. As the nervous traveller awaited embarkation at Harwich he wrote an unwitnessed will declaring his intention to leave £100 for the Apothecaries' Physic Garden and to promote the herbarizings and lectures. Petiver lived for another seven years and failed to mention the Society in his last will. With the future of the Garden bleak, members of the Court looked to the renowned physician, collector, antiquary, scientist and botanist, Sir Hans Sloane, for assistance. He had taken advantage of the Society's Laboratory and Garden in his youth; he was the friend and correspondent of several Apothecaries; and in 1713 he acquired the Manor of Chelsea.[41]

Sloane and Miller
The Apothecaries had made several approaches to the Lord of the Manor and freeholder of the site of the Physic Garden, Lord Cheyne, with a view to obtaining an extension of the lease on the Garden. Negotiations were afoot in 1696, were resumed in 1698, lapsed, and were revived in 1707. Cheyne, who had gained a fortune by marrying the daughter of the Duke of Newcastle, refused to part with the reversion of the property for less than £400, so the matter was dropped.[42] Dr Hans Sloane's purchase of the Manor of Chelsea from Lord Cheyne in 1713 gave the Garden a more sympathetic landlord and a potential patron.

Following earlier overtures, the Master, Henry Smith, called on Sloane in June 1718 to discuss settling the Garden on the Society in perpetuity. A meeting was arranged between the Society's Clerk, John Meres junior, and Sloane's lawyer but it was another four years before the conveyance was signed. This allowed Sloane plenty of time to devise a contract that secured the future of the Physic Garden, provided for a collection of at least 2,000 specimens from it, stimulated scientific interest and had the effect of tightening its management. In February 1722 Sloane conveyed the property to the Society for £5 per annum on condition that fifty new plants in the form of dried specimens grown in the garden each year were submitted to the Royal Society for listing in *Philosophical Transactions* and for preservation as a collection – the Natural History Museum now holds 3,150 specimens obtained according to this agreement. The obligation served to generate activity: the Society of Apothecaries, animated by Sloane's gift, redoubled its efforts to improve the Garden and stock it with plants from all parts of the world. New specimens were obtained, carefully cultivated and the Society's Demonstrator was responsible for listing and presenting them to the Royal Society. A further condition imposed by Sloane removed the possibility of developing the Garden for other purposes: if the Apothecaries were unable to maintain it as a Physic Garden it was to pass to the Royal Society, the College of Physicians or to Sloane's descendants.[43]

Sloane's conveyance was the act of a far-sighted benefactor; he also ensured the immediate improvement of the Garden by introducing Philip Miller as Gardener, and he showed his continuing concern for the Garden by contributing towards the building and repair funds for the greenhouse.[44] On the recommendation of Dr Patrick Blair to Sloane, Philip Miller, "the greatest botanical horticulturalist of the eighteenth century" was engaged as Gardener at Chelsea in 1722 with a salary of £50 a year, his predecessor having been summarily dismissed.[45] Miller's appointment coincided with a new set of rules for the management of the Garden and the raising of subscriptions, followed by the publication of an engraving of the Garden by Sutton Nicholls (1725) featuring the proposed new greenhouse – this version was unexecuted.[46] The subscriptions were to pay for the intended improvements, namely the greenhouse that was to include a room for books and collections, and a new gate in the Garden's west wall. It was also suggested that the quarters into which the Garden plants were divided should be enclosed and secured with doors and locks.

Isaac Rand was appointed *Praefectus Horti* in 1724 with responsibility for demonstrating the plants to Apothecaries and their apprentices in the Garden twice-monthly in summer and submitting fifty specimens to the Royal Society annually. Miller, meanwhile, established his reputation by compiling *The Gardeners' and Florists' Dictionary* (1724) which ran into eight editions (1731–68) and explained the author's methods for cultivating and improving all manner of gardens including physic gardens and vineyards. In the first edition, dedicated to Sloane, Miller warmly acknowledged his debt to his patron and his gift of the garden to the Apothecaries. Miller's next publication, *Catalogus Plantarum Officinalium quae in Horto Botanico Chelseyano aluntur* (1730), was dedicated to the Master, Wardens and Society of Apothecaries, and its frontispiece showed the ornamental garden gates with a glimpse of the late-seventeenth-century greenhouse beyond. *The Gardener's Kalendar* appeared in 1731, the first of seventeen editions, and it too was dedicated to the Master and Wardens. Nevertheless, relations between Miller and the Society soured over the publication of Isaac Rand's catalogue in the same year as Miller's – Miller accused Rand of plagiarism and nursed a grievance for many years. Apart from this conflict of interests, Rand's duties were those of instructor in botany, whereas Miller concentrated on the introduction and cultivation of new and exotic species. He journeyed to Holland to purchase some 200 plants in 1727 and was constantly exchanging seeds and plants with fellow-botanists and corresponding with experts. Sloane and Miller arranged for the Society to give £20 per annum towards the collection of plants, trees, dyes and drugs in

Georgia and in Spanish America. Miller's brother Robert was despatched to Georgia for this purpose, taking with him a shipment that included a tub of white mulberry plants, cotton seeds, vines, an olive tree, caper plants and madder root – the cotton seeds were particularly successful. Robert Miller managed to send a few reciprocal specimens back to Chelsea before war with Spain halted such exchanges in 1740.[47]

Pineapples (popular at the Society's dinners) and coconuts were grown at Chelsea; fig trees, guavas, mangoes, tea-plants and Arabian jasmine were nurtured in the hothouses. Another of Miller's specialities was to grow tulip

Portrait of Isaac Rand F.R.S. attributed to John Ellys (1732). Rand was appointed the Society's first *Praefectus Horti* at the Physic Garden in 1724.

and narcissi bulbs in water, but above all he valued shrub roses and especially *rosa gallica officinalis*, the Apothecary's Rose. He was one of the first to draw attention to the importance of insects in fertilization and he was keen to promote vineyards in this country; his tan stoves, fuelled with tanbark obtained from a tannery, were legendary and his advice was widely sought.

The engraving published in 1725 to advertise the Society's projected greenhouse had the desired effect in that it persuaded members and patrons to reach into their pockets. Sloane gave 100 guineas, the Royal College of

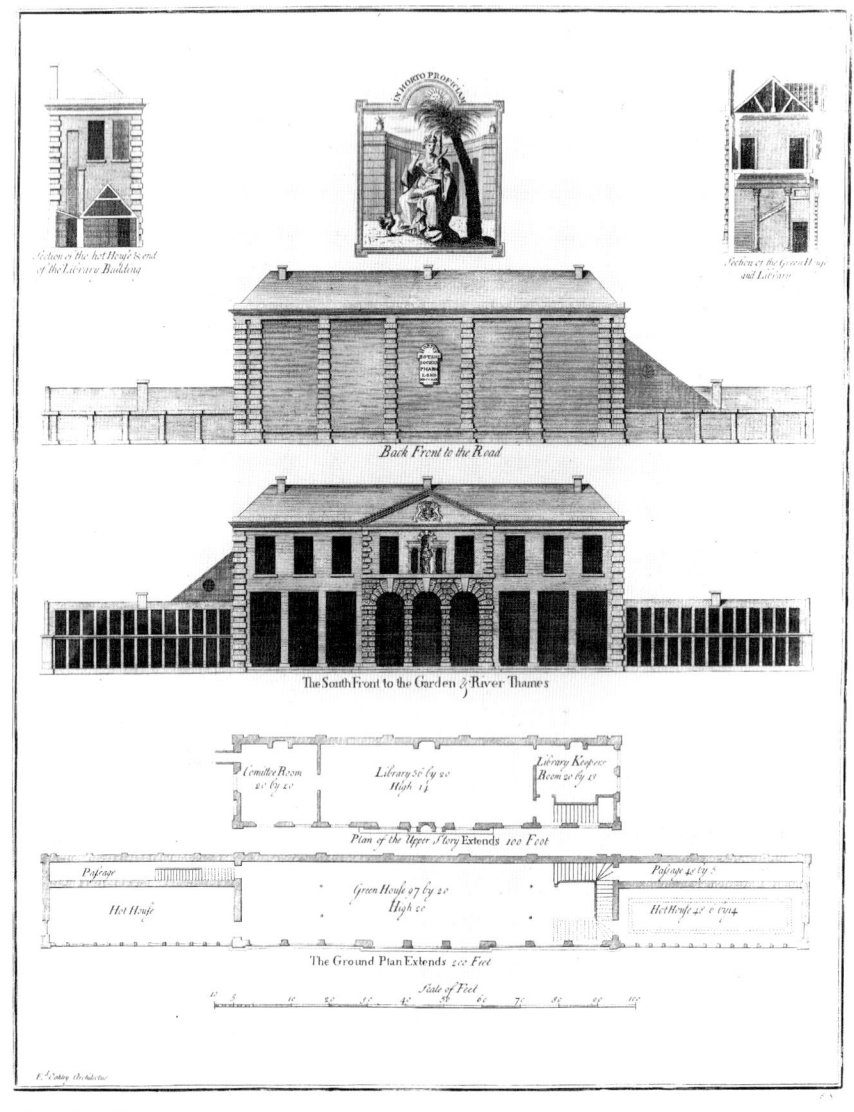

Edward Oakley's plans and sections for the proposed greenhouse and library at the Physic Garden (1732).

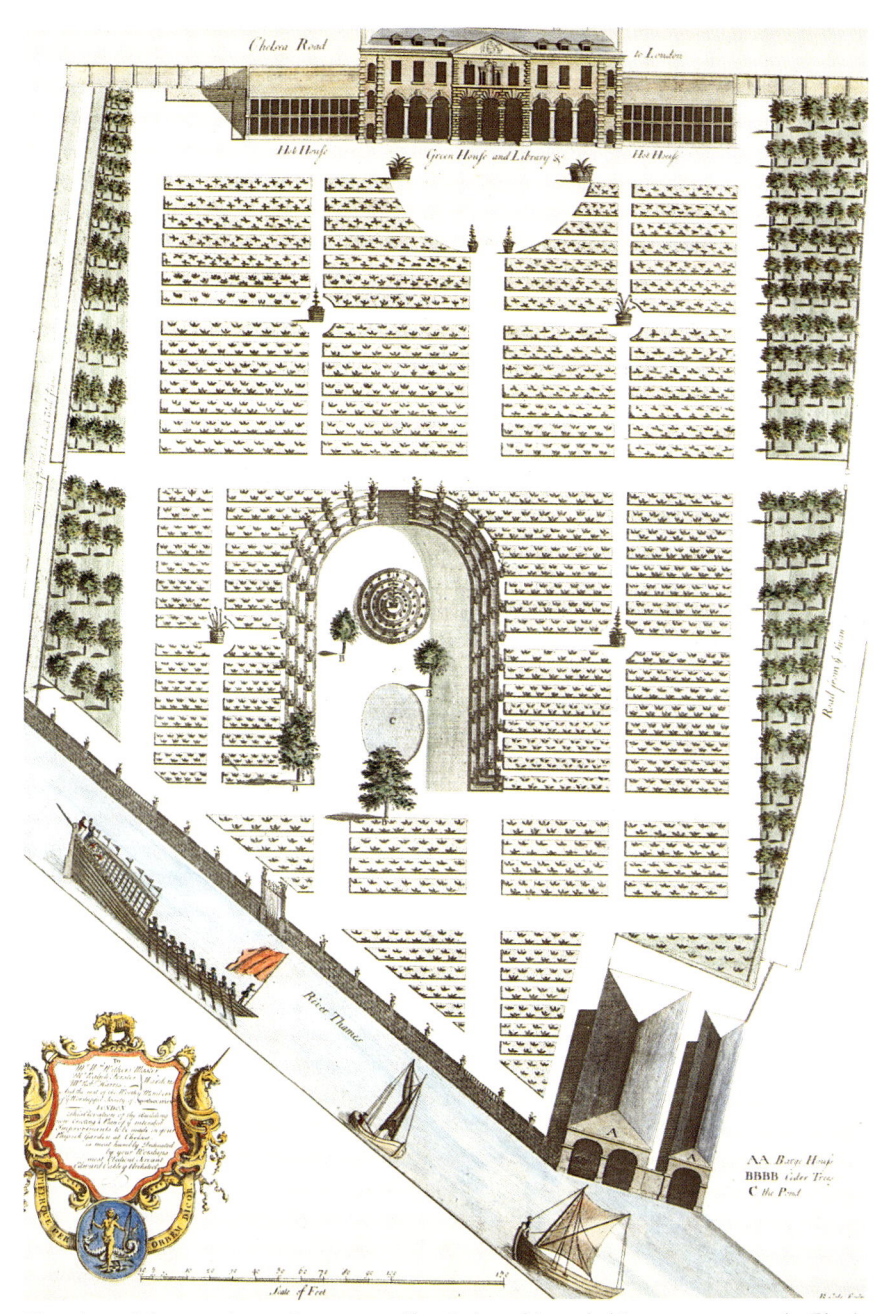

Elevation of the greenhouse "now erected" and plan of intended improvements at the Physic Garden, by Edward Oakley, architect (1732), engraved by B. Cole. AA marks the barge-houses, BBBB indicates the four cedar trees, C is a pond.

Physicians, the Royal Society and a stream of noble lords and physicians who appreciated the Garden contributed, raising some £2,000. A modified design for the building was then produced by Edward Oakley, whose drawings of 1732 show an elegant orangery or greenhouse flanked by hothouses with a total length of nearly 200 feet (100 feet shorter than the previous plan). The central greenhouse contained a Library, committee room and accommodation for the Gardener on the upper floor (although Miller chose to live in Swan Walk between 1733 and 1762). Oakley's designs show slightly differing versions and it is clear that Miller demanded alterations to the original (taller chimneys, staircases), increasing the cost from £1,550 to £1,891.[48]

The foundation stone for the new greenhouse was laid by Sloane in August 1732 and the completion of building work was marked by the commissioning of his statue from Rysbrack in 1734 – the choice of sculptor was Sloane's and the Apothecaries' Clerk had difficulty with the spelling of "Risbank" "Ricebank".[49] The mighty figure of Sir Hans Sloane was intended for a niche in the centre bay of the orangery, facing the Garden, but the marble statue was too heavy so was placed on a pedestal. When the greenhouse was condemned as dangerous in 1748 the statue was moved to a central position in the Garden, enclosed by rails (1751) and given an inscription.[50] It had been intended to protect the figure with a sail cloth or tarpaulin but as it happened the weather and pollution took its toll. To prevent further damage the statue was removed to the safety of the British Museum in 1984 and a replica was placed in the Physic Garden (another replica presides over Sloane Square).

The new greenhouse provided limited accommodation for the Gardener and for a Library. The nucleus of the Apothecaries' Library dated from 1633 when Thomas Johnson presented a copy of his edition of Gerard's *Herbal*, and the post-Restoration surge of interest in botany and chemistry persuaded the Society to find room in the gallery at the Hall for a "repository for books" in 1682. Its counterpart at the Physic Garden expanded with the presentation of Samuel Dale's collection (1739), followed by gifts from Isaac Rand's widow, Joseph Miller and Dr John Wilmer among others. Sloane, as Dale's executor, advised the Garden Committee on the storage of the legacy, insisting that separate presses be provided[51] (a large cupboard survives) and by 1769 when the collection was catalogued by Stanesby Alchorne, the Library at the Physic Garden comprised 266 volumes, many of them rare.

After less than a decade, the greenhouse was in danger of collapse. The Society treated the matter seriously, consulting James Gibbs (who had designed St Martin-in-the-Fields), and George Dance senior (architect of the Mansion House and Clerk of the City Works). They reported that it was "absolutely necessary" to pull it down and rebuild it according to the drawing, at a cost of £300. Alarmed by the expense, the Court chose to disregard the advice of the experts, preferring the opinion of the bricklayer Charles Atkins

Samuel Dale, artist unknown, *circa* 1730. Dale was a botanist, topographer, author and an apothecary of Essex who left a bequest of his library, collections and portrait to the Society on his death in 1739. He had been apprenticed through Apothecaries' Hall but did not take up his freedom.

and Benjamin Hillyard, the carpenter employed by the Society, that the work was not urgent.[52] As a result the buildings decayed further so that in 1747 Miller estimated that rebuilding would cost £933 15s. Faced with these daunting figures at a time of financial crisis, the Master and Clerk approached Sloane, then living in retirement at Chelsea Manor House. Alarmed by the rumour that the Society was considering "throwing up the garden", Sloane donated £150 insisting "in the strongest manner" that the repairs be executed forthwith. Miller then produced an estimate for the most necessary repairs (£175 5s) and was authorized to put these in hand as soon as the weather permitted, and to notify Sloane.[53] These repairs did not alter the appearance of the orangery, as John Haynes's survey of 1751 shows, although the hothouses on either side had been modified. Haynes provided a key or "explanation" to the layout of the Garden indicating two wildernesses, blocks of perennials, glass cases, frames, etc. (opposite).[54]

As word of Miller's achievements at the Physic Garden spread, visitors came to see for themselves: Carl Linnaeus (the Swedish botanist whose system of classification Miller eventually adopted) was there in 1736, obtaining the plants and specimens he desired. Gilbert White, author of *The Natural History of Selborne* called on Miller for advice on growing melons. Pehr Kalm was in Chelsea in 1748 to see Sloane's collection of curiosities at the Manor House and Miller's exotics at the Physic Garden. He was impressed by the stoves fed with the bark of oak trees (tan stoves), and by the Gardener's reputation – "the principal people in the land set a particular value on this man".[55]

In addition to students, overseas visitors and botanists, artists were attracted to the Chelsea Garden to make accurate drawings of plants. Jacobus van Huysum lived in Chelsea between 1720 and 1740, taking advantage of the Physic Garden plants to illustrate John Martyn's *Historia Plantarum Rariorum*. The German artist G.D. Ehret was given access to the Garden in the 1730s to make drawings for the steady flow of flower paintings and engravings which earned him the patronage of the aristocracy, and in 1738 he married Philip Miller's sister-in-law. Another German artist, J.S. Miller (originally Müeller) worked closely with Philip Miller, producing 300 copperplates "accurately engraved after drawings taken from nature . . . their flowers and seed vessels drawn when they were in their greatest perfection", published in *Figures of Plants* (1755–60). The purpose of such books was instructive and the plates illustrated plants that were curious in themselves, useful in medicines and largely unknown to former botanists.

The artist Elizabeth Blackwell came to live nearby in Swan Walk in order to draw the plants and trees found in the Physic Garden "taken from the life" for *A Curious Herbal* (1737–38) which acknowledged the encouragement she had been given by Dr Richard Mead and the Apothecaries Sherard, Rand, Joseph Miller and Robert Nicholls. Her *Herbal* contained 500 illustrations of plants used in the practice of physic, and was followed by *Herbarium Blackwelliarum* (1750–56) – the profits from her labours enabled her to rescue her husband from prison. John Quincy, the author of *The English Dispensatory* which ran into twelve editions (1721–42), acknowledged the assistance of Miller – "a very worthy Apothecary and a most judicious Botanist" – for corrections and improvements to his work. Another author and botanist, Richard Warner,

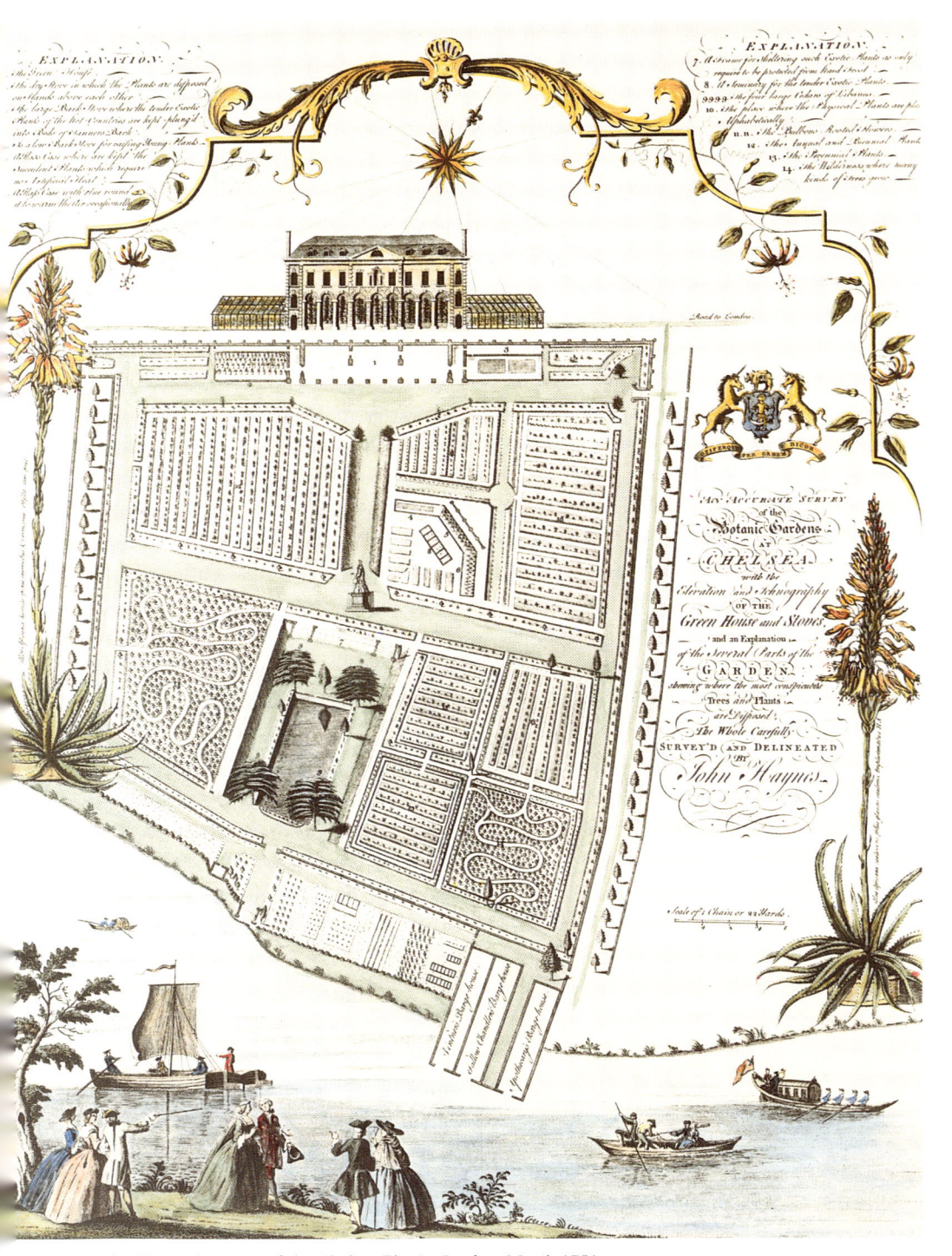

John Haynes's survey of the Chelsea Physic Garden, March 1751.

who was a friend of Miller, dedicated his book *Plantae Woodfordiensis* (1771) to the Society of Apothecaries, acknowledging the favours granted in the prosecution of his botanical amusements.

The eighteenth-century botanical artists provided an instructive and exquisite record of plants cultivated by Miller at the Physic Garden. The decorative quality of their work lent itself to porcelain, notably the pieces being produced at the Chelsea Porcelain Manufactory, not far west of the Physic Garden, in the 1750s. These were advertised as "enamelled from Sir Hans Sloan's plants" (1758), suggesting that the artists drew the plants at the Garden. Some porcelain was evidently painted directly from plants but a great deal of the decoration was taken from Ehret's engravings. Either way, many pieces of mid-eighteenth-century Chelsea porcelain record in a decorative and valuable form an achievement to which Sloane, Miller and the Society of Apothecaries contributed.

Visitors were met at the Garden gate by Miller who escorted them for a small fee. He still complained that he was out-of-pocket, and he aired his grievances in a "Humble Memorial" submitted to the Court of Assistants in 1767. He claimed to have found the Physic Garden in great disorder in 1722, overgrown with the suckers of fruit trees and being used in part for a nursery garden. He had purchased over 300 pots of plants and personally paid for their carriage to Chelsea. He had incurred expenses on his trip to purchase plants in Holland, and he was particularly upset that having worked fourteen hours a day for six months to produce a catalogue of plants, Mr Rand had taken the credit with the publication of his work.[56] Miller was duly compensated with a gratuity of £50 but his relationship with the Society of Apothecaries was soured.

As well as a discontented Gardener the Court had to deal with the complaints of members about riotous herbarizings: many were deterred from sending their apprentices on the Society's botanical expeditions because of the "irregularity and indecent behaviour" of some apprentices who treated the day out as a holiday.[57] Stricter discipline was introduced on herbarizing days, and in a similar mood the Apothecaries began to exercise tighter control at the Garden.

Miller's resentment festered as the Society's tentacles took a closer grip on the Physic Garden. A special committee was formed to undertake an inventory of the plants, each one being marked with a stick. One of those on the committee was John Channing (Master 1771–72), a scholarly Apothecary of Essex Street who translated Arabic medical texts in his spare time. Miller resented the interference of this committee of experts and refused to co-operate. John Chandler F.R.S., Past Master, botanist and author of a treatise on the common cold, produced a critical report on the management of the Garden and of Miller in particular – he was apparently "very refractory" and " would give the present committee no assistance".[58]

Therefore he was to be removed. Miller, aged seventy-nine, remained obdurate until his unauthorized felling of a plane tree sealed his fate. He resigned, contrite, in November 1770 and the following February he surrendered the keys of the Garden. He continued to enjoy herbs grown there and he obtained repayment for the cistern bearing the date 1670. Miller lived in Chelsea for the remaining year of his life and he was buried in Chelsea Old Churchyard near to his patron, Sir Hans Sloane, where they were to be joined by the body of another of the Society's Gardeners, William Anderson, in 1846.

Gardeners, patrons and Demonstrators
On the recommendation of the Duke of Northumberland, the Society engaged William Forsyth as Miller's successor in 1771. Mindful of Miller's recalcitrance, the Society imposed rules on Forsyth: they began by stressing obedience and ended with the prohibition of wine or strong liquor being drunk in the Garden.[59] Forsyth was given an allowance to pay for two or more under-gardeners but he was no more satisfied with his lot than Miller had been and resigned after fourteen years at Chelsea to become Superintendent of the royal gardens at St James's and Kensington. He was also one of the founders of the Royal Horticultural Society and is remembered in the flowering shrub that was given his name.[60]

Meanwhile the Botanical Demonstrator, William Hudson, resigned and, in the absence of a suitable successor, a member of the Society, Stanesby Alchorne, took responsibility as Honorary Demonstrator. The year of his appointment, 1771, saw the felling of the two northern cedar trees, also some limes and oaks, which Alchorne replaced with fifty young trees. With the new regime came the filling of the lily pond with rubbish to make a swamp for plants of American origin, and the embankment of the riverside. Robert Mylne, architect of Black Friars Bridge, and George Wyatt, a successful surveyor and builder, were consulted before the embankment was undertaken by the Society's builder, John Severn. At the same time defence against the Thames and the craft that plied it was provided by raising the river wall 5 feet and the construction of new piers for the river gates. The Master, John Lisle, laid the first brick in June 1771, having first placed two coins of His Majesty's realm underneath. The alterations are outlined on a plan drawn by Alchorne in 1772 (see page 137).[61]

Miller had grown "pyne apples" for the Society's dinners, and Forsyth was ordered to plant young peach and nectarine trees and to raise quantities of melons and rhubarb – the rhubarb was for medicinal use, the melons were for herbarizing dinners.[62] Forsyth had convinced the Court of Assistants that his quarters in the greenhouse were dangerous and that the chimneys must be rebuilt. He and his family moved into a house nearby and he opened a shop in Paradise Row where he sold seeds, flowers, roots and fruit trees "at the most reasonable rates". During Forsyth's first summer at Chelsea he was presented with a bag of seeds delivered by Mr Banks and Dr Solander: the two had recently returned from a voyage to the islands of the South Pacific and *Terra Australis Incognita* with Captain Cook on the *Endeavour* (Solander was a pupil of Linnaeus and latterly Sir Joseph Banks's librarian). The following year, on his return from Iceland, Banks presented the Garden with a quantity of lava (used as ballast on the return voyage). This was to be used to build a rockery at the Physic Garden, with flints and chalk presented by John Chandler (Master briefly in 1768) and about 40 tons of old stone purchased from the Tower of London by Alchorne during the demolitions there (Alchorne was later Assay Master of the Royal Mint at the Tower). The "artificial rock work" was Alchorne's project, carried out by William Curtis (who succeeded as Botanical Demonstrator in December 1772), with the help of Uriah Bristow (to be Master 1803–04), and the Gardener, Forsyth. The Court agreed that the steps on each side of the toolhouse (the original greenhouse was by this time being used for tools and storage) were a nuisance, so should be removed and the second rockery in this country (the first was at Orford near Warrington, 1767) was created south of Sloane's statue on the spot marked H on Alchorne's diagram. It was completed in August 1773.[63]

Sir Joseph Banks, President of the Royal Society from 1778 to 1820, became a regular patron of the Physic Garden, presenting over 500 specimens of plants and seeds. In a letter to the Society he expressed his appreciation of the Garden – "an Establishment important in the highest degree to the advancement of the science of Botany as well as to the instruction of those who are educated in the medical line" and he referred to his own instruction by Miller "in that laudable and most useful establishment". Banks's connection with the Physic Garden was perpetuated in a cast taken from Garrard's bust of him, presented in 1824 and placed beside the rockery.[64]

William Curtis found his duties as Botanical Demonstrator onerous. He was obliged to superintend the Garden and Library at Chelsea and to encourage the knowledge of botany. Instruction continued to be of paramount importance and Curtis was to demonstrate plants, their names and uses to the apprentices at least once a month between April and September. He was also to conduct the students on five herbarizings in summer, "preserving strict decorum", to prepare and organize the general herbarizing for members of the Society and their guests, to devise other methods of instruction if he could, to attend meetings of the Garden Committee, to pursue an extensive correspondence at home and abroad, to enlarge and improve the Garden, to prepare the fifty specimens annually for the Royal Society and to dry another twenty for the late Mr Rand's collection. These responsibilities proved overwhelming. Curtis failed to deliver the specimens to the Royal Society between 1774 and 1776 and resigned in 1777. His major work, *Flora*

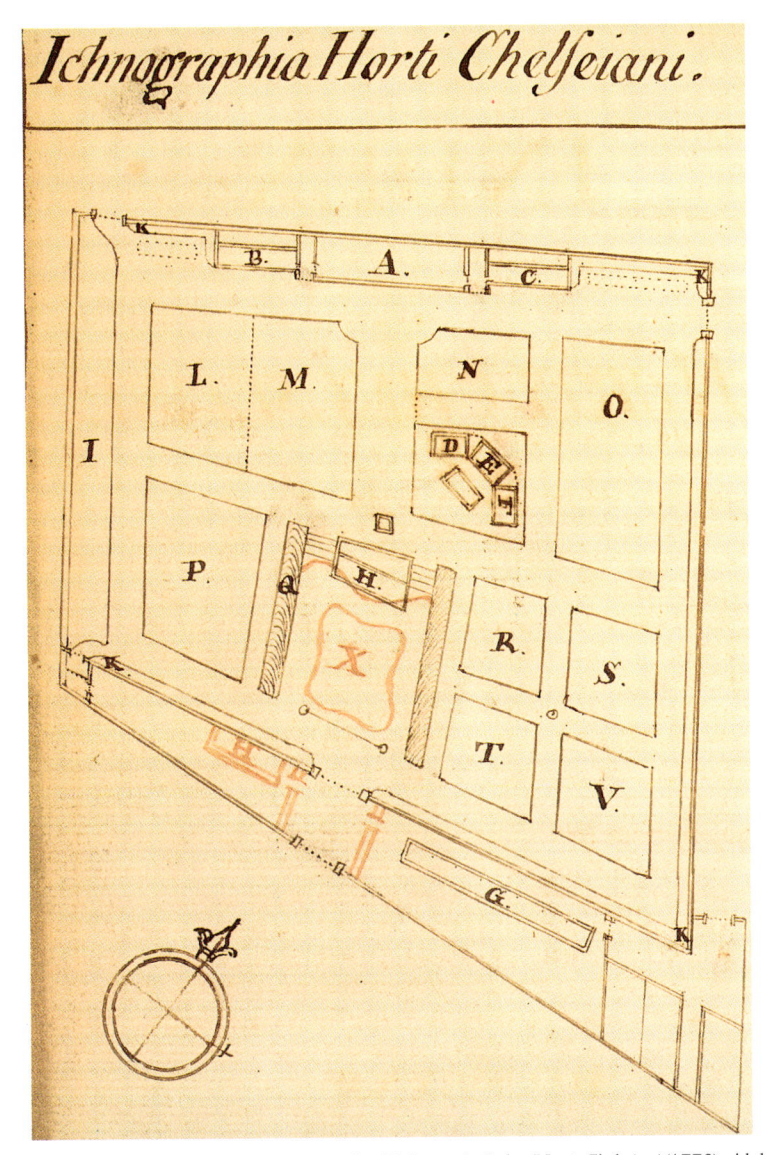

Plan of Chelsea Physic Garden from Stanesby Alchorne's *Index Horti Chelseiani* (1772). Alchorne was Honorary Demonstrator at the Physic Garden (1771–72) and from 1789 Assay Master of the Royal Mint at the Tower of London.

KEY: A - The greenhouse. B – The dry stove. C – The great tan stove. D – The little tan stove. E – The middle glass case. F – The end glass case. G – The light frames. H – The cold frame. I – The shrubbery. K – The great border. L – Annual quarter, the eastern division sown 1772. M – Annual quarter, the western division sown 1773. N – The small perennial quarter. O – The officinal quarter. P – The Wilderness including the trees round the annual quarters. Q – The slope. R – The first large perennial quarter. S – The second large perennial quarter, formerly called the holly quarter. T – The third large perennial quarter, formerly called the Bee quarter. V – The wood including the trees around the eastern quarters. X – The swamp. Y (omitted on the diagram) – Exotic annuals. L and M were appended to the original index.

Londinensis, was published in the same year and he went on to establish botanic gardens at Brompton and Sloane Street, and to found the *Botanical Magazine* in 1787. The memorial window erected in his memory at St Mary's church, Battersea, is illustrated opposite.[65]

Thomas Wheeler took on Curtis's mantle as Botanical Demonstrator in 1778, initiating the long and successful reign of Wheelers. Thomas Wheeler F.L.S. became Master of the Society (1823–24) and two of his six sons were Masters in the 1860s. The third son, James L. Wheeler F.L.S., succeeded his father as Botanical Demonstrator in 1821, published a Catalogue of the medicinal plants in the Physic Garden (1830) and was later appointed Superintendent of the Society's Chemical Laboratory. A grandson, Thomas Rivington Wheeler, was Secretary to the Court of Examiners from 1877 to 1883.

With characteristic energy, Thomas Wheeler implemented lectures in botany at Apothecaries' Hall or in the Library of the Physic Garden, and whipped up enthusiasm for the Society's herbarizings. Wheeler was Apothecary to Christ's Hospital, then to Bart's from 1806 to 1820, when the latter became the regular starting-point for herbarizings at 6 a.m. Umbrellas were scorned but metal boxes (*vasculi*) and botanical knives were essential. Wheeler, "a delicate, spare man", was invariably clad in long leather gaiters, breeches and waistcoat, a threadbare coat, an old hat and massive spectacles. Thus he attended the Society's herbarizings for some fifty-five years, latterly following the lead of his son James. The old man was pedantic about the correct pronunciation of Latin names, lavish with moral axioms and just as attentive to the physical well-being of his disciples. The apprentices enjoyed breakfast en route and substantial lunches of meat, pudding and ale – it was decreed in 1816 that the Society would undertake the expense of the herbarizing dinner for the "young gentlemen" apprentices, who were entitled to a bottle of wine, a bottle of cider and beer shared between four.[66] Afterwards, Wheeler would open his large metal box to reveal the specimens he had collected and instruction commenced. Tea concluded the proceedings – eel pies at The Star and Garter in Putney were a favourite. While Thomas Wheeler and his son held the post of Demonstrator the herbarizings were well-attended – as many as ninety apprentices might be expected, who had to be disciplined and closely watched. On one occasion an apprentice nearly drowned, trapped when a boat capsized; fortunately Wheeler spotted the potential disaster. At the end of the season the prize of a copy of William Hudson's *Flora Anglica* (1762) was presented to the young man most successful in discerning and investigating the greatest number of plants.[67]

The general herbarizing in July was a more dignified gathering of members of the Society to which eminent botanists were invited as guests. The climax to the exertions of the day was the ample dinner of venison, fowls, hams,

William Curtis was the Demonstrator of Plants at Chelsea Physic Garden (1773–77) and author of *Flora Londinensis* (1777). He is commemorated in a modern stained glass window at St Mary's church, Battersea.

tongues and fruit from the Physic Garden. Dinner bills that survive for the early nineteenth century tell of extravagant feasts involving the barge, musicians and careful planning. Dinner at Blackheath or the Highbury Tavern was enjoyed by some 200 members and guests who consumed haunches of venison laced with currant jelly and gravy (the dinner was sometimes referred to as the venison feast). Ale, beer, wine, port, sherry, cider and brandy were offered in plenty, making work for some sixty servants. The greater part of the cost of the entertainment – usually in the region of £200 – was shared between the Stewards appointed to organize the event, supplemented by a small contribution from corporate funds. Undaunted, or perhaps revelling in their responsibilities, the Stewards treated themselves to an ordering dinner and a settling dinner on either side of the main event.[68]

At the Garden a survey of 1785 told of decayed buildings, so an appeal was launched to which members of the Society contributed £539, mostly spent on re-slating the greenhouse, the installation of new tan stoves by Sanderson and repairs to the wall by a bricklayer called Britton under the surveillance of Messrs Nokes and Carr, surveyors.[69] Admission tickets were issued for the first time in 1786 – fanciful engraved cards depicting the orangery and palm trees (see page 141). Cautiously, admittance to the Garden was extended to medical students – in the early summer of 1830 some 150 students came to the Garden each Wednesday – and a course of botanical studies was inaugurated leading to an examination with prizes. These initiatives could not disguise the fact that

Thomas Wheeler F.L.S. by H.P. Briggs *circa* 1790. Thomas Wheeler was Botanical Demonstrator to the Society (1778–1821) and Master (1823–24).

plants and trees were deteriorating – the Gardener admitted to the local historian, Thomas Faulkner, that the plants were suffering from overcrowding and from the thick and smokey air (deposits from the neighbouring cement and lime works had a detrimental effect), and the two remaining cedar trees were diseased. Nevertheless, Faulkner found there was much to admire at the Apothecaries' Garden – one of the most beautiful oriental plane trees in England, cork trees, a nettle tree and an old pomegranate. He readily acknowledged that the eminence of the Garden was due to "the steady patronage and laudable exertions of the Society of Apothecaries".[70]

The Professor of Botany at London University, John Lindley F.R.S., F.L.S., F.G.S., was appointed Demonstrator in 1836. His book, *Introduction to the Natural System of Botany* was dedicated to the Society of Apothecaries, for whom he produced a dismal report on the state of the Garden (1837): the collections were in "lamentable confusion" and many species were missing. Lindley reported that it was impossible to find the plants he required to illustrate his lectures and he expressed a lack of confidence in William Anderson F.L.S., the Gardener. Anderson had entered the Society's service with an excellent reference ("a gardener of the very first rank") from Sir Joseph Banks, although his reputation took a tumble in 1835 when he was found to have colluded with a student prior to examination. Professor Lindley, who was renowned for his hot temper, complained of Anderson's hostility and the two men were at loggerheads. The Emperor of Russia, on the other hand, had nothing but praise for Anderson's special care of his orange trees, showing his appreciation by the gift of a diamond ring (later pawned by Anderson to help a friend in financial difficulties).[71]

Admission tickets to the Physic Garden were first issued in 1785 when a copperplate was commissioned for the purpose, "suitably ornamented and embellished" with the assistance of Uriah Bristow (Master 1803–04).

Anderson's successor at the Chelsea Garden in 1846, Robert Fortune F.R.S., came with the blessing of Professor Lindley. He found the Garden in a ruinous state, overgrown with weeds, the botanical arrangements in confusion and the exotics in the greenhouses languishing. During his two-year curatorship a pond for water plants was dug and plants from China were introduced.[72] Fortune was an inveterate traveller with previous experience in China, and when approached by the East India Company with a commission to return there to collect tea-plants and seeds he resigned from his post at Chelsea and departed.

Chinese tea-plants had already been introduced to India but had not been successful: Fortune's achievement was the use of Wardian cases to transport the plants safely and in good condition – he arranged for the transportation of some 20,000 tea-plants thus, forming a sound basis for the development of the Indian tea industry. Wardian cases, modelled on the principle of a bottle but shaped like the old plant cabins with glass sides and tops, were the invention of Nathaniel Bagshaw Ward F.R.S., F.L.S., Master of the Apothecaries (1854–55), who was largely responsible for a revival at the Physic Garden during the 1860s. His invention – cases that were virtually miniature greenhouses – had been proved successful as a means of transporting plants on deck and unwatered during voyages to Australia and back between 1833 and 1834, and they were to revolutionize the transfer of living plants over long distances.

The Society's herbarizings for the apprentices were discontinued after 1834, the tradition of three centuries halted by urban sprawl and lack of enthusiasm – many apprentices only appeared as the dinner hour approached. With the cancellation of herbarizings it was hoped that the apprentices would pursue botanical studies at the Garden, open 9 a.m. to noon two days a week between April and August when the Demonstrator was in attendance; recognized teachers and their students were also encouraged.

These changes were made on the assumption that students and apprentices would find plenty to interest them in the Garden but, as Professor Lindley had discovered, this was not always the case. More fundamental still was the decline in the importance of botany to medical students – the medical schools were opening up new and more exciting fields of study. At the same time, amateur botanists were finding more accessible alternatives to the Apothecaries' Physic Garden. The Botanical Society of London, for instance, founded in 1836, was popular with physicians and Apothecaries – Thomas Moore, the Society's Curator was a staunch supporter.[73] And under the Directorship of Sir Joseph Banks the Royal Botanic Gardens at Kew became a national institution and the most important storehouse of plant specimens in the world (the Apothecaries toyed with the idea of abandoning the Chelsea Garden in favour of a plot at Kew in 1838, an idea that was revived by the Commissioners for Metropolitan

N. Bagshaw Ward F.R.S., F.L.S. painted by A.A. Hunt 1867. Ward was a botanist and medical practitioner of Whitechapel and the inventor of the Wardian case for transporting plants long distances in good condition. He was Master of the Society (1854–55).

Improvements in 1843). The Royal Botanic Society of London, with eighteen acres at Regent's Park including a lake, conservatory, library, museum and medical garden, likewise detracted from the prestige of the Chelsea Physic Garden. The Natural History Museum was to open in 1881, and there were botanical and horticultural publications and societies, such as the Royal Horticultural Society, springing up to cater for the interests of botanists and horticulturalists. None of this augured well for the future of the Physic Garden where improvements were needed if standards were to be upheld.

Uncertainty about proposed metropolitan improvements also dampened enthusiasm for the Garden. It seemed that the Chelsea Garden had outlived its purpose and represented little more than a financial drain. In these circumstances the Court readily accepted the recommendation from the Finance Committee that the Garden should be relinquished (1852). Accordingly, negotiations for the transfer of the Garden were opened with Earl Cadogan, the freeholder of the site. Meanwhile, expenditure at the Garden was reduced to the lowest possible level: no fuel to heat the greenhouses, no lectures, no prizes and no dinners. The post of *Praefectus Horti* was abolished and no more than £250 was to be allocated to the Garden annually.[74]

The construction of a sewer along what is now Royal Hospital Road adversely affected the foundations of the orangery or conservatory as it was sometimes called, precipitating the decision to demolish it in 1853. The Society was in no position to rebuild on a grand scale – a modest house for the Curator, flanked by lean-to greenhouses cost just £315. The sewer also had a detrimental effect on the trees, depriving them of water. The third cedar deteriorated and was blown down, apparently in 1853, and the last remaining one was dying slowly.[75]

South view of the two remaining cedar trees at the Apothecaries' Physic Garden, Chelsea. From a painting by J. Fudge exhibited at the Royal Academy in 1845.

While statutory authorization for the construction of the Embankment was pending, another threat loomed in the notice issued by the West London and Pimlico Railway Company warning that land on the Chelsea riverside would be required for a proposed new railway line. With the Thames Embankment (Chelsea) Act of 1868, the construction of the Embankment took priority and the owners and occupants of riverside properties at Chelsea faced compulsory purchase orders.

Still casting round for a means to be rid of the Physic Garden, in 1861 the Master and Wardens notified the Royal Society and the Royal College of Physicians of their resolve to relinquish it. Neither of those institutions wished to assume responsibility, so it was left to Charles L. Wheeler, Master (1862–63), to rally support for the Garden and in this he was backed by Past Master Nathaniel Bagshaw Ward. Spurred on by the fact that students continued to use the Garden, Wheeler managed to drum up enthusiasm at Apothecaries' Hall for the proposed expansion of the collection of plants, the conversion of old greenhouses and the construction of a new one. The Curator, Thomas Moore, a prolific author and an expert on ferns, joined in the spirit of revival by contributing a voluminous list of the medicinal plants he wanted to cultivate in a plantation in the north-east of the Garden.[76]

At Ward's suggestion, dozens of conifers were planted, lining the two avenues that crossed the Garden. Within a couple of years many of them had died – "such trees will not succeed here", Moore concluded gloomily, so they were replaced by ornamental deciduous trees. This bout of activity included "rock work" in the greenhouses and outside for which Moore recruited the help of "a person who is clever at throwing up rock banks". The old bank was taken down, indicating, it would seem, the demolition of the rockery created in 1773 in favour of an "irregular rocky slope with grass in front, next the walk", evidently using the original materials. Alterations extended to the building of gardeners' rooms which doubled as committee rooms when required, a new greenhouse known as the "Wardian House" and the lowering of the interior riverside wall.[77]

In 1871 heavy construction work commenced on the Embankment separating the Physic Garden from its water supply and depriving it of a riverside frontage. The Society was opposed to the project from the start and made a claim for £14,000 in compensation, to which the Board of Works would not agree. The building of the new thoroughfare with sewers beneath took three years, and the issue between the Society and the Board of Works was not settled for another three. The Chelsea Embankment was formally opened by the Duke and Duchess of Edinburgh in May 1874 at a ceremony watched by a large party of Apothecaries in the Physic Garden, and the banners from the Society's barge were retrieved from the Hall to be paraded.

The Garden was cordoned off from the new thoroughfare by wooden fencing while negotiations between the Metropolitan Board of Works, the Society, solicitors, architects and surveyors dragged on, producing a final settlement whereby the Garden gained a strip of land along its southern edge and the Board of Works paid for the new wall, railings and gate facing the Embankment. The Society's architect, Henry Dawson, failed to agree with the surveyor of the Board of Works (George Vulliamy), so Charles Barry (the younger) was called in to mediate. Dawson's report of March 1877 mapped out the alterations to the Garden, with the old river wall kept as a retaining structure. He proposed planting the margin of land between the two walls with flowering shrubs and evergreens and recommended the demolition of the barge-houses.[78] The Garden had been neglected due to economies and the plants suffered as the result of the lower water-table but the Gardener was hopeful that the sowing of grass seed and new shrubs from Jackman and Sons of Surrey would be effective. Two young cedar trees had been planted on the high ground beside the central walk in 1875, replacing two of the ancient trees, although the Curator did not hold out much hope for them after the severe winter of 1879–80. The last of the old cedars was reported to be declining in 1896 but remained *in situ* for another seven years.[79]

Once a settlement was reached between the Society and the Board of Works, the new wall and gate along the Embankment went up, with the Master's name inscribed on the sturdy new gate piers and the Society's coat of arms on the gates (1877). The Court of Assistants marked the end of the disruption by requesting Dr R.H. Semple to update Henry Field's *Memoirs of the Botanic Garden at Chelsea* (1878). This version included a catalogue of plants in the Garden and a plan showing that the north-eastern corner was devoted to medical plants, and the central plots to hardy herbaceous plants, trees and shrubs. Two lean-to greenhouses and a cold frame were planted "à la Ward"; there were two warm propagating pits, a cold pit and frames. A tank for water plants, a bed of yuccas and mixed borders and grassy slopes ran south to the low inner wall with a holly hedge between that and the new Embankment wall.[80]

The Physic Garden was a heavy financial burden, nevertheless the Society continued to promote it as an educational facility. The botany prizes were extended to young women, granted access to the Garden to further their knowledge of botany in 1876. This gesture towards female education received an enthusiastic response – seventy-three women competed for the prizes in June 1878 (see page 248).

The increasing cost of maintaining the Garden and its buildings in the face of the higher price of fuel, manure and escalating wages, combined with the lack of water and increasing pollution, caused the Society to re-examine the possibility of renouncing the Garden. It would require a Bill in Parliament to allow the sale or development of the Garden and this was discussed in 1887 only to be dismissed by Counsel as unwise. Economies and its poor condition

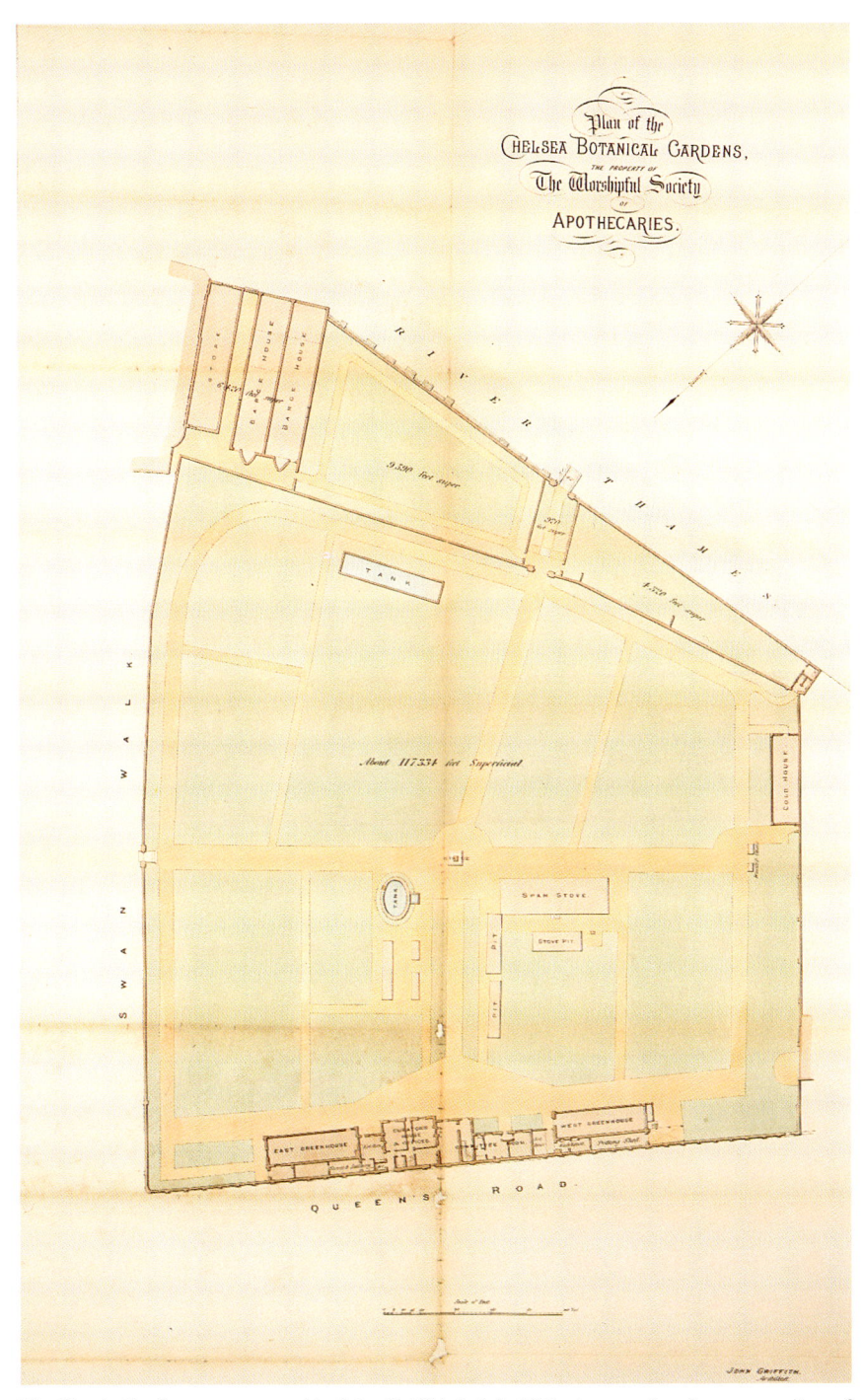

The Physic Garden was surveyed by John Griffith in July 1871, the year that the construction of Chelsea Embankment commenced, separating the Garden from the Thames.

forced the closure of the Garden in the summer of 1890 amid rumours that it was to be sold and covered with bricks and mortar.[81] Earl Cadogan had expressed an interest in the property – for development, it was said, but in view of the public outcry he withdrew. By May 1892 the Society had determined that the Physic Garden must be abandoned – the reason given was "the sterility of the soil and the dilapidated state of the walls and buildings", and the Charity Commissioners were notified of the intention. The Society sought permission from the Commissioners to sell the Garden to the best advantage and to obtain unfettered control of the funds arising for the advancement of science, research and teaching. It was proposed that two-thirds of the proceeds should pay for laboratories, a lecture room and library at Black Friars, and the residue would be applied to the advancement of science and research in connection with medicine, with special reference to the vegetable kingdom. The Charity Commissioners did not approve.

A Treasury committee appointed to investigate the matter heard evidence from the Society's Clerk that the local surroundings and conditions prevented the Garden from serving the purposes envisaged by Sir Hans Sloane. The Clerk's claim was contradicted by Sir William Thisleton-Dyer, Director of Kew Gardens, who alleged that the Garden was mismanaged and neglected. The Apothecaries were aggrieved: they had hoped to be relieved of the Garden and to obtain financial recompense for the large sums spent on it since 1673. The Charity Commissioners would not countenance this, yet they could find no solution. As patience wore thin, the Court advised the Charity Commissioners that if a settlement was not achieved shortly the Society would voluntarily abandon the Garden.[82]

A solution was achieved through the personal effort of William Hayes Fisher, M.P. for Fulham and later Baron Downham. Among his many concerns he was a trustee of the recently inaugurated London Parochial Charities (the City Parochial Foundation), and he urged his fellow-trustees to assume responsibility for the Apothecaries' Garden, stressing its importance as an open space and an asset to the new polytechnics. Once the trustees were convinced, the Charity Commissioners devised a scheme of management alleviating the Society of Apothecaries of financial responsibility for the Garden (1899). The arrangement required the City Parochial Foundation to give an annual grant of £800 to the Physic Garden (augmented by £150 from the Treasury and £10 from London University) and to elect over half the members of the Management Committee.[83]

The Garden as a charity
The Physic Garden, although no longer the Apothecaries' Physic Garden, remained true to the principles of its foundation: the promotion and study of botany through general education, scientific instruction and research. The first

View of the Chelsea Physic Garden in 1895 showing the statue of Sir Hans Sloane in the centre. The statue, commissioned from J.M. Rysbrack in 1734 and completed in 1737, originally stood in the greenhouse. It is now in the British Museum and a replica has been placed in the garden.

meeting of the Management Committee in May 1899 recommended a radical change of staff, leading to the appointment of William Hales, formerly of Kew Gardens, as Curator. William Hayes Fisher took the Chair and sought advice from E.G. Rivers, surveyor at Kew Gardens, and Professor J.B. Farmer F.R.S., of the Royal College of Science. Rivers condemned most of the buildings at the Garden as out of repair and the lean-to greenhouses as "absolutely useless".[84] With the promise of a loan of £4,000 from the City Parochial Foundation, plans were laid for a new laboratory, lecture theatre, a glasshouse similar to those at Kew, a propagating house, pits and alterations to the Curator's house. The sale of a slip of land for widening Queen's Road (Royal Hospital Road) yielded an additional £2,000, used to rebuild the Curator's house, the northern garden wall was rebuilt and the old greenhouse removed.[85] At an intellectual level, the Garden benefited from the assistance of Professor Farmer, who advised on new regulations and the role of the Garden in the twentieth century: its educational purpose was strongly re-affirmed. The Physic Garden officially re-opened with a ceremony in July 1902 attended by

Earl Cadogan, William Hayes Fisher, Professor Farmer, Sir William Thisleton-Dyer and 500 others.[86]

The reports of the Committee of Management reveal an increasing number of students and teachers taking advantage of the Garden. Lectures were organized, Francis Darwin F.R.S. (Reader in Botany at Cambridge University) undertook research there and a seed catalogue was published for circulation to similar establishments. Unfortunately, several trees in the Garden were suffering from fungus, the last of the cedar trees among them. On the recommendation of Professor Farmer the afflicted trees were removed during the winter of 1903–04, whereupon the Mayor of Chelsea was quick to apply for cedar wood to make a chair.[87] The City Parochial Foundation made regular increases in its annual grant to the Physic Garden, reaching £2,000 in 1921. A few years later 50 feet of the wall fronting Swan Walk was rebuilt and a new "intermediary plant house" was erected in 1930. The Society of Apothecaries' association with the Garden was maintained by a representative on the Management Committee (alternately with the Royal College of Physicians) and by grants. Members of the Court kept their own keys to the Embankment gate until 1929 when these were replaced by admission tickets (the Master retained his privilege for the meanwhile).[88]

Bomb damage in the Second World War necessitated the removal of plants to Kew; consequently the maintenance grant to the Chelsea Garden was reduced. With the resumption of normality after the war the City Parochial Foundation agreed to accept responsibility for repairs to the buildings. The Curator replenished stock and was able to report in 1950 that 50,000 botanical specimens had been supplied by the Garden to London schools and colleges for educational purposes. The Library was reinstated at the Physic Garden in 1953 including the valuable bequest of Samuel Dale – books had been siphoned off to Apothecaries' Hall from 1750 and removed there entirely in 1832.

By the mid-1970s the trustees faced the same problems that had defeated the Apothecaries: the escalating and continual cost of maintenance. The City Parochial Foundation was essentially a philanthropic charity for the benefit of the deserving poor, and it was questionable whether the Physic Garden fulfilled this criterion. A committee reviewing the future of the Garden recognized that funds from the Foundation could assist its modernization but that the Foundation wished to withdraw its long-term support. The trustees explored a number of alternatives to ensure its future, considering a Garden School, a Centre for Plant Studies, or alternatively its perpetuation as a National Trust property. Eventually an independent body of trustees was formed in 1981, agreeing to take over the Physic Garden which received grants totalling £200,000 from the Charity Commissioners to meet the estimated running costs for the next four years.[89]

The scheme came into operation on 1 April 1983 with Dr David Jamison, a Liveryman of the Society, as Chairman of the trustees. The following year the new regime was celebrated by a Garden Party attended by His Royal Highness The Prince of Wales who agreed to become an Honorary Fellow, with his grandmother as Patron of the Physic Garden. An appeal was launched for £1.25 million to endow the Garden and public support was enthusiastic, resulting not only in the raising of funds but also in the regular opening of the Garden to visitors who paid £1 each to enjoy the facility on summer afternoons.

The destruction wrought by the storm of October 1987 was a set-back, but notwithstanding this, the Garden recovered to maintain and extend its role in education and research. Plant samples are regularly supplied to the Glaxo Wellcome Medicine Research Centre, the Natural History Museum's department of botany grows species for taxonomic research at the Garden, and Imperial College conducts studies into fungal research there. The establishment of a "Garden of World Medicine" takes the original concept of the Physic Garden a step further, while the association with Glaxo Wellcome concerning the screening of plants for new pharmaceuticals looks far into the future. The English Garden School is based at the Physic Garden, special events and lectures are organized, parties of schoolchildren are shown round and visitors can join a tour or just wander, on Wednesday and Sunday afternoons between April and October. With a grant from the National Lottery Fund a new education and research centre was built and formally opened by H.R.H. Princess Alexandra in May 1997.[90]

The Chelsea Physic Garden is the second oldest surviving botanical garden in England. Having been founded and sustained by the Society of Apothecaries for its first 226 years the Garden is now an independent charity managed by a committee of twelve trustees, including a representative of the Society, which gives annual grants for the production and distribution of the seed list. The achievement of the Apothecaries' Gardeners and Botanical Demonstrators is perpetuated by the Philip Miller section, and other displays commemorate the contributions of Curtis, Hudson, Moore, Lindley and Fortune. Miller, who was responsible for introducing so many foreign plants to this country including the periwinkle *vinca rosea*, widely used in the treatment of disease, gave his name to the genus *Milleria*, and several Apothecaries are similarly remembered.

The influence of the Physic Garden has been, and still is, felt world-wide. Every year seeds gathered there are sent to over 200 botanic gardens and universities in dozens of countries. Work at the Garden has furthered the boundaries of botanical, medical and pharmaceutical knowledge and the Apothecaries' emphasis on the importance of plants in medicine is more valid than ever.

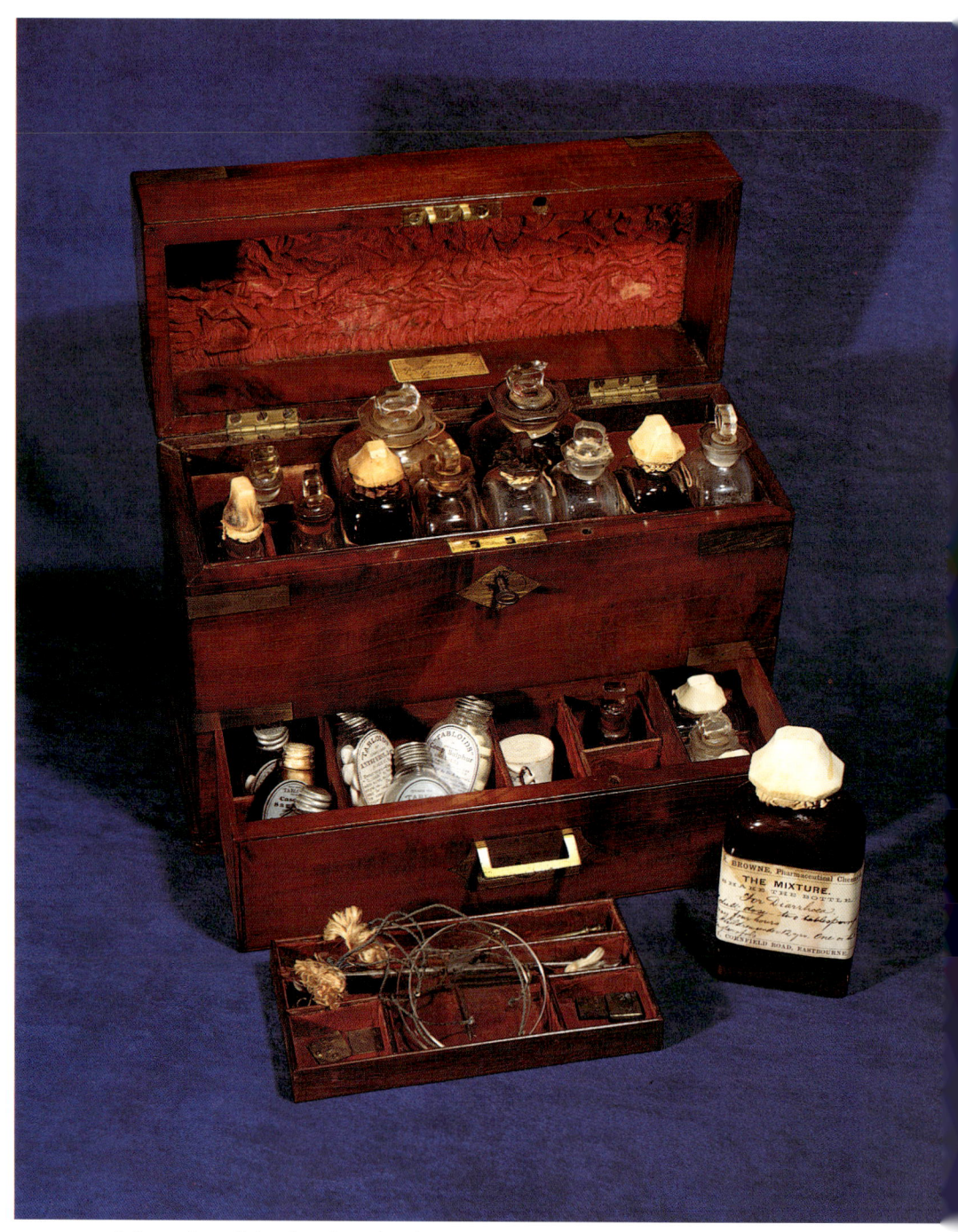

A domestic medicine chest from Apothecaries' Hall *circa* 1820–50. It contains a balance and pans for weighing drugs, a pill, and bottles of medicines including "The Mixture", supplied from the Hall.

Chapter 6

The trade

The livery companies of eighteenth-century London faced a struggle for survival as traditional ties between the trade and the guild eroded. A decline in membership numbers was accompanied by financial problems rooted in the demands made upon the City by the Stuart kings. The reign of Queen Anne brought a long and costly war in Europe; the reign of her successor King George I witnessed two major crises – the Jacobite rebellion and the South Sea Bubble (1720) which generated shivers of economic and political insecurity through the country. During the second half of the century there was rebellion in America, a naval campaign raged in the West Indies, troops were fighting in India from 1754 and were deployed in the City of London during the Gordon Riots of 1780. At the close of the century war against France brought high taxation and retrenchment in the livery halls.

Even the peaceful years were marred by high unemployment and the social consequences of the industrial revolution. Large property-owners, the wealthiest merchants and livery companies were shielded to some extent from hardship yet none were impervious: the possibility of bankruptcy loomed over the Haberdashers' Company, the Stationers faced challenges from within and the Leathersellers were forced by the great weight of taxes to demolish their Hall.

All the more remarkable, therefore, was the relative prosperity of the Society of Apothecaries, sustained as it was by the trade of the two stock companies – the Laboratory Stock from 1672 and the Navy Stock from 1703. These companies were able to take advantage of recent advances in chemical pharmacy, to exploit the expansion of trade and the drive for Empire. Beginning with the foundation of the Laboratory at the Hall to manufacture medicines and drugs for the benefit of members, the commercial enterprise expanded with contracts to supply the navy, the East India Company, hospitals and the army.

The trading activities of the stock companies dominated Apothecaries' Hall, yet there were clear signs pointing the Society in another direction. The House of Lords sanctioned an Apothecary's right to practise medicine in 1704 and with the failure of the Society's Bill to extend its control over chemists and druggists in 1748, it became evident that the future of the Society lay not so much in trade as with the medical profession. The decision to restrict the Livery to medically practising members, taken in 1774, made this explicit. For the time being, however, there were profits to be made from trade, and as late as 1881 the Court was reluctant to abandon this aspect of the Society's activities.

The Elaboratory
The provision of reliable, good-quality medicines and drugs had always been the Society's concern — the elimination of "unwholesome, hurtful, deceitful, corrupt and dangerous medicines" was cited in the royal charter of 1617. Thereafter members of the Court of Assistants made regular searches of Apothecaries' shops to inspect the contents and confiscate defective medicines; the Court also took steps to ensure that apprentices were properly trained. It was consistent with this policy that in 1623 leading members formed a committee for the good ordering, furnishing, provision, preparation, mixing and embellishing of simples (herbs and plants used for medical purposes).[1]

The committee of 1623 consisted of the Master and Royal Apothecary J.W. Rumler (his duties at Court meant he was often represented by a deputy), the Wardens Barton and Harris, the Society's benefactor, Gideon de Laune (Master 1628–29, 1637–38), Past Masters Edmond Phillipps and Stephen Higgins, Lewis Le Mire (another Royal Apothecary), Richard Bacon (Master 1623–24) and his successor Thomas Fones or Fownes. This influential group became responsible for supplying, preparing and mixing medicines, presumably for the benefit of other members of the Society. It may be that the operation centred on a dispensary or pharmacy organized under the auspices of the Society but the records are silent as to the location (the Society did not yet own a Hall) and to the success or failure of the enterprise.[2]

The demand for just such a facility was endorsed by Edward Cooke (Master 1639–41) and one of the wealthiest trading Apothecaries, who in 1641 proposed to give £500 to establish a Laboratory where medicines and drugs could be manufactured on the Society's waste ground beside the Thames.[3] The year that witnessed the execution of the king's chief minister, rebellion in Ireland and the emergence of Oliver Cromwell in the House of Commons was not favourable to fresh investments or building projects. The Court of Assistants was preoccupied with the provision of arms and ammunition at the Hall, and a tenant was found for the riverside site where Cooke had envisaged a laboratory.

When the Restoration of the monarchy and recovery from the Great Plague and the Great Fire permitted such considerations, the Apothecaries' need for a Laboratory was pressing. In addition to the obvious advantage to members of a ready supply of good-quality drugs and medicines, there was by this time a demand for chemical medicines requiring specialist preparation in a laboratory. Arising from the influence of Paracelsus (1493–1541), chemical preparations (as opposed to the traditional herbal or vegetable remedies known as simples or galenicals) had gradually become accepted as effective medicines. Processes for the distillation of volatile substances such as alcohols, spirits and oils had improved and another development was the discovery that strong mineral acids such as oil of vitriol and spirits of salt could be used to create metallic and mineral compounds. Thirdly, new mining and metallurgic techniques were producing ample supplies of mercury and antimony, used in many of the new medicines – for instance calomel (*mercurous chloride*) became a popular purgative.

Sir Theodore Mayerne, probably the best-known Physician of the period, was an early protagonist of chemical medicines, for which he had been condemned by the orthodox physicians of Paris in 1603. The London *Pharmacopoeia* of 1618 included mineral acids, calomel and iron preparations, and more chemical medicines were added to the 1650 edition. The work of one of Paracelsus's disciples, Van Helmont, was published in English in 1662; J. Beguin's book *Tyrocinium Chymicum*, aimed at medical students and apothecaries, appeared in English in 1669, and there were other important works by Croll, Glauber and Glaser revealing the secrets of the new chemical methods. Even so, when Nicholas Le Fèvre arrived in England at the behest of Charles II he found there were few comprehensible text books dealing with the preparation of chemical medicines – a situation he was soon to rectify. Le Fèvre, "Royal Professor in Chemistry to His Majesty and Apothecary in Ordinary to His Hon Household" (1660–69) and a Fellow of the Royal Society from 1663, had been trained in pharmacy and chemistry by his father, an apothecary. His most important work, *Traité de la Chymie* was translated into

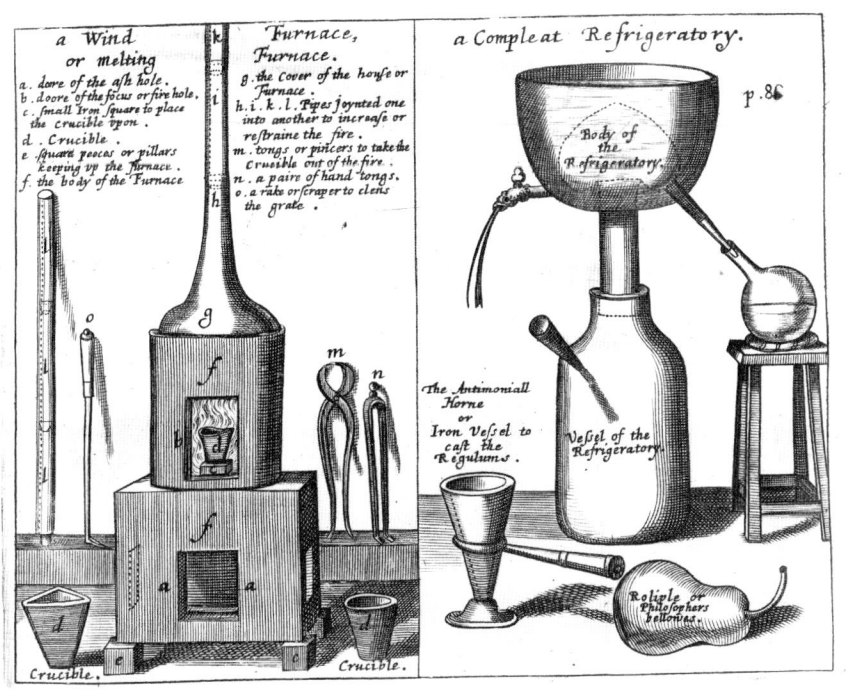

Illustrations of late-seventeenth-century laboratory equipment from N. Le Fèvre's *Compleat body of Chymistry* (1670), a work dedicated to apothecaries. Le Fèvre was Professor of Chemistry and Apothecary to King Charles II.

English as *A Compleat body of Chymistry* (1664, 1670) providing Apothecaries with a text book containing diagrams of the vessels and furnaces required in a chemical laboratory, an explanation of chemical characters and instructions on the preparation of chemical remedies such as the distillation of sulphur, the calcination of gold, the sublimation of antimony (a brittle metallic element popular as antimony wine), and the mixing of "rubies of arsenic".

Le Fèvre's book, conveying the work of contemporary German chemists to English readers, was specifically dedicated "to the use of all Apothecaries" indicating that its author saw the potential of chemical pharmacy in the hands of the Apothecaries. To enforce the point he included an epistle addressed to "the Apothecaries of England" in the hope that chemistry, applied to pharmacy, might "redound to the glory of medicine". When the Society of Apothecaries established the Laboratory at Apothecaries' Hall in 1671 Le Fèvre's book was the obvious guide.

Apothecaries' laboratories, shops and physic gardens in London and Oxford played an important part in the scientific advances of the late seventeenth century as centres of instruction, experiment, study and consultation on matters botanical and chemical. In Oxford the interests of Boyle, Petty and Hooke were fostered by their apothecary landlords prior to the foundation of the Royal Society, for whom Dr Jonathan Goddard conducted experiments in the laboratory at Gresham College. He also compounded his own remedies there, the most famous being "Goddard's Drops" (spirit of hartshorn, allegedly laced with the skull of a hanged person, dried viper, etc.). Goddard's contemporary, Dr Christopher Merrett F.R.S., an Honorary Freeman of the Society of Apothecaries, was another skilled chemist.

Recognizing the advantages of possessing a laboratory where the new medicines and drugs could be prepared, the College of Physicians established its own laboratory in the College garden in the 1650s, where the Apothecary William Johnson was employed. The Society of Apothecaries was not averse to the arrangement provided that Johnson promised not to meddle in galenical medicines.[4] Johnson's special antidote proved no defence against the plague, to which he succumbed, and the College laboratory was destroyed in the Great Fire of 1666. When the College was rebuilt, a resident chemist was installed in a laboratory there but by this time the Laboratory at Apothecaries' Hall had been established and was well on the way to making a profit.

The tide of interest in chemistry and chemical pharmacy extended beyond the portals of Apothecaries' Hall, the Royal Society and the College of Physicians. King Charles II created the new royal office of Chemical Physician and took an interest in the laboratory at Whitehall Palace. Prince Rupert, members of the aristocracy, ecclesiastics, pseudo-chemists and quacks also dabbled in the new science. A number of them formed the Society of Chemical Physicians in 1665, in the hope of founding a new profession.[5] This novel Society lacked credibility and failed to obtain a charter; nevertheless, it was a manifestation of the widespread interest in chemical medicines.

The demand for chemical medicines was difficult for individual Apothecaries to meet: the necessary equipment and materials were scarce and expensive, not to mention the expertise required for their preparation in a laboratory. The rebuilding of Apothecaries' Hall after the Great Fire provided the perfect opportunity to establish a Laboratory and a shop with accommodation for an Operator around the corner in Glasshouse Yard.

On 8 September 1671 it was ordered "that the laboratory be erected and finished", in one breath as it were. Richard Litlar (Master 1668–69) had been responsible for the planning and he explained to the Court how the business was to be managed and financed with £100 from corporate funds, augmented by subscriptions from interested parties – Assistants subscribed £25 each, Liverymen £15 and Yeomen £10, raising £1,205 from seventy shareholders. The undertaking appears to have been achieved with ease, largely due to the leadership of Litlar, who presented formal orders for the Laboratory for the approval of the Court on 4 January 1672. The orders for the government of the Laboratory Stock were defensive in tone: the preface claimed that Apothecaries had been "publicly traduced" i.e. slandered by the "pseudo-chymists" for their ignorance in "spagirick" (the science of alchemy or chemistry). To vindicate the Society's reputation and to reassure the Physicians, patients and the public, the Apothecaries promised that their chemical preparations would be skilfully and exactly made and sold by an Operator of their fraternity at the Hall under the inspection and government of the Master, Wardens and a committee. The committee was headed by Past Masters as supervisers, and a good deal depended on the Treasurer. The job of preparing the medicines and drugs was fulfilled by an Operator who initially received no salary – on the contrary, he was expected to contribute £200 by way of security. Members of the management committee volunteered for the duties of Registrar and Steward, while the Renter Warden collected subscriptions. The committee consisted of twenty-seven members of the Society and the business of the Laboratory could legitimately be conducted by a quorum of five.[6]

The main reason for establishing the Laboratory was the Apothecaries' concern that medicines and drugs, especially the new chemical preparations, had to be of good quality, and skilfully and exactly made and sold. In addition to this philanthropic aspect there was an educational purpose in that subscribers were allowed free access to the Laboratory "to inform themselves by what they shall there see in the knowledge of the chemical part of pharmacy".[7] Subscribers must also have been aware of the financial benefits to be derived from the large-scale manufacture of medicines and drugs under the umbrella of a reputable livery company.

The Apothecaries had few practical examples to follow. Le Fèvre's *Compleat body of Chymistry* was a useful guide but there were few operational laboratories to look to. In this country Robert Boyle was the chief inspiration: his chemical discoveries were numerous and he introduced a new spirit into chemistry that was particularly relevant to medicine. During the planning of their Laboratory, the Apothecaries may have had access to Boyle's laboratory (at the rear of Lady Ranelagh's house in Pall Mall) but it was hardly an appropriate model, being used primarily for experiments whereas the Apothecaries' Laboratory was to be a commercial operation. There had been a laboratory at Gresham College and another at the College of Physicians before both were destroyed in the Great Fire, and enthusiasts such as John Lockyer and Thomas O'Dowde, chemical physicians, also owned laboratories. A quack chemist called Christopher Packe (father of the famous map-maker) operated a laboratory at the sign of The Globe and Chemical Furnaces in Little Moorfields where he presided as a self-styled Professor of Chemical Medicine, but he is unlikely to have had any credibility among Apothecaries. King Charles II's laboratory demonstrated the royal interest in chemistry, and being in Whitehall it escaped the Great Fire. It is marked on Vertue's plan of Whitehall Palace as "The King's Laboratory and Bath" – but as his private indulgence it bore little relevance to the commercial enterprise the Apothecaries had in mind.[8]

The Laboratory established at Apothecaries' Hall in 1672 was an important and pioneering enterprise for the Society. In the post-Fire rebuilding of the City the Apothecaries' Laboratory was on the map before that of the College of Physicians and was running at a profit several years before Ashmole's laboratory at Oxford was functioning. It gave birth to the Laboratory Stock and the Navy Stock companies, and formed the basis of the Society's trading activities throughout the eighteenth century and beyond. Richard Litlar was the driving force in establishing the Laboratory and was one of its supervisors (1673–74). He was supported by Walter Pelling (Master 1671–72), his co-supervisor Lt Colonel Rosewell (a Past Master) and John Battersby (Master 1674–75 and well-known as a manufacturing chemist at the sign of The Golden Helmet in Fenchurch Street). The compounding of medicines was endemic to the Apothecary's craft and there had always been some who made their fortunes from the manufacture of patent medicines. Gideon de Laune had produced de Laune's pills in his shop at Black Friars; Job Weale and George Haughton manufactured *lac sulphuris* in the 1630s and, like Edward Cooke, Hicks and Edwards, they were successful traders. Cooke, Richard Holland and their apprentices Battersby and Benyon exported medicines as far afield as Russia and Robert Benyon later played a significant part in the expansion of Russian pharmacy.[9]

The Society's first Chemical Operator, Samuel Stringer, was appointed on 29 January 1672 although the Laboratory was not yet operational. Ovens had to be moved and furnaces installed, a labourer and foundry-man employed, materials purchased and a catalogue of the preparations compiled and submitted to the College of Physicians. By April the Laboratory shop was established in one of the houses on the north side of Glasshouse Yard where Stringer and his family were accommodated. The location of the shop, down what was then a narrow passage, was not conducive to business so it was moved in 1674 to the "end of the walks under the gallery" as far as the first pillar of the colonnade (later extended to the third pillar).[10]

In January 1673 the Court asserted its hold over operations at the Laboratory, requiring Stringer to give details of the materials he needed. The right of the President and Censors of the College of Physicians to view the materials was asserted and Stringer was reminded that the Master and Wardens must approve the medicines before they were put on sale and that he must give advance warning when anything "of moment that is chemical" was to be prepared. The Court also wanted to know what text books he was consulting and asked him to produce a catalogue of remedies available from the shop.[11] These demands and the lack of a salary did not suit Stringer. Negotiations about his contract took place less than a year after his appointment, resulting in his resignation in March 1673. The Court endeavoured to change his mind but Stringer "openly declaring that he was resolved to leave the place" was discharged.[12] This was a blow at a difficult time, for the Society was beset by domestic problems – the Clerk and the Bedel were at each other's throats, and worse, the Clerk, John Burton, was found guilty of specific "crymes". Having served the Society for over twenty years the extent of Burton's misdemeanours was suddenly revealed in 1673. He was accused of antedating apprentices' indentures and allowing records to be removed from the Hall and copied. He had failed to secure an assignment of lands in Kent, had reviled and abused Past Master Pelling along with other Assistants, and had said "he would sell the Company man by man for half crown apiece".[13]

John Meres senior replaced Burton as Clerk in January 1673 and two months later Stringer left his post, continuing to be a Liveryman of the Society and a member of the Court of Assistants (1687–89). His successors at Apothecaries' Hall were to be salaried, to have an assistant, and to be instrumental in the expansion of manufacturing at the Laboratory.

Meanwhile, the Apothecaries' Physic Garden was being created at Chelsea, with support from the Laboratory Stock. Subscribers to the Laboratory considered the contribution of £50 towards building the wall round the Physic Garden a sound investment, for they anticipated a regular supply of herbs from the Garden. In the autumn of 1672 Battersby transported bags of rosemary for the Laboratory, stored until needed in the garret over the Court Room, and quantities of mint, pennyroyal and marjoram were supplied from the Chelsea Garden for use in the Laboratory.[14]

The manufacturing activities in the Laboratory were potentially dangerous, as a fire at the Hall in May 1676 demonstrated. This was caused by the overheating of the Laboratory chimney. The chimney wall was subsequently altered in the interests of safety and eighteen fire buckets and a hand spout were purchased as fire precautions.[15] The preparation of chemical medicines, if not dangerous, could certainly be unpleasant. Tenants and neighbours complained of the smell arising from the preparation of sulphur which made them "so sick that they are not able to endure it". The burning of sulphur in the kitchen was then prohibited and the chimneys were again altered.[16]

By 1677 the Apothecaries' Laboratory was a commercial success, producing a profit of £29 on the £100 invested from corporate funds in 1672. The success of the Laboratory had attracted the interest of the king. The Court of Assistants ordered that "some good dispensation" be prepared to show His Majesty during his intended visit to the Hall; equally important was the provision of a collation to tempt the royal appetite.[17]

The dividend paid to subscribers rose to 30 per cent in 1681, in addition to which members of the Society obtained a discount on their purchases provided they were not in debt to the Laboratory (the collection of debts was to be a major problem). The following year the sale of preparations from the Laboratory was opened up to Physicians, surgeons, druggists and apothecaries who were not members of the Society.[18]

The Operators

The manufacture of chemical preparations required the services of a skilled Operator. Originally the post was held by an Apothecary, latterly by a chemist or pharmacist who was given the title of General Superintendent from 1881. After Samuel Stringer's brief tenure of office, his successor Samuel Hull, fared better with an annual salary of £40. Hull, who had competed for the post in 1672, agreed to carry on the work of the Laboratory if he could have the help of Mr "Stall" and a labourer.[19] "Stall" was none other than Peter Stahl, a chemist from Strasbourg introduced by Robert Boyle to the Oxford circle of scientists as a teacher of chemistry. Stahl's pupils included Boyle, Wren, Locke, and Anthony à Wood, who described Stahl as "a great hater of women, and a very useful man".[20] Stahl's classes and laboratory at an apothecary's house in Oxford (1649–59) blossomed into the Royal Society where Stahl acted as Operator (1665–70). After a brief spell back at Oxford he returned to London to give Hull assistance at the Apothecaries' Laboratory. The terms of his engagement are unclear: he was given lodging and storage space for herbs in the garrets above the kitchen at the Hall, and he was thanked for his care and attendance in April 1674, possibly marking his retirement, for he died *circa* 1675.[21]

After the deaths of Hull and Stahl, Hull's apprentice Symonds managed the Laboratory until a new Operator was found in Nicholas Staphorst, who had been taught chemistry by Stahl, a fellow-countryman. In 1679 Staphorst was occupying the lodgings provided by the Society (the Operator's house was now on Water Lane, closer to the shop), sharing the accommodation with a nineteen-year-old student called Hans Sloane, recently arrived in London to further his education. According to Sloane's first biographer, it was from Staphorst that Sloane acquired "a perfect Knowledge of the Preparations and Uses of most chemical medicines". This was to stand him in good stead as Physician to Queen Anne, George I, George II and many lesser mortals.[22] Little is heard of Staphorst before 1683 when he was instructed to compile a catalogue of the medicines available from the Laboratory. This was intended as a rebuttal to the "quack chemists" who, with their "sham catalogues", did a good deal of mischief. Staphorst printed the catalogue at his own expense, dedicating it to the Master and Wardens and Society of Apothecaries; the work was published in 1685 as *Officina Chymica Londinensis* and a copy went to Robert Boyle. Staphorst "behaving himself well and performing his duty" had his contract renewed for seven years from 1684 with a salary of £80 per annum.[23] As a sideline Staphorst translated botanical books from German for Sloane, and for the botanist John Ray, and his son maintained the association with Sloane by foraging for rare plants overseas on his behalf.

In the first years of the eighteenth century Staphorst was replaced by Francis Condy or Condee, formerly apprenticed to Walter Pelling (Master 1671–72). Condy was described as "an ingenious chemist of Apothecaries' Hall whose Elaboratory I saw often". The visitor to the Laboratory was James Yonge, who as a young man lodged with the Apothecary William Clarke (Master 1682–83); Yonge was later a surgeon and Mayor of Plymouth.[24] Condy was soon joined (or succeeded) by Ambrose Godfrey Hanckwitz, previously a chemical assistant to Robert Boyle. Known in this country as Mr Godfrey, he made his name and fortune by the manufacture and sale of phosphorous and was the founder of the family business, Godfrey and Cooke. How far Godfrey pursued his experiments with phosphorous in the Laboratory at Apothecaries' Hall is a matter of speculation – the length and precise nature of his engagement is also vague. His name is strangely absent from the Court Minutes and there is just one contemporary report of his being the Society's Operator: when he showed Dr C. Erndtel round the Laboratory in 1706 he was described as having formerly been Master or Operator of "the place where all the Apothecaries take their medicines, as well as the great Compositions, as the Chymical".[25]

It is likely that Godfrey came to work in the Society's Laboratory around the time of Boyle's death (at the house of Thomas Smith, an apothecary in the Strand, 1691). Godfrey's son was given the name of Boyle, and Godfrey

Portrait of Ambrose Godfrey Hanckwitz F.R.S., the Society's Chemical Operator *circa* 1690–1706. An engraving by G. Vertue after Schmutz (1718). Hanckwitz was a well-known drug manufacturer, chemist, analyst and founder of the business later known as Godfrey and Cooke.

acknowledged how much he owed to Boyle, "my kind Master and the generous Promoter of my Fortune, whose memory shall ever be dear to me". Boyle had experimented with phosphorous but it was Godfrey who perfected the skill of producing it in a solid, transparent form – he claimed to be the first in this country to manufacture it thus on a commercial scale. Godfrey's "Chemical and Pharmaceutical Formulary" survives and the prescriptions (for Lord Derby, pills for Mr Wagoner for the stone, the Earl of Marchmont's toothpowder and distilled water for Lady Betty Germain) confirm his claim to "prepare all sorts of remedies, chemical and galenical". It opens with a formula involving four cut vipers put into a retort with sand, contains instructions for both chemical and herbal preparations, advises on apparatus, gives a recipe for a "glew" used on broken dishes and explains the uses of various medicines.[26] This versatile Operator also developed a "fire annihilator" (the first fire extinguisher) which failed at its first demonstration, but was successful the second time. Sir Hans Sloane and the Apothecary Isaac Rand were Godfrey's proposers for Fellowship of the Royal Society in 1730, by which time Godfrey was to be found in Southampton Street, Covent Garden, where he had established his own Laboratory and chemical manufacturing business in 1706–07. The appearance of the interior of this working Laboratory, known as The Golden Phoenix by the middle years of the century, gives some idea of the Laboratory at Apothecaries' Hall (see pages 164, 165). A German tourist, Von Uffenbach, reported that Godfrey's laboratory in Covent Garden was finer than those belonging to the Royal Society and the Apothecaries. He thought the Chemical Laboratory at Apothecaries' Hall "the largest and best but the Galenicum is very small and wretched and so is the Apothecaries' shop".[27]

When Ambrose Godfrey forsook the Apothecaries' Laboratory to set up his own establishment, Thomas Field replaced him as Operator – he was to leave £50 to the Physic Garden in his will. His successor, Thomas Wilford, preferred working in the shop to the Laboratory, for the sake of his health. The appointment was subsequently held by William Randolph (1742–50), Michael Clarke (1750–81), and Stephen Griffin (1781–91). It was then Francis Moore (1791/2–1816) who took the Laboratory into the nineteeenth century when there was both a Chemical Operator and a Galenical Operator working in two separate departments until, following the formation of the United Stock, the posts amalgamated.[28] W.T. Brande F.R.S., giant of the Royal Institution, was Superintending Chemical Operator and Professor of Chemistry and *materia medica* to the Society from 1813. Shortly after the amalgamation of the two stock companies into the United Stock he wrote a booklet on *The Origin, Progress and Present State of the Various Establishments for Conducting Chemical Processes and Other Medicinal Preparations at Apothecaries' Hall* (1823) and he became Master in 1851 (see page 184).

An engraving of *circa* 1728 showing the interior of Hanckwitz's laboratory in Southampton Street, Covent Garden. The west side was equipped with apparatus for the preparation of phosphorous for which Hanckwitz was famous.

The Laboratory Stock and the Navy Stock

The Apothecaries of London flourished in times of pestilence and war. Apothecary spicers and pepperers had served the king and his army in the thirteenth century, and the sea-surgeons of the Elizabethan navy relied on supplies obtained by the Barber-Surgeons' Company from the apothecaries' shops of Bucklersbury. As the country prepared for civil war in 1644 the House of Commons directed the Barber-Surgeons and the Apothecaries to ensure that able, fit and properly equipped surgeons were ready to serve on land and sea. With the formation of a regular army at the Restoration, the Royal Apothecary George Solby became responsible for providing "fitting medicaments for surgeons' chests to be used by the King's forces on land and sea". Solby, a freeman of the Society since 1637, was awarded this lucrative commission for life, although the Barber-Surgeons pointed out that naval surgeons were entitled to make their own arrangements for stocking their medicine chests – a situation that was soon to change.[29]

Solby's extensive responsibilties caused delay at first and he was advised to recruit the help of his fellow-Apothecary Charles Watts. Samuel Pepys was called in to investigate the delay, whereupon Solby redoubled his efforts, was redeemed, and continued to supply plasters, ointments, oils, instruments, syringes, galley-pots, glasses, bean and barley flour, as well as powders, medicinal syrups and confections to the navy.[30] Solby's monopoly did not go unchallenged. Soon after the start of the third Anglo-Dutch War, four members of the Society of Apothecaries presented their proposals to fit out surgeons' chests for His Majesty's Fleet to the Court of Assistants. The idea was endorsed and a committee was directed to make application to the king (1673).[31]

The east side of Hanckwitz's laboratory, known as The Golden Phoenix, Southampton Street, Covent Garden *circa* 1728.

The supply of medicines and drugs to the army was handled similarly, by the Apothecary General Richard Whittle, by his successor Isaac Teale, and William Morris, who furnished regimental medicine chests and provided supplies for the "marching hospitals" in Ireland and Flanders. Charles Angibaud, a Huguenot, was apothecary to King Charles II for five years (1684–89) before being appointed Apothecary General to the army and military hospitals in Ireland. He was owed over £489 by the Crown in 1702, and was Master of the Society of Apothecaries (1728–29). In the eighteenth century descendants of another Huguenot refugee, Isaac Garnier, monopolized the post of Apothecary General to the army.

The authorities usually relied on the College of Physicians for advice on medical supplies for the troops, but when there were problems with a batch of drugs sent to the forces in Ireland (1691) a group of enterprising Apothecaries stepped into the breach. Jonathan Lee (Master 1712–13), Robert Gower (later Colonel, and Master 1719–20 and 1726–27), Edward Harle and James Anderson explained to a Special Court in February 1692 that they had already agreed to supply the army and were looking to supply the navy and naval hospitals: the Court encouraged them, appointing a committee to "stir therein". Perhaps as a result of "stirring" by the Master, Wardens, James Chase M.P. and Peter Gelsthorp (Master 1701–02 and 1703–04, whose portrait hangs at the Hall), a clerk in the Navy Office called Richard Gibson recommended that the navy should obtain its medicines from Apothecaries' Hall (see below). The Lee/Gower syndicate, meanwhile, supplied drugs and medicines to the military hospitals in Flanders, for which some £5,888 was due to them in 1697.[32]

The persistent loss of seamen through disease, particularly during the disastrous West Indies expedition of 1693, and complaints about the negligence and ignorance of medical officers to the army prompted moves towards reform. Gibson's memorandum of 1693 contained the novel proposal that medicines for His Majesty's ships should be provided at government expense and that sea-surgeons should obtain from Apothecaries' Hall, "such medicines for each ship as shall be settled by Surgeons' Hall".[33] Gibson's recommendations were fowarded to the king by Samuel Pepys, the personal friend of several Apothecaries (see page 63). Before Gibson's proposals could be implemented, peace was achieved by the Treaty of Ryswick (1697) and the Board responsible for sick and wounded seamen was disbanded. The medical administration of the navy then reverted to the Admiralty which was at odds with the College of Physicians on the question of medicines, so with the exception of individual Physicians such as Sir John Colbatch and Dr William Cockburn, whose cures were invaluable to soldiers and seamen, the Admiralty troubled the College no further. This left the door open for the Society of Apothecaries when the next round of warfare commenced.[34]

In October 1701 the Commons voted to raise a large number of men for the army and navy and re-armament began. It cannot have escaped the Apothecaries' notice that those being called up to fight the French would need medical supplies. The Laboratory at the Hall had been making a steady profit and in the spring of 1702 the management adopted new rules for its better administration. The stock was increased to £2,000 by a new share issue, subscribers were offered a 5 per cent discount as long as their bills were paid promptly, a salesman was appointed for the shop and the General Committee of Management was reconstituted.[35] This formal organization of the Laboratory Stock was achieved in the week that war against King Louis XIV was officially declared. The war necessitated the reconstitution of the Sick and Wounded (Sick and Hurt) Board of five Commissioners who bore responsibility for the medical care of seamen and prisoners. An Apothecary called Richard Lawrence was quick to apply to the Commissioners with an offer to provide all the medicines required at the naval ports. Lawrence being a member of the Society of Apothecaries, the Commissioners consulted the Master and Wardens for a reference. The report was not good: on a recent inspection of his shop some mithridate (an antidote against poisons and infectious disease) had been confiscated and his distilled waters were suspect. In conclusion, the Master and Wardens opened negotiations by offering to view any medicines for the Fleet gratis.[36]

Having failed to secure a contract from the Commissioners, Lawrence became a thorn in the Society's flesh. He negotiated with the Dispensary of the College of Physicians to supply medicines to the West Indies in 1704, and matters between him and the Society came to a head in 1708 when he called the Master a villain, proclaiming that the members were all rogues and that the Navy Stock made false Gascoyne's powder, and bought Jesuit's bark at 3 shillings and sold it to the surgeons at 20 shillings. The Court disciplined him by forbidding him to take apprentices and excluding him from the Livery.[37]

Instead of the volatile Mr Lawrence, five Apothecaries were appointed in August 1702 to "serve" medicines for the sick and wounded seamen and prisoners of war at the ports: Francis Dandridge (Master 1708–10), James Sherard F.R.S. (an Assistant in 1720), Thomas Robinson (twice Warden), Henry Halstead and Robert Baskett. Sherard was urged to prepare the medicines for the forces in the West Indies (some 4,000 men) and the Master and Wardens were asked to go to his shop in Mark Lane to inspect the goods jointly with the Master and Wardens of the Surgeons' Company.[38]

In December 1702 the eccentric Earl of Peterborough was appointed Captain General and Governor of Jamaica and Admiral of the Fleet in the West Indies. His Physician, Sir Thomas Millington, President of the Royal College, proposed that the College Dispensary should supply Peterborough's expedition with drugs. This retrogressive suggestion rekindled the smouldering relations between the College and the Society of Apothecaries. As soon as the Society heard that the College Dispensary planned to assume the Apothecaries' traditional privileges, it protested. A missive was laid before the Secretary of State registering the Society's objections and claiming that members had always been employed in, and contracted to supply, the Fleet and that the Master and Wardens oversaw the mixing of medicines by their members for the army. "It is therefore humbly hoped that this business may proceed in its ancient channel and such apothecaries be chosen for this service as shall be able and willing to undertake and perform the same with all expedition".[39]

While the Master, Thomas Gardener (Mr Deputy Gardener, a senior Common Councilman), left the Society's memorandum on the desk of the Secretary of State, Lord Nottingham, Charles Bernard (Sergeant-surgeon to Queen Anne and Master of the Barber-Surgeons) and James St Amand (Master and Alderman 1687–88 and former Tory M.P.) used their influence with the queen.[40]

In the event, the Earl of Peterborough's commission to the West Indies was cancelled, the queen listened to her advisers and the issue was addressed by her husband, Prince George, in his capacity as Lord High Admiral. The outcome was favourable to the Apothecaries, as the Master reported to the Court in February 1703 – the queen intended that the Society should serve the Fleet with medicines and drugs according to the proposals submitted.[41] The importance of good-quality medical supplies for the navy was highlighted when several surgeons' chests were found to contain medicines "wholly unfit to be made use of" and these were sent to Apothecaries' Hall for inspection.

Previously, naval surgeons had obtained their medicines, drugs and instruments wherever they pleased and the temptation was to do so as cheaply as possible. Consequently the quality, quantity and suitability were not guaranteed. Prince George voiced his concern, reinforcing the queen's proposals with a series of directives to ensure that medicines for the navy were of the purest quality. His Council's agenda was forwarded to Apothecaries' Hall with instructions that all naval surgeons' chests were to be prepared at the Hall, approved by the Commissioners with two Governors of the Surgeons' Company, then sealed to prevent embezzlement.[42]

The Apothecaries' Clerk, John Meres junior, drew up Articles of Agreement for the Navy Stock in line with the proposals put forward by the Prince's Council. The new stock company was to have the use of three houses on the south side of the courtyard at the Hall and was to obtain all medicines and drugs from the Laboratory. The business was to be managed by a committee of the Master, Wardens and twenty-four others (eight Assistants, eight Liverymen and eight Yeomen) with responsibility for the buying, inspection, composition and preparation of the best medicines and medical necessities for the navy. Subscribers were asked for contributions of between £30 and £50 each in order to raise £6,000 capital for what was essentially a commercial undertaking.[43]

Two years later John Meres drew up a similar document for another stock company – this was for the construction and sale of a newly invented machine "for raising water by fire". Meres's work with the Sick and Wounded Board on behalf of the Navy Stock brought him into contact with Thomas Savery, the inventor, who became Meres's personal friend and colleague – they were both Fellows of the Royal Society. On Savery's death in 1715 Meres secured patent rights for Savery's invention, a steam-operated pump. This had been developed and demonstrated by Savery in his manufactory in Salisbury Court, south of Fleet Street and not far from Apothecaries' Hall. Meres had taken an interest and with his legal training, scientific mind and experience of the Apothecaries' stock companies he was able to exploit the invention by launching a stock company in 1716 for building a number of the steam engines. While Meres was the organizing genius behind the venture, another Proprietor, Thomas Newcomen, had much to contribute. Meres having obtained the patent and constituted the stock company, Newcomen's practical expertise resulted in the construction of steam engines at collieries throughout Britain between 1715 and 1733. The business of this innovative consortium was based at Apothecaries' Hall from where Meres conducted the correspondence, drew up agreements, negotiated with customers and where meetings were held. After Meres's death in 1726 his successor as Clerk, Cornelius Dutch, assumed the same responsibilities and by the time the patent expired in 1733 at least 100 steam engines had been built and were operating

An impression of the trade mark of the Navy Stock.

in Britain, Belgium, France, Germany, Hungary, Sweden and Austria. The invention was gradually superseded by Watts's engine, but the initiative, groundwork and risks associated with the introduction of the steam-operated pump owed not a little to the Society's Clerk, John Meres junior.[44]

The business of the "Navy side" at Apothecaries' Hall expanded slowly with a contract to fit out surgeons' chests for both hospital ships and the garrisons at Gibraltar and Lisbon. The British Fleet in the Mediterranean was desperately short of medicines in 1704 when, as a matter of urgency, the Navy Stock was instructed to supply internal and external medicines which were to be transported by the next convoy leaving for Lisbon. From there Vice-Admiral Sir John Leake was to distribute the chests to thirteen of Her Majesty's ships in the Mediterranean.[45]

James Sherard (whose brother Dr William Sherard was one of the most active Commissioners for the Sick and Wounded 1702–03) held onto the supply of the naval hospital at Jamaica during his lifetime and, after his death, the contract was given to the Navy Stock. By the end of the century naval surgeons' chests from Apothecaries' Hall had been sent to Newfoundland, Minorca, Jamaica, Gibraltar, Lisbon, to the ports of the East Indies and had even reached Australia (see pages 180–82). At home, medicines were supplied from the Hall to Greenwich and Chelsea Hospitals, to the Royal Naval Hospital Haslar at Gosport, and to civilian customers.[46]

The early years of the Navy Stock company were not easy. Tradesmen clamoured for payment for raw materials delivered to the Hall yet the authorities were notoriously slow in meeting debts to the Apothecaries: the account for medicines sent to Gibraltar in 1704 was still unpaid in 1710 along with over £7,300 due for supplies to hospital ships and ports.[47] In 1706 there was "a very slender stock for the continuing and carrying on" of the business and, in 1712, £2,200 of South Sea stock had to be sold to pay tradesmen. The Clerk, Reginald Dennison, claimed that the Navy Stock was of little advantage to the Proprietors (shareholders) for the first forty years and that discussions took place during that period with a view to its dissolution. This is confirmed by the figures: in the 1730s profits were modest – in the region of £175 per annum, with the exception of 1739–40 when they surged to £843, followed by an increase in the capital of the company the next year. As a result of the East India Company's contract profits reached £1,677 for 1766–67 and shareholders received good dividends.[48]

The naval surgeons (some 500 qualified at Barber-Surgeons' Hall each year) resented the high prices charged for medicines and drugs which they were obliged to obtain from Apothecaries' Hall: it could cost between £80 and £90 to fit out one chest. "The Navy Surgeons' Memorial" of 1708 alluded to the Apothecaries of Black Friars as "fumbling old miserly curmudgeons" abetted by their "mercenary saucie and imperious clerk". There were other complaints about the system of certificates, delays, burnt hartshorn and insufficient supplies.[49]

Despite the initial difficulties and complaints, the reputation of the Apothecaries' medicines brought an overture from the East India Company for chests for the surgeons with the Indiamen (1706) and in 1736 various medical practitioners and hospitals applied to the Navy Stock for supplies.[50]

The years of peace (1713–39) brought a lull during which new Articles of Agreement were drawn up for the Laboratory Stock, and fire precautions were installed following a fire in the Laboratory (1734).[51] By the middle years of the century the organization of the two stock companies was complex: the Rough Minutes of the Laboratory Stock reveal the workings of a sophisticated operation headed by a Court of Proprietors, with a committee of managers, a purchasing committee, an inspection committee and another to regulate prices. There were three different furnaces to be maintained in the Laboratory where three labourers were employed and in the interests of quality the Operator sometimes visited the source of supply, to see the wormood burnt and the ashes packed, for example.[52] Such measures enhanced the Apothecaries' reputation for good-quality medicines and drugs – and made them expensive. The medical author and Apothecary John Quincy, for one, appreciated "the care of the Apothecaries' Company; who with a joint stock have these medicines made at their Hall under such careful Management and Inspection as cannot give any possible Opportunities for Impositions".[53]

The prospect of peace after two years of war against the French in India (1746–48) caused anxiety at Apothecaries' Hall, for it was anticipated that there would be a resulting decline in the business of the Navy Stock. This was all the more serious because the Society had been in financial difficulties for several years and the membership was declining. It was suggested that the business of the stock companies might be sustained by establishing permanent open trade at the Hall – the sale of drugs and galenical medicines for ready money was tempting and a precedent had been set earlier in the decade when Physicians, surgeons, chemists and all apothecaries were permitted to buy galenical medicines at the shop. However in 1749 the Court of Assistants asserted its pre-eminence, forbidding the proposal on the grounds that if all medicines were available, ready-mixed, the apprentices would learn nothing and eventually members would be ignorant of their profession.[54]

The decision in favour of the education of apprentices rather than immediate commercial gain by extending the trade was auspicious. It represented a closing of the ranks on the part of medically practising members and anticipated the important part the Society was to play in medical education between 1815 and 1858.

The decision not to open up the trade at the Hall came in the wake of a setback: the failure of the Society's Bill in Parliament to extend its powers. Concerned at the decline in the number of apprentices and hence the membership of the Society, a large number of the Livery and Yeomanry had addressed a remonstrance to the Court in December 1746 expressing fears that the Society was in danger of extinction. Responding, and possibly overreacting, the Court raised subscriptions towards the drafting of a Parliamentary Bill to oblige all apothecaries, chemists and druggists making and keeping medicines for sale in the capital to be examined and, if successful, to be admitted to membership of the Society.

During the debate the Bedel outlined the problem to a committee of M.P.s: there were about 700 apothecaries' and chemists' shops in London and its suburbs, of which half were kept by non-members of the Society (men untrained in the art and mistery of the Apothecary). The proposed Bill, if passed, would bring all chemists and druggists in London under the control of the Society at one stroke establishing the Society's monopoly of the trade, increasing its membership and improving its finances. It can have been no surprise to find that the Royal College of Physicians opposed the Apothecaries' Bill, introduced its own, causing delay, and when Parliament was prorogued in May 1748, the Society's Bill lapsed and the possibility of its supremacy as a trading association evaporated.[55] The chemists and druggists were left to pursue their own course until the next outburst against their encroachments at the turn of the century, resulting in the Apothecaries' Act of 1815 (see Chapter 7).

The war years 1739 to 1748 and 1756 to 1762 brought increased profits to the Navy Stock as surgeons' chests were restocked according to the expert advice of Drs Mead and Cockburn, each item being carefully calculated according to the size of the ship and the number of seamen. However, Prince

George's edict making it compulsory for surgeons of the Fleet to furnish their medicine chests at Apothecaries' Hall was not a watertight monopoly. Individuals supplying medicines included Dr Cockburn, whose patent remedy for "the flux" (gastro-enteritis/dysentery) was carried by every ship of the Fleet. James Sherard sent medicines from his shop in Mark Lane to the navy in the West Indies, and an Apothecary of Gosport, Henry Halstead, was supplying sick and wounded seamen in that town between 1704 and 1707. However, in 1743 the edict of 1703 in favour of supplies from Apothecaries' Hall was re-iterated, by which time the Navy Stock at the Hall had extended its trade to the naval hospitals in Jamaica and at Gosport.[56]

At the outbreak of the Seven Years' War the business of the Navy Stock was challenged by a local apothecary called William Cookworthy who succeeded in obtaining the contract for the hospital ship at Plymouth, to the annoyance of the Apothecaries of Black Friars. The Master and Wardens complained to the Admiralty that the Commissioners of the Sick and Wounded Board had agreed that the *Rupert* hospital ship was to be supplied by Cookworthy, a druggist of Plymouth, instead of by the Navy Stock at Apothecaries' Hall – the Society had already taken a warehouse at Plymouth and sent there a store of the best drugs and medicines in anticipation of the war.

The Commissioners were unmoved, hinting at unsatisfactory service from Apothecaries' Hall in terms of quantity and delay, and expressing a cynical view of the Apothecaries' motives in acquiring a warehouse at Plymouth on the eve of war. They reserved the right to "treat elsewhere" for drugs and medicines, as they had done for the *Enterprise* hospital ship during the last war – especially if supplies could be had as good and cheaper, as at Plymouth. Cookworthy thus continued to supply the navy from his highly successful Plymouth business – to the tune of £700 a year in 1778.[57]

Cookworthy had been apprenticed to Sylvanus Bevan of the Plough Court Pharmacy, Lombard Street, and his Plymouth business was originally a partnership with the Bevans. Sylvanus and his brother Timothy Bevan were both members of the Society of Apothecaries but not shareholders in the Navy Stock, which they were sure they could undercut to their own advantage. The Bevans' proposition to the Commissioners in 1742 claimed that they had a large magazine of medicines and drugs already in Jamaica, which they would sell at 35 per cent less than the equivalent from Apothecaries' Hall. Alternatively, the Bevans estimated they could supply direct from their London pharmacy at prices 20 per cent less than was charged by the Navy Stock. This bid to wrest business from the Navy Stock was unsuccessful but Timothy Bevan's manufacturing and wholesale business went from strength to strength in this country, the West Indies and America. Under the name of Allen & Hanburys from 1856 the pharmaceutical business founded by the Bevans became known world-wide before being absorbed by Glaxo in 1958.[58]

From Black Friars to Bombay

The East India Company put quality first when considering the supply of medicines to India. Representatives from the Company inspected the surgeons' chests at Apothecaries Hall in 1706 but there is no news of a contract in the Court Minutes. An invective of 1748 suggests that the East India Company *had* previously dealt "for several thousand pounds a year with these emulsioneers, this bunch of pulp-pated pill gilders" of Black Friars, before taking its custom to the Bevans of Lombard Street and Johnson of Fenchurch Street, finding them cheaper. The situation was reversed in 1766 when the Directors of the East India Company awarded a contract to the "Best-side Banditti of Black Friars", as the anonymous pamphleteer described the Society.[59]

The scale of operations in India had escalated with the development of Madras and Clive's adventures in Bengal – during the Seven Years' War there were some 20,000 troops in India. The pacification of Bengal in 1766 brought generous dividends to shareholders in the East India Company and on this wave of affluence the Directors looked to the Society of Apothecaries who had produced an enticing catalogue of the chemical preparations available from the Hall. The Directors, meeting in the splendour of East India House, Leadenhall Street, decided in October 1766 that in future the outposts of the Company would be supplied from Apothecaries' Hall "with the drugs and medicines that may be wanted for the several Presidencies, notwithstanding their prices exceed those of other persons, as there is a certainty of being supplied by them with the best of medicines and drugs, every article coming under the inspection of a deputation from the College of Physicians and the Surgeons' Company". As a further precaution the East India Company employed its own Inspector of Medicines, who with the officers of the Royal College of Physicians, the Physician to Greenwich Hospital and the First Commissioner for the Sick and Wounded were given places of honour at the Apothecaries' dining table for the eighteenth-century equivalent of corporate hospitality.[60]

The East India Company suffered a reversal in fortune at the end of the eighteenth century with armed conflict in central India and mismanagement in London. The Company was stripped of its trading privileges in the early nineteenth century, yet medical supplies were still needed for an Indian Army of approximately 300,000 men in 1820. The Society of Apothecaries was proud to boast that "the whole army of India (we believe exclusively) is served under the direction of the Hon United India Company from our establishment" – a privilege that yielded the Navy Stock an average of £20,160 a year for the first decade of the nineteenth century.[61] In one year alone 10,000 pounds of Glauber's salts (sulphate of sodium used as a purgative), 28,000 pounds of Epsom salts, ointments, large quantities of citric acid, terebinth and arsenic were part of the Indian order made up and packed at Apothecaries' Hall for shipment to Bengal, Bombay, Madras, Canton, Fort Marlborough, Prince of Wales Island and St Helena. After the Indian Mutiny the Council of India renewed the contract for drugs and medicines, providing the United Stock with a regular income until the final payment of just £19 in 1881 concluded the business. In that year the United Stock was dissolved and thenceforward the Society's trade relied on contracts from the Crown Agents, the Army Medical and Veterinary Departments, merchants, hospitals and retail customers.[62]

The expansion of trade
The buoyant trade of the 1760s resulted in dividends of 20 per cent supplemented in boom years by bonuses. By 1777 the trade had outgrown itself and a committee was appointed to find a way of enlarging the premises of both the Laboratory and Navy Stocks.[63] The freehold of Mrs Thornicroft's property on the north side of Glasshouse Yard was purchased and redeveloped (1778), and in the 1780s the south and west sides of the Hall courtyard were rebuilt to accommodate the trade of the stock companies (see Chapter 4).

The award of the East India Company contract called for new Articles of Agreement in December 1766 allowing for an increase in the capital of the Navy Stock to £12,000. Only Liverymen who were Proprietors of the Laboratory Stock were permitted to take up the new shares, a condition that elicited an angry response from the disgruntled Yeomanry. The case was referred to lawyers, accompanied by a biased memorandum from the Clerk, Reginald Dennison. He pointed out that the original Proprietors of the Navy Stock had taken a risk, "so hazardous was the undertaking then deemed by many that only 112 could be prevailed upon to subscribe and thirteen of them only £40 apiece". He claimed that for the first forty years the project had been of little advantage; the recent prosperity, however, had excited the envy of junior members eager to participate in the profits. This was denied them and "the great increase and extension of the trade", continuing during the Napoleonic wars at the end of the century, was to be of greatest benefit to Liverymen Proprietors of the Navy Stock.[64]

With the trade premises enlarged and rebuilt by 1786 (see Chapter 4), the stock companies were well-prepared to deal with the medical requirements of the Fleet during the war at sea (1793–1802). The medical care of the navy improved slowly with the issue of lemon juice, soap and, from 1796, some drugs and medicines for the surgeons' chests were provided at government expense. With the peace of 1802 official enquiries revealed the corruption and mismanagement of naval administration and the resulting reforms reduced the monopolistic position of the Navy Stock at Apothecaries' Hall.

Nevertheless, substantial orders were still received and between 1806 and 1811 the cost of drugs, medicines, pill tiles, bottles, corks, galley-pots, mortars and pestles, needles, funnels, sponges, etc. supplied to the navy from the Hall averaged £24,917 per annum, being the largest account.[65]

The booming trade of the late eighteenth century spilled out of the south and west sides of the Hall into the courtyard itself and any other available space. An opportunity to extend the trade premises north along Water Lane was taken in 1801 with the purchase of a site for the Mill House and engine room, and a large building on the south side of Glasshouse Yard was acquired in 1808. It has been supposed that the so-called "Apothecaries' Mill" in Lambeth – an eighteenth-century windmill with outbuildings – was the Society's Mill House. The only connection was an indirect one through John and Henry Field (John was Master 1785–86, his son Henry was Apothecary to Christ's Hospital and Treasurer to the United Stock), who used the Lambeth mill for grinding drugs. The Mill House adjoining Apothecaries' Hall was to provide the facility the Laboratory needed, complete with three pony-powered stone mills and other machinery.[66]

Continued prosperity persuaded the Laboratory Stock to take a lease of premises at Saffron Place, between Great Saffron Hill and the Fleet River in Holborn (1808). The conditions of the contract prohibited the use of the premises for a gin shop or alehouse – the preparation of Glauber's salts was

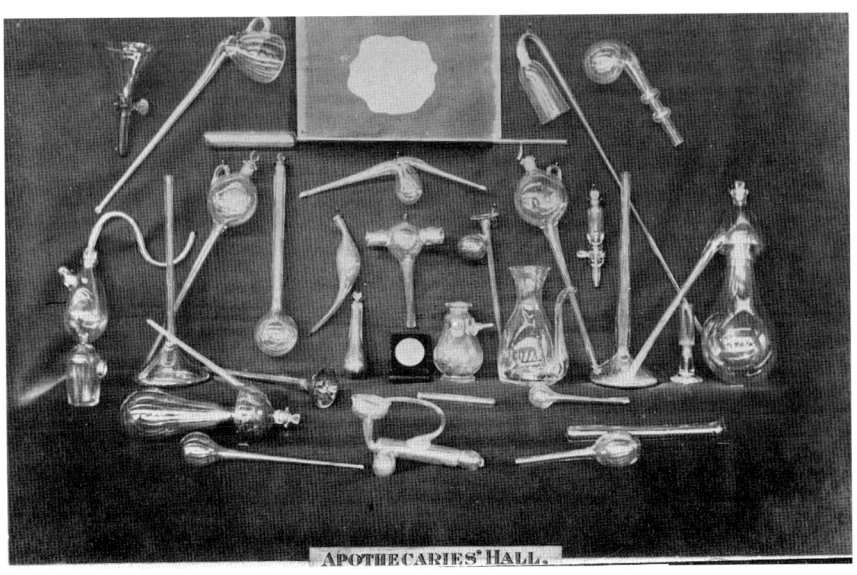

Chemical glassware used by Professor Brande, Henry Hennell and Robert Warington in the Laboratory at Apothecaries' Hall (1810–42). The exhibits won a bronze medal and Diploma in the Universal Exposition at St Louis (1904). The glassware also gained a Diploma of Merit at the Turin International Exhibition of 1911.

what the Society intended.⁶⁷ This was part of a general expansion of the trade premises to increase manufacturing and warehousing facilities for the stock companies in response to the war at sea (1793–1802) followed by the war on land (1802–15),⁶⁸ bringing the prospect of a contract from the army in 1810. An approach from the Army Medical Board received a quick response from the Master and Wardens, affirming that medicines for an army of 30,000 men could be supplied from Apothecaries' Hall within ten days. The officers of the Society called upon William Huskisson M.P. (the former Under Secretary for War who later went down in history for being run over by a locomotive). Negotiations continued in bureacratic fashion while the Duke of Wellington's campaign in the Spanish Peninsula lurched from crisis to victory. The Peninsular War ended without an agreement between the Society and the Army Medical Board, the main stumbling block being that the Apothecary General, George Garnier, held a sinecure of medical supplies for the army.⁶⁹ When it came to the notice of the Apothecaries that the old man was ill, in December 1819, the Master and Wardens renewed their efforts to grasp the contract to supply the army. Garnier obligingly died forthwith, and the Society approached the Treasury.⁷⁰ Once again the manufacturing methods and prices were subject to military inquisition and a decision was slow – according to the United Stock Accounts the first contract from the Army Medical Board was received in 1843, soon followed by one from the Army Veterinary Department.

Reward came in full during the Crimean War when supplies were shipped to troops wounded at Sebastopol or dying of disease in the barrack hospital at Scutari where Florence Nightingale was working miracles. From an annual average of £4,000 spent by the Army Medical Board on drugs, medicines, phials, mortars, etc., from Apothecaries' Hall (1849–53) the bill soared to £40,882 for 1855.⁷¹ One of the scandals of the Crimean War was the lack of supplies through inefficient distribution. However much was ordered, packed and shipped from Apothecaries' Hall, only a small proportion found its way to the suffering soldiers. One shipload of medical supplies sank in a hurricane, and large quantities were looted from the beach or vanished at the Turkish customs. The remaining proportion that reached the distribution centres was delayed by officials and the difficulties of transport in an inhospitable terrain.⁷²

Such matters were investigated by a Royal Commission and as a result the Army Medical Board was re-organized (1858–59). The United Stock company at Apothecaries' Hall managed to cling onto the military contract (almost lost through production delays in 1871) until in the spring of 1891 the Director of Army Contracts declined the Apothecaries' tender. This was all the more serious because Admiralty orders had ceased in 1871 (having previously lapsed for ten years), as part of the reform of the pharmaceutical service of the navy.⁷³

a Brick Athanor for Sand-heat

1.1. the flew for the Smoke
2.2. 2 plates of Cast iron
3. the Register
4. Cast iron tower fill'd with Charcoal keeps fire 24 hours
5. the Stopple
6. the place for retorts fill'd with Sand 8 Inches Deep 8 Inches wide
7. the Door of the fire place
8. the Grate which takes out and in
9. the Door of the ash hole.

Above and pages 178, 179: drawings of the fire-place, a portable furnace, retorts, receivers and other equipment used in the Laboratory at Apothecaries' Hall. The drawings date from *circa* 1810–25, the equipment may be older.

Medicines to America and Australia

The demands made on other City livery companies to support the early-seventeenth-century schemes to colonize Londonderry and Virginia came too early to involve the Society of Apothecaries. Nevertheless, individual members supported the settlement of North America: one of the subscribers to the Virginia Company was Anthony Hinton (Master 1675–76), who shared

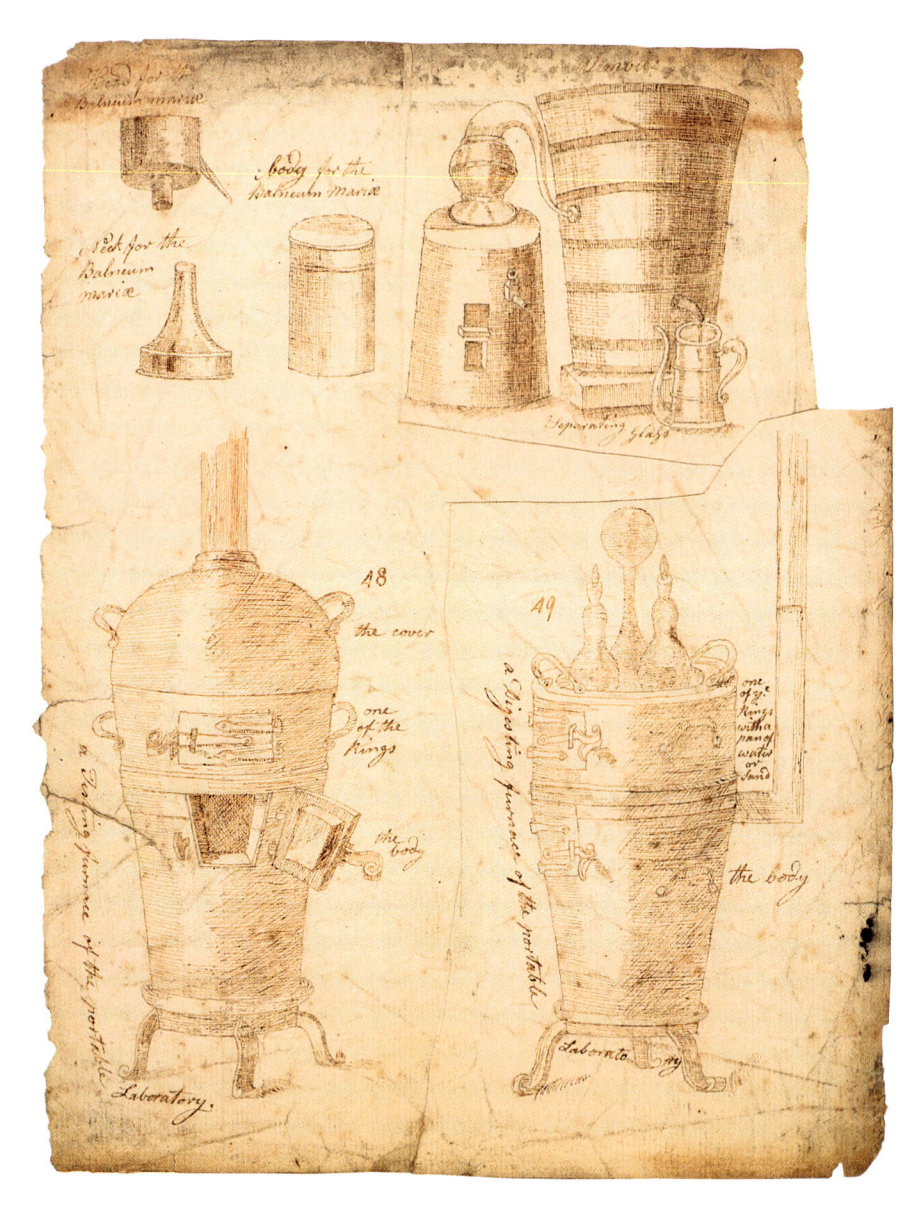

responsibility for the medical care of the colonists, giving directions and sponsorship to the physicians, surgeons and apothecaries there. In the ensuing years there was a shortage of medical practitioners, medicines and apothecaries in the colony. Contact with London, such as it was, was maintained by the trading companies and by the Crown, and was largely dependent on personal recommendation. Edward Cooke, the wealthy Master of the Apothecaries (1639–41), wrote to John Winthrop, the first Governor of Connecticut, introducing Mr Birde who "was desirous of setting up as a physician to the colonists" in 1640. Winthrop had trained as a lawyer and had lodged with his uncle, the Apothecary Thomas Fones (Master of the Society 1624–26), whose daughter he married. He must have absorbed some knowledge from Fones, for he became one of the first pharmaceutical and chemical manufacturers in North America, where his medical expertise and prescriptions were greatly valued. Dr John Pott, who became Governor of Virginia in 1628, took apothecaries as apprentices, and he too must have possessed the skills of the apothecary.[74]

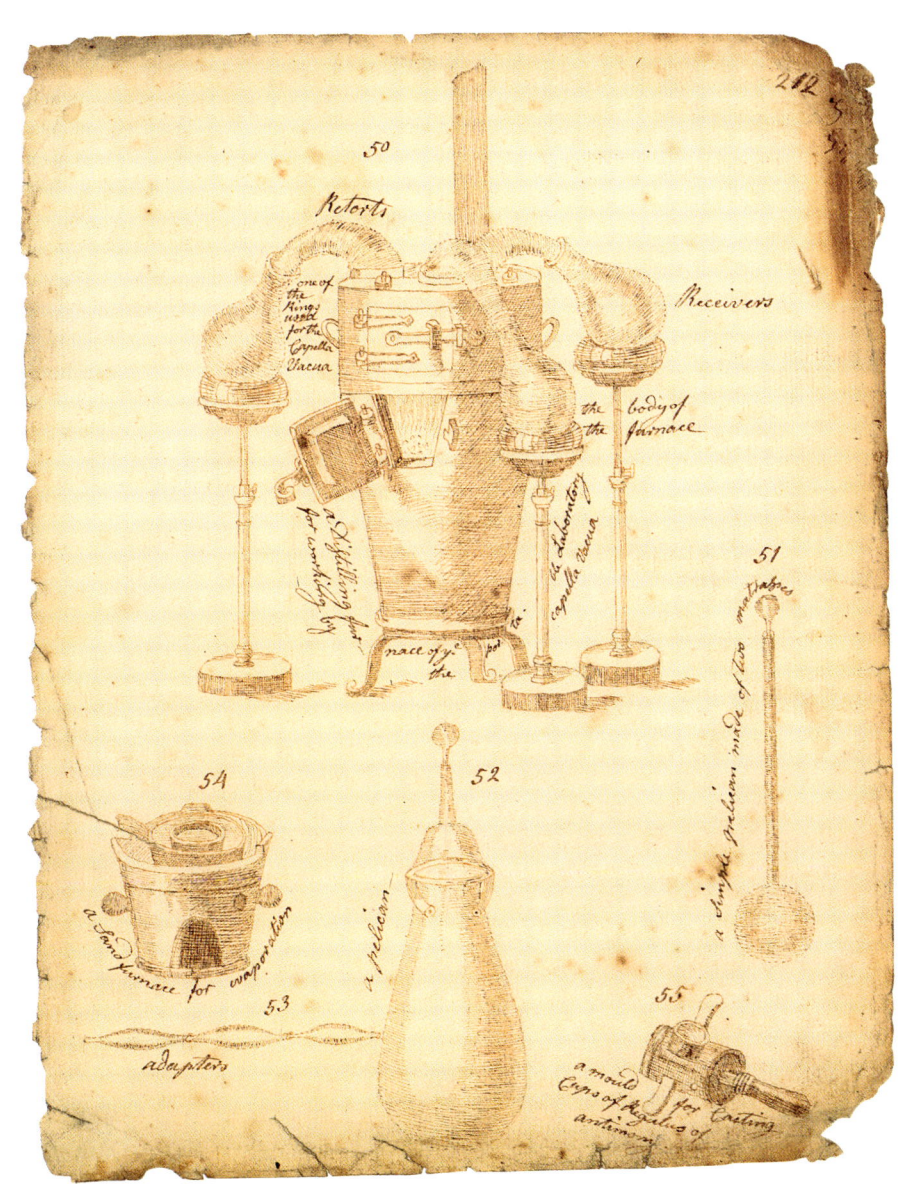

Medical practitioners and apothecaries colonizing the New World learnt to make use of indigenous materials. But there were some, like Dr Daniell De Hart, a physician of New York, who ordered medicines from London. In 1677 Dr De Hart contacted the Apothecary Moses Rusden, a freeman of the Society living in Westminster, asking for a box of "the best and fresh medicines" to be shipped to New York. Rusden obliged, and the list of twenty-six medicines provides what is probably the earliest evidence concerning remedies employed by physicians in North America.[75]

During the eighteenth century several members of the Society set off for the New World with the blessing of the Court. In 1736 Henry Williamson requested the Court to grant him a certificate to recommend him to the trustees of the colony of Georgia as a suitable person to manage the medicine chest (he had served his apprenticeship and duly gained his freedom). Ten years later, William Shirley, another member of the Society, told the Court he intended to settle in Virginia and desired a diploma under the Society's seal as testimony that he had been examined and gained his freedom. Another Apothecary, Samuel Danforth had been apprenticed to Isaac Rand, the Society's *Praefectus Horti*, before emigrating to Boston where he worked as an inoculator.[76]

By the time that His Majesty's navy was drawn into the American War of Independence the Apothecaries of Black Friars were pre-eminent in the supply of medicines and drugs for naval surgeons' chests. When a confrontation with a few rebels turned into an international war (1778–83) the sickness and inadequate victualling of the British Fleet was a major factor in its loss of command at sea. This aspect of the American War was subsequently reviewed, leading to the reform of naval medicine according to Sir Gilbert Blane's recommendations – his list of medical stores for ships ran to sixty-five items.

The loss of the American colonies was a hard lesson to learn, forcing a re-adjustment of ideas about Empire. Geographically, attention turned to the Middle East, Africa and Australia, the latter continent being fixed upon as the destination for transportable convicts. Captain James Cook's voyage in the *Endeavour* (1768–71) made him famous as an explorer and cartographer; he was also an expert on naval hygiene and diet, and was much concerned with the health of his passengers and crew. His mission to the southern hemisphere had the backing of the Admiralty, hence His Majesty's barque the *Endeavour* was well victualled and medical supplies were doubled. Having raised the flag at Botany Bay in April 1770, the *Endeavour* sailed next to Batavia (Jakarta), Cook having noted with pride that hitherto he had not lost one man through sickness. The record was broken when seamen and passengers contracted tertian malaria and dysentery. Cook, Banks and Solander were among those afflicted, and the ship's surgeon, William Monkhouse (Munkhouse), died. Cook instructed the surgeon's mate to take over Monkhouse's duties and to inspect the medicine chest so that the quantity and quality of the remaining medicines could be ascertained and valued, on return, at Apothecaries' Hall. Monkhouse had clearly equipped his medicine chest from the Navy Stock at the Hall where it would be returned for re-fitting. Not surprisingly, after two years and three months, the contents of the chest were reported to be deficient and so were replenished locally.[77] Whether it was due to the poor quality of medicines obtained in Batavia or the virulence of the "bloody flux", twenty-four died before the *Endeavour* reached Cape Town in March 1771.

Cook's voyage with the *Resolution* and the *Adventure* (1772–75) was well-provided with medicines, including the eighteenth-century equivalent of the aspirin, Dr James's fever powder, and ten chests of "rob of oranges and lemons" from Apothecaries' Hall. This was the fruit juice reduced to a syrup and preserved with sugar – there was not one death from scurvy on this voyage. For Cook's third voyage, this time to Antarctica (1776–80), chests of rob of oranges and lemons were again ordered, although apparently they were not used – Cook himself had more faith in sauerkraut as an antiscorbutic.[78]

The First Fleet of eleven ships transporting 759 convicts, marines, crew and supplies to Australia also carried medicine chests from Apothecaries' Hall. The medical care of all personnel was the responsibilty of Surgeon John White, who asked that the medicines and necessities for the transport ships should be supplied in the usual manner – from Apothecaries' Hall. One of White's assistants was the apothecary Thomas Arundell or Arndell, a member of the Wheelwrights' Company who gave his profession as apothecary on his freedom certificate of the City. Arundell set up as an apothecary in St Martin's-le-Grand, qualified as a surgeon and ventured east aboard one of the East India Company's ships. He worked as assistant surgeon for the duration of the voyage to Australia and after arrival at Sydney Cove in 1787 Arundell set up the first hospital, becoming the official apothecary to the colony and a substantial landowner by the time of his death in 1821.[79]

Another of Surgeon White's assistants, Dennis Considen, achieved fame as a pioneer of pharmaceutical research in Australia for his collection of and experiments with native plants. Dysentery was treated with red gum from the eucalyptus trees (one variety is *eucalyptus consideniana*), yellow gum was effective in the treatment of lung infections and a local berry was used to cure scurvy. For some cures, however, the settlement remained reliant on H.M. stores, which by July 1788 were very depleted. White sent a list of his requirements to Lord Sydney: "I have to entreat your Lordship will be pleased to cause the medicines to be sent from Apothecaries' Hall where they are sure to be genuine and fresh";[80] he also drew attention to the importance of careful packing and a dry passage. Unfortunately, White's faith in Apothecaries' Hall crumbled when inferior and old drugs reached him, so he recommended instead Wilson, Hodgkins and Marshall, druggists of Snow Hill. Meanwhile, the most urgent requirements (flour and medicines) were obtained from Cape Town and Batavia, sustaining the community at Sydney Cove until the arrival of the Second Fleet in 1790, which brought hundreds of seriously ill convicts. Sixteen chests of medicines had been loaded onto the *Juliana* and the *Guardian* before the two ships left Britain, but many of them were lost or thrown overboard when the *Guardian* struck ice. Those waiting anxiously for supplies were mortified when the *Juliana* unloaded her shipment of "so unnecessary and unprofitable 222 females" instead of the anticipated provisions.[80]

The Third Fleet arrived in 1791 and the colonization of Australia proceeded apace: some 84,000 convicts reached New South Wales, 67,000 went to Tasmania and 9,720 to Western Australia between 1786 and 1868. Medical care en route improved as a result of William Redfern's report of 1814 and during the 1820s and 1830s the Colonial Office took pains over the details of transportation. The Society of Apothecaries pressed for the employment of fully qualified medical practitioners to care for the emigrants, meaning one of the new breed of general practitioners holding the dual qualification of M.R.C.S. and L.S.A. The appointment of naval Surgeon Superintendents, issued with instructions for the health and welfare of their charges, eased the mortality rate, although a basic problem – the enfeebled state of convicts at the time of embarkation – remained. Their diet was improved and medical supplies were adequate, indeed John Haslam, Surgeon on the convict ship *Mariner* (1816), testified that there was an abundant supply of medicines "and the different articles were of the very best quality having been furnished from Apothecaries' Hall".[81]

The Apothecaries obtained a regular contract to supply "the convict establishment" in Australia from 1823, providing some £500–£600 worth of medicines and drugs annually until the end of that decade. A small quota was destined for Van Dieman's Land (Tasmania) in 1830 and in 1839 the United Stock was owed £4,772 for medicines aboard eight ships taking 2,400 emigrants to the colonies.[82] By the 1820s and 1830s colonists in Australia were setting up their own dispensaries and chemists' shops – for example John Tawell, transported for forging banknotes, opened Australia's first pharmacy in 1820.

The settlers in Australia took their own medicine chests if they could, some of which doubtless came from Apothecaries' Hall. It was in the emigrants' interest to take a well-stocked chest as this boosted the valuation of their property entitling them to a land grant. Colonial surgeons such as Dr John Ferguson in Western Australia usually requested medicines from Apothecaries' Hall because these were most likely to arrive in good condition – an order could take fifteen months to be delivered. One order shipped on the *Chieftain* in 1840 consisted of 119 separate items from calico bandages to arsenic.[83] A pioneers' medicine chest originally used on a ship and then transported to Arcoona Station in South Australia sometime after 1872 is displayed at the Woomera Heritage Centre. It measures 119 by 59 cms and is 68 cms tall (almost 4 feet by 2 feet and over 2 feet tall). Still inside, crammed onto rows of shelves are eighty glass bottles of various sizes, some with medicine remaining inside, along with tins, bandages, splints and in the centre is a smaller emergency box of supplies. According to a torn label at least some of the medicines and possibly the entire chest came from Apothecaries' Hall; the splints bear the name Evans and Wormull, surgical instrument makers of Stamford Street London S.E.1 *circa* 1870. An advertisement in the Perth *Inquirer* of May 1879 indicates that all manner of medical goods could be ordered from Apothecaries' Hall: ointments, balsam, castor oil, the essential quinine, hair-restorer, tobacco and perfumes.[84]

The United Stock
The business of the two stock companies being so closely related it was proposed in 1822 that a joint company would serve with greater economy and advantage: the United Stock of the Society of Apothecaries of the City of London. The agreement was the opportunity for a special dinner "to promote harmony" held in November 1822.[85] The background to the new arrangement was the assignment of a lease of dwellings, stables and an iron foundry in Glasshouse Yard, behind the Hall. The foundry, in a brick building about 50 feet square and with a central chimney rising 100 feet, had recently been used for the manufacture of ships' boilers and hearths.[86] It was fire-proofed with a lining of iron, then given a new floor as part of its conversion into the chemical laboratory known as the Great Laboratory. Adjoining it was the Still House for processes involving distillation and evaporation, a chemical warehouse and a mortar room.[87] The former Great Laboratory under the Great Hall became a warehouse, and the prescription and retail departments were given a new entrance on Water Lane as part of the improvements designed to set the United Stock on a prosperous course.

The Society's trade interests were now overseen by a Committee of Management (the Master, Wardens and thirty Proprietors); a buying committee ordered and purchased drugs, medicines and other wares, a committee of inspection examined the quality of medicines and chemicals while a committee for pricing fixed their cost. A committee of accounts reported to the Treasurer and Deputy Treasurer and shareholders were limited to 120 first-class Proprietors investing £420 each and 220 second-class Proprietors investing £60 a share.[85]

Immediate prospects for the United Stock were hardly rosy. After protracted enquiries the proposed contract from the army failed to materialize and another blow came in September 1823 when the Commissioners for victualling the navy took their custom elsewhere – "in consequence of the very high prices". The Apothecaries registered their extreme surprise and endeavoured to retrieve the situation by embarking on a public relations exercise. Professor Brande was commissioned to trace the origins and progress of the Society's trade, with emphasis on recent improvements, and John Field (Deputy Treasurer of the United Stock) was to contribute an account explaining the Society's historic role in the provision of genuine medicines. Brande's booklet was published at the end of 1823 whereupon copies were circulated to the king, every member of the House of Lords, every Commissioner of the Victualling Board, every Lord of the Admiralty, every Director of the East India Company, other trading companies, merchants and the College of Physicians.[88] The publicity given to the "greatly enlarged and much improved state of the laboratories and apparatus" failed to produce the desired results: the annual reports on the Society's trade between 1824 and 1830 tell of "the continued and increasing depression of all branches".[89] John Nussey, Master 1833–34 and Royal Apothecary, used his influence to win back the Admiralty contract; nonetheless this was not as profitable as in the past. Apart from its main customer at the time, the East India Company, the Society relied on the business of the retail and prescription department, yet this was diminishing on account of general competition and the fact that customers, "the upper classes of the population of London", now lived in the West End. The idea that a branch establishment (a shop) might be opened west of Temple Bar was dismissed as degrading.[90] The Society was absorbed with the education of the medical profession and those responsibilities, coupled with its role as a City livery company, precluded it from competing with the increasingly commercial pharmaceutical houses of Victorian London.

The enquiries of a Select Committee of the House of Commons on Medical Education (1834) left no doubt about the important part being played by the Society in the education of medical students, and the Society's academic reputation was bolstered further by Professor Brande's longstanding commitment as Professor of Chemistry, lecturer, and Superintending Chemical Operator to the Society. Brande's diligence had earned him a Fellowship of the Royal Society at the age of twenty-one and he succeeded Sir Humphry Davy at the Royal Institution in 1813, the year in which he gave his first lectures at Apothecaries' Hall as Professor of Chemistry. Brande's scientific expertise found expression in a stream of publications, not least *A Manual of Pharmacy* (1825), dedicated to the Society of Apothecaries.[91]

Brande's colleague in the Laboratory at Apothecaries' Hall was Henry Hennell, another F.R.S. who also contributed papers to *Philosophical Transactions*. Hennell combined the posts of Galenical and Chemical Operator from 1825, undertaking original research in the Society's Laboratory where he discovered sulphovinic acid. Like Professor Brande, he was concerned with the application of chemistry to medicine and the utilitarian aspects of science. Tragically, Hennell's career came to an end in the back yard of Apothecaries'

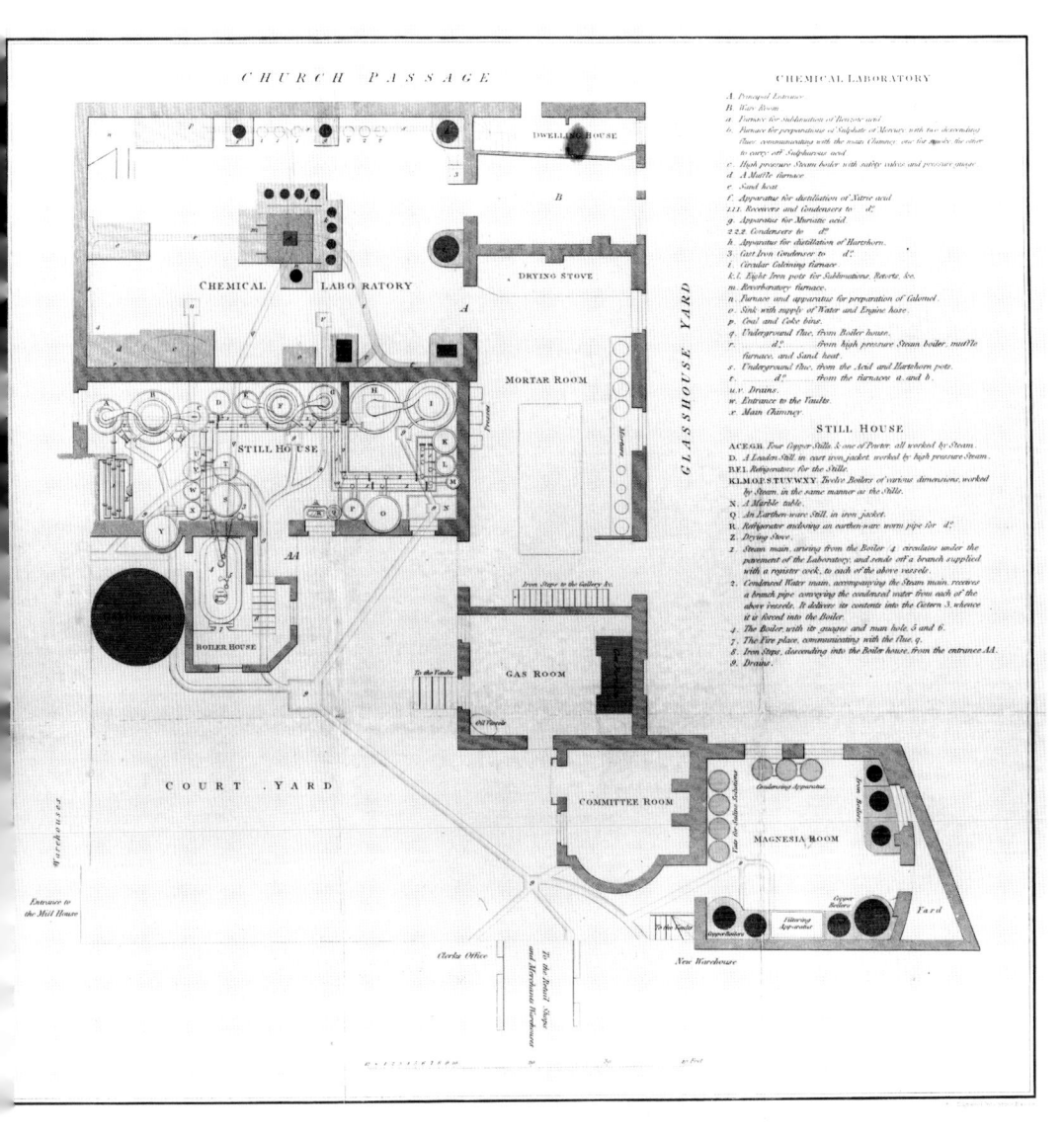

Plan showing the premises occupied by the United Stock from an explanatory booklet tracing the Origins, Progress and Present State of the various establishments (1823).
KEY to the main features of the Chemical Laboratory: A – Principal entrance. B – Ware room. a – Furnace for sublimation of Benzoic acid. b – Furnace for preparations of sulphate of Mercury. c – High pressure steam boiler. d – A muffle furnace. e – Sand heat. f – Apparatus for distillation of Nitric acid. g – Apparatus for Muriatic acid. h – Apparatus for distillation of Hartshorn. i – Circular calcining furnace. k,l – Iron pots for sublimating. m – Reverberatory furnace. n – Furnace and apparatus for preparation of calomel. x – Main chimney.
KEY to the main features of the Still House: A,C,E,G,H – Stills worked by steam. D – Lead still worked by high pressure steam. B.F.I. – Refrigerators for the stills. K,L M,O,P,S,T,U,V,W,X,Y – Boilers. N – Marble table. Q – Earthenware still. R – Refrigerator. Z – Drying stove. 1 – Steam main from the boiler (4).

Hall while he was preparing fulminate of mercury for percussion caps (detonating appliances on gunlocks) required by the East India Company, allegedly for use in the Afghan War. A slip of the hand caused a series of explosions which struck Hennell below the chest, carried away his right arm, face, the top of his head and some internal organs so that his chest lay open, exposing his heart and lungs. The right arm was found later on the roof of the Hall, a finger was retrieved from Union (now Apothecary) Street and other parts of Hennell's anatomy were scattered around the neighbourhood. The United Stock paid for the funeral and awarded Hennell's widow an annuity to recompense for the "very melancholy and fatal event".[92]

It was pointed out that the preparation of fulminate of mercury had been undertaken by Hennell as a matter of urgency and was contrary to usual practice. The Accounts tell no tale of explosives or armaments being manufactured at the Hall, only of "medicines delivered" to the East India Company, although the Chemical Superintendent's sideline in "refractions of saltpetre" is suspect. Hennell's fatal accident raises the question of what exactly was included in the supplies sent from Apothecaries' Hall to the Niger expedition (1841) and to those fighting in the first opium war in China (1839–41).[93]

In 1843 the United Stock company at the Hall at last secured the confidence of the Army Medical Board, and the contract ushered in a prosperous period for the trade. The new steam engine installed on the advice of Professor Brande (1853–54), the huge demand for medical supplies during the Crimean War (1855–56) and the Indian Mutiny (1857–58) gave the United Stock "an accumulation of business" during Robert Warington's term as Operator of the Laboratory (1842–66).[94] Warington was essentially a pharmaceutical chemist, joint founder of the Chemical Society and elected a Fellow of the Royal Society in 1864. He has been credited with the invention of "the parlour aquarium" which in truth owed more to N.B. Ward (see page 142). Under Warington's supervision high standards were maintained at the Society's Laboratory – he liked to boast that only the best quality ingredients were purchased, to be ground and prepared under his scrupulous eye.

With the trade departments at Apothecaries' Hall in full swing during the middle years of the nineteenth century, the scene was recorded in the pages of Charles Dickens's periodical, *Household Words*: "the great mill stones powder rhubarb, rows of steam pestles pound in iron mortars, steam rollers mix hills of ointment, enormous stills silently do their work, calomel sublimes in closed ovens, magnesia is made and evaporated, crucibles are hot and coppers all heated by steam are full of costly juices from all corners of the world". Medicated brews were fermented in the cellars, delicate scientific tests took place in a private laboratory, warehouses and packing rooms were heaped with boxes of drugs to be sent by the next ship to India, to kill or cure – "these are the premises of the United Stock".[95]

After the Mutiny, the Council of India replaced the East India Company as the Society's best customer, with orders doubling in the years leading up to Queen Victoria's triumph as Empress of India in 1876. The rapid decrease in Indian orders thereafter was a major factor in the decision to dissolve the United Stock in 1881.

Overall, the Proprietors of the United Stock did well financially. George Hogarth Makins (Master 1889–90), calculated that a Proprietor investing £420 received an average annual dividend of 15¾ per cent on his investment between the years 1823 and 1878. As the decline in the trade became evident after 1876 the Proprietors were wise to vote for the dissolution of the United Stock and the return of their capital.[96]

Decline and closure

The profits of war sustained the Society's trade in the mid-nineteenth century but in the longer term the Society's commitment to the medical profession was overriding. The two pursuits were incompatible: the Society could not compete as a trading company in a commercial world *and* fulfil its role as a medical licensing body. It was not until 1878 that the conflict of interests was identified as a problem and even after the dissolution of the United Stock in 1880 the Court of Assistants would not forsake the Society's trading interests.

Apart from the difficulty of reconciling commercial and professional interests, there were flaws in the operations of the United Stock, such as restricted space, primitive book-keeping and the concentration of power in the hands of the Master, Wardens and Assistants, who were not necessarily interested in the trade. Business methods were out-dated and despotic: the auditors' suggestion that double entry accounts be introduced went unheeded in 1867 and had to be repeated in 1891, and when a member of the Committee of Managers asked to see a balance sheet in 1872 the request was dismissed as abnormal. By the time the point was conceded in 1879 there was a crisis.[97]

The Treasurer blamed the decline in the business of the Society on the great pressure applied by the Departments of State and the competition of other establishments. Pressure had come from the Council of India and the Army Medical Department, both complaining of delays in orders. A committee of inquiry admitted that there was a lack of authoritative superintendence in the manufacturing department, a want of method and accuracy in the records and irregularites in the management of correspondence.[98]

A valiant effort was made to attract business from Proprietors, hospitals, dispensaries and minor public institutions, and in 1878 the question of a branch establishment was raised again. In rejecting the proposal, the Society identified the crux of the problem: as one of three "Great Portals" through which those aspiring to the medical profession had to pass, the Society could not or would not use the tactics of salesmen to attract customers and increase

Drug manufacturing at Apothecaries' Hall in 1915 and (opposite) at the closure of the trade in 1922.

trade. How, then, was the trade to survive at a time when the quantity of drugs used in the treatment of disease was shrinking generally and "the stores" were cornering the retail market? The decline of the trade over the preceding fourteen or fifteen years became a matter of urgency in 1879 when a conference was held at the Hall to confront the issue. There were accusations of mismanagement and cumbrous staffing, and it was discovered that there was not, nor ever had been, a profit and loss account.

In the subsequent shake-up the Treasurer resigned and after consultation with every Proprietor, the United Stock was dissolved at the end of 1880. Yet there were those who would not admit defeat: the Court of Assistants decided to carry on the trade for the sale of pure drugs, chemicals and pharmaceutical preparations for one year at least and at its own risk under the management of a new General Superintendent, Robert H. Davies.[99] Davies was chosen from fifty-six applicants and he was highly qualified – a silver medallist and he had recently been Demonstrator to the Pharmaceutical Society. The new broom swept clean with the re-organization of the Great Laboratory for general order work by the clearing of the ancient equipment; old invoice books were thrown out and the Accountant was moved into an office under the Great Hall. Matthews the carpenter carried out £300 worth of repairs to the Laboratory, a universal kneading machine was purchased and employees were forbidden from sleeping in view of the public during the dinner hour.[100]

Good profits still remained elusive. The Council of India account was withdrawn in 1881, leaving the Society dependent on the Crown Agents for the Colonies (frequent orders, problems with packaging and safe transport to remote areas), the Army Medical Department (dwindling and soon to cease), the Army Veterinary Department (a small account, also soon to cease), merchants, hospitals and private clients. By 1887 the retail department was in decline. The Clerk drew the Master's attention to the gradual decrease in its business, which he attributed to the custom "which almost universally prevails of medical men prescribing and not compounding and dispensing medicines".[101]

William Chattaway's appointment as General Superintendent in 1893, and the modest success of the analytical department, persuaded the Society to continue trading into the twentieth century. Furthermore, the freehold reversion of the Great Laboratory had been purchased in 1894 and old dwellings in Fleur de Luce Court were sold. The Trade Committee Minutes give the impression that there was little to worry about except the urinal installed against the wall of the Society's premises in Playhouse Yard and the manufacture of toothpaste according to a secret formula.[102]

Davies had died of tuberculosis in 1893 and his successor, Chattaway, died only eleven years later in 1904, aged forty-three, whereupon the post of General Manager and Superintendent of the Trade was discontinued. Frederick Farey Shelley, who had been a pharmacist in New South Wales, was the last to oversee the trade at Apothecaries' Hall in his capacity as Manager and senior analyst. The final era makes sad reading. Reduced from manufacturing large quantities of medicines for shipment to India, Australia and obscure corners of the globe, the Society had come to rely on problematic orders from the Crown Agents, contracts from assurance companies, local vestries, lunatic asylums, school boards (which had to be renegotiated every six months or annually) and the meagre charges for dispensing prescriptions for individual customers. As business drew to a close, the Duke of Wellington and Lord Cholmondley ranked among the debtors.[103]

The depression that followed the Boer War had repercussions on the drug trade and the Apothecaries' profits fell to £500 for 1902–03 with dividends cut to 3½ per cent. The prevailing depression had no respect for the humanitarian aspects of the Society's trade in supplying vaccine to Uganda, ivory points for immunization against smallpox to the Zambesi Medical Mission and anti-malarial tablets to West Africa. Profits for the year ending in December 1910 amounted to £333, compared to £1,934 for 1909, a reduction that was blamed on severe competition.[104]

The First World War meant the loss of staff as they enlisted, worries about the import of chemicals from Germany and the loss of exports. The diminution of trade had been a major concern since 1907 when the Trade Committee admitted that sooner or later trading profits would disappear. In these circumstances, the trade premises were identified as the Society's main asset and their demolition/redevelopment/sale was the subject of various reports, surveys and plans.

In the midst of decline the Society embarked on a new speciality – a laboratory for the biological testing of drugs on living animals, under the supervision of Dr Bambridge. A licence was obtained and the facility was advertised to the medical profession. At the same time a report underlined the laxity of operations at the Hall. After a mix-up between castor oil and glycerine, the pots in the pharmacy were arranged in alphabetical order and bottles and jars containing poison were distinctly marked – a precaution that was long overdue.[105]

The demolition of the Mill House in 1915 and the redevelopment of the site as Cobham House produced welcome rents but prospects for further rebuilding receded during the war years. The announcement of a loss of £36 for the accounting year ending in December 1919 put paid to ideas of amalgamation with another corporation or of becoming a government department.[106]

The last nails in the coffin were driven by the employees' repeated demands for pay increases; the tool they used was to strike without warning for a fortnight in May 1920. The trade department barely survived into 1921, and the revelation in February of a net loss of £2,695 for the last year prompted the decision to close the trade as soon as possible.[107] Manufacturing came to an

The retail shop, Apothecaries' Hall, *circa* 1920.

end in March, the warehouse remained busy "finishing up" until May and on 27 June the Minutes conclude: "This is the last meeting of the trade committee which has been established for so many years", followed by the names of the seven attending the funeral.

Randall and Wilson of Southampton purchased the Society's process book and the wholesale connection for £50; the retail business with prescription books, formulae and goodwill passed to Messrs Cooper Son and Co, and Orridge and Co (chemists' transfer agents and valuers of Ludgate Hill) organized the sale of fixtures, utensils, implements of pharmacy and stock in trade valued at £2,761 10s 4d. The fittings of the pharmacy (long mahogany counters, cabinets and brass lamps) sold for £25 and Shelley paid £50 for the analytical apparatus.[108] All was disposed of by the summer of 1922 when the shop was converted into offices, indicating the beginning of another era.

The chimney of the Great Laboratory with the dome of St Paul's behind, in the early years of the twentieth century.

Chapter 7

The age of reform

By the close of the eighteenth century the Apothecary's role as a general medical practitioner had taken shape. His legal right to practise had been recognized by the House of Lords in 1704 and thenceforward the Apothecary's professional and social status advanced so that by the 1830s he was acknowledged as being a well-educated gentleman and a qualified general practitioner. A major force compelling Apothecaries in this direction was the proliferation of untrained practitioners of medicine, especially chemists and druggists. Following an Act of Common Council in 1712 chemists and druggists who were free of the City (but not freemen of a livery company) could legitimately trade in the capital, competing with Apothecaries to supply medicines and attend patients. Their usurpation of the Apothecary's living became a major issue in the agitation for reform, precipitating the Apothecaries' Act of 1815.

The Physicians of the Royal College, meanwhile, remained an élite whose high charges and small number placed them out of the reach of most Londoners. As Adam Smith pointed out in 1776, "the apothecary was the physician of the poor in all cases, and of the rich when the distress or danger is not very great".[1] In these circumstances many Apothecaries styled themselves Doctor, for example Sylvanus Bevan of the Plough Court Pharmacy, who was an Apothecary in medical practice, whereas his brother and descendants took the alternative route as druggists and chemists (later forming the pharmaceutical business of Allen & Hanburys).

R. Campbell, writing in 1747, recalls how easy it was for an Apothecary to set up shop, make large profits and pursue a medical career: "The Army of Apothecaries of this Age scorn to confine themselves to the dull scene of their profession. They are no sooner equipped with a shop than they commence Doctor; they prescribe in all common cases and only call in the Doctor to be present at the Death of the Game which they have run down".[2]

The onward march of the Apothecary was assisted by the passivity of the Royal College of Physicians and more actively by Dr Richard Mead F.R.S., the most prosperous and fashionable Physician of King George II's reign. He recognized the value of Apothecaries as practical medical men and his consultations with them at the coffee-houses added to their knowledge and credibility as medical practitioners.

While the interests of a proportion of the Society lay in medical practice, the trading arm remained strong, particularly during the second half of the eighteenth century. However, the Apothecaries' Act of 1815 made it clear that the Society's future lay in the regulation of education within the medical profession rather than in business – although it was another 100 years before the trade at the Hall closed.

The rising status of Apothecaries has been traced to the recruitment in the early eighteenth century of a high proportion of apprentices who were sons of clergymen[3] and to the Society's insistence that apprentices were proficient in general knowledge and Latin. Once apprenticed, the practical training in pharmaceutical skills was complemented by attendance at lectures and classes, anatomical dissections, home visits and instruction in botany and chemistry. Thus equipped, members of the Society were well-qualified as Apothecaries and medical practitioners, and many of those who ascended the hierarchy as Liverymen became Fellows of the learned societies, botanists, authors and men of science.

Practising Apothecaries consolidated their position at dinners of the Friendly Medical Society (F.M.S.) founded in 1725 "to preserve a good understanding and friendship amongst members of the Company of Apothecaries" and by supporting the Medical Society of London on its

Thomas Rowlandson's satire, "The Quack Doctor" (1814), depicts the interior of an early-nineteenth-century apothecary's shop. The sign above the doorway on the left indicates Apothecaries' Hall. The drug jars are labelled as poisons (canthari, arsenic, opium, nitre, vitriol). The apothecary's assistant, the skeleton death, pounds a mortar behind the curtain. A rhyme below the print (not shown) reads "I have a secret art to cure/ Each malady which men endure".

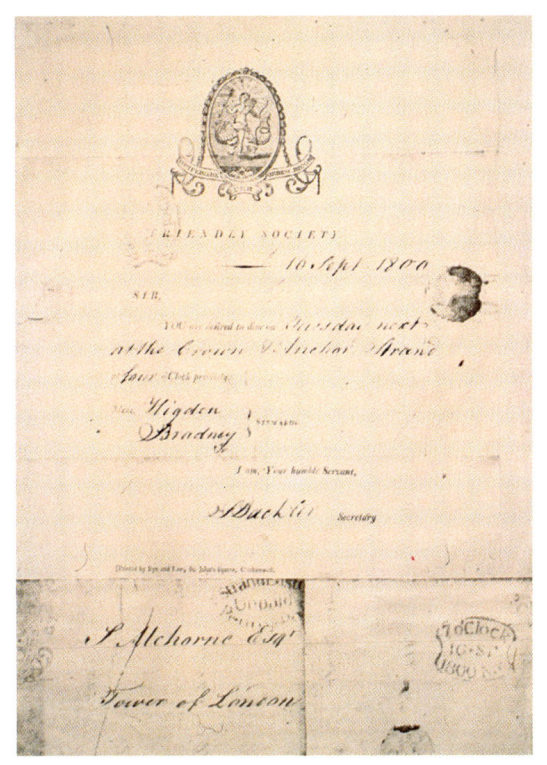

Invitation to Stanesby Alchorne to attend a dinner of the Friendly Medical Society at the Crown and Anchor in the Strand, 16 September 1800. The Friendly Medical Society was founded in 1725 as a dining club for medically practising members of the Society.

formation in 1773. The ascendancy of medically practising Apothecaries within the Society was confirmed the following year, when the Livery was restricted to practising members.

The Friendly Medical Society was a social dining club unique to the Society of Apothecaries. Its membership – limited to twenty-six Assistants and Liverymen, plus the Clerk – formed an élite. Sir William Watson, George Man Burrows, Dr Joseph Adams and Stanesby Alchorne were among the stalwarts who dined together four times a year. The Crown and Anchor in the Strand, "the birthplace of the general practitioner", was a favourite rendezvous although the centenary dinner in 1825 was held at The Star and Garter in Richmond. Speaking on that occasion, the Master, Edward Browne, proclaimed that the Apothecary was no longer merely a compounder of medicine but an accredited character with a classical and medical education.[4] Parallel to the leaning of Apothecaries towards general medical practice and away from pharmacy, was the rise in number and reputation of Surgeon-Apothecaries. These men were qualified surgeons who practised as apothecaries – many of them gained wide experience through service in the forces and when disbanded they turned to general practice. It was the alliance of Apothecaries with Surgeon-Apothecaries under the leadership of George Man Burrows that called for a distinct authority to superintend their professional interests (1812). Three years later the Apothecaries' Act gave the Society of Apothecaries that responsibility.

The Apothecaries' Act 1815
The need for the reform of the medical profession surfaced in 1794. Some 200 medical practitioners converged on the Crown and Anchor Tavern in the Strand to protest against the encroachments of chemists and druggists and the need for regulation. Not the least of the Apothecaries' grievances was the diversion of profits into the pockets of chemists and druggists who sold all manner of "cures" to the unsuspecting public – it was alleged they were depriving each Apothecary of nearly £200 per annum. Urged on by John M. Good F.R.S., those present at the Crown and Anchor formed the General Pharmaceutical Association of Great Britain with the aim of securing reform by legislation. Good's proposals were published,[5] but legislation was elusive.

The demand for the reform of the medical profession was taken up in the early nineteenth century by Dr John Latham of the Royal College of Physicians and Dr Edward Harrison of Lincolnshire. The Royal College devised a sweeping programme to extend its control over the whole profession, a proposition that was hardly likely to be acceptable to other institutions, whilst Harrison secured the support of Sir Joseph Banks and canvassed the Royal Colleges and the Society of Apothecaries. The Society agreed that improvement was desirable but in defensive mood a Special Court recited the Society's regulations, conveyed satisfaction with its own organization and lack of interest in other branches of the medical profession.[6] If the Apothecaries' response was passive, the attitude of the College of Physicians was negative, with the result that in 1811 Harrison retired from the fray.

It was left to a member of the Society of Apothecaries, George Man Burrows, to take up the cause. The Crown and Anchor was once again the meeting place of the reformers, this time protesting against a new tax on glass "almost equivalent to another income tax". Coming on top of other war-time taxes, this hit Apothecaries hard as they relied on a constant supply of glass bottles. Anthony Todd Thompson, who was busy founding a dispensary and infant school in Chelsea and who later became the first Professor of *materia medica* at University College, diverted attention to the subject of medical reform. This banner was upheld enthusiastically over the next three years by some 3,000 medical practitioners who joined the Association of Apothecaries and Surgeon-Apothecaries under the Chairmanship of Burrows actively supported by R.M. Kerrison, Henry Field, James R. Upton and many members of the Society of Apothecaries. Their main complaint was that the kingdom teemed with ignorant pretenders, druggists and their hired assistants who not only sold cures but also visited and administered to the sick, thus usurping the Apothecaries' role. Secondly, the Apothecaries were aggrieved that they were restricted to charging for medicines only. The proposed solution to these and other problems was to achieve reform by placing Apothecaries, Surgeon-Apothecaries and practitioners of midwifery under the direction of a controlling body. The reformers also sought a new term to describe the Apothecary/Surgeon/midwife or "mixed practitioner" they represented. The term "general practitioner" seems first to have been used in a pamphlet of 1714, was taken up by Kerrison in 1813[7] and by the 1830s the title was accepted and understood to mean someone who held qualifications from both the Society of Apothecaries (L.S.A.) and the Royal College of Surgeons (M.R.C.S.).

Burrows and the London Committee of the Association of Apothecaries and Surgeon-Apothecaries were set on reforming legislation and they recruited the parliamentary support of William Wilberforce, John Calcraft, Samuel Whitbread and George Rose. According to R.M. Kerrison, three-quarters of the members of the Society of Apothecaries stood behind the reformers, and a memorandum signed by ninety-one of them set out their concern "to prevent by legislative enactments, uneducated persons from practising as they do at present throughout the kingdom in every department of medicine". They urged the Master, Wardens and Court of Assistants to liaise with the Royal College of Physicians to this end.[8] The enthusiasm of these members did not extend to the Court of Assistants: it upheld the *status quo* and would not back the reformers. Opposition from the higher echelons of the Society, the two Royal Colleges and a committee of chemists and druggists made it clear that the creation of a new medical corporation to superintend the professional interests of Apothecaries, Surgeon-Apothecaries and practitioners of midwifery would not be permitted. The entrusting of their interests to the Society of Apothecaries, however, was acceptable.

This proposal emanated from Dr John Latham who replaced Sir Francis Milman as President of the Royal College of Physicians in October 1813. Latham was in favour of medical reform generally and under his direction the College of Physicians raised no objection to the vesting of new powers in the Society of Apothecaries provided that the proposals were submitted to the College for approval prior to the application for a Bill in Parliament.

Fired by the prospect of a major role in the regulation of the medical profession, the Society swung into action with the appointment of an Act of Parliament Committee in February 1814.[9] Negotiations with the Royal College of Physicians proved tiresome, particularly when the College insisted on a clause making it compulsory for Apothecaries to dispense Physicians' prescriptions, and ultimately the College withdrew its support. Having introduced the Bill, the Rt Hon George Rose found he was too busy to promote it wholeheartedly; Sir James Shaw abandoned it, the Royal College of Physicians, the Committee of Chemists and Druggists, and some Associated Apothecaries petitioned against it, and members of the House of Lords insisted on amendments before the Apothecaries' Act was passed by one vote on the last day of the session. It received the royal assent on 12 July 1815.

From 1 August the Society of Apothecaries became responsible for carrying out the provisions of the Act, most importantly by granting a certificate to medical students successful in examination for the Licence of the Society of Apothecaries (L.S.A.). The Act was criticized from the start, by reformers, by the Royal College of Physicians and by its perpetrators. It contained defective provisions and was hastily cobbled together, as the Society's Act of Parliament Committee was the first to admit. The Committee's report revealed how the Bill for enlarging the Society's charter for the better regulating of the practice of Apothecaries had emerged with a contorted title and "very material alterations" engineered during its progress through Parliament "which it had with great difficulty twice travelled". The report cited the opposition of the Royal College of Physicians, who having thrown the burden of reform onto the Society, then insisted on modifications: "the jealousy on the part of the Physicians which has existed towards the Apothecaries and which appears from the Records, continues with unabated force". The result was an Act likely to be "be defective in its operation in many particulars" and which should be regarded as "an experiment only".[10]

More recently the Act has been variously assessed as "enlightened . . . the most immediately successful and satisfactory of all medical statutes"; "the first Parliamentary effort to set standards of professional education in England and Wales"; "a major obstacle to the improvement of the general practitioners' status", "the zenith of the Apothecary in history", "reactionary" and "the abortive outcome of over twenty years' agitation by general practitioners".[11]

Although it was criticized from the start, chiefly on account of the five-year apprenticeship clause introduced by the House of Lords, there is no denying that, in due course, the Apothecaries' Act had the effect of raising the standard of medical education: it gave structure to the profession and impetus to medical reform.

Examinations and examiners
It has been claimed that the Society had greatness thrust upon it in 1815. It could also be said that the Act merely extended the Society's educational function which had been part of its ethos since 1617.[12] Both claims are valid: the Society had always taken the education of its apprentices seriously and the Act of 1815 forced it to formalize a curriculum and to appoint Examiners to

As a result of the Apothecaries' Act of 1815 the Society became an examining body for the medical profession. Successful candidates were awarded a certificate of qualification licensing them to practise in England and Wales. This example is for 1822.

administer a compulsory exam to be taken after a five-year apprenticeship. If successful, the candidate (male or female) was awarded a certificate enabling him to practice as an Apothecary in England and Wales.

By the end of July 1815 a Court of Examiners was elected and examination regulations were issued. Of the twelve Examiners, three were Fellows of the Linnean Society, three were members of the Royal College of Surgeons, three were keen botanists, one was the Royal Apothecary and seven among them were reformers in the sense that they belonged to the Association of Apothecaries and Surgeon-Apothecaries that had set the ball rolling in 1812. All were members of the Society of at least ten years' standing and two were on the Court of Assistants.[13]

The first examination regulations specified that following a five-year apprenticeship to an Apothecary the candidate must demonstrate his competence in Latin by translating parts of the *Pharmacopoeia Londinensis* and Physicians' prescriptions; he was also to be examined in the theory and practice of medicine, in pharmaceutical chemistry and in *materia medica*. He must produce testimonials of his apprenticeship, his age and moral conduct. Certificates to show he had attended for six months at least a medical practice, public hospital, infirmary or dispensary were also required – the Society was the first licensing body to demand such a thorough practical training. The candidate was also expected to have attended two courses of lectures on anatomy and physiology and two courses on the theory and practice of medicine, one course of lectures on chemistry and another on *materia medica*. Those wishing to qualify as Apothecaries' Assistants in compounding and dispensing medicines were required to translate Physicians' prescriptions, parts of the *Pharmacopoeia Londinensis* and to answer questions in pharmacy and *materia medica*.[14]

The imposition of apprenticeship and compulsory examinations provoked immediate opposition. Surgeons already practising with the army and navy claimed exemption and persuaded the Secretary at War to take up their case; students at the Anatomical Theatre in Blenheim Street objected to compulsory apprenticeship for those who had already undergone and paid for medical training. Other objectors to the new regulations resorted to the forging of indentures, impersonation or practising without a licence.

As the Court of Examiners wrestled with such problems, one of their number caused a rumpus. This was George Man Burrows, a pugnacious character who was disappointed by the Apothecaries' Act, yet as a member of the first Court of Examiners he was dedicated to its execution. He had taken a leading part in the movement for reform but had no previous experience of the Society's affairs which may explain why he found the authority of the Court of Assistants so irksome. He crossed swords with William Simons who was in a position of power as Master (1816–17), Chairman of the Court of

George Man Burrows painted by J.G. Middleton (1851). As Chairman of the Association of Apothecaries and Surgeon-Apothecaries Burrows was instrumental in the movement for medical reform that resulted in the Apothecaries' Act of 1815. He was a member of the Society's first Court of Examiners from 1815 to 1817.

Examiners, Treasurer of the Navy Stock, Chairman of the Act of Parliament Committee, a manager of the Physic Garden and was also involved with the chemical department. Matters came to a head when Burrows refused to examine a candidate who had been apprenticed (albeit for seven years) to a chemist and druggist as opposed to an Apothecary, as the Act specified. Burrows presented his argument to the Court of Assistants and somehow his letter was leaked to the Press. Burrows was held responsible and he was summoned before the Court on 25 March 1817 whereupon he promptly resigned as an Examiner. His bitter account of the affair pointed to the oligarchic constitution of the Society, the age, nepotism and irregular record-keeping of the Examiners, and a lack of zeal in prosecuting unlicensed practitioners (some of his criticisms were valid and later rectified). Although no longer an Examiner and unlikely to proceed to the Court of Assistants, Burrows remained a member of the Society until 1823 when he was disfranchised on becoming a licentiate of the Royal College of Physicians, the Society generously remitting the fine.[15]

In his refusal to admit a candidate who did not conform to the regulations, Burrows had a case (he claimed half the Court of Examiners agreed with him). Yet from the beginning, some candidates who did not conform in every respect with the regulations, were successful. The first candidate to be examined, George Smyth, was no youngster, having been a naval surgeon for five years. He had attended lectures on anatomy, physiology and the theory and practice of medicine but could claim no formal instruction in chemistry or *materia medica*. Nevertheless, his experience and testimonials from naval officers stood him in good stead and he obtained the first L.S.A. on 10 August 1815 despite his shortcomings. The second candidate was another naval surgeon and thereafter candidates trickled through at the rate of one a week, with the first two rejections at the end of the month. Over the next six months thirty-one candidates were examined (two others could not produce the requisite testimonials) and twenty-six received certificates, five being rejected for their inadequate Latin. A prize was proposed as an incentive and after one year the Court of Examiners reflected with justifiable pride that "the Act has already tended to the increase of Industry and application among the students of medicine and that it will eventually be the means of raising up a class of well-educated practitioners in every part of the Kingdom".[16]

The number of students examined (for a fee of 10 guineas for London students, 6 guineas for country candidates) rose steadily to 584 for 1859–60 after a hiatus in 1846 when the number dropped to 285. This temporary fall was attributed to large numbers practising without a licence in the expectation that no legal proceedings would be taken, and to the uncertainty generated by the various proposals for medical reform in circulation.[17]

Candidate number 189, John Keats, presented himself for examination on 25 July 1816. He was not quite twenty-one, the age specified by the regulations, so either deception, kindness or ignorance was at work. Having been apprenticed from the age of fifteen to Thomas Hammond, his grandparents' medical practitioner in Edmonton, Keats completed his medical training at Guy's and St Thomas' before presenting himself at Apothecaries' Hall as a candidate for the Society's Licence. Henry Stephens, a fellow medical student,

The earliest surviving portrait of John Keats: a charcoal drawing by Joseph Severn *circa* 1816. Keats produced the required testimonials and sat the Society's examination in July 1816.

recalled that Keats "surprised many of us by his passing that examination as he had appeared to pay so little attention to his profession but he was very quick in acquiring anything and his knowledge of the Classics helped him a good deal in that examination, for it was the examination in Latin which the students most feared". Keats was examined by Everard Brande (Royal Apothecary) in the presence of the whole Court – the ordeal lasted about one and a half hours after which Keats, the 168th candidate to be examined and approved, was granted the certificate. He subsequently took a post as a

> July 25th 1816.
>
> 189 MR. *John Keats of full age* — CANDIDATE for a CERTIFICATE to practise as an APOTHECARY in *the Country*.
>
> An APPRENTICE to MR. *Thomas Hammond of Edmonton* APOTHECARY for *5* Years.
>
> TESTIMONIAL from *Mr. Thos. Hammond*.
>
> LECTURES.
> 2 COURSES on ANATOMY and PHYSIOLOGY.
> 2 —— THEORY and PRACTICE of MEDICINE.
> 2 —— CHEMISTRY.
> 1 —— MATERIA MEDICA.
>
> HOSPITAL ATTENDANCE.
> 6 MONTHS at *Guy's & St. Thomas's*
> as
> MONTHS at
>
> 168 *Examined by Mr. Brande & approved*

John Keats's examination entry, 1816. The Mr Brande referred to in the last line was Everard A. Brande, Royal Apothecary.

surgeon's dresser at Guy's Hospital but his unsuitability to medicine soon became apparent – the gruelling tasks of the early-nineteenth-century surgeon offended the poet's sensibility. Therefore, in 1817 Keats abandoned thoughts of a medical career in favour of poetry and his first volume of poems was published that year. He viewed his last operation with some pride – "the opening of a man's temporal artery. I did it with the utmost nicety, but reflecting on what passed through my mind at the time, my dexterity seemed a miracle, and I never took up the lancet again". When the muse escaped him Keats toyed with the idea of reverting to the "apothecary line", a possiblity that was dismissed as the poet lapsed "into an idle-minded, vicious way of life ... in no period of my life have I acted with any self will but in throwing up the apothecary profession. That I do not repent of ... My occupation is entirely literary". And so it was to remain until his death from consumption in Rome (1821).[18]

The examination curriculum for the Society's Licence was extended by new regulations of September 1827 which introduced a course on medical botany. Nine instead of six months' attendance was required at a dispensary and students were earnestly recommended to attend one or more courses on midwifery and the diseases of women and children. Two courses of anatomical demonstrations and attendance at clinical lectures were compulsory and if a candidate's ability in Latin was doubtful he would be asked to translate from one of the easier Latin authors. This was extended in 1831 when translations from Celsus and Gregory became the norm – "the very imperfect acquaintance of a great number of candidates with the Latin language" was the most common reason for failure. Translations from Latin authors became part of the preliminary exam in classics and maths, suspended briefly between 1845 and 1849 when the Latin translations were wrapped into the general exam. Once the Preliminary Arts Exam resumed it included passages from Virgil, Cicero, Greek translations and maths. The number of lectures attended by students increased to 100 for each of the main subjects in 1841, and the Examiners stressed the importance of organic chemistry and botany and wanted proof that students had dissected the whole human body at least once.[19]

Thus the Examiners regularly adjusted the course of study, meeting weekly for that purpose and to conduct the examinations in the afternoon. To begin with the nervous candidate faced the whole Court who were entitled to question him in turn, although the certificate named only the principal Examiner. As the numbers to be examined increased the Court divided into four tables of three Examiners, each table examining one candidate under the direction of a chief Examiner. If the three Examiners found the candidate unsatisfactory he was referred to a majority of the Court and those who failed that test could re-take after six months.[19]

Examination candidates had to prove their competence according to the published curriculum and examination, yet the competence of the Examiners was unspecified apart from ten years' membership of the Society. This aspect was seized upon by the outspoken editor of the *Lancet*, Thomas Wakley, who as M.P. for Finsbury (1835–52) campaigned vigorously for medical reform. He called on his readers to emancipate the medical profession from the domination of the "company of ignorant, mercenary pharmacopolists . . . incorporated tradesmen" of Apothecaries' Hall and he alleged that the Society had benefited from examination fees totalling nearly £30,000 by 1828. Wakley specialized in nicknames, labelling the Apothecaries "the Old Hags of Rhubarb Hall". "Which of the Old Hags possesses such knowledge of chemistry, *materia medica*, botany, anatomy and physiology"? he questioned. Others took the same line – a naval surgeon, disbanded after Waterloo, wrote to protest at the indignity of examination by the "drug-pounders of Black Friars", and Dr Ramadge, a former Censor of the Royal College of Physicians, joined the chorus of criticism with a derisory account of the uselessness of the searches of Apothecaries' shops by the Censors and the Wardens of the

Society, "men worn down with age and infirmities without much knowledge of the genuineness of the articles they inspected". One had lost his sense of smell and taste, another had dropsy and they were all more interested in concluding the day at the tavern than inspecting the shops.[20]

The cholera epidemic of 1831–32 diverted attention to fundamental issues of public health, and in its wake came the gargantuan enquiries into medical education beginning with the report of the Warburton Committee in 1834. As it reflected upon the Society's execution of the Apothecaries' Act, the verdict of the Committee was laudatory. Many witnesses, including Sir Henry Halford, Physician to four monarchs and President of the Royal College (1820–44), expressed the view that the Society's examinations had raised the educational standards of general practitioners and that the Examiners fulfilled their duties conscientiously.[21]

Coincidentally with the parliamentary enquiries, the Apothecaries' Examiners displayed a new toughness, rejecting sixty-five candidates out of 448 examined in 1834: twenty-four for incompetence in Latin, and forty-one for inadequate professional knowledge. The following year the Examiners faced the ire of a tumultuous assembly of students who held a protest meeting at The Crown and Anchor to demonstrate against the rejection of one of their number in a recent examination. The failed candidate, Thomas Smith, accused one of the Examiners, John Ridout, of coarse and contemptuous language; Wheeler and Watson were also criticized for their rudeness (Watson, Secretary to the Examiners, was ill and soon to resign). No sooner had the Society recovered from this unwelcome publicity than another student struck out, literally, "in wanton and unprovoked manner" inflicting severe wounds on three Examiners; he was consequently restrained in the Giltspur Street Compter. The Bedel and Porter also had to cope with the students' ebullience and on one occasion the Porter was overpowered by an intoxicated candidate forcing an entry.[22]

The Examiners Bacot and Ridout, meanwhile, found their loyalties divided between the Society and the University of London where a medical school was being established at University College. At the Hall, the Clerk took umbrage because he was not thanked for his work as Secretary to the Examiners and resigned that post. Professor W.T. Brande, a star in the Society's firmament, also threatened resignation if his recommendations for changes to lectures at the Hall were not heeded.[23]

The Court of Examiners' workload intensified according to the increasing number of candidates, the revisions and extensions of the curriculum and particularly with the introduction of written papers for the Arts Exam (1839–40). Following recommendations from the newly constituted General Council of Medical Education and Registration of the United Kingdom (G.M.C.), the Society's preliminary examination in classics and maths was made compulsory from 1861 to ensure "an efficient bar against the admission of illiterate persons into the profession", and there was an immediate rise in the number of medical students enrolling for examination at the Hall. The professional or main exam was also extended from 1861 by division into two exams, written and oral, lasting five hours altogether and embracing the new subjects of forensic medicine, toxicology and morbid anatomy.[24]

The Examiners congratulated themselves that their Preliminary Arts Exam had anticipated the G.M.C.'s recommendations. Three special Examiners in arts were appointed in 1861 to test the ability of students in English history and language, maths, natural philosophy and the Latin language (the traditionalists lamented that Greek was no longer compulsory).[25]

A challenge to the Society's position came in 1861 when the Royal College of Physicians stirred from a period of torpor and initiated a reform whereby its licentiates were permitted to dispense as well as to prescribe medicines. The Apothecaries resolved that it was their duty not to permit "the hostile and injurious proceedings of the College of Physicians to pass unquestioned" and warned the College it would prosecute new licentiates found to be dispensing as well as prescribing medicines. The threat proved hollow and a new breed of Physicians qualified to attend, prescribe and dispense began to emerge from the Royal College.

The Society, in its wisdom, remained quietly dissatisfied with the legal opinion in the Royal College's favour but chose not to challenge it by prosecution. The *British Medical Journal* sympathized with the Society that had "done far more than other medical corporations to elevate the standard of medical education . . . it has created the general practitioners of this country, demanding from them an education equal to that of a university". Now that the Society's position was undermined, the editor predicted that its days were numbered and that Black Friars would soon cease to be the nightmare of aspiring students: "The College licence now gives every privilege to its holder which the Company [Society] licence gives excepting that of keeping a shop". In witnessing "the blossoming of the College and yellow leaf of the Company" the main problem was identified: "It is no blame to it that the Company perishes, for it bore within it from its birth the fatal weapon of its own destruction. Its connexion with trade was its fatality. If it could have shaken off that incubus and met the growing aspirations of a liberal profession it would have survived".[26] The Society confounded this dire prediction of imminent demise but it did eventually abandon its trading activities.

A challenge of a different form soon faced the Court of Examiners in the shape of Elizabeth Garrett, better known as Mrs Elizabeth Garrett Anderson. Daunted but not defeated by the fact that no medical school admitted female students, Elizabeth Garrett commenced a course of private instruction in

Elizabeth Garrett was awarded the Society's Diploma in 1865 and gained a medical degree from Paris in 1870. As Mrs Elizabeth Garrett Anderson M.D. she was the first English woman doctor. This engraving, published in *The Graphic* 26 November 1870, is from a portrait by Laura Herford.

APOTHECARIES' HALL. *Sept 28th 1865.*

Questions for the Second Examination.

PRACTICE OF MEDICINE AND PATHOLOGY.

1. What are the causes and Pathology of the different forms of Jaundice? Sketch a case and give the treatment.

2. How may air find its way into the pleural cavity? What are the physical signs of the existence of Pneumo-hydrothorax?

3. What are the causes and Pathology of Epilepsy? Sketch an attack & give the treatment.

4. What are the physical signs of disease of the Aortic valves? Give the pathology of Cardiac dropsy.

An example of the examination in medicine and pathology, part of the qualification for the L.S.A. Elizabeth Garrett sat this paper 28 September 1865, successfully.

1860. Her enquiries into the possibility of being examined at Apothecaries' Hall caused consternation: the introduction of female practitioners had never been contemplated. Counsel's opinion that, according to the Apothecaries' Act of 1815, the Society's examinations were open to all "persons" provided they conformed to the regulations, was in Elizabeth Garrett's favour, for the word person included women. Elizabeth Garrett duly passed the Society's Arts Examination in 1862, the first part of the professional exam in March 1864 and the second part on 28 September 1865 when she gained her medical Diploma – the first woman to do so in Britain. As she reported to her friend Emily Davies: "I heard a cheering account of the hall examination yesterday.

Two of the examiners told Mr C. that it was a mercy they did not put the names in order of merit as in this case they must have put me first. I am very glad, though the exam was too easy to feel elated about". Elizabeth Garrett went on to receive a full medical degree from Paris (1870), became the Dean of the London School of Medicine for Women (L.S.M.W.), and the first female mayor in England.[27]

Such revolutionary events persuaded the Court of Examiners to take precautions against further inroads by women: "their introduction through the portals of this Society is alike derogatory to its character and lowering to the position of its members and licentiates". Thus the Court of Examiners declined to admit any more female candidates to examination. This rearguard action was prompted by the success of three women in the Preliminary Arts Exam of January 1867 and with the prospect that they might follow in Elizabeth Garrett Anderson's footsteps, the Examiners again resorted to Counsel, who pronounced that women could not be excluded from the Society's examinations if they possessed the requisite testimonials and certificates. The Examiners managed to circumvent the ruling by advertising that they would no longer accept as valid certificates of attendance at lectures delivered privately (effectively excluding women candidates).

Isabel Thorne sat the Arts Exam in April 1868 but found herself barred from the professional exams (she was later to join Mrs Garrett Anderson at the L.S.M.W.). Mrs Thorne held no grudge and in 1887 wrote to the Clerk congratulating the Society on the extension of its licence (following the Medical Act, 1886) and expressing the hope "that Cinderella [the Society] will not be too much elated by her alliance with the State to recognize a still younger sister [L.S.M.W.]".

The foundation of the London School of Medicine for Women in 1874, was soon followed by the easing of restrictions against women in the medical profession by an Act of Parliament giving them the right to be placed on the medical register (1876) and two years later women were admitted to all degrees of London University. Fanny Saward was the first woman to gain admission to the Apothecaries' Assistants' exam (1887) and the Society conceded to the unconditional acceptance of female candidates applying to take its Licence in 1888, when Isabella Macdonald became the second woman to receive the Society's Licence and the first to be successful in the recently established exam in surgery.[28]

Discounting their attitude to women, the Court of Examiners demonstrated remarkable flexibility – with the exception of Burrows who had exited promptly. In general, they became gradually more liberal in their interpretation of the Apothecaries' Act when faced with competent candidates with irregular qualifications and they adjusted the curriculum to accommodate new subjects. It was, of course, "the age of improvement" or at least the expectation of improvement. There was a growing corpus of knowledge to be absorbed, particularly in anatomy, physiology and pathology; new vaccines became available, anaesethesia came into use. Cholera, tuberculosis, typhus, typhoid and diptheria had to be tamed and the medical demands of a burgeoning population catered for, with the hitherto unknown problems of pollution and industrialization creating unsuspected health hazards. Particularly towards the end of the century, fresh research and unexplored subjects had to be taken into account, not least the work of Louis Pasteur and Joseph Lister.

The Court of Examiners registered these changes by adapting the curriculum and examinations and occasionally it showed the way forward. For instance, the preliminary exam, originating as Latin medical classics (1835) and general knowledge in arts subjects (1851) had predated the recommendations of the G.M.C. As early as 1827 candidates were advised to attend lectures in midwifery, in 1832 exams were extended to the diseases of pregnant and puerperal women, and three years later certificates were required to prove that candidates had attended in cases of labour. The introduction of forensic medicine and a practical exam in pathology (1866–67) were likewise innovations. The Court of Examiners pressed for an examination in surgery before this became a requirement under the 1886 Medical Act and the following year the Society tried to establish a Diploma in Public Health. A similar spirit of enterprise lay behind the lectures at the Hall given by Past Master Timothy Lane F.R.S. in 1803, by Dr Joseph Adams (famous for his treatise on morbid poisons), by Professor Brande from 1813, and by Professor Roscoe of Owens' College, Manchester, who spoke on chemical philosophy in 1867.[29]

The scientific conversaziones at Apothecaries' Hall were another new departure, centred on the wonders of the microscope. Guests (among them the Lord Mayor, Presidents of learned societies and M.P.s) were invited to the entertainment, bringing if possible a microscope and submitting curiosities such as scientific novelties, unusual specimens or rare apparatus. Students mixed with professors and it was not uncommon for 700 guests to attend on one day (ladies were admitted the following morning). A journalist from the *City Press* reporting on one of these "banquets of science" was impressed by the variety of specimens: aquatic vegetables, the scalp of a negro, a cat's tongue and stereoscopes that created illusions of a château and mountain scenery. The experience convinced him that

> "the parish Hippocrates has been transformed from a rough, boorish half-educated bi-ped into a thoroughly presentable gentleman well-up in most of the discoveries and accomplishments of the nineteenth century . . . the absurdity of the apothecary has died out and the licentiate of the Hall may now take his place among gentlemen".[30]

A Scientific Conversazione at Apothecaries' Hall in April 1855. Guests were invited to bring a microscope, a lamp and to provide interesting exhibits such as scientific novelties or apparatus.

Apothecaries were educated and respectable but the examination system for the medical profession remained muddled. The Medical Act of 1858, even after it had been amended, failed to establish a uniform standard of examination. There remained nineteen different licensing corporations in England, Scotland and Ireland each with its particular idiosyncracies and standards. Both Wakley in the *Lancet* and the National Association of General Practitioners pressed for a conjoint examination to give uniformity to medical education. Although the 1858 Medical Act did not achieve this, it sanctioned the concept, and in 1870 the Society came very close to forming a conjoint examining board with the two Royal Colleges. As the result of a nudge from the G.M.C., the Royal College of Physicians produced a comprehensive but complicated scheme for conjoint examinations, followed by a second scheme involving just the two Royal Colleges and the Society of Apothecaries. The Master relayed the invitation to a receptive Court and a deputation was formed to arrange and establish a conjoint board to examine in medicine, surgery and midwifery. By March 1871 the plan allocated exams in medicine to the Royal College of Physicians and the Society of Apothecaries, anatomy and physiology were to be the province of the two Royal Colleges, midwifery exams were to be conducted by the Surgeons and Apothecaries, *materia medica*, medical botany, pharmacy, chemistry and forensic medicine by the Physicians and Apothecaries. Fees were agreed, the number of examiners fixed and the whole was sanctioned and approved by the Apothecaries' Court of Assistants.[31] The Society's lawyers then found an obstacle: the conjoint scheme was beyond the scope of the Society's powers as defined by the Act of 1815. So the Royal Colleges proceeded with their plans, excluding the Society of Apothecaries. These "grave circumstances which now threaten the very existence of the Society as an examining body"[32] prompted protests to the G.M.C. and efforts to repeal the restrictive clauses of the Apothecaries' Act, achieved by Act of Parliament in 1874. For the moment the government stalled, waiting on the report of a Royal Commission on medical legislation.

The Society's Court of Examiners in 1880. Back row left to right: Dr Burges, Dr Crocker, Dr Hensley, Dr Taylor, Dr Thorowgood, Dr Lavies, Dr Fowler, Dr Savage. Front row left to right: Dr Sherwood Stocker, T.R. Wheeler Esqre (Secretary), Dr Semple (Chairman), Dr Randall, Henry Bullock Esqre F.R.C.S.

The Royal Colleges of Physicians and Surgeons took the matter into their own hands, establishing a conjoint scheme and holding the first examinations for the L.R.C.P and M.R.C.S. in January 1885.

In common with other livery companies the Apothecaries were threatened by the Royal Commission of 1880–84, appointed to enquire into the wealth and usefulness (or not) of what many suspected were merely self-indulgent dining clubs: the concluding report pronounced thirteen City livery companies extinct. With its existence as a livery company under scrutiny, the Society was at the same time in danger of being eliminated as a medical licensing body by the formidable alliance of the Royal Colleges and by the provisions of the 1886 Medical Act. The Clerk approached the universities, hoping to join forces as an examining board, and when that failed, applied to the G.M.C. for permission to hold examinations in surgery as well as medicine and midwifery in order to comply with the Medical Act of 1886. The Apothecaries' Examiners had long been in favour of an examination in surgery, insisting on an exam in the subject from January 1885, and surgical and medical scholarships were offered from the winter of 1883–84. Midwifery, henceforward one of the three subjects of the new qualification under the 1886 Medical Act, had been promoted as an essential element of the Society's curriculum since 1827, so in some respects the Society could claim to have pre-empted the 1886 Medical Act.[33]

In promoting surgery and midwifery in addition to medicine, the Examiners were in line with, or even ahead of, current thinking. Be that as it may, the Society struggled to maintain its place as an independent licensing body. It was only by raising a petition with the overwhelming support of licentiates, by the appointment of special Examiners in surgery and by the forceful representation of Robert Brudenell Carter to the G.M.C.[34] that the Society emerged unscathed by the events of the 1880s. The Society had rallied and pursued an independent course but it had suffered a snub from the Royal Colleges. Its overtures had been finally and firmly rejected in a letter to the Master: "a combination of the two Colleges with the Society of Apothecaries, is, for examination purposes, unnecessary, and in the unanimous opinion of the committee, is also undesirable". By way of response, the Society made it clear it would compete – undoubtedly the case for as long as its examination fee stood at 6 guineas, compared to a fee of some 35 guineas charged by the Conjoint Board. After canvassing the universities (unsuccessfully), the Society bolstered its position by securing new Examiners in surgery, by vigorously opposing the proposed new charter for the Royal Colleges and by building examination rooms behind the Hall, although they hardly compared with those opened by the Physicians in 1886.[35]

A Royal Commission of 1882 had stressed the value to medical students of a broad education and in the wake of these recommendations the Society's

Preliminary Arts Exam gained in popularity, the number of candidates increasing from 201 in 1885 to 755 in 1887 with a corresponding increase in Examiners and Assistant Examiners to seventeen. The Arts Exam reached a peak of popularity in the 1880s when candidates wrote papers on the English language, English history and modern geography, Latin, maths and elementary mechanics, and chose an optional subject – French, German, Greek or elementary chemistry. The Society was obliged to prune the syllabus in 1885 by eliminating English history and modern geography, and new regulations of 1893 further refined the exam to English, Latin, arithmetic, algebra, geometry and an optional language or logic. The large number of candidates taking the Arts Exam was a clear sign of its popularity, yet the failure rate was high (fifty-seven out of ninety-one failed the compulsory subjects in 1893, although they could re-take). Administrative costs meant the Examiners made a loss of £91 on the Arts Exam in that year and with the number of candidates falling in the 1890s, the G.M.C. recommended that it be discontinued, a point that was finally conceded in December 1895.[36]

The G.M.C.'s education committee was making its presence felt. It launched an enquiry into the conduct of the conjoint exam of the Royal Colleges as well as the Society's exams. The Society objected strongly to the abolition of its Arts Exam and the Royal College of Physicians registered disquiet at the harassment of the licensing bodies by the Council, to no avail.[36] Along with the disappearance of the Arts Exam, the Society faced a decline in the number of candidates sitting its professional examinations: the conjoint exam of the Royal Colleges had greater appeal (over 80 per cent of registered medical students took it in 1890). The Society's Examiners claimed this was because the conjoint exam was easier, so they sought to make their own more attractive. Botany, once one of the Apothecaries' chief interests was abandoned as a subject for examination and prizes, as were the examinations and prizes in *materia medica* and pharmaceutical chemistry (1895). On a more positive note, emphasis was given to the Apothecaries' Assistants' exam by the appointment of a special board of Examiners (1892), a new certificate in mental science was under discussion and it was resolved to recruit teachers at the medical schools as new Examiners.[37] A few years later revised regulations had to be issued in line with the G.M.C.'s insistence on a longer, five-year curriculum for medical students from January 1896 (officially marking the demise of the five-year apprenticeship).

When C.R.B. Barrett concluded the first history of the Society in 1904 there were three bodies in London granting the triple Diploma in Medicine, Surgery and Midwifery: the University, the Conjoint Board of the Royal Colleges and the Society of Apothecaries.[38] All students underwent the same course of study at the medical schools and the Society's Examiners were drawn from those schools. The exams at the Hall were divided into the primary (held quarterly) and finals (monthly), when patients were imported from hospitals to test the students' clinical skills – some concern was expressed regarding patients' resilience to withstand the ordeal. The clinical exams were held in the Great Hall, the operative and pathological parts in the Brande and Wheeler rooms – the grand surroundings were thought to have a good effect on the candidates by impressing them "with the dignity and importance of the Society whose diplomas they are anxious to obtain." In other respects, Apothecaries' Hall was not the ideal location for examinations: young women employed by the tenants were liable to flirt with the examinees by leaning out of the windows and showing "a great deal of black stocking", which was roundly condemned.[39]

Unlicensed practitioners
Although the examinations at Apothecaries' Hall gave medical practitioners a recognized qualification and initials after their names, they were still not permitted to charge a fee for medical advice or attendance, only for medicines. This deprivation and the economic encroachments of chemists and druggists were longstanding grievances which the Apothecaries' Act had failed to redress. The absurdity of the financial arrangement between apothecary and patient was illustrated by the case of "Old Q", fourth Duke of Queensberry, a wealthy rogue who died in 1810. For the last seven and a half years of his life he insisted on the personal attendance of his Apothecary, Mr Fuller, who made a claim to the executors for £10,000 to cover 9,340 visits and 1,700 nights at the late Duke's house in Piccadilly. The verdict was in the plaintiff's favour, although the Judge made the point that this was an exceptional case and an apothecary did not generally have a claim to payment for attendance.[40]

It was another twenty years before the issue was resolved conclusively by the case of James Handey, a surgeon and apothecary of Waterloo Bridge Road, who sought to recover £7 0s 6d from a patient for medicines and attendance. The verdict in this case gave legal recognition to an apothecary's right to a fee for medical advice and treatment, acknowledging the professional status of the dispensing apothecary/general practitioner as distinct from the chemist/druggist. The right to charge a fee removed the temptation to which apothecaries were prone – of supplying rivers of mixtures and mountains of pills in order to recover expenses.[41]

The legal right to charge fees gave the apothecary professional dignity and distinguished him from chemists and druggists. Nevertheless, chemists and druggists remained a section of the medical profession until effectively excluded by the Medical Registration Act of 1858. Their reputation had improved with the founding of both the Chemical Society and the Pharmaceutical Society of Great Britain in 1841. The Society's Chemical

Operator from 1842 to 1866, Robert Warington, was the moving spirit behind and Secretary of the Chemical Society, and the Society's Professor of Chemistry, W.T. Brande, was President (1847–49).[42] Brande was also closely involved with the Pharmaceutical Society which had been founded by Jacob Bell, the owner of a famous pharmaceutical business. The Society had no objections to the Chemical Society but the Pharmaceutical Society posed a threat as a new examining body. While condoning the better education of chemists and druggists generally, the Court of Assistants wished to see this achieved "without the formation of a new body which appears to the Society not only to be unnecessary but in many respects highly objectionable".[43] With the establishment of the Pharmaceutical Society, the Apothecaries made a point of re-naming their awards in *materia medica* and pharmaceutical chemistry (previously referred to as *materia medica* and therapeutics), and asserted the Society's position by successfully prosecuting a chemist and druggist called Greenough of St Helens for practising as an apothecary in 1841. He was reported to have attended over 300 patients (one had died while undergoing treatment), yet he possessed no formal qualification. A decade later the Society reinforced its stand against chemists and druggists by firmly opposing the Pharmacy Bill; the Pharmaceutical Society took revenge by excluding licentiates from its membership.[44]

The pharmaceutical chemists went from strength to strength: the Pharmaceutical Society obtained a royal charter in 1843; a School of Pharmacy with Jonathan Pereira L.S.A. as the first Professor of *materia medica* advanced the education of chemists and druggists, as did the foundation of the Royal College of Chemistry in 1845. These developments marked the separation of pharmacy from medicine and henceforward pharmacy formed a distinct profession with its own discipline and organization, raising problems for the Apothecaries' Assistants in the next century (see Chapter 8, pages 229–35).

There remained a scattered bunch of disreputable, unqualified chemists, druggists and medical practitioners who constituted a danger to the public. The Act of 1815 had specified that an apothecary/druggist/chemist practising medicine without the Licence granted by the Society was liable to a penalty of £20, but the enforcement of this clause was a duty the Society found difficult to fulfil. Cheats and impersonators who presented themselves for examination at the Hall were relatively easy to detect and bring to book – as was a teacher who tried to steal exam papers from the printer.[45] The unlicensed medical men of England and Wales were harder to trace and the process could be lengthy and expensive. George M. Burrows alleged that in its approach to unlicensed practitioners "the fear of expense pervades every determination and paralyzes all energy" on the part of the Society.[46] Reacting to this criticism the Society instigated the first prosecution under the Act in 1818. The costs were not recovered but the action was productive in that the accused took the Society's exam and passed at the second attempt. A report of 1825 emphasized not the expense so much as the practical difficulties in pursuing unlicensed practitioners: in the previous ten years there had been sixteen successful prosecutions, chiefly in the provinces. In many other instances, however, the endeavours of the Society had been frustrated by the unwillingness of parties to give evidence or come forward as witnesses. The Clerk, R.B. Upton, confirmed that one of the flaws of the Apothecaries' Act was the lack of effective machinery to pursue, check and fine unqualified persons. It was beyond the Society's power to institute frequent prosecutions so it had to be content with making an example of an individual from time to time.[47] Sometimes an admonitory letter was a sufficient deterrent and the offender relinquished their practice, promised to quit or agreed to sit the examination. Alternatively, witnesses were called and evidence produced – the Clerk's notes record how unsatisfactory this was: "evidence not furnished", "no evidence found", "too insignificant" or occasionally "action taken" which could entail expensive legal proceedings.[48]

The Society pressed for effective legislation aimed at unqualified practitioners and in the meantime encouraged licentiates to act as informers. Rival practitioners were the usual source of a complaint, and it then fell to the Apothecaries' Clerk to investigate the matter, usually with difficulty. John Nussey told the Select Committee of 1834 that the Society had only recovered £130 in penalties from unlicensed practitioners since 1815, and he cited a recent prosecution that had cost the Society £400. It was therefore not surprising that the Society "had no occasion to be over-active in making inquiries".[49]

The case of William Rowe, a chemist and druggist of Devonport who misdiagnosed and mistreated Mrs Munro, resulting in her death, attracted the attention of the Press, chiefly because Rowe went free. An editorial in the *Lancet* of 17 October 1846 drew attention to the fact that offenders such as Rowe could not be dealt with successfully by criminal indictments: "the Apothecaries' Society has the onus for prevention and punishment. They are the only persons empowered by law to prevent and punish the unqualified who attempt at general practice". Wakley went on to accuse the Master, Wardens and Assistants of "blameworthy supineness in enforcing the powers with which they are entrusted".[50]

Conscious that accusations of failure were valid yet lacking adequate means of restraint, the Apothecaries took legal advice and subsequently encouraged others to institute prosecutions against unlicensed practitioners.[51] The situation eased once the Medical Act of 1858 demanded the registration of qualified practitioners, although there was still no penal restraint on the unqualified. The various general practitioners' associations took steps against individual unqualified persons, in particular the Medical Defence Association

Watercolour of the west elevation of Apothecaries' Hall by T.H. Shepherd (1855).

persuaded the Society to institute a series of prosecutions against chemists and druggists in the 1870s. For a time it seemed that open warfare was being conducted in the courts by the Society of Apothecaries on behalf of the Medical Defence Association and by the Pharmaceutical Society representing the Chemist and Druggists' Trade Association -a truce was called in 1878. Meanwhile the Society's internal discipline stiffened with the power to strike off its list of licentiates anyone found guilty in a court of law of infamous conduct – an Apothecary in a Lancashire gaol provided an immediate target.[52]

Unlicensed practitioners found themselves increasingly isolated – by medical registration, by disqualification from appointment by the Poor Law Commissioners, in the army, navy and East India Company, and by the possibility of prosecution. Nevertheless, members of the public still resorted to unqualified practitioners when and where there was a shortage of qualified men, and there would always be some who did not conform to the system, whether they called themselves apothecaries, bone-setters, faith-healers or herbalists.[53] Those styling themselves apothecaries trod on dangerous ground, and the description continued to be jealously guarded.

Towards reform

The Society's Act of Parliament Committee was quick to point out the defects of the Apothecaries' Act. The Court of Assistants, however, preferred to proceed cautiously for the first ten years. Then in 1825 the Society petitioned the House of Commons for revisions and, although the Bill encountered difficulties, temporary amendments to the Act were secured. Most importantly, practising naval surgeons and apothecaries to the army and the East India Company were given exemption from the Society's examinations, but graduates of the Scottish universities were not.[54]

There was pressure from all sides for reform, beginning with the accoucheurs of London and Westminster who in 1826 urged the Society to take responsibility for regulating the practice of midwifery. The Society was sympathetic and consistently stressed the importance of midwifery as one of the most important branches of the general practice of an Apothecary. As yet, however, legal opinion decided that examination in the subject lay outside the Society's powers. The best that could be done was to insist that candidates for the Licence answered questions on the subject as part of the examination in anatomy and physiology. When the Royal College of Surgeons instituted an optional Diploma in Midwifery in 1852 the Society's Examiners were outraged at the impudence. They raised their serious objections to this invasion of their domain in a memorandum to Lord Palmerston, Secretary of State at the Home Office, and altered the wording of the Society's certificate making it clear that its qualification was in the science and practice of medicine and midwifery.[55] More than thirty years later the Medical Act sanctioned midwifery as part of the new triple qualification.

Like the accoucheurs and the Obstetrical Society, the general practitioners' associations looked to the Society to support their cause and to instigate reforms. In principle the Society chose not to initiate medical legislation, preferring instead to give its support to the large body of general practitioners it had been instrumental in educating, acting as a mouthpiece and representing their interests in the political arena.

Reform, including medical reform, was high on the political agenda during the 1830s and 1840s. The Reform Act of 1832 extended the franchise and the Whig government went on to investigate municipal corporations and to threaten the livery franchise. The Royal Commission on Municipal Corporations (1833–34) examined the activities of the City, compelling the Apothecaries' Clerk to submit a statement of income and expenditure, details of membership and other statistics. At the same time, eminent members of the Society were called to give evidence to the Select Committee on Medical Education (the Warburton Committee, dealing with many aspects of the medical profession). As might be expected, medical education and reform were the issues that engrossed the Society's Act of Parliament Committee under the leadership of William Simons, J.G. Ridout F.L.S. and John Bacot (all at one time or another on the Court of Examiners and Masters). The Clerk, R.B. Upton, also took a keen interest in the various proposals for medical reform and issued a statement of the Society's position in 1844 (see below).

By the 1830s the general practitioner was identified by the initials M.R.C.S. and L.S.A after his name: in 1834 it was estimated that over one half of the Society's licentiates also held the M.R.C.S. The dual qualification was known as "the College and Hall" and it identified the general practitioner. Dr John Jobling in *Martin Chuzzlewit* stood as Dickens's example of the properly qualified, socially acceptable, immaculately dressed general practitioner as distinct from the poor village apothecary/grocer: "We know a few secrets of nature in our profession, sir. Of course we do. We study for that; we pass the Hall and the College for that; and we take our station in society *by* that".[56]

Medical practitioners qualified by the "College and Hall" formed local and national associations to promote their interests: the Metropolitan Society of General Practitioners (1830), the first British Medical Association (1836) and its more permanent successor founded in 1856, and the National Association of General Practitioners (1844), which hoped to establish a royal college. The Society of Apothecaries, taking pride in the fact that it had been largely responsible for providing some 10,000 well-educated practitioners dispersed throughout the country by 1842, gave its wholehearted support to the general practitioners' efforts to establish a new corporation with a royal charter. Between 1844 and 1845 this came close to fruition – there were simultaneous proposals for a Royal College of Apothecaries and Wakley alleged that a National Institute of Medicine, Surgery and Midwifery was about to be spawned as an offshoot of the Society.[57] As with the rest of the proposed medical reforms of the 1840s, these plans failed to materialize and it was not until 1952 that the Royal College of General Practitioners was founded and given temporary accommodation at Apothecaries' Hall. Nevertheless, the episode emphasized the identical interests of the Society of Apothecaries and general practitioners; it also demonstrated the pioneering yet self-effacing character of the Society: on this occasion and on many subsequent issues the Society, having done the groundwork, relinquished responsibility to a larger corporation.

Those giving evidence to the Warburton Committee on medical education in 1834 confirmed the beneficial effect of the Society's exams in raising the standard of education of medical practitioners. John Nussey, Royal Apothecary and later Master (1845–46), testified that the Society was an advocate of medical reform and wished to see several clauses of the Apothecaries' Act removed; on the national issue of medical education he spoke in favour of a uniform system. John Bacot, Chairman of the Court of Examiners at the time and later Master, told of the Society's consistent promotion of courses in midwifery.[58] For all of its three volumes of evidence (and more besides, lost in the fire that destroyed the Palace of Westminster in October 1834) the Warburton Committee failed to achieve any tangible reform of the medical profession.

Between 1840 and 1858 fifteen Bills aiming at the reform of the medical profession were presented to Parliament. Their tortured passage was closely tagged by the Society's Act of Parliament Committee which declared its deep interest in Sir James Graham's proposals and resolved to meet the subject of medical reform upon broad and liberal principles. During this period the Society and the Royal Colleges tabled an Amendment to the Act of 1815. Deputations from the Society consulted with Sir James Graham and Sir George Grey Bt at the Home Office in the 1840s, presenting the Society's views on medical reform and pushing for a college of general practitioners, and the Society's representatives took part in conferences with the other medical corporations to discuss reform. In 1844 the Clerk issued a printed statement which left no doubt that the Society advocated reforms to modify apprenticeship, to abolish searches of Apothecaries' shops and that it wanted to see a uniform system of medical education in England, Wales and Scotland. The Society was also in favour of the examination of general practitioners by their own profession and the introduction of a penal act to protect the public from unqualified practitioners.[59]

Thomas Wakley writing in the *Lancet* and voicing his opinions in the House of Commons from 1835, was sceptical. He did not believe the Apothecaries would agree to a full reciprocity of practice in the three kingdoms, alleging that the Society was bent on a punic war against their Irish and Scots brethren. The National Association of General Practitioners, on the other hand, paid tribute to the "enlightened policy" of the Society and applauded its conduct during the discussions on medical reform.[60]

The Crimean War then interrupted the movement towards medical reform and, when the subject was resumed, a compromise was reached with the existing medical corporations by establishing the G.M.C. (1858). The Medical Act of 1858 failed to secure a uniform standard of examination in the United Kingdom and failed to impose penal restraints on unlicensed practitioners. It did establish registration and the G.M.C., which after a languorous start and many amendments to the Act, assumed overall supervision of education for the medical profession. In so doing, it deprived the Society of Apothecaries of the leading role it had taken in medical education since 1815, although the Society remained a licensing body represented by one member on the Council. Past Master John Nussey, Apothecary to Queen Victoria, was elected as the Society's first representative, succeeded by George Cooper, who was to be Master for two successive years (1866–68). Cooper, a surgical dresser to the famous Astley Cooper, had taken the young John Keats under his wing many years before.

No-one denied the valuable contribution the Society had made to the education of the general practitioner during the preceding forty-three years. The Society had also been influential in raising standards of medical teaching at hospitals, dispensaries and medical schools in England and Wales. At the opening of the nineteenth century medical teaching in London was conducted in private, profit-making medical and anatomy schools such as the Great Windmill School, and at three hospitals – Bart's, the united St Thomas' and Guy's, and the London. With the creation of the L.S.A. in 1815 candidates were required to have completed at least six months at a hospital, infirmary or dispensary and there was consequently an increased number of students requiring instruction, leading to the expansion of medical schools. In 1814 thirty-eight medical students were under instruction by Physicians at seven London hospitals; in 1832 the number stood at 326. By 1858 there were twelve London hospitals with teaching schools attached – the London Hospital Medical College in Whitechapel, founded in 1785 through the efforts of Sir William Blizard, was the first complete medical school, and Charing Cross was the first hospital to open with the specific intention of teaching medicine (1831). The first provincial medical school was established at Manchester in 1824, followed in the 1830s by seven others scattered round the country. While the foundation of new hospitals and medical schools probably owed more to the Victorian ethos of improvement than to the Society of Apothecaries, there is no doubt that the Society's examinations had a stimulating effect on the teaching of medicine in England and Wales. The growing number of students aspiring to the L.S.A. had to be catered for and the Society wielded direct influence in the medical schools through its Examiners who inspected the hospital schools and dispensaries to ensure standards were adequate.

The Society accepted students' certificates of attendance at dispensaries as well as at hospitals – the dispensaries at Islington, Aldersgate Street and Carey Street were renowned as centres of medical teaching, and students in the provinces found instruction at local dispensaries where there were as yet no hospital medical schools – at York and Wakefield, for example. One licentiate, Jonathan Pereira, was pre-eminent in the education of medical students in *materia medica* and chemistry. As soon as he had obtained his certificate from the Society (in 1823 aged nineteen), he returned to his *alma mater*, the Aldersgate Street Dispensary to instruct. He went on to lecture in chemistry at the London Hospital, was the first Professor of *materia medica* to the Pharmaceutical Society, became a Fellow of both the Royal and the Linnean Societies, and his publication *The Elements of Materia Medica* (1839) became a classic. After his death in 1853 he was commemorated by the Pereira Medal, awarded by the Pharmaceutical Society for researches or proficiency in *materia medica*.

The University Dispensary opened in 1828, expanding to become University College Hospital and the first institution to provide a university education for general practitioners. It was closely followed by King's College, and the Society expressed approval of the latter by donating £300 towards its foundation. The Society's Examiners were included on the committee to arrange a plan of medical study for the University and the link was maintained by two members of the Court of Examiners having seats on the Senate. The year after the University Dispensary was founded the Examiners of Apothecaries' Hall visited the Royal Western Hospital to assess its competence as a school of practical medicine. It failed to comply with the Society's definition of a hospital even though it had 100 beds, and was for the meanwhile classified as a dispensary.[61] Similarly, in 1852 the Society's Examiners refused to accredit St Mary's, Paddington, as a teaching hospital because there was no Apothecary on the staff. Far from being negative, the Examiners expressed their "every wish to encourage the clinical teaching in this metropolis" and were happy to recognize St Mary's as a *bona fide* medical school as soon as it appointed a qualified resident Apothecary.[62] One of the first Examiners, John Ridout, testified to the Select Committee of 1834 that the Society deliberately encouraged the establishment of medical schools in the great provincial towns: "we have reason to believe that the establishment of those provincial schools has been of considerable advantage not only to the students but to the practitioners of medicine living in the neighbourhood".[63]

In accordance with this policy, the Society issued a list of recognized teachers and medical schools: in 1833 some 100 hospitals and forty-three schools were of an acceptable standard. The famous Great Windmill School, founded by William Hunter in 1770, survived until 1836 but by the 1860s the private schools had been superseded by the public hospitals and the attached medical schools.

The Society encouraged and influenced the medical schools and from 1874 recruited Examiners from their staff. The Apothecaries' Amendment Act of 1874 removed the condition that Examiners for the L.S.A. had to be members of the Society of ten years' standing, thus allowing teachers from the medical schools onto the Court of Examiners. The Act of 1874 also removed the necessity for a five-year apprenticeship as a prelude to the Apothecaries' Licence – the Society had never sought to impose this clause and had recommended its removal.

The example of the Society of Apothecaries stimulated the Royal College of Surgeons to reassess its qualification, resulting in its first printed curriculum issued in 1819. The Apothecaries of Dublin, granted a royal charter in 1745, also followed the example of those of Black Friars in establishing a laboratory and courses of lectures and granting certificates of competence. The Medical Act of 1858 recognized the Dublin Apothecaries' Hall as a licensing body but with the passage of the 1886 Act, the Dublin Hall Apothecaries, like those of Black Friars, were threatened with extinction. The G.M.C. sought a solution to such problems in the form of a conjoint board of the two Royal Colleges with the Apothecaries of Dublin and Black Friars. This was not to be: the Society at Black Friars clung to its qualification and Apothecaries' Hall Dublin conferred its own Diploma in Medicine, Surgery, Midwifery and Pharmacy (L.A.H. Dublin) until the 1970s.[64]

The Society in London was not averse to joining forces with the College of Physicians to promote the public interest or the education of medical students. Both institutions supported the Anatomy Act, petitioning for a legal supply of corpses for anatomical study. This new educational facility was achieved in 1832 and was a great improvement on previous arrangements with body-snatchers or "resurrection men".[65] The Society also sought the improvement of medical care aboard emigrant convoys to Australia (particularly with regard to pregnant women), recommending that all ships' surgeons should possess the Society's Licence. On another front, the Society petitioned that parish apothecaries caring for the poor up and down the country should be properly qualified.[66] The Society's influence was thus widely felt – in medical education, public health, in the drive for medical reform and in the medical schools and dispensaries of Victorian England. Individual licentiates also left their mark on the Victorian medical scene. The last Apothecary to Bart's, Frederick Wood, emerged as a hero when the dreaded cholera returned to the capital in 1848: he remained at his post while others fled and was reputed to have seen between 100 and 350 patients each day. His contemporary, another practitioner qualified by the "College and Hall", John Snow, was also instrumental in the fight against cholera. His investigations demonstrated that diseases such as cholera could be transmitted by contaminated water and, although his publication *On the mode of communication of cholera* (1849) did not prevent later outbreaks, Snow's work was central to the improvement of health and sanitation in Victorian England. Snow later transferred his attention to the scientific use of chloroform, which he twice administered to Queen Victoria during childbirth (he also anaesthetized Professor Brande).

One young recipient of the Society's botany prize, Sir William Jenner Bt F.R.S., achieved fame for his work on typhoid and typhus fever (1850). His expertise brought him to the bedside of the fading Prince Albert and he was appointed Physician to the Queen the following year. Another licentiate, John Hughlings Jackson F.R.S., was revered as "the father of English neurology"; he was also renowned for his eccentric reading habits – he tore up and discarded the books he read, page by page.

The culmination of the nineteenth-century movement for medical reform came in the 1880s with the foundation of the Conjoint Examining Board and the Medical Act Amendment Act. The Society of Apothecaries was excluded from the Conjoint Board, yet survived the snub and maintained its status as an independent licensing body. When the Medical Act Amendment Act was mooted in 1883 the Society raised no objection in principle until it discovered that it was to be denied a representative on the reformed Medical Council.

The Court of Assistants (1899–1900). Back row left to right: J.B. Baker, John Charles Thorowgood, Edwd Parker Young, Albert Bryan Day, Clarence Cooper, Henry Veasey, James Richard Upton (centre), J.S. Burton, William Parson, C.H. Slaughter, S.A. Richards, R.B. Wall, James Henry Jeffcoat. Front row left to right: Edward Tegart, J.R. Withecombe, Samuel Clewin Griffith, William Shillito, Charles Brownes (Senior Warden), Sherwood Stocker (Master), T.E. Burton Brown (Junior Warden), J.W. Robinson, F.R. Gibbes.

Action was immediate and a petition against the Bill was drafted registering the Society's sense of injustice. The Rt Hon Henry Fawcett M.P. and Sir Trevor Lawrence took up the Society's cause in the Commons, a deputation from the Society confronted the Marquis of Salisbury as Lord President, the Rt Hon A. Mundella, Vice President of the Privy Council was approached and Robert Brudenell Carter put the Society's case to the G.M.C. These efforts resulted in success. The Society secured its seat on the enlarged G.M.C. and obtained permission to appoint three Examiners in surgery, enabling it to offer the new qualification in Medicine, Surgery and Midwifery. And so the Society "continued in its present satisfactory position as one of the great Examining bodies of this country".[67]

Chapter 8

The twentieth century

The Society of Apothecaries had been threatened on three fronts in the late nineteenth century. Firstly, its role as a medical licensing body was undermined by the alliance of the Royal Colleges in forming a Conjoint Examining Board, excluding the Apothecaries. Secondly, the trading activities carried on at the Hall by the United Stock went into liquidation at the end of 1880, at which point the Society took over the precarious trade at its own risk. Thirdly, as a City livery company, the Society found its affairs being scrutinized by the Royal Commission investigating livery companies generally. Remarkably, the Society survived on all counts: it continued to act as an independent licensing body for the medical profession and it maintained the trade at the Hall until 1922, as well as justifying its existence as a City livery company to the Commissioners.

The Society weathered the vicissitudes of the late nineteenth century but the future was not promising. Following the Boer War the country was gripped by an economic depression which adversely affected trade at the Hall. The Clerk for the last twenty-eight years, J.R. Upton, died suddenly in India in 1901 and three years later the unexpected death of William Chattaway, General Superintendent of the trade at the Hall, left a gap that was not filled. Worse was to come when Upton's successor as Clerk, his son Archer Mowbray Upton, disappeared. The Master was surprised to receive official notification that an order in bankruptcy had been filed against A.M. Upton and Co, the firm of solicitors headed by the errant Clerk. Upton re-appeared only to face charges of converting to his own use sums amounting to over £12,000, for which he was sentenced in the central criminal court to five years' penal servitude (1916). The Society lost an officer it had trusted and was relieved to find that its funds were untouched by Upton, whose disgrace terminated his family's eighty-two years' association with the Society.[1]

On a more positive note, the Society obtained an Act of Parliament in 1907, altering the title of the L.S.A. to L.M.S.S.A. to give a more accurate description of the qualification. There was much discussion in the early years of the century about titles and distinctions, arising from the case of a licentiate, H.K. Hunter, who was prosecuted for calling himself a Physician. Although he lost his case, Counsel's opinion was that the description Physician or Surgeon was legitimate for licentiates of the Society of Apothecaries. This prompted the formation of the Association of Physicians and Surgeons in 1902, a core group within the Society led by Dr A. Rivers Willson as President. It was he who first proposed an alteration in the wording of the Society's Licence to indicate the legal qualification of licence-holders in medicine, surgery and midwifery. The proposal was approved by the Court of Assistants and

Sir Thomas Boor Crosby, Master of the Society and Lord Mayor (1911–12). He had previously been Master of the Turners' Company.

supported by 767 licentiates who signed a petition forwarded to the G.M.C. The necessity for an Act of Parliament caused delay and expense (£500 – of which half was raised by the Association of Physicians and Surgeons, with the remainder coming from the funds of the Court of Examiners), and by the time the new licence was authorized it had been abbreviated to Licentiate in Medicine and Surgery of the Society of Apothecaries.[2]

Efforts to obtain the prefix Royal for the Society (1897, 1901 and recurring) and the title of Fellow for selected members were not successful, but there was the gratification of the election of Sir Thomas Boor Crosby as Master and Lord Mayor in 1911. He had been Master of the Turners' Company (1900–01), and was admitted to the freedom of the Society of Apothecaries by redemption in 1906 (he had been a licentiate since 1852). Strangely, Crosby refused a call to the Livery in 1909, yet was not averse to taking the fast track to the Mastership two years later to coincide with his mayoralty. Dr Arthur Long, who in the normal course of events had expected to be Master for the year, gallantly stood aside "for the benefit of the Society", fulfilling instead the position of Deputy Master. This allowed Sir Thomas Crosby to be elected Master shortly after Lord Mayor's Day in November 1911. At the advanced age of eighty-two he was the first Physician to be Lord Mayor. His year of office saw the sinking of the Titanic and a coal strike that threatened to develop into a national disaster.[3]

Dispensers of medicines
Traditionally an apothecary kept a store of spices, herbs and drugs which he prepared, compounded, dispensed and sold. His role developed over centuries into that of general medical practitioner yet he refused to sacrifice his right to dispense medicines. During the first decades of the twentieth century the Society fought to preserve this right and mounted a vigorous campaign to defend the position of Apothecaries' Assistants who were being displaced and relegated to a lower order by qualified pharmacists.

Among its many provisions, the Apothecaries' Act of 1815 made the Society responsible for the education and examination of Apothecaries' Assistants (dispensers). It formalized the existing arrangement whereby an Apothecary trained his assistant, by instituting an oral examination which qualified the Assistant as competent to translate and dispense prescriptions. The navy had recognized the value of Apothecaries' Assistants, under the title of Dispensers, from 1713, possibly earlier. They had to be men who were "bred Apothecarys . . . capable of making and Compounding all things usually made and Compounded by People of that Profession". The Dispensers' duties at the naval hospitals were defined by instructions of 1742 and there are instances of the examination of potential Dispensers and Assistant Dispensers by the Court of the Society of Apothecaries in the mid-eighteenth century. Once armed with the qualification from Apothecaries' Hall, Dispensers held respected positions at the large naval hospitals such as Greenwich and Haslar.[4]

The Apothecaries' Act of 1815 made it compulsory for those intending to qualify as Apothecaries' Assistants to take an examination testing their ability to translate parts of the *Pharmacopoeia Londinensis*, Physicians' prescriptions, their knowledge of pharmacy and *materia medica*; if successful the candidate obtained a certificate. To begin with few thought the qualification necessary: between 1815 and 1834 not more than eight applied to take the exam; there were only two candidates in 1858, rising to seventy-seven in 1888.[5]

From the middle years of the nineteenth century pharmacists were being trained at the Pharmaceutical Society's School of Pharmacy, or in prosperous businesses such as the Plough Court Pharmacy or John Bell's in Oxford Street. By the early 1900s there were several educational institutions in London offering courses in pharmacy leading to qualification and registration by the Pharmaceutical Society. Thus qualified pharmacists replaced the hospital apothecary and, with the backing of the Pharmaceutical Society, they formed an expanding, well-qualified profession. Nevertheless, general practitioners dispensing their own medicines still needed Apothecaries' Assistants, as did dispensaries and public institutions throughout the country. "Lady Dispenser (Hall)" appeared frequently in the situations vacant column of the *Chemist and Druggist* – it was a post suited to a young lady willing to work as the handmaiden of the doctor for little pecuniary reward. Particularly during the First World War women dispensers were in great demand owing to the shortage of manpower. The Assistants' certificate, known as "Hall", was the best adapted for this purpose for it offered a qualification to young women of sound general education who could produce proof of six months' instruction in practical pharmacy, for a modest fee of 3 guineas.[6]

Early-twentieth-century legislation did not deal kindly with Apothecaries' Assistants, favouring instead the qualified pharmacist. The Poisons and Pharmacy Act of 1908 limited the compounding of certain medicines to pharmacists who had taken the examination of the Pharmaceutical Society at the age of twenty-one or over, having three years' practical experience behind them. The Society had opposed the Bill vehemently as "an irreparable and unjustifiable injury", and the Act of Parliament Committee was instructed to take all necessary steps to prevent it becoming law on the grounds that it would marginalize the many holders of the Assistants' certificate employed by practitioners, public dispensaries, hospitals, poor law institutions and shops.[7] The pharmacists won the day when the Act was passed in 1908, although a by-law provided a loop-hole (if it could be enforced) allowing the possibility of registration for Apothecaries' Assistants, and military and colonial Dispensers.

Three years later Lloyd George's National Health Insurance Act dealt a second blow to Apothecaries' Assistants and imposed severe restrictions on general practitioners' traditional and lucrative role as dispensers. Modelled on the German example, the Act extended state medical care by compulsory health insurance for working people earning up to £150 a year. Their health was thenceforward entrusted to "panel doctors" who were paid 7s 6d per patient but at the same time were deprived of their right to dispense medicines, except in rural areas where a chemist was inaccessible. Highly contentious at first, the Act proved acceptable to most general practitioners who stood to benefit from a secure income from the state and who might continue with private dispensing. Apothecaries' Assistants, on the other hand, had nothing to gain because the Act of 1911 placed the supply of medicines and drugs for insured patients in the hands of qualified chemists and pharmacists. For this reason, and because the proposals challenged "the supremacy of the Society in matters relating to dispensing", the Apothecaries and the British Medical Association opposed the National Health Insurance Bill. The Apothecaries received an evasive reply to their objections from Lloyd George, and the B.M.A. threatened to boycott the Act when it came into operation in 1912.[8]

Forced to accept the National Health Insurance Act, the Society continued to complain about its provisions, particularly the supervisory authority of the Insurance Commissioners who "interfere injuriously with the rights and proper independence of the medical profession".[9] In time general practitioners and their associations found the Act workable and the bulk of private dispensing remained in the hands of local practitioners and their Assistants. Nonetheless, the Act did severely limit employment opportunities for Apothecaries' Assistants. Disconcerted by state interference, the Society considered a Bill in Parliament to extend its powers to examine and grant certificates for dispensing medicines (1913).[10]

At the outbreak of the First World War the Society was deadlocked with the Pharmaceutical Society over the issue, its overtures having met with "a very evident feeling of hostility".[11] While the Pharmaceutical Society acknowledged the ability of the Society of Apothecaries to determine the fitness of a person to act as an Apothecary or an Apothecary's Assistant, the Pharmaceutical Society decreed that it alone was "by knowledge and experience the proper body to judge the fitness of a person to conduct a pharmacy".[12] Such persons were qualified pharmacists, not Apothecaries' Assistants, to whom there were to be no concessions. Nor was there much hope for the future of the trade at the Hall with the prospect of war and a profit of only £46 8s for 1912–13. By 1914 part of the Society's premises on Water Lane was being demolished, and all public entertainments at the Hall were cancelled during the First World War apart from a breakfast held on 6 December 1917 to commemorate the tercentenary of the granting of the charter. Students aspiring to take the Society's Diploma profited by some leniency owing to the shortage of teaching

The Society's fire brigade in the courtyard at the Hall (1913). One of the helmets worn by members of the brigade survives.

staff, although the exams for Assistants were extended in 1918 as part of the drive to improve their status.[13]

Apothecaries' Hall escaped the air-raid that damaged Ironmongers' Hall in July 1917, but on Whitsunday the following year during the last raid by German planes shrapnel from anti-aircraft guns damaged the Parlour window and a skylight over the retail shop. At the conclusion of the Great War a roll of honour was inscribed with the names of members who served in the forces and the Court of Assistants recorded its "profound thankfulness to Almighty God" for victory.[14]

The World War was over; the contest with the Pharmaceutical Society was not. The Master was informed by the Director General of Medical Services that only pharmacists were to be employed in the larger hospitals and that the Society's request for Apothecaries' Assistants to be on the same footing was not acceded to. The Society then sought to find a way forward for its Assistants through a by-law allowing their conditional registration. The prospect aroused strong feelings between the Society of Apothecaries and the Pharmaceutical Society, as well as within the ranks of dispensers. The pharmacists regarded Apothecaries' Assistants as second-rate and ridiculed them, and some pressed for the Pharmaceutical Society to establish its own Assistants' exam to make the Apothecaries' certificate redundant. At a rowdy meeting of some 700 to 800 members of the Pharmaceutical Society in the summer of 1919 the question of whether to allow Apothecaries' Asssistants onto the register and on what terms was debated. The pharmacists alleged this would dilute the register and cheapen the qualification, so would only allow the Apothecaries' Assistants a small window for advancement: admission to the register without examination after seven years' continuous employment in an approved establishment. The concession was of limited duration and cost 14 guineas an applicant. By 1921 only fifty-two Apothecaries' Assistants had taken up the offer.[15]

There remained a large number of women who were content to take the Assistants' certificate offered by Apothecaries' Hall – those who wanted to earn a little without a long period of training and who were resigned to working under the supervision of a doctor or pharmacist for a low wage. In 1917 nine men and 233 women registered for the Apothecaries' Assistants' examination, among them Agatha Mary Clarissa Christie. As part of the war effort Agatha Christie worked first as a nurse and then in the Dispensary of the Red Cross Hospital in Torquay (1917–18). She was instructed by the pharmacists there, enabling her to take the Apothecaries' Assistants' examination at the Hall. Once qualified, she returned to the Red Cross Dispensary and, when not busy, started to draft her first detective story, *The Mysterious Affair at Styles*, published after several rejections in 1920. As Dame Agatha's readers know, poisons were her speciality and in her first story she demonstrated her knowledge of drug incompatibility (strychnine and bromide) which together caused the death of Mrs Inglethorpe.[16]

During the year 1920–21 the Clerk estimated that between 5,000 and 6,000 men and women held the Apothecaries' Assistants' certificate; some of them worked in 155 different public hospitals and institutions, others worked under the supervision of private doctors and for pharmacists. These statistics were gathered and used with other arguments in the continuing drive to improve the dispensers' position and training. The Society even contemplated instituting a school of dispensing or pharmacology, but took the less radical step of adding a practical exam in chemistry to the Assistants' syllabus.[17]

The Dangerous Drugs Acts (1920, 1922) and the Poisons Amendment Act (1923) exacerbated the difficulties of Assistants, who were not permitted to purchase cocaine or opium for use in the dispensaries or institutions where they worked. Mr Graham Bott of the Association of Certified Dispensers of Apothecaries' Hall took an aggressive stance, pressing for a Bill in Parliament and a statutory register to make Apothecaries' Assistants eligible for appointments under the terms of the recent restrictive legislation. Bott argued (with some foresight) that, if nothing was done, the powers of the Society with regard to dispensing would in time be abrogated by the Pharmaceutical Society. Sir George Buchanan at the Ministry of Health (he was to be Master of the Society on his retirement in 1934) was not encouraging and Bott's campaign was brought to a halt in 1923 with a statement from the Master acknowledging the need to improve the status of Apothecaries' Assistants but not by legislation. It had to be recognized that the Society's certificate was not as rigorous as the Pharmaceutical Society's qualification and there was no point extending the Assistants' course merely to flood the market with dispensers. He offered the solace that the Society was performing a public utility by "meeting the requirements of large numbers of young women who cannot afford or do not wish to spend three years training, who want to earn as soon after leaving school as possible".[18] When the provisions of the National Health Insurance Act were reviewed by a Royal Commission (1924–26) the Apothecaries' Assistants were put in their place by the Commissioners' declaration that their certificate was inferior to that of a registered pharmacist.[19]

The discovery of new remedies and drugs such as salvarsan in the early years of the century, followed by the emergence of modern pharmaceuticals in the 1930s and the subsequent expansion of the drug industry, demanded greater scientific and academic knowledge and a training that exceeded the scope of the Society of Apothecaries' Assistants' exam (the ambitious and clever could always undergo further training to make them eligible for the qualification of the Pharmaceutical Society). Shortly before the introduction of the National Health Service in 1948 the Society was awarding an annual average of 151 Assistants' certificates but the extension of state medical care led to a fall in the dispensing of private medicines to less than 10 per cent. It was not therefore surprising that the annual average of certificates issued from the Hall fell to forty-nine in the 1950s.[20]

The change of name to Dispensing Assistants, a tougher exam and the founding of the Apothecaries' Hall Dispensers' Association raised standards and status during the 1950s and 1960s. The examination regulations for 1960 specified a one-hour written paper and an oral exam in pharmacy, a two-hour practical exam, a written paper and an oral in *materia medica*, all of which had to have been preceded by a minimum course of 120 hours of part-time or evening classes.[21] However, the pharmacists' qualification was extended in parallel to cater for the wider range and complexity of drugs on the market, and from 1967 pharmacy became a profession composed of graduates.

The certificate from Apothecaries' Hall then faced competition from the City and Guilds Institute offering an easier and cheaper exam. The situation became more complicated with the founding of the Business Technical Education Council and later the National Vocational Qualifications. Following protracted negotiations about salaries and employment, culminating in the Whitley Council Agreement, the Society's Dispensers changed their title to Pharmacy Technicians in 1966, compromising at Dispensing Technicians twenty years later. By that time relations with the Pharmaceutical Society had improved, largely due to the influence of T.D.

Whittet, the first pharmaceutical Master of the Society of Apothecaries (1982–83). He was a man of broad interests and capabilities – the driving force on the Pharmacy Technicians' Committee, the Society's representative at the Physic Garden and at the City and Guilds Institute. He was a supporter of the Faculty of the History and Philosophy of Medicine and Pharmacy, gave the Society advice on the training and examining of Dispensing Assistants and was the author of many publications on different aspects of the history of the Society.[22]

In the 1970s candidates for the Society's certificate in dispensing stood at between 100 and 200 a year, despite competition from the City and Guilds exams. The organization of regional examination centres encouraged candidates to apply – the Assistants' exams had been held in Leeds during the Second World War, after which they were held in Sunderland, as well as in London.[23] The examination of pharmacists for Messrs Boots proved to be a flash in the pan and, with the death of T.D. Whittet in 1986, the Dispensing Technicians of Apothecaries' Hall lost a pillar of support. The number of candidates fell in the 1990s, and therefore the laboratory used for the practical exam was converted into the Brande room, and a minimal laboratory for the dispensing exams was provided next door. Supremacy in the training and examination of Dispensing Technicians, by whatever name, having passed to others, the last of the certificates in dispensing were awarded in January 1998. The laboratory previously used for the practical exam was already being put to good use by the Society's Archivist.

Diplomas

The administration of the Society's Licence and the certificate for Apothecaries' Assistants, or Dispensing Technicians as they were later called, formed the backbone of the Society's business. It was a time-consuming exercise involving the Registrar, meetings of the Court of Examiners and of the Examinations committee, and the exams themselves, held at the Hall for a few days every month in the early years of the twentieth century.[24] At this time, sixteen universities granted medical degrees and the M.B. was the preferred qualification. Nevertheless a great number obtained the registrable qualification offered by the English Conjoint Board, the Society of Apothecaries, the Scottish Board and two authorities in Ireland.

In the list of twenty-five universities and licensing bodies for the medical profession in the British Isles (1936–37), the Society of Apothecaries ranked eighth in order of numbers admitted to the final examination (115 candidates compared to 1,178 for the English Conjoint Board exam), and was proud to be the corporation with the lowest, toughest pass rate (48.15 per cent).[25] The popularity of the Society's Licence rested on the fact that it could be taken earlier than medical schools' finals, and was thus viewed as a sensible insurance

The entrance to Apothecaries' Hall from Black Friars Lane, 1998. This side of the courtyard was rebuilt in the 1780s.

policy for less confident medical students. It was also more accessible to overseas students than other qualifications.

During the Second World War the L.M.S.S.A. final exams continued to be held at the Hall and the Assistants' exams were redirected to Leeds. In wartime mode, the Society adopted the 167th City of London Field Ambulance Unit, constructed air-raid shelters and paid teams of firewatchers to guard its premises. The Firewatchers' Report of June 1941 testified to the stamina of

The courtyard, Apothecaries' Hall, 1998.

one W.F. Hill, who was on duty for thirty-six hours during which fourteen incendiary bombs threatened the Hall and the water supply for the fire brigade failed.[26] No casualties were reported on that occasion and staff and firewatchers at the Hall escaped the war lightly, with the exception of Ernest Busby, Bursar at the time (he became Acting Clerk and Registrar in 1941, and was confirmed as Clerk and Registrar 1945–77). He was seriously injured by an explosion as he returned home from the Hall in November 1940, as the result of which his right leg was amputated.

Before hostilities ceased, the extension of state medical care and the future of the country's medical schools were under review. Representatives of the Society assisted the Interdepartmental Committee on Medical Schools (1941–44),[27] enquiries which brought the Society's future role under close scrutiny. The appointment by the Court of a committee to inquire into the Society's future activities, leading to the creation of the Faculty of the History of Medicine and Pharmacy, followed. Meanwhile, the Society embarked on a fresh initiative: the granting of postgraduate diplomas. The specialization of medicine had accelerated in the nineteenth century, as could be seen from the many different hospitals established in London at that time. The Infirmary for the Relief of the Poor Afflicted with Fistula and other Diseases of the Rectum (St Mark's, founded in 1835) and The Hospital for Stone (St Peter's, opened in 1860) were just two examples in the long list of specialist medical institutions.

The demand for specialists was met in part by the foundation of postgraduate diplomas in particular branches of medicine, first granted by Trinity College, Dublin (State Medicine) and Cambridge University (Public Health) in the 1870s. The Society of Apothecaries' attempt to establish its own Diploma in Public Health in 1887 was thwarted by the Conjoint Board's Diploma in the same subject, and a similar fate met the Society's proposals for Diplomas in Tropical Medicine and Dentistry in 1911. Tropical medicine was a popular new subject, inspired by Dr Patrick Manson and supported by the Colonial Office and Ronald Ross at the School of Tropical Diseases, Liverpool, from 1899. However, while the Society was petitioning the G.M.C. and the Privy Council for the right to grant a Diploma in Tropical Medicine, the Royal College of Physicians stole its thunder.[28]

The Society's next attempt proved more successful and this was in a subject close to its heart – midwifery.[29] The Medical Act of 1886 had made the triple qualification of Medicine, Surgery and Midwifery compulsory for registration with the G.M.C., and with the Midwives Act of 1902 the status of midwives improved. However, the standard of medical teaching in obstetrics remained low. Maternal mortality rates barely improved between 1891 and 1914, and the great majority of pregnant women still went without any ante-natal care in the 1920s. Sir William Fletcher Shaw first promoted the idea of a Diploma in Obstetrics for general practitioners but, without the support of the Royal Colleges and without their own college, neither obstetricians, gynaecologists nor midwives were in a position to take the idea further. Obstetricians and gynaecologists began to move towards founding a college in 1925 and, while plans were still in the melting pot, the Apothecaries' Senior Warden, Alfred Hepburn, suggested to the Court of Assistants that the Society might institute a Diploma for proficiency in midwifery and gynaecology. The suggestion appears to have grown out of discussions among the Examiners for an Honours Certificate in Obstetric Medicine, evolving into a proposed Diploma in Obstetrics and finally the Mastery of Midwifery (M.M.S.A.). The G.M.C. raised no objection, although there was some doubt that any Diploma other than the L.M.S.S.A. was within the Society's scope, and the Privy Council found that legislation would be necessary. Undeterred, the Society circumvented the obstacles and by 1927 the Examinations Committee was drawing up regulations designed for assistant medical officers, particularly those connected with ante-natal and child welfare clinics. Timing was crucial for the successful launch of the Diploma: the Society managed to organize the first examination for twenty-five candidates in October 1928 when the two Royal Colleges were still contemplating with horror the prospect of a new sister in the College of Obstetricians and Gynaecologists, while gingerly exploring the possibility of their own Diploma. The Society's M.M.S.A. was a stringent exam, "so that admission to the Mastery should indicate distinction", and Dr Cecil Wall designed special gowns for Masters of Midwifery modelled on those worn by the Court of the Leathersellers' Company in the seventeenth century.[30]

Once registered as a College in 1929, the Obstetricians and Gynaecologists instituted a special qualification that superseded those offered by the Royal Colleges and the Society of Apothecaries. The Apothecaries' Mastery of Midwifery was thus put in the shade. Only two Diplomas were granted in 1934–35 and, with such a small number enrolled for the M.M.S.A. in 1960 the decision was taken to discontinue the qualification after November 1963, at which point it was calculated that a total of 177 Diplomas had been granted.[31]

The M.M.S.A. was the blueprint for several of the Society's Diplomas: the Bio-Physical Assistants' Diploma in electro-therapeutics (B.P.A.S.A.) was set up in 1929 following a request from the G.M.C. for a register, but dropped when the Chartered Society of Physiotherapy (originally the Chartered Society of Massage and Medical Gymnastics) extended its qualification in 1932. The Society then abandoned its B.P.A.S.A., maintaining the listing (which amounted to 1,117 names when it was last published in 1935), and then passing responsibility to the B.M.A., which kept the register of Medical Auxiliaries.[32] An attempt to revive the Diploma in 1945 failed amid continuing bitterness towards the Chartered Society of Physiotherapy who, "after specific promises not to", had set up the qualification that made the B.P.A.S.A. redundant.[33]

The Diploma in Industrial Medicine suggested by Dr Roche Lynch in 1945 was established in consultation with the Ministry of Supply, a medical officer from Imperial Chemical Industries, the medical officer for Harrods and a medical inspector of factories. An efficient health service for industry was in line with the extension of state medical care and the revitalization of the country after the war. The first exam in February 1946 was open to medical practitioners, members of H.M. forces, those with experience in occupational medicine, those who were or aspired to be factory doctors and, by the 1950s, overseas candidates were sitting the Diploma. In 1962 the Association of Industrial Medical Officers came into the picture, followed in 1978 by the Faculty of Occupational Medicine established by the Royal College of Physicians (it had granted its own Diploma in Industrial Health from 1946). That Faculty rapidly became the chief guardian of education in occupational medicine, and the duty of conducting postgraduate examinations naturally passed to it in 1987. Having issued its Diploma for forty years to 521 successful examinees, the Society of Apothecaries graciously conceded future responsiblity to the Faculty of Occupational Medicine.[34]

The Diploma in Medical Jurisprudence, nurtured by Dr Macdonald Critchley in 1961–62, has been consistently popular and led to examinations being held in Hong Kong in 1996. A Mastership in the subject was established in 1993, now awarded on the basis of a 20,000 word thesis. In the 1970s the Faculty of the History and Philosophy of Medicine and Pharmacy generated two Diplomas (see pages 244–45), and what began as a Diploma in Venereology in 1973, re-named Genitourinary Medicine and dealing with sexually transmitted diseases, attracted a record number of forty-eight candidates (1995–96) who sat a reorganized, objective, structured, clinical exam (O.S.C.E.). Sports Medicine, a promising subject, was introduced as a Diploma in 1988 yet has never found a large following.

The recently established Diploma in Musculoskeletal Medicine was awarded in 1996 to eight enthusiasts. Regulatory Toxicology, demanding an ability to design, assess and evaluate toxicity programmes for a range of substances with reference to health and the environment is perhaps the most esoteric of the Society's Diplomas and has yet to attract any candidates. On the other hand, the Diploma in the Medical Care of Catastrophes, established in 1993, has grown steadily more popular with civilian and military doctors aiming to give specialized medical treatment at the scene of disasters, whether natural or man-made. The Diploma in Clinical Pharmacology, established in 1996 for practitioners who already have experience in that branch of medicine, points to apparently limitless horizons in the administration of new chemical and biological substances and experimental drugs, and is especially relevant to those working in the pharmaceutical industry.[35]

The Society is to be credited with initiating diplomas which have subsequently been adopted by a more appropriate authority. Of those remaining under its sponsorship, some have been successful in terms of the number of candidates, others have limited appeal because of their specialized nature. Many proposed diplomas have never reached fruition – twenty-six suggestions received between 1963 and 1993 never materialized for various reasons (subjects have ranged from higher dentistry to nuclear medicine). Wherever there is a perceived gap or demand for a postgraduate qualification, the Society gives the proposal serious consideration, and if the diploma is approved, it will provide the administration, organization and facilities to encourage its success.

The Faculty

The post-war period was one of reconstruction combined with uncertainty about the future. Peace after six years of international war demanded a fresh sense of direction and the readjustment of goals. The creation of the Faculty of the History of Medicine and Pharmacy (as it was originally called) was a major new enterprise for the Society, resulting from a hard look at its future role and the decision that it should concentrate its activities in the medical sphere. A committee was appointed in March 1944 to explore possible fields of future development, with Professor Charles Dodds F.R.S. (later a Baronet) as its Chairman.[36] Dodds was appointed to the new chair of Biochemistry at London University aged twenty-five and he developed the synthetic oestrogen, stilboestrol, before he was forty.[37] His facility for attracting the attention and support of influential people from many fields proved helpful in arrangements for the revival of lectures at Apothecaries' Hall during the winter of 1944–45, and in establishing the Faculty of the History of Medicine and Pharmacy in 1959.[38]

In 1947 the lectures at Apothecaries' Hall were extended to a course of twenty on modern therapeutics reflecting the recent "therapeutic revolution" in medicine. These were attended by general practitioners, postgraduates, representatives from the Commonwealth and those returning from the armed forces, each paying 15 guineas for the course. Dodds himself lectured, along with Drs Richard Trail and W.S.C. Copeman, and all three were to become involved with the foundation of the Faculty. Howard Florey (Lord Florey, a Nobel prizewinner and recipient of the Society's Galen Medal in 1946) also lectured, on "Recent advances in the laboratory investigation of penicillin".[39]

After a decade of these winter lectures on medical subjects, thoughts turned to historical topics, starting with the first Gideon de Laune lecture given by Sir Zachary Cope in November 1955 on "The Society of Apothecaries and medical education – a historical survey".[40] As interest in the medical lectures ebbed, a sub-committee reviewed the position and Dr W.S.C. Copeman was elected Master. He had nursed the idea of a Faculty of Historical Medicine for several years and, as Master he directed attention towards the foundation of a Faculty of the History of Medicine and Pharmacy with the aim of organizing lectures, recruiting a research fellow and attracting interested medical students.[41] With a personal gift of 1,000 guineas he put the Faculty on its feet.[42]

The first meeting of the Faculty of the History of Medicine and Pharmacy took place in the Parlour of Apothecaries' Hall on 3 April 1959. It undertook to administer the Gideon de Laune lecture and establish others. The next proposal, the sponsorship of a Research Fellow, brought Dr F.H.K. Green of

Miniature portrait of Dr W.S.C. Copeman, the founder and first Chairman of the Faculty of the History of Medicine and Pharmacy (1959–64). He wears the silver gilt badge of the Chairman of the Faculty, made by Garrard in 1960.

the Wellcome Trust and Dr F.N.L. Poynter, of the Wellcome Institute Library, into the discussion. The Research Fellow of the Faculty, sponsored by the Trust and given accommodation at Apothecaries' Hall, was appointed promptly: R.S. Roberts who was working on the early history of the drug trade.[43]

The first of the Faculty's lectures was founded in 1960 and named after the seventeenth-century clinician Sir Thomas Sydenham, and was followed by the establishment of the Osler lecture in 1967, commemorating Sir William Osler F.R.S., the first Professor of Medicine at Johns Hopkins University in Baltimore and latterly Regius Professor at Oxford. The new Faculty was soon able to offer the Maccabaean Prize of 25 guineas (now £200 annually) and a bronze medal for an original essay by a student under thirty on a subject connected with the history of medicine or pharmacy. Honorary Fellowships were instituted, and the first Society of Apothecaries' lecturer was appointed at St Thomas' Hospital (there are currently thirteen lecturers at medical schools, and one visiting lecturer). The first British Congress on the History of Medicine and Pharmacy was held at Apothecaries' Hall in 1960 with the theme "The Evolution of British Medical Practice" – the proceedings of this and subsequent conferences were published. The activities of the Faculty were financed by individual subscriptions of 10 guineas, by annual subscriptions of £200 from pharmaceutical firms, and by support from medical schools and corporations.[44]

The enthusiasm and energy of Dr Copeman and Dr Poynter brought the Faculty to the notice of medical schools, the Pharmaceutical Society and medical historical societies. The network extended to affiliation with the Veterinary History Society and the Faculty was one of the founders of the British Society for the History of Medicine, Dr Copeman being elected its President in 1967. Noel Poynter, as he was known, was ideally placed as editor of *Medical History* (1961–73) to publicize the Faculty's programme; he was President of the International Academy of the History of Medicine and in line with his work for the Faculty he developed the Wellcome Institute Library as an internationally important centre for the study of the history of medicine. The subject had long been neglected, the enthusiasm of the Faculty membership was contagious and the formula of the Wellcome Trust in conjunction with the Society of Apothecaries brought generous sponsorship from the pharmaceutical industry, combined with excellent facilities and gravitas. As Copeman was proud to point out, "no similar academic body had existed anywhere in the Commonwealth to maintain interest in and knowledge of the history of the medical profession's fight against ignorance and disease through the ages, nor to maintain the traditions and ethic which are based upon this story".[45]

The tenth Annual Report of the Faculty recorded its success: seventeen founder members, ten Honorary Fellows, five institutional members, seventy-one corporate and 342 personal members (including founders). The Faculty was attracting eminent lecturers such as Dame Veronica Wedgwood, an annual dinner was held at the Hall and a Diploma in the History of Medicine was the next step.

Dr Poynter, appointed Director of the Museum and Library at the Wellcome Institute for the History of Medicine in 1964, was the first to raise the question of a diploma, the aim being to establish a course that would give a good general grounding in the history of medicine with emphasis on the last 150 years. The qualification was designed to equip the successful candidate to teach the history of medicine up to and including university level, and the first Diploma examination was held in November 1970, a few weeks before the death of Dr Copeman, "he who while Master conceived the idea of the Faculty and so found a new and singularly appropriate role for that ancient Society".[46] His successor as Chairman, Dr Poynter, had the satisfaction of reporting that there were nine successful candidates in the first Diploma examination, five of whom were doctors. The Diploma soon attracted enquiries from Australia and Canada (one enthusiast travelled from Ottawa once a fortnight to attend the seminars of 1978–79), and a lecturer was appointed in Athens. The course presently involves regular instruction, includes an essay of between 4,000 and 6,000 words, and culminates in two three-hour exams in November as qualification for the D.H.M.S.A.

The scope of the Faculty's lectures expanded with the Sloane biennial lecture, now one of six eponymous lectures. The Gideon de Laune, the Sydenham, and the Osler have been mentioned; in 1967 the Monckton Copeman lecture was established in memory of Dr Sydney Monckton Copeman F.R.C.P., F.R.S. who had died twenty years previously. This lecture was intended to reinforce medical-historical ties between the Society of Apothecaries and the City. The John Locke lecture was the last to join the programme in 1978, following the inauguration of a course in the philosophy of medicine.[47]

The extension of the Faculty to embrace philosophy arose out of conversations between Sir Gordon Wolstenholme (Chairman of the Faculty 1973–75, Master of the Society 1979–80, and Director of the Ciba Foundation), and the Reverend Edward Shotter, then Director of the Institute of Medical Ethics and now Dean of Rochester. The original idea concerned a Diploma in Medical Ethics, at a time when issues such as abortion were being hotly debated. The plan that emerged was to extend the existing Faculty of the History of Medicine to embrace the Philosophy of Medicine.[48]

The Society now insisted on a clearer definition of the relationship between the Faculty and the City livery company that had acted as its catalyst. Originally, the Faculty's status was that of an autonomous committee of the Society, but from 1976 it was governed by a new constitution asserting the Society's influence as the ruling body and allocating to the Clerk the office of Honorary Treasurer.[49] In the vital role of Honorary Secretary, Professor Sydney Selwyn and then Mr Robin Price devoted extended periods of service to the Faculty. The former also appears on the roster of recent Presidents, alongside such figures as Dr J. Dickson Mabon and Professor Michael D. Biddiss.

With the constitution of the Faculty re-defined in the mid-1970s, the course in the Philosophy of Medicine was born. It was to explore such current issues as the morality of abortion, infanticide, euthanasia, the limits of experimentation and the extent of freedom to be exercised by practitioners. Prebendary Shotter, Dr Raanan Gillon (later Professor of Medical Ethics, London University), Professor Richard Hare of Oxford University and Dr Whittet mapped out the new Diploma, choosing "a good young philosopher to run the course" – Dr Michael Lockwood from Oxford.[50] A two-year course was introduced for postgraduate students in 1978, eight of whom obtained Diplomas and the letters D.P.M.S.A. after their names.

One of the aims of the Faculty was and is to arouse the interest of medical students, and therefore visits were organized to the Museum and Library at the Wellcome Institute. However, students failed to respond in any significant number to the initiative. Nevertheless, the Faculty persisted, pressing for the inclusion of the history of medicine in the student curriculum in a paper submitted to the G.M.C. in 1965,[51] and more recently by organizing three-day courses in the subject for students of London University. The number of the Society of Apothecaries' lecturers in the history of medicine at the medical schools was increased and they now meet annually to liaise and plan ways of promoting the subject in the undergraduate curriculum. In this respect, the G.M.C.'s recommendations on undergraduate medical education (1993) were favourable in that they encouraged diversity in the medical schools and the development of special study modules,[52] and figures confirm a recent surge of interest in the history and philosophy of medicine and pharmacy. After a brief lapse, the course in the philosophy of medicine re-emerged in October 1993 and eleven students were enrolled for 1996–97, while thirty attended the history course. Not all of those who attend the course sit the Diploma examination; a good proportion do, and if successful, obtain a D.H.M.S.A. or D.P.M.S.A., as appropriate. Plans to create courses in the U.S.A., Canada and Australasia proceed, and lectures – varying in subject from "Elizabeth I and the Spanish Armada – the Apothecaries' Painting" to "The History of Gastric Acid", are well-attended. The Faculty was registered as a charity in 1960, its finances have been carefully stewarded, and the relationship between The Worshipful Society of Apothecaries and the Wellcome Institute for the History of Medicine has proved both fruitful and promising.

Charity

The provision of charity is and always has been fundamental to City livery companies. Members of the same mistery supported one another professionally and socially, meeting together to regulate and govern the craft to mutual advantage. Those falling on hard times would usually be helped, and sometimes their widows and families applied for assistance. Records of the Apothecaries' charitable giving begin in the 1620s with the gift of 6d to the poor of Kingsland Spitalhouse (hospital) and the purchase of the Society's poor box. Once established in the Hall at Black Friars, the Court of Assistants regularly authorized a few shillings to be extracted from the box and given to the poor of Ludgate. Into the fund went the fluctuating sums paid by an Apothecary as he ascended the hierarchy of the Society – on admission to the Livery and to the Court, for example. In effect, this constituted a modest charitable fund providing annuities to freemen and their widows and help for the needy of the neighbourhood.[53] The principle has since been extended and presently takes the form of the Amalgamated Fund and the Charitable Company.

The financial demands of the late seventeenth century (loans to king and Parliament, rebuilding and furnishing the Hall, the maintenance of the Physic Garden and commissioning of the Society's barge) put a strain on corporate and individual funds and it was not until the early eighteenth century that charitable giving took on significant porportions. The provision of free medicines to the sick poor at the infirmary of the Bishopsgate Workhouse (1701–06) was ostensibly an act of charity, although the Court was well aware that this scored points for the Society in its contest with the Royal College of Physicians.[54]

The initiative for creating a charitable fund specifically for impoverished members of the Society came in 1711. Peter Gelsthorp (Master 1701–02 and 1703–04), Treasurer of the Navy Stock, was due £20 from the Laboratory Stock, but, being a wealthy and generous Past Master, he returned the £20 bond "with the intention that the Company shall forever pay the sum of £1 4s to such poor members of the Society as they shall think fit". Gelsthorp was thanked for his kindness and the Renter Warden was charged with the duty of investing and distributing the largesse.[55] This was the origin of the Widows' Fund, soon to be augmented by gifts and legacies from other members and occasionally their relatives, by corporate contributions, by a gift from the Friendly Medical Society and by every member holding a share in the trading stock of the Society. Among the most generous benefactors to the fund (and the Society generally) was John Allen, Apothecary to three King Georges, who gave six donations amounting to £800 to increase the pensions, £50 to the Physic Garden, his portrait, and bequeathed £1,000 in his will of 1774.[56]

Another notable benefactor was the Apothecary who had served two kings, Everard A. Brande, whose trust of 1854 provided £300 for a pension for Elizabeth Yonge, the widow of a freeman, James Yonge, until her death in 1858 after which other widows stood to gain.[57]

The freemen's widows who benefited from the fund were usually over sixty years of age; they or their representative came to the Hall once a quarter to receive and sign for the pension. This was raised regularly so that by 1819 eleven widows were each taking home £3 15s a quarter; by 1826 £5 each.[58]

The other charity administered by the Society was the brain-child of John Bacot, formerly on the Court of Examiners and Master (1845–46). This was created in direct response to "a most painful case of destitution in one of our Liverymen". Bacot, W.T. Brande and N.B. Ward were the leaders of a group of eight Liverymen who took pity on this unnamed, destitute Liveryman. They circulated other Liverymen and initiated a fund "for the relief of decayed and destitute members" in February 1863. Launched with personal donations amounting to £78 3s, the Distressed Members' Fund was transferred to the corporate administration of the Society, becoming a well-endowed charity through the bequests and gifts of sympathetic members.[59] The Widows' Fund and the Distressed Members' Fund amalgamated in 1967, and because there have been so few applications for assistance, the amalgamated fund is also available for medical education.

Widows and distressed members were not the only ones to be grateful for the Society's charity. The Court received a stream of unsolicited applications for donations – particularly in the mid-nineteenth century when the Society gave financial assistance to a variety of good causes such as local schools, St Paul's Cathedral, the Medical Benevolent Fund, the poor of Chelsea and, at times of national emergency or disaster, contributions were always forthcoming.

The Sustentation Fund was founded in 1947 at the suggestion of Duncan C.L. Fitzwilliams (Master 1949–50) to boost the Society's financial position after the war. He made an appeal to members suggesting they remember the Society in their wills by gifts and legacies. As he pointed out, "they cannot take the money with them and their families will scarcely grudge their leaving something to meet the needs of the Society where they have spent so many delightful hours". The Fund that accumulated as a result helps to fortify the Society's activities, and to assist freemen, preserve the Hall, its furniture and treasures.

The most recent fund, known as the Charitable Company (1982), is purely for charitable giving. Three times a year a tall pile of applications is carefully considered and divided into medical, City, and non-medical causes. The recipients of grants are often little-known charities with a special project in mind. Among the well-known causes have been the MacMillan Nurses Fund and the hospice movement, while individual students may also benefit. The plight of poverty-stricken medical students is regarded with compassion if, through no fault of their own, they have fallen on hard times – by the death or illness of a parent, for example. Six grants of between £500 and £1,000 have recently been awarded to such cases.

Prizes and awards

From the early nineteenth century the Society's apprentices were offered prizes in botany, in the form of books presented by the Court. The apprentices were so keen that at one point the number of prizes had to be restricted to four and it was agreed to give them to the younger boys.[60] A more generous attitude prevailed after 1830 when the Society gave gold and silver medals as well as books to medical students excelling in the botany exams held each summer. The fifteen-year-old William Jenner attended the examination at the Hall in 1830 and was rewarded with the Society's gold medal. Another well-known name on the list of prizewinners was that of Thomas Huxley. He took the trial very seriously, studying first under Dr Lindley at Chelsea Physic Garden and spending nine hours at the Hall in August 1842 to complete the exam to his satisfaction. He was the youngest of the six candidates and his silver medal paved the way for a scholarship at Charing Cross Medical School.[61]

W.T. Brande, who as Superintending Chemical Operator and Professor to the Society was in a strong position to argue his case, wanted to see his subjects given as much emphasis as the botany examinations and prizes. He suggested the introduction of examinations and medals for students of *materia medica* and pharmacy and he capped his recommendations with a threat of resignation if he did not have his way.[62] Accordingly, the exams and prizes were established from 1841, although the Society adjusted the wording to emphasize pharmaceutical chemistry. The first prize, a gold medal, was engraved by William Wyon R.A. of the Royal Mint, whose particular skill was portraiture. He took his design from the bust of the Greek physician Galen at the Royal College of Physicians. A silver medal, also by Wyon, and books, were offered as second and third prizes.[63]

Responding to the official enquiries of the 1880s, the Clerk cited the Society's prizes in botany, *materia medica* and pharmaceutical chemistry as its contribution to general and technical education, pointing out that the cost of the awards with the Examiners' fees had amounted to £75 12s in 1879. A recent innovation was botany prizes for young women. George H. Makins (Master 1889–90) recorded in a personal notebook that they were "started with a view of encouraging the extension and improvement of female education", botany being "particularly fitted for the female mind. In aid of this object the Society opened their Garden at Chelsea for their use, not to enable the Students to acquire a Knowledge of Medical Botany as a stepping stone to a further acquisition of Medical Knowledge, but of General Botany as an improving and refining acquirement". No less than seventy-three young women took the first botany exam in June 1878. So many excelled that a second, more severe exam had to be held, the eventual winners gaining medals and books.[64]

The Society's prizes fell victim to the reorganization of the medical

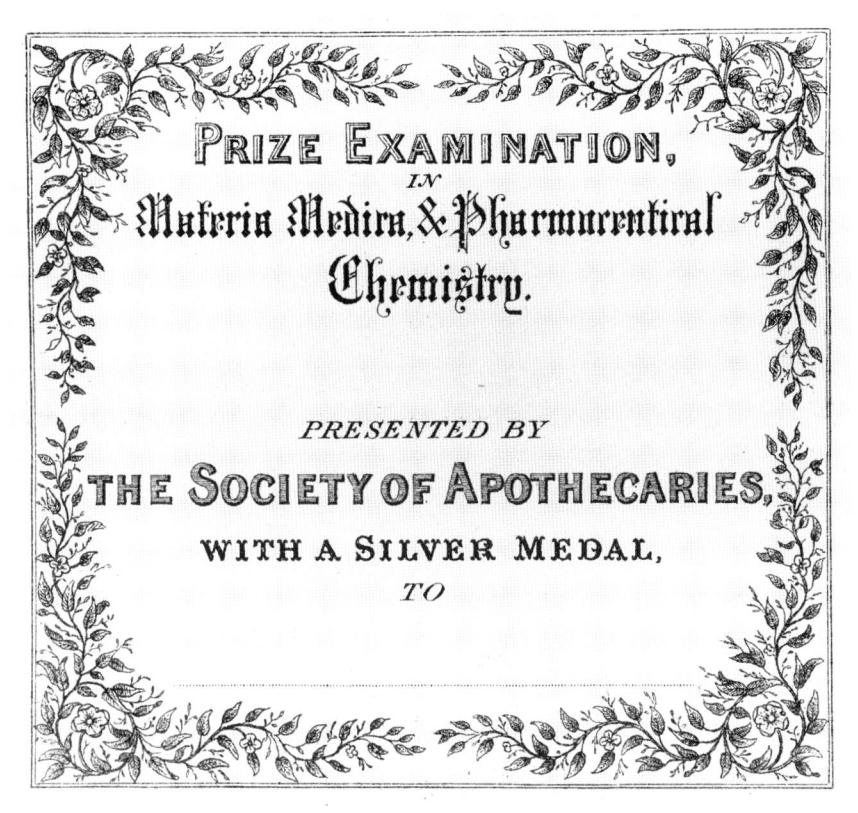

> PRIZE EXAMINATION,
> IN
> Materia Medica, & Pharmaceutical
> Chemistry.
>
> PRESENTED BY
> THE SOCIETY OF APOTHECARIES,
> WITH A SILVER MEDAL,
> TO

A bookplate for one of the Society's prizes in *materia medica* and pharmaceutical chemistry. Prizes in this subject were awarded from 1841 to 1895.

curriculum recommended by the G.M.C. in the 1890s. New subjects had by then superseded botany, conformity was the order of the day and the last examinations for the Society's prizes in botany, *materia medica* and pharmaceutical chemistry were held in 1895.[65]

Similarly, two scholarships instigated by the Society in 1883 were rendered redundant by the provisions of the 1886 Medical Act. The scholarships had been suggested in 1882 by George Makins and were known as the Medical Scholarship (i.e. clinical medicine, midwifery and therapeutics) and the Surgical Scholarship (including surgical pathology, major and minor operations). Each was worth £100 and the first candidates came to the Hall to compete for the Medical Scholarship in the summer of 1883, and for the Surgical Scholarship early in 1884.[66]

Dr William Gillson evidently approved of the Society's management of its awards and scholarships, for in his will of April 1899 he left a bequest to found a scholarship in his name. Gillson was a licentiate of the Society and a surgeon at Westminster Hospital who seems to have ended his days an embittered man:

The Galen Medal in Therapeutics or the Society of Apothecaries' Medal, instituted in 1925.

"As none of my relations have at any time given me any help whatever (with the exception of my mother's adopted daughter)", he left them nothing in his will. The Master, Wardens and Assistants of the Society of Apothecaries, however, were instructed to establish a scholarship in pathology financed by Gillson's bequest, which amounted to £3,472 in 1900. While the Society was making plans to administer this, the benefactor's aggrieved step-sister appeared from Russia pleading penury, and was given £30. The first award under Gillson's bequest was made for original research in any branch of pathology. It had an annual value of £105 and was presented to H.S. French, the Medical Registrar of Guy's Hospital in 1902.[67] The scholarship is now awarded triennially and has a value of £1,800.

A similar arrangement was made by Dr Joseph Rogers, a surgeon who died in 1889 leaving a legacy of £500, payable on the death of his widow to establish the Rogers Prize which was to be given "to such person who the trustees judge to have written the best or only good essay on the treatment of the sick poor of this country and the preservation of the health of the poor of this country or either of each (*sic*) subjects".[68] Dr Rogers' concern for the relief of the sick poor was the subject of articles in medical journals, and he was Chairman of the Poor Law Medical Officers' Association. The first Rogers Prize was awarded to Dr Hugh MacCurrick in 1926 when the £500 bequest yielded £157 10s – he was one of thirty-six competitors. The President of the Royal College of Physicians and the Master of the Society of Apothecaries are responsible for offering the award every ten years, but interest in the sick poor

The reverse of the Galen Medal features a female figure representing Science.

has declined: only two essays were submitted in 1986 and none in 1996.

Dr Joseph Strickland Goodall, licentiate, Examiner from 1903 to 1931 and Liveryman of the Society from 1919, played an important part in the advancement of cardiology, having been responsible for installing an electrocardiogram at Middlesex Hospital (where he was Lecturer and Sub-Dean) as early as 1910. After his death in 1934 colleagues, friends and patients showed their appreciation of his life and work by raising a fund for a memorial lecture and gold medal in cardiology. The Society of Apothecaries undertook to act as trustee and in 1936 organized the first Strickland Goodall memorial lecture at the Hall for members of the medical profession and senior students. Once it had been successfully launched, responsibility for administering the Strickland Goodall Trust eventually passed from the Apothecaries to the British Cardiac Society in the 1980s.[69]

The Greek physician Galen originally featured on the medal awarded to students winning first prize in examinations of *materia medica* and pharmaceutical chemistry (1841–95). The idea was revived in 1925 as the Galen Medal in Therapeutics or The Society of Apothecaries' Medal. The original design, the work of Wyon, was taken as a basis for a new one by T.H. Paget who created a weighty and attractive token of esteem that is awarded for distinguished achievements in the science of therapeutics.[70] The honour has been accepted by men of world renown, Sir Alexander Fleming and Lord Florey for example, in 1946, and by specialists such as Professor John Jacob Abel (1928) of Johns Hopkins University in Baltimore, whose work paved the way for the treatment of kidney disease by dialysis. Abel was unable to attend the presentation ceremony, so the American Ambassador in London was delegated to receive the medal on his behalf.[71]

The presentation of the Galen Medal was formerly the highlight of a summer soirée at Apothecaries' Hall, becoming a more formal occasion in 1992 with a dinner for distinguished guests and members of the Society. In that year the recipient was Dr C.D. Marsden F.R.S., who received it for his work in clinical neurology and pharmacology and its therapeutic applications. After dinner other awards were made: Sir Roger Bannister, a Liveryman, received an Honorary Diploma in Sports Medicine, and an Honorary Diploma in Medical Jurisprudence was given to Dr D. Jenkins, retiring Examiner in that subject. In 1995 H.R.H. The Princess Royal was pleased to accept the Galen medal in recognition of her outstanding contribution as President of the Save the Children Fund.

Coincidentally with the institution of the Galen Medal in therapeutics came the introduction of the first Honorary Diploma (L.M.S.S.A) presented to H.R.H. The Prince of Wales at St James's Palace in 1926. The Prince of Wales was attracting a good deal of publicity at the time, not least on account of his relationships with unsuitable women. Nevertheless, he was a popular recipient of honours and fellowships – the Royal College of Surgeons made him an Honorary Fellow and he was briefly Master of the Stationers' Company before succeeding to the throne as King Edward VIII in 1936.[72]

Honorary Freedoms of the Society were first awarded in the seventeenth century, the Presbyterian minister of St Ann's Black Friars, William Gouge, being the first recipient in 1633. Dr Christopher Merrett F.R.S., whose vitriolic publications did the Society no good, Dr Thomas Wharton, an anatomist who stood by the victims of the Great Plague, and another minister of St Ann's parish, Mr Gibbons, were all made Honorary Freemen in September 1659. The honour was revived at the beginning of this century, starting with a Nobel prizewinner who as a young man had failed to pass the L.S.A. at his first attempt – Sir Ronald Ross. As he explained in his autobiography, "having obtained the M.R.C.S. with only three days' reading I decided to read for the L.S.A. early on the morning of the examination. But there was no time to go through the poisons and their antidotes. The *viva voce* commenced but the examiner took me – on poisons and antidotes! I failed". Without the Society's Licence, Ross missed his chance of competing for the Indian Medical Service in 1879, and after a few years as a ship's surgeon he returned to London to study, passing the L.S.A. in 1881. Inspired by Dr (later Sir Patrick) Manson, Ross tested Manson's hypothesis on malaria and on 20 August 1895 ("Mosquito Day") he solved the problem in Secunderabad. He was awarded the Nobel prize for his discovery of the role of the mosquito in transmitting malaria in 1902, and was made an Honorary Freeman of the Society of Apothecaries in 1915.[73]

The Honorary Freedom of the Society was awarded to Sir Ronald Ross in 1915 in recognition of his discovery of the role of the mosquito in transmitting malaria.

The Society was generous with Honorary Freedoms at the close of the First World War, conferring them upon Surgeon Vice-Admiral Sir William Norman, Lt General Sir Thomas Goodwin and Sir George Newman, the new Minister of Health. There are presently nine Honorary Freemen of the Society, including the Duke of Kent, and two Honorary Diplomates.

The Society, the profession, the City

Lloyd George had visualized the National Health Insurance Act as the first of a series of measures leading to a comprehensive state medical system. Lord Dawson's report of 1920 on "The Future Provision of Medical and Allied Services", the B.M.A. Proposals for a General Medical Service for the Nation (1930) and the organization of Emergency Services during the Second World War formed the prelude to the National Health Service. In 1941 the Master of the Society, Thomas B. Layton, was the first to alert members to the forthcoming reorganization of medical care in this country and the threat this could pose to the future of the Society. His New Year's Letter used strong language intended to provoke a positive response and hence avert the possible extinction of the Society of Apothecaries. "We cannot continue to exist merely as dispensers of entertainment ... as a picturesque backwater of the past. If we do not find something else to do in the interests of the Health of the People we shall cease to exist".[74]

The Society's existence as an examining body for the medical profession had to be defended in the face of the proposed reforms and competition. An opportunity to take part in the government's post-war medical policy came with the work of the Interdepartmental Committee on medical schools under the Chairmanship of Sir William Goodenough. A committee of the Society headed by Sir Stanley Woodwark (Master 1941–44) and Lionel V. Cargill (Master 1939–40) gave evidence and contributed a report focusing on hospitals and medical schools.[75]

Sir Stanley Woodwark encouraged the Society to "do all in its present power to retain its right to examine". He encouraged the Future Activities Committee in its task and supported the course of lectures on medical subjects held at the Hall. On his retirement as Master in 1944 he assured the Court that the financial position of the Society had improved. He was still not confident about the Society's future as an examining body and he went on to call attention to another matter that the Society needed to address: "the increasingly important position which women hold".[76]

As the Society faced the prospect of the N.H.S., there were some who were opposed to change and expected the Apothecaries to resist the looming "menace of a full time state medical service". Doctors Basil and Russell Steele wrote to the Master expressing their opposition: "in our view the state medical service would be a disaster for the nation, for medical men and for the patients".[77] The Society and general practitioners were apprehensive but in principle the Court was in favour, putting it on record that "the Court welcomes the establishment of a National Health Service and is prepared to co-operate with the Minister in its development."[78]

The other subject that needed to be tackled was women, as Sir Stanley Woodwark had pointed out in 1944. After consultation with the membership,

Common Hall was called in December 1946, when a narrow majority voted in favour of the admission of medical women as freemen. By the custom of the City a female was entitled to the freedom of the Society by patrimony, yet on the rare occasions that an application had been made, the Master and Wardens had preferred to purchase the woman's freedom of another livery company rather than to admit her to the Society of Apothecaries.[79]

Once the door was opened to women in 1947, with the first admission in 1949, the Society sought a woman for a figurehead, choosing none other than Princess Elizabeth. She politely refused the Honorary Freedom, owing to "many other similar applications" and her sister also replied in the negative.[80] In 1972, when a vacancy occurred on the Court due to the resignation of Sir Cecil Wakeley, the election of women to that body was discussed. As a result, a by-law was altered to allow this. In 1989 the last discriminatory elements were removed from the Society's by-laws so as to permit the admission by patrimony of offspring of a female line. In this respect the Society can be credited with a more broad-minded approach than many other livery companies; as yet there are no women members of the Courts of any of "The Great Twelve" companies, whereas Mrs Enid Taylor F.R.C.S., D.O. has been a member of the Society's Court of Assistants since 1989, posing the prospect of the first female Master of the Society.

More problematic to the Society than the N.H.S. or the admission of women, were the burdensome requirements of the G.M.C., whose recommendations of 1947 stipulated fifteen subjects in more exacting and intensive examinations for medical students. Furthermore, the Medical Act of 1950 gave the G.M.C. the right to appoint visitors to inspect and report on the conduct and standards of these exams. The Inspector's report for 1954 on the examinations for the Society's Licence was not good (at this time these exams were held at the Hall every month except September and the failure rate was 50 per cent). The clinical examination was reported to be "very unsatisfactory" and "short and scrappy", and that in midwifery and gynaecology "insufficient". The other subjects were satisfactory, although few candidates sat the exams. Further inspections over the next few years were more favourable but the qualification still failed to attract many candidates.[81] The G.M.C. later admitted that its recommendations of 1947 were too stringent. Consequently those issued in 1957 were more liberal and were welcomed by the medical schools. Nevertheless, some changes to the final exams of the Conjoint Board and the Society were required.

For three years from 1957 to 1960 the Society's examinations for its Licence were held in Hong Kong, for the convenience of a large number of Chinese doctors. The somewhat eccentric arrangement was impractical and was not condoned by the G.M.C. An attempt to revive the idea in 1988 failed. One deluded candidate in Mexico City imagined that the Society organized exams for its L.M.S.S.A. there. He sat the exam in 1975 and when his Diploma was not forthcoming he telephoned the Clerk at Apothecaries' Hall only to find that he had been the victim of a fraud – Dr J. Franks Anasoh, alias J.A. Franks, had set imaginary papers and supervised the examinations for a fee of Can. $6,428 (£2,500).[82] In 1985 the number applying to take the Society's examinations was so high as to make a waiting list necessary. Reforms were to follow, namely the removal of the clinical exams to St George's Hospital Medical School (1988–89) and the reorganization of exams at Apothecaries' Hall to be held four times during the year. Neither the exams conducted by the Royal Colleges nor those by the Society were financially profitable. The problem called for a joint working party (1977–78) to investigate means of reducing costs, and one obvious remedy was to increase the examination fees, supplemented by an injection of many hundreds of pounds from the Society.

The most important point to emerge from the G.M.C.'s inspections of medical licensing bodies in the 1980s was the need for uniformity, and hence the movement towards a truly conjoint examining board was revived. This time the Society of Apothecaries was a member – with the Royal College of Physicians of Edinburgh, the Royal College of Physicians of London, the Royal College of Physicians and Surgeons of Glasgow, the Royal College of Surgeons of Edinburgh and the Royal College of Surgeons of England – of the United Examining Board formed in 1993.[83]

The new arrangement made sense although it was with some nostalgia that the last of the Society's old-style examinations were held, and with some trepidation that the Registrar's office at Apothecaries' Hall assumed the honour of sole responsibility for the administration of the exams of the U.E.B. These were first held in February 1994 and they entitle successful candidates to full registration with the G.M.C. Those who have taken the U.E.B. examinations in London, and passed, are awarded the L.R.C.P. Lond., L.R.C.S Eng., L.M.S.S.A. Lond.

The establishment of a United Board did not solve every problem – the operation continues to run at a loss and candidates from overseas still face difficulties in finding clinical attachments at medical schools. The viability of the examination depends on it being self-funding which depends on the number of entries which in turn depends on the availability of attachments to medical schools for those coming from abroad.

The Society was drawn into the organization of a new examination in the 1980s. The unattractive acronym PLAB (Professional and Linguistic Assessments Board) describes a test for foreign doctors. Since the Second World War an increasing number of doctors from all parts of the world have sought registration in this country. From time to time allegations were made which cast doubt on the competence of those who had qualified overseas and had managed to obtain registration here. The G.M.C. investigated the

The entrance hall featuring a display of drug jars. The staircase dates from the rebuilding of Apothecaries' Hall after the Great Fire.

problem in 1971, its report confirming that there were indeed difficulties and that standards needed improving. Representatives from the Society of Apothecaries were invited to discussions with the G.M.C. on the possibility of subjecting doctors from overseas to a systematic test of linguistic and professional competence. As a result, written and oral exams were introduced in 1975 when they were known as the TRAB tests (Temporary Registration Assessment Board). These soon revealed that failure was usually due to lack of professional knowledge rather than to difficulty in communicating in English.[84] The PLAB tests were reorganized in 1986 to be held at three centres in London, including Apothecaries' Hall, and three in Scotland. Some 2,500 candidates sit the tests annually and, if successful, they are deemed to be sufficiently qualified to undertake employment at senior house officer level in a British hospital.

The running of PLAB tests, the U.E.B. exams and specialized diplomas forms the essential business of the Registrar's office at Apothecaries' Hall – thus the Society maintains its role as an examining and licensing body. It also fulfils an advisory role by contributing expertise on medical issues, as it did to the Royal Commission on Venereal Disease (1913), to the British Pharmacopoeia Commission (1959) and to the Royal Commission on the N.H.S. (1977). Papers have regularly been submitted to the G.M.C. and to the Ministry of Health, for instance on Medical Education (1965) and on Hospital Scientific and Technical Services (1967). The Society has had representatives on the G.M.C., the British Postgraduate Medical Federation, the City and Guilds of London Institute and other bodies to which Apothecaries can usefully contribute.

Lectures have been part of the tradition of the Society since the early

The Great Hall set for a Livery dinner, January 1998.

nineteenth century when, as a result of William Prowting's bequest of 1794, Timothy Lane F.R.S. (Master 1801–02) spoke at the Hall. The tradition was revived between 1944 and 1945 and ultimately gave rise to the foundation of the Faculty of the History of Medicine and Pharmacy. During the 1960s the Society hosted courses of lectures for general practitioners under the aegis of the British Postgraduate Medical Federation, and 1969 saw the first John Keats memorial lecture. This, like the Macdonald Critchley lecture, is held biennially, but whereas the John Keats lecture has its subject defined, the Macdonald Critchley lecture ranges widely, from Marcel Marceau on "The art of mime" to Enoch Powell on "Medicine and Politics". An annual Wellcome lecture was founded in 1993 and another is given to the Society of Occupational Medicine.

Apothecaries' Hall is more than an examination centre and an attractive venue for lectures. It was intended to be and remains primarily the home and headquarters of a City livery company, a meeting place for kindred spirits and a source of hospitality. The Hall has also provided a base for the Spectacle Makers' and the Turners' Companies since the 1940s, and the meetings of the Council and committees of the newly founded Royal College of General Practitioners were held at the Hall in the 1950s. Since the redevelopment of the Society's properties in the 1980s the solicitors Rowe & Maw have occupied the offices on Black Friars Lane and around the courtyard. Improvements to the Hall and adjoining properties made at that time have not only brought good rents but also good Hall lettings – there is a constant demand for the use of the Hall for social functions, from wedding receptions to bankers' dinners.

For members of the Society there are five Livery dinners each year, a Livery lunch, a Yeomanry dinner, a ladies' dinner and opportunities to entertain guests, attend lectures and church services. The Society's social calendar received an injection of energy following the appointment of the Livery Committee as a new link between the Court and Liverymen in 1981, and the introduction of a carol service and the occasional ball. Alas, the herbarizing dinner, formerly held in July and unique to the Society, is no more, although the tradition was rekindled once during the Mastership of Dr James Fisher (1987–88). The quarterly dinners of the Friendly Medical Society, also unique to the Society and held for almost 200 years, were discontinued after 1922.

With the largest membership of any livery company, standing at 1,707 in November 1997 (430 Yeomen, 1,277 Liverymen), these and other functions are well supported. Membership of the Society is open to all British subjects who belong to the medical profession – those in other professions may gain admission provided that the non-medical membership does not exceed 15 per cent of the total. The composition of the Court of Assistants consists of up to twenty-four senior members of the Society, of whom not less than twenty-two must be registered medical practitioners. Within this body, the Master and two Wardens form the Private Court and are elected each year on the basis of seniority.

The royal charter of 1617 laid down that every year on 20 August or within eight days of that date, three of "the more wise and discreet Men of the said Society" should be chosen as Master and Wardens. The election of the new Master and Wardens still takes place in August and the inauguration of the new reign is celebrated on Master's Day in October (near enough to the feast day of St Luke, patron saint of doctors, surgeons and artists) when members attend a service at St Andrew-by-the-Wardrobe.[85]

In the late eighteenth century the ceremony on Master's Day, then called Confirmation Day, was an elaborate performance requiring the attendance of a "band of musick" at four stately processions. Sustained by sirloin of beef at noon, the first procession led the company to church and, when the service and sermon ended, gifts were distributed to the poor. Dinner at the Hall was in strict order of precedence and after the toasts a procession formed to perambulate the Great Hall, seeking out the new Master to place the coronet on his head. The two Wardens were similarly honoured, their healths drunk and oaths taken before the last procession retreated to the strains of "The conquering hero".[86] Two hundred years on, the formalities of Master's Day are less demanding, but the tradition of the church service followed by lunch at the Hall is maintained, providing an opportunity to pay tribute to the Past Master and to congratulate the new incumbents.

Anniversaries are an important part of the Society's history and are always celebrated. The tercentenary of the granting of the charter by King James I was the reason for an extravagant "breakfast" feast in 1917, despite war-time shortages. The 350th anniversary in 1967 warranted a whole week of celebrations, the climax being a dinner on 6 December attended by Her Majesty Queen Elizabeth The Queen Mother. Two new stained-glass windows were installed in the Court Room, the courtyard was re-paved and Dr Copeman delivered the Gideon de Laune lecture "In praise of Apothecaries", on which his history of the Society was based.

The Apothecary's evolution from the spicers and pepperers of London justified the celebration of the octocentenary of the Pepperers' Guild in 1980, when the Court dined with the Court of the Grocers' Company in the presence of H.R.H. The Duke of Edinburgh. The Society also held a garden party that summer at the Chelsea Physic Garden in the presence of H.R.H. The Duke of Gloucester, and commissioned commemorative salt-and-pepper-shakers.

The Society of Apothecaries is unique in combining the duties of a licensing body for the medical profession not only with even wider educational endeavours but also with the civic, social, ceremonial and charitable responsibilities of a City livery company. The Society was incorporated in 1617 to regulate, govern and uphold the art and mistery of its fellowship, which it continues to do, and, with an unrestricted number of Liverymen, the Society is set to maintain its position as the City livery company with the largest membership. In the twentieth century the Society's professional membership has supported two Apothecary Lord Mayors of the City, in 1911 and in 1995. On the first occasion Sir Thomas Boor Crosby, previously Master of the Turners' Company, became the first Physician to be Lord Mayor. On the second occasion Alderman Sir John Chalstrey, the Immediate Past Master,

Alderman Sir John Chalstrey, Master of the Society (1994–95), Lord Mayor (1995–96), painted by June Mendoza in 1996.

Liverymen of the Society taking part in the procession on Lord Mayor's Day, November 1995.

became the first Surgeon to be Lord Mayor, and Lady Chalstrey the first Liveryman Apothecary to be Lady Mayoress. In 1911 Sir Thomas Crosby's escort included a small contingent from the Society as part of the procession on Lord Mayor's Day which featured pageants of the victorious historical epochs in the history of the British army and navy from Sir Francis Drake to the Duke of Wellington.[87] In November 1995 the Lord Mayor's Show was led by the Society's float of giant Apothecaries' jars filled with medicinal plants. Liverymen in their gowns formed a dignified escort while the less serious members were disguised as man-sized medicine bottles and capsules sporting cork hats and wielding over-sized spoons.

As Master of the Society of Apothecaries and as Lord Mayor the following year, Sir John Chalstrey represented his livery company in the City of London. Thus he personified that unique combination of professional and civic interests to which the Society remains true. As the charter of incorporation granted by King James I had stated in 1617, it was the duty of the Apothecary to "provide for the safety and public good of our subjects". Nearly four hundred years later that obligation continues to be central to the work of the Society.

Abbreviations and Notes

AHA	Apothecaries' Hall Archive.
BL	British Library.
BL Ms	British Library Department of Manuscripts.
BMJ	*British Medical Journal.*
Clark	Clark, George N., and Cook A.M., *A History of the Royal College of Physicians* 3 vols (1964–72).
CLRO	Corporation of London Records Office.
CM	Court Minutes, Society of Apothecaries. Volumes for 1617–1926 form GL Ms 8200 (see below). Later volumes at Apothecaries' Hall.
CME	Minutes of Court of Examiners, Society of Apothecaries. Volumes for 1815–99 form GL Ms 8239. Later volumes, and Examinations Committee Minutes at Apothecaries' Hall.
DNB	*Dictionary of National Biography.*
EAU	Underwood, E.A., Cameron, H.C., and Wall, Cecil, *A History of the Worshipful Society of Apothecaries of London* vol i 1617–1815 (1963).
EAU notes	Typescript and manuscript notes by E.A. Underwood deposited at the Wellcome Institute for the History of Medicine Library, ref PP/EAU F1–8, F39–46.
GCM	Minutes of Chelsea Physic Garden Committee, Society of Apothecaries. Volumes for 1731–1862 form GL Ms 8228. Later volumes at Apothecaries' Hall.
GL Ms	Guildhall Library Department of Manuscripts.
HRNSW	Bladen, F.M., (ed) *Historical Records of New South Wales* vols i–iii (1892–93).
Keevil	Keevil, J.J., *Medicine and the Navy 1200–1900* vols i–iv (1957–63).
NMML	National Maritime Museum Library, Greenwich.
PRO	Public Record Office, Kew.
TLMAS	*Transactions of London and Middlesex Archaeological Society.*
WA	Wardens' Accounts, Society of Apothecaries. Volumes for 1626–1812 form GL Ms 8202.

Notes

Apothecary with a capital letter denotes a member of the medieval mistery, and from 1617 a member of the Society; apothecary in the lower case is used in the wider sense. The same applies to other guilds and livery companies.

Dates are given according to the modern (post-1752) calendar.

Notes to chapter 1, pages 11–27.

1. Nunn, John F., *Ancient Egyptian Medicine* (1996) p.132.
2. The Goldsmiths were fined 45 marks. See Unwin, George, *The Gilds and Companies of London* (1963) p.48.
3. Kingdon, J.A. (ed), *Facsimile of the first volume of the Manuscript Archives of the Worshipful Company of Grocers of the City of London 1345–1463* (1886) part 1 p.xviii.
4. Matthews, Leslie G., *The Royal Apothecaries* (1967). Riley, H.T., *Memorials of London and London Life 1276–1419* (1868). Sharpe, R.R. (ed), *Calendar of Letter-Books preserved among the archives of the Corporation of the City of London* (1899–1912) and *Calendar of Wills proved and enrolled in the Court of Husting London* (1889). Thomas, A.H., and Jones, P.E. (eds),

Calendar of Plea and Memoranda Rolls 1323–1482 6 vols (1926–61).
5. John Stow, in his *Survey of London* (1598) claimed the lane was so-called because of the soap makers there.
6. Matthews, Leslie G., *The Royal Apothecaries* (1967). Trease, G.E., "The Spicers and Apothecaries of the Royal Household" in *Nottingham Medieval Studies* vol iii (1959) pp.19–52 and Appendix 1. For the Montpellier family see Trease, G.E., "A 13th century family of Court apothecaries" in *The Pharmaceutical Journal* 4 April 1959.
7. *Calendar of Charter Rolls* vol i (1903) p.292.
8. Nightingale, Pamela, *A Medieval Mercantile Community. The Grocers' Company and the Politics and Trade of London 1000–1485* (1995) p.95.
9. Beaven, A.B., *The Aldermen of the City of London* 2 vols (1908–13). Masters, Betty M., *The Chamberlain of the City of London 1237–1987* (1988).
10. Sharpe, R.R. (ed), *Letter Book E* (1903) p.232. There is no apparent explanation for the high number of Apothecaries and low number of Grocers. Pamela Nightingale (note 8 above, p.162) suggests that the Mayor was wary of the Apothecaries' ambivalent attitude towards him.
11. Riley, H.T., *Memorials of London and London Life 1276–1419* (1868) pp.344–45. The lack of records of the Fraternity of St Anthony/the Grocers' Company for the years 1358–73 may indicate a decline in their fortunes.
12. Matthews, Leslie G., *The Royal Apothecaries* (1967). Trease, G.E., "The spicers and apothecaries of the Royal Household" in *Nottingham Medieval Studies* vol iii (1959) pp.19–52.
13. Based on a list of twenty-six spices, twenty-seven drugs, five sugars, etc. supplied by John Donat, spicer-apothecary of Bucklersbury and Lombard Street, to King John of France during his imprisonment in England (1359–60). See Matthews, Leslie G., "King John of France and the English Spicers" in *Medical History* vol v (1961) pp.65–76.
14. William de Staines provided saltpetre and sulphur to manufacture gunpowder intended for the attack on Calais (1346, 1347), see Keevil vol i p.23.
15. Matthews, Leslie G., *The Royal Apothecaries* (1967) and Gottfried, Robert S., *Doctors and Medicine in Medieval England 1340–1530* are the sources for much of this section. See also Myers, A.R., *The Household of Edward IV* (1959) and for Burton's will Sharpe, R.R. (ed), *Calendar of Wills proved and enrolled at the Court of Husting* vol ii (1890) p.555.
16. "A Book of plaisters, spasmadraps, pulthes etc devised by the King's Majestie, Dr Butts, Dr Chambre, Dr Cromer, Dr Augustin", Sloane Ms 1047, BL Ms. Transcribed in Thompson, C.J.S., *The Mystery and Art of the Apothecary* (1929) pp.168–178. Bayles, Howard, "Notes and Accounts Paid to the Royal Apothecaries in 1546 and 1547" and Stubbs, S.G. Blaxland, "Henry VIII and Pharmacy" in *Chemist and Druggist* 27 June 1931 pp.792–96.
17. *Calendar of Letters and Papers Foreign and Domestic, Henry VIII* vol xxi part 2 (1910) pp.394–99. Alsop was a Warden of the Grocers' Company (1552–53) and later on the Court, see Matthews, Leslie G., "Royal Apothecaries of the Tudor Period" in *Medical History* vol viii (1964) pp.170–80.
18. Grocers' Company, "Calendar to the Court Minute Books 1556–1692" Ts compiled by William Le Hardy *circa* 1930 vol i part 3, 26 June, 24 July 1584. Matthews, Leslie G., *The Royal Apothecaries* (1967).
19. Hanbury, Daniel, "The Spices, Groceries and Wax of a Medieval Household AD 1303–10" in *Science Papers* (1876) pp.478–85.
20. Harvey, Barbara, *Living and Dying in England 1100–1540. The Monastic Experience* (1993).

21. Riley, *op cit* pp.273–74.
22. Power, D'Arcy (ed), Arderne, John, *Treatises of Fistula in Ano (1376)* (1910).
23. Skeat, Walter W. (ed), *Chaucer. Complete Works* (1976) p.424. The OUP classics edition (1986) translates thus: "Ever at hand he had apothecaries/ To send him syrups, drugs and remedies/ For each put money in the other's pocket -".
24. Kingsford, C.L., *Stonor Letters and Papers 1290–1483* vol ii (1919) p.107.
25. Thrupp, Sylvia, "The Grocers of London", in Power, Eileen, and Postan, M.M. (eds), *Studies in English Trade in the Fifteenth Century* (1933). In one case at least (1433) an apothecary earned more than the physician in attendance on a dying man (a draper called Tatersall), see Rawcliffe, Carole, "Medicine and Medical Practice in Later Medieval London" in *Guildhall Studies in London History* vol v no 1, October 1981 p.20.
26. The value of Hexham's inventory (£5 3s 7d) has been compared to that of a jeweller's shop – £5 11s 6d (1381) and a haberdasher's – £3 10s 7d (1378), see Getz, F.M., "The Pharmaceutical writings of Gilbertus Anglicus" in *Pharmacy in History* vol 34 no 1 (1992) p.22. Trease, G.E., and Hodson, J.H., "The inventory of John Hexham, a Fifteenth Century Apothecary" in *Medical History* vol ix (1965).
27. Saunders was powdered sandalwood. For a transcription of Ashfield's fine see Heath, Baron, *Some Account of the Worshipful Company of Grocers* (1869) p.423.
28. Grocers' Company, "Calendar" *op cit* vol i part 1, 20 May 1564.
29. Preface to *Pharmacopoeia Londinensis* (1618).
30. Grocers' Company, "Calendar" *op cit* vol i part 3, 28 May 1587, 26 February 1589. For apothecaries in the Grocers' Company see Jacques, David, *Essential to the Pracktick Part of Physic: the London Apothecaries 1540–1617* (1992) chapter 3 and table 1.
31. Grocers' Company, "Calendar" *op cit* vol i part 3, 15 March 1588. Royal College of Physicians of London, Annals (1581–1608) f.72, 12 February 1588.
32. Grocers' Company, "Calendar" *op cit* vol i part 1, 4 March 1563.
33. The figures are taken from Weinstein, Rosemary, *Tudor London* (1994) and Roberts, R.S., "The London Apothecaries and Medical Practice in Tudor and Stuart England" PhD London University 1964, Appendix 1.
34. Recorde, Robert, *The Urinal of Physick whereunto is added an ingenious Treatise concerning Physicians, Apothecaries, and Chyrurgians, set forth by a Dr in Queen Elizabeth's Days* (1651) p.158.
35. Bullein, William, *Bulwarke of defence against all sickness* (1562).
36. Stow, John, *A Survey of London* (1598) reprinted from the text of 1603, edited by Kingsford, C.L., vol i (1971) p.260.
37. Thornbury G.W., and Walford, E., *Old and New London* vol i part 2 (1883–85) p.435.
38. Shakespeare, William, *Romeo and Juliet* (1597) Act v Scene 1.

Notes to chapter 2, pages 29–55.

1. There were three Peter Chamberlens. The eldest was surgeon/accoucheur to Queen Anne. His younger brother, Peter II, married Sara de Laune (Gideon's sister). Their son was Peter III (1601–83). The family lived at Black Friars. Peter the elder is generally credited with the invention of the Chamberlen midwifery forceps. See Aveling, J.H., *The Chamberlens and the Midwifery Forceps* (1882).
2. The date has been erroneously given by Dr E.A. Underwood and others as 1607. The misunderstanding has arisen because the documents refer merely to the fourth year of King James. He came to the throne of England 24 March 1603, the fourth year of his reign therefore spanned March 1606 to March 1607, thus a document of April

in the fourth year is April 1606. This is confirmed in the Grocers' Company Court Minutes 11 April 1606, GL Ms 11,588 vol ii f.437, and in House of Commons, *Report of the Livery Companies' Commission* vol iii (1884) p.1.

3. Grocers' Company, "Calendar to the Court Minute Books 1556–1692" Ts compiled by William Le Hardy *circa* 1930 vol ii part 3, 15 June 1610.

4. *Ibid* 29 April 1614. Jacques, David, *Essential to the Pracktick Part of Physick: The London Apothecaries 1540–1617* (1992) chapter 4.

5. CM 11 July 1648.

6. Lansdowne Ms 487 ff.388–89, BL Ms. Grocers' Company, "Calendar" *op cit* vol ii part 3, 29 April 1614.

7. GL Ms 8251 f.69. Jacques, David, *op cit.*

8. GL Ms 8251 f.75.

9. *State Papers Domestic 1611–18* pp.307, 312–13, 326. Rumler and Lobel were brothers-in-law; Lobel was related to Mayerne by marriage. For the Overbury scandal see Somerset, Anne, *Unnatural Murder: Poison at the Court of James I* (1997).

10. Grocers' Company, "Calendar" *op cit* vol ii part 3, 22 June 1614; vol iii part 1, 7 February 1617.

11. For a comparison of draft versions of the charter see Journal 30, ff.299–306; Letter Book GG 1617–20 ff.1–8 and printed copy (1825), CLRO. Rot.Pat. c66/2136, PRO. GL Mss 8251, 8256, 8252. Goodall, Charles, *The Royal College of Physicians of London* (1684) p.119. The most reliable version is GL Ms 8252, being a late-seventeenth-century translation of the original. It is the most likely source for the transcription given in Barrett, C.R.B., *The History of the Society of Apothecaries of London* (1905) pp.xix-xxxix (with one mistake over the name George Haughton Mace). The original, sealed document belonging to the Society is at the Hall but is partly folded and difficult to read. The different versions, and the occasional repetition of a name has led to the number of founder members of the Society being variously given as 123 or 125, incorrectly.

12. Lord Chancellor Bacon was charged with bribery and corruption and condemned by the House of Lords in 1621. Among other charges, it was alleged that he had received £200 from the Grocers' Company and £100 from the Apothecaries with a taster of gold worth £40–£50 and a present of ambergris (a product cast up by whales or found in their intestines). He was imprisoned briefly and never again sat in Parliament.

13. Grocers' Company, "Calendar" *op cit* vol iii part 1, 13 December 1620, 3 January 1621.

14. Higgins was later dismissed from the Court of Assistants for being in dispute with de Laune, but was Master 1638–39 when Nicholas Culpeper was one of his apprentices (he broke his indentures in 1640). BL Ms Harley 1454 contains the accounts of the Apothecary Stephen Huggins or Higgins who supplied medicines to the aristocracy and courtiers such as Viscount Cranborne and Lord Burleigh from 1594 to 1604. Thomas Fownes or Fones lived alongside his pharmacy at the sign of The Three Fawns, Old Bailey. His nephew, John Winthrop (later a Fellow of the Royal Society and Governor of Connecticut), lodged with him and married his daughter Martha. Another daughter, Elizabeth Winthrop, was the subject of Anya Seton's novel, *The Winthrop Woman* (1968). Whittet, T.D., "Apothecaries and their Lodgers", in *Journal of the Royal Society of Medicine* vol 76 supplement 2, 1983. Black, R.C., *The younger John Winthrop* (1966).

15. George Shiers, J.W. Rumler, Ralph Clayton (retired), Gideon de Laune, Lewis Le Mire, Joliffe Lownes. Stephen Chase and John Parkinson were to be Apothecaries to

Charles I, see Matthews, Leslie G., *The Royal Apothecaries* (1967). Whittet, T.D., "The Charter members of the Society of Apothecaries" in *Proceedings of the Royal Society of Medicine* vol 64, October 1971 p.1064, and pre-publication typescript, AHA. Poynter, F.N.L., *Gideon De Laune and his family circle* (1965).

16. *State Papers Domestic 1611–1618* p.507.
17. Grocers' Company, "Calendar" *op cit* vol ii part 1, 12 April 1619.
18. *State Papers Domestic 1619–23* p.171. Members of the Grocers' Company continued to trade in apothecaries' goods e.g. Robert Batt, apothecary and Grocer, whose goods and chattels were valued at £314 15s 1d in 1655. The valuation/inventory comprises two folios listing the contents of his shop, MCI/85 no. 202, CLRO.
19. 6 March 1624, GL Ms 8292. *State Papers Domestic 1619–23* p.229.
20. Cobbett, William, (comp), *The Parliamentary History of England* vol i 1066–1625 (1806) 22 James I (1624) 1503. For Bacon's downfall see note 12.
21. Society's suit in the Star Chamber 1622–23, GL Ms 8285. For a detailed account of the case and the archives see EAU pp.225–242.
22. CM 12 December 1617, GL Ms 8200 vol i. The charter of 1617 referred to the new corporation of Apothecaries as "one Politic and Corporate Body", the "Art, Mistery or Faculty of Apothecaries", "the Company" and "the Society". The earliest Court Minutes and Wardens' Accounts use the word Company, which tends to be superseded by Society from 1684. It has been been claimed that the Society of Apothecaries was so-called after the *Societa Scientifica* of Naples founded 1540, see Rolleston, Henry, "History of medicine in the City of London" in *Annals of Medical History* vol iii (1941) p.3.
23. The Court Minutes for 1617 to 1651 record such matters.
24. At a rent of £10 p.a. with 2s 6d for the Beadle, see WA 1626–27 and Englefield, W.A.D., *The History of the Painter Stainers' Company of London* (1950) pp.15, 107.
25. CM 12 October 1620. WA 1626–27. From time to time spoons were sold or exchanged for other pieces of plate.
26. WA 1631–32.
27. *Ibid* 1626–27.
28. From September 1626 when they begin, the Wardens' Accounts record gifts, loans and regular expenses and payments, GL Ms 8202.
29. CM 15 November 1622. WA 1633–34, 1634–35, 1635–36. EAU p.37.
30. WA 1630–31, 1633–34, 1634–35.
31. *Ibid* 1629–30, 1630–31.
32. *Ibid* 1626–27, 1627–28, 1660–61.
33. A seventeenth-century list of the order of the City companies (CLRO Ms 963) lists the Apothecaries as number fifty-eight out of eighty-four livery companies at that time. The Society remains at number fifty-eight in a list of 100 (1997).
34. The Merchant Taylors rank sixth or seventh in the order of precedence, the order having been settled in 1516.
35. WA 1630–31. For the Society's barges see pages 113–16.
36. The date usually cited for the Society's first herbarizing is 1633 (erroneous), see CM 30 May 1620: "Thursday after Whitsunweek was appointed for ye simpling day". Whitsunday was 3 June in 1620. Whitsunday, Monday and Tuesday were known as Whitsuntide. The Thursday after that week would have been 14 June. There may have been earlier, unrecorded simpling days – the Court Minutes for the period are brief and chiefly concerned with binding apprentices, granting the freedom and discipline. The note in the margin to CM 9 June 1623 "the first simpling" may refer to the first simpling of the summer, or be an oversight. For early-nineteenth-century herbarizings see pages 138–39.

37. *DNB*. Jeffers, Robert H., *The Friends of John Gerard* (1967). Kew, H.W., and Powell, H.E., *Thomas Johnson* (1932).
38. CM 12 December 1633. The copy has since disappeared from the Society's Library, presumed destroyed in the Great Fire (a copy of the second edition, 1636, remains). The frontispiece featured the bananas with which Johnson was associated. Johnson was elected to the Court of Assistants in 1640. He should not be confused with Thomas Johnson, Apothecary of Friday Street, who obtained his freedom in 1628.
39. *State Papers Domestic 1611–18* p.555. Gideon de Laune obtained a grant of arms 7 March 1613.
40. CM 18 August 1642, 11 July 1648, 23 May 1676.
41. GL Ms 8252.
42. CM 20 April 1643.
43. The Master, Wardens and three Assistants who advised the College were Phillipps, Higgins, Fones, Parkinson, Sherriff, Darnelly – all of them experienced Apothecaries. They were not called upon until February 1618. The *Pharmacopoeia* was reported to be on the point of completion the previous September. See Clark vol i p.228 and Urdang, George, *Pharmacopoeia Londinensis 1618* (1944). Parkinson's claim was made during the investigations surrounding the *Quo Warranto* (1634–35), EAU pp.289–90 and GL Ms 8286.
44. August 1631, see WA 1630–31. Proceedings in Star Chamber against several members of the Apothecaries' Company (1635), GL Ms 8286.
45. The dispute with the College of Physicians is dealt with in greater detail in EAU chapters 4 and 9, also EAU notes F45. GL Ms 8286 is a source for both. During the investigations it was stated that Cooke had for seven or eight years "served the Emperor of Muscovia and divers of his Peers and Nobility with all kinds of physic".
46. CM 15 March 1664.
47. *Ibid* 30 May 1665.
48. *Ibid* 22 February, 8 March, 15 June 1670.
49. Merrett, a Fellow of the College of Physicians, was Keeper of the Harveian Library at the College before the Great Fire. Following a dispute with the College he was expelled from the Fellowship in 1681. The pamphlets airing the differences between Physicians and Apothecaries included Goddard, Jonathan, *Discourse setting forth the Unhappy Condition of the practice of Physick* (1670). Merrett, C., *Self-Conviction* (1670) and *The Accomplisht Physician, the Honest Apothecary and the Skilful Surgeon* (1670). Stubbe, H., *Lex Talionis* (1670) and *Campanella Revived* (1670). See also Cowen, David L., "Pharmacists and Physicians: An Uneasy Relationship" in *Pharmacy in History* vol 34 no 1 (1992) pp.6–7.
50. CM 24 August, 7 October 1675.
51. *Ibid* 7 November 1677. The College of Physicians was granted a royal charter in 1518; its charter of 1663 referred to "the King's College of Physicians". The title Royal College of Physicians came into use from 1674.
52. Badger aired his grievances against the Society in a Broadsheet, "Dr Badger's Vindication of himself from the groundless Calumnies and Malicious Slanders of some London Apothecaries" (1701). Whittet, T.D., "John Badger Apothecaryite" in *Pharmaceutical Historian* vol iii no 1, May 1973 pp. 2–4.
53. CM 29 January, 14 February 1689.
54. *Ibid* 6 March, 14 April 1690. Apothecaries' draft petition against Surgeons' Bill 1690, GL Ms 8290. EAU pp. 370–74. Hilton Price, F.G., "Signs of Old London" in *London Topographical Record* vol iv (1907) p.89.
55. CM 10 March 1698.

56. *DNB*. Wheatley, H.B., *London Past and Present* vol i (1891) pp.55–56.
57. CM 6 November, 19 November 1701, 6 January, 18 February 1702, 4 July 1706. The London or Bishopsgate Workhouse was on the site of Liverpool Street Station. It was founded in 1649 for the relief and employment of the poor. Demolished *circa* 1830.
58. CM 28 April 1684.
59. Clark vol ii pp.442–43. EAU pp.131–32.
60. Brown, J., *Reports of Cases in the High Court of Parliament 1701–1779* (1779) pp.78–80. EAU pp.132–35, 389–402. Anon, *Observations upon the case of William Rose* (1704). Clark vol ii pp.476–79.

Notes to chapter 3, pages 57–73.

1. Bell, Walter, *The Great Plague in London in 1665* (1951) estimated that this figure, taken from the Bills of Mortality, was probably short of the truth by 30,000. Boghurst, William, *Loimographia. An account of the Great Plague of London in the year 1665* (1666), edited by Payne, J.F., (1894).
2. WA 1634–35, CM 5 April, 27 July 1636.
3. *Ibid* 15 May 1640. WA 1640–41.
4. WA 1641–42.
5. CM 6 November 1641.
6. *DNB*. Kew H.W., and Powell, H.E., *Thomas Johnson* (1932). Thomas Johnson, herbalist and Royalist, should not be confused with Thomas Johnson, an Apothecary of Friday Street, who was made free in 1628.
7. CM 18 April 1661. Parsons, F.G., *The History of St Thomas's Hospital* vol ii (1934) pp.59–60.
8. CM 24 February, 22 April 1646, 17 August 1652. *DNB*. Hearne, T., *Notes and Remarks* vol viii (1907) p.403 and vol ix p.220. Dick, Oliver Lawson (ed), *Aubrey's Brief Lives* (1950) p.205. Whittet, T.D., "Apothecaries and their lodgers: their part in the development of the sciences and of medicine" in *Journal of the Royal Society of Medicine* supplement no 2, vol 76 (1983), and "Sir Thomas Clarges, apothecary and envoy" in *Journal of the Royal Society of Medicine* vol 81 August 1988 pp.464–67. I am grateful to Dr Southwood for drawing this to my attention. Scott, J.M., *The Book of Pall Mall* (1965) p.20 claims that Clarges was the first to occupy 79 Pall Mall *circa* 1664–65.
9. CM 19 December 1633, 28 August 1649. *DNB*.
10. CM 20 April 1643.
11. *Ibid* 17 December 1648.
12. WA 1648–49.
13. *Ibid* 1650–51.
14. *Ibid* 1651–52.
15. *Ibid* 1659–60, 1660–61. CM 3, 22 May 1660. Nicholas Bannister paid for the king's arms at the Hall (1664), Benefactions Book, GL Ms 8231.
16. Dekker, Thomas, *A Rod for Run-Awayes* (1625).
17. Merrett, C., *A Short View of the Frauds and Abuses Committed by the Apothecaries* (1669, 1670).
18. Hodges, Nathaniel, *Loimologia or an Historical Account of the Plague in London, 1665* (1720).
19. CM 8 September 1659. Clark vol i p.341.
20. CM 22 June 1665, 22 March 1666.

21. Latham, Robert, (ed), *The Shorter Pepys* (1987) pp.250, 543, 648. Whittet, T.D., "Samuel Pepys and his Apothecaries" in *Die Vorträge der Hauptversammlung* (1965) pp.273–81, AHA.
22. Whittet, T.D., *The Apothecaries in the Great Plague of London 1665* (1965).
23. CM 26 May 1666.
24. O'Rourke, D.T., "John Houghton 1645–1705, Journalist, Apothecary and FRS" in *Pharmaceutical Historian* vol ix no 1, April 1979.
25. Boghurst, William, *Loimographia. An account of the Great Plague of London in the year 1665* (1666), edited by Payne, J.F. (1894).
26. Burnby, J.G.L., "John Conyers. London's First Archaeologist" in *TLMAS* no 35 (1984) pp.63–80. Conyers was admitted to the Livery in 1667.
27. Bell, Walter, *The Great Plague in London in 1665* (1951), see note 1.
28. The Wardens' Accounts for 1669–71 refer to payments for the return/transportation of plate, pewter and other possessions held for safekeeping from the time of the Great Fire until the Hall was rebuilt. See also GL Ms 8204. John Lorrimer's portrait had been presented in 1663 and now hangs in the Great Hall.
29. De Beer, E.S. (ed), *The Diary of John Evelyn* (1959) p. 496.
30. Malcolm, J.P., *Londinium Redivivum* vol iv (1807) p.76.
31. CM 2 October 1666.
32. *Ibid* 4 June, 15 August, 3 September 1667, 2 April, 1 October 1668.
33. WA 1667–68.
34. CM 1 July 1673.
35. *Ibid* 10, 24, 28 April 1684.
36. *Ibid* 16, 26 February 1685. Copy of charter naming Edward Fleetwood, City's Enrolled Charters vol i f.276, CLRO.
37. *Ibid* 6, 11 May 1685. Lists of Liverymen, 1685, 1688, GL Ms 8257.
38. *Ibid* 7, 19, 22 October 1687. James Chase was the king's first apothecary; Lightfoot was formerly apothecary to Charles II, and Catherine of Braganza (the Queen Dowager).
39. *Ibid* 3 March 1688.
40. *Ibid* 28 November 1688.

Notes to chapter 4, pages 75–111.

1. CM 20 February, 8 August 1621. The Benefactions Book lists seventeen members' subscriptions of £5 or £8 towards the purchase of a Hall in 1621, GL Ms 8231.
2. WA 1631–32, 1632–33. CM 19 October 1633.
3. CM 27 November, 3 December 1632.
4. For details of the gallery see Colvin, H.M. (ed), *The History of the King's Works* vol iv part 2 (1982) p.55.
5. Conveyances of messuages built by Hardrett 1624, 1635, 1662, Box 31 nos 2, 6, 44, CLRO. Expenses of re-tiling and building work 1632–34, GL Ms 8251. CM 22 February 1633. Articles of Agreement between the Clerk and William Stevens (joiner), 12 September 1682, GL Ms. 8288.
6. *State Papers Domestic 1546* part 1 504 (35).
7. The topography of the site and the archives relating to it are transcribed in Feuillerat, Albert, "Blackfriars Records", *Malone Society Collections* vol ii (1913) and Smith, Irwin, *Shakespeare's Blackfriars Playhouse* (1964). See also Clapham, A.W., "On the Topography of the Dominican Priory of London" in *Archaeologia* vol 63 (1912). Norman, Philip,

"Medieval Remains found at Blackfriars, May 1900" in *London Topographical Record* vol i (1901) pp.1–9. Martin, William, and Toy, Sidney, "The Black Friars in London" in *TLMAS* vol v (1929) pp.353–79.

8. Norman, Philip, "Recent Discoveries of Medieval Remains in London" in *Archaeologia* vol lxvii (1916) pp.13–14. Bluer, Richard V., and Allen, Patrick, "Archive Report, Apothecaries' Hall, 20–26 Black Friars Lane", Department of Urban Archaeology, Museum of London APO 81, March 1985. *London Archaeologist* vol iv no 14, spring 1984 p. 385. I am grateful to Bruce Watson of the Museum of London Archaeological Service for his contribution on the archaeology of the site.

9. Nichols, John, *The Progresses and Public Processions of Queen Elizabeth* vol ii (1788). The queen's visit to Black Friars was the subject of a painting by Marcus Gheeraerts which shows a building tentatively identified as Cobham House, see Ilchester, Earl of, "Queen Elizabeth's visit to Blackfriars June 16 1600" in *Walpole Society* vol ix (1921) pp.1–19.

10. Petitions of the inhabitants of Black Friars 1596 and *circa* 1619 transcribed in Smith, Irwin, *Shakespeare's Blackfriars Playhouse* (1964).

11. *Ibid* p.110. Downes, John, *Roscius Anglicanus* (1708) edited by Knight, J. (1886) p.20. Hotson, Leslie, *The Commonwealth and Restoration Stage* (1928) pp.142, 145. Latham, Robert, and Matthews, William, *The Diary of Samuel Pepys* vol ii (1970) p.130 and vol x (1983) p.439. Nethercot, A.H., *Sir William D'Avenant* (1938) alleges that Davenant had used Apothecaries' Hall for plays before the civil war. There is no reference to Davenant's Company in the Court Minutes or Wardens' Accounts. Lady Davenant had previously been married to the Apothecary Thomas Crosse. Their son Paul was admitted to the freedom in 1667; Thomas Crosse junior became Davenant's secretary.

12. Stow, John, *A Survey of the Cities of London and Westminster* (1598) edited by J. Strype part 1 (1720) pp.187–88.

13. CM 7 June 1633.

14. GL Mss 8251 and 8230 both contain the accounts of Job Weale, Treasurer, of the purchase and restoration funds for the Hall 1632–34. Ms 8251 is more detailed and may have been the rough copy. It gives a figure of £1,033 6s 8d for the first instalment paid to the Commissioners for Lady Howard, November 1833; the Court Minutes cite £1,040, CM 16 November, 3 December 1632.

15. CM 22 March, 4 April 1633.

16. GL Ms 8251. WA 1632–34, CM 1632–33.

17. CM 12 January 1633. Lord Hertford's garden was south of the Hall.

18. CM 28 September 1641, 20 April 1642, 14 August 1643, 11 July 1648, 23 August 1655. GL Ms 8233.

19. WA 1651–52, 1667–68. Peter Mills's involvement in surveying the site after the Great Fire is detailed in the London Topographical Society's publication (1967), see note 35 below.

20. CM 2 October, 16 December 1666, 3 September 1667. One new house at Black Friars was being rebuilt only a week after the fire, see Porter, Stephen, *The Great Fire of London* (1996).

21. CM 4 June, 20 October 1667.

22. 23 July 1667, GL Ms 8201. WA 1667–68.

23. *Ibid* 4 August 1667. WA 1667–68. Jerman "came not" to the first rendezvous with members of the rebuilding committee but attended the second, with P. Sambrooke.

24. 27 April 1668, GL Ms 8201. Kirbie or Kirby has been identified by H.M. Colvin as Richard Kirby, responsible for a house in Snow Hill for Paul Wickes (1671). His name occurs only in the Rough Court Minutes, GL Ms 8201 vol i. EAU pp.319–20. C.R.B.

Barrett's History of the Society (1905) gives the surveyor/architect as Cook, a misreading of the name Lock.

25. Gunther, R.T. (ed), *The Architecture of Sir Roger Pratt* (1928). Metcalfe, Priscilla, *The Halls of the Fishmongers' Company* (1927). Lock was employed as carpenter at three of Wren's City churches: St Magnus the Martyr, St Mary at Hill and St Mildred Poultry, see Colvin, H.M., *Biographical Dictionary of British Architects 1600–1840* (1978) p.523. T. Lock is mentioned in Robinson, Henry, (ed), *The Diary of Robert Hooke 1672–80* (1935).
26. CM 20 October 1668, 10 May 1669.
27. *Ibid* 18 January 1670.
28. WA 1668–71. CM 19 January 1670.
29. The fretwork on the ceiling cost £100, GL Ms 8288. Joiner's bill for the Court Room £141 4s (1673), GL Ms 8257.
30. CM 18, 24 January, 22 June 1671. WA 1669–73. For Young's career see Colvin, H.M., *A Biographical Dictionary of British Architects 1600–1840* (1978) pp.965–66; Gunnis, Rupert, *Dictionary of British Sculptors 1660–1851* (1968); Imray, Jean, *The Mercers' Hall* (1991); Knoop, D., and Jones, G.P., *The London Mason in the Seventeenth Century* (1935) and *Wren Society* vol xx (1943) p.267. Young reclaimed land from the Thames for a new wharf, CM 22 July 1673. Gates were set up at the lower end of the great stone stairs in 1692, CM 30 June 1692. Young submitted a bill for £5 10s for "Mr de Laune's head" but was paid only £4, CM 23 May, 23 November 1676. John Young was Master of the Masons' Company in 1657, his two sons were to follow suit. Nicholas was the mason for five of Wren's churches including St Martin Ludgate (1677–87).
31. CM 14 July, 17 August 1671. WA 1671–72.
32. CM 2 July 1672. Phillips was paid £36, WA 1673–74.
33. EAU p.72 supposes that Spanish tables meant Cuban mahogany. It seems more likely that they were Spanish oak (as used in the gallery, 1682). WA 1668–70. CM 23 May, 15 August 1676. Snelling was paid £15 for drawing King James's picture and 28s for procuring the copy to draw from, CM 10 October 1676 (the figure 28 has sometimes been misread as 20). Corbett's kitchen, CM 10 June 1672.
34. CM 15 August 1667. WA 1667–68. Lease of 1671, GL Ms 8233. Deeds etc 1671–1801, GL Ms 8266.
35. Ground taken from Apothecaries, 8 March 1668 and surveying of foundations by Peter Mills, London Topographical Society, *The Survey of Building Sites in the City of London after the Great Fire of 1666 by Peter Mills and John Oliver* 5 vols (1967).
36. CM 19 May 1670. GL Ms 8233. Walter Pelling was a close friend of Pepys, see Latham, Robert, (ed), *The Shorter Pepys* (1987).
37. Articles of Agreement 1671, GL Ms 8269.
38. CM 20 May 1623, 12 October 1641.
39. *Ibid* 8 September 1671, 18 December 1677.
40. *Ibid* 22 July 1673, 1 July 1682. Plan by John Oliver (1682), AHA.
41. Hatton, Edward, *A New View of London* vol ii (1708) p.593.
42. Strype, J., *A Survey of the Cities of London and Westminster* vol i (1720) p.194.
43. CM 25 September 1729, 27 July, 20 August 1730, 14 March, 20 June 1734, 21 October 1785. Insurance with Sun Life, 19 July 1734 policy 64344 describes the Great Laboratory under the Hall and counting house adjoining, a house fronting the street, a timber shed and various rooms in the Hall including "a little room ... on the common staircase and two rooms over the same", a warehouse over the Company's Parlour, the chemical shop, long garret etc. GL Ms 11,936 vol 41. Photograph of the document, AHA.
44. CM 8, 18 December 1746. Remonstrance addressed to the Master for 1746–47,

NOTES

William Lake, AHA.

45. CM 19 August 1746.

46. *Ibid* 16 June, 18 August 1757, 10 January 1758.

47. Inventory of estates, GL Ms 8233. Title to wharf deeds 1671–1770, AHA. CM 19 June 1683.

48. *Ibid* 12 August, 21 October 1762, 6 December 1763. Conveyance and plan 14 June 1764, AHA. George Wyatt (d.1790) was a successful builder, Surveyor of Paving for the City and one of the proprietors of the Albion Mills. Robert Mylne was surveyor to St Paul's Cathedral (1766) and to the Stationers' Company from 1776.

49. CM 10 December 1767, 20 October 1768, 15 June, 30 October, 22 December 1770, 19 March 1771. Elevation of east side Chatham Place attached to enfeoffment to Society, 13 July 1770, AHA. Cf. elevation of east side "Apothecary's ground", Comptroller's City Lands Plan 125B, and other plans for the northern approaches to Black Friars Bridge attributed to Mylne, Comptroller's City Lands Plans 85A,B,C, 125A,B, 147, CLRO.

50. CM 3 August 1773. Report by Burchett CM 11 December 1775. Barlow developed another site on the north side of Earl Street/corner of Water Lane (1774), Box 22 no 22, CLRO.

51. CM 12 June 1776, 29 May, 25 June 1778. WA 1775–76, 1777–78.

52. Possibly John Nash, carpenter-builder and later architect to King George IV? He entered into a speculative building enterprise in Bloomsbury in 1775 and was bankrupt in 1783. The last payment of rent by John Nash to the Society was in 1785.

53. These issues dominate the Court Minutes 1859–64.

54. Negotiations opened in 1762, CM 10 June 1762. Mrs Thornicroft's property was purchased for £1,200, CM 27 August 1777, 29 May 1778. GL Mss 8267, 8269. Reconstruction of GL Ms 8267, AHA.

55. The Court Minutes for 1779–82 are missing. The proceedings can be followed in the Rough Court Minutes i.e. 13 March 1777, 16 May 1782, GL Ms 8201 vol xiii. See also Minutes of Building Committee 1781–85, GL Ms 8232 vol i; WA 1781–85; GL Ms 8203 vol i pp.17–18g; CM 1782–86. For Norris's career see Colvin, H.M., *Biographical Dictionary of British Architects 1600–1840* (1978) p.596 and *The Gentleman's Magazine* part 1, January 1792 p.91.

56. 16 May 1782, 19 June 1783, GL Ms 8201 vol xiii. Articles of Agreement and plans, July 1782, AHA.

57. CM 16 May 1782, 1784–86. GL Mss 8203 vol i pp.17–18 and 8232 vol i.

58. The Society had dealt with George Wyatt in the 1760s. Wyatt was paid £79 15s 4d for stuccoing in 1783, WA 1783–84. "Great court" given Higgins's stucco and Wyatt to finish, 23 May 1783, GL Ms 8232 vol i. Messrs Adam refers to the firm of William Adam set up in 1764 as developers and builders' merchants. The architect Robert Adam was the principal director, in partnership with William, John and James. Payment to Adams of £34 for "artificial stone" 28 December 1785, GL Ms 8203 vol i. CM 15 March 1785. Adams consulted about proposal to stucco the front of the Hall, 30 June 1785, GL Ms 8232 vol i. Thomas Carr of 7 Hatton Garden continued to act as surveyor to the Society in the 1780s. Possibly he was a relative of James and Henry Carr of Clerkenwell.

59. Bradley, Simon, and Pevsner, Nikolaus, *The Buildings of England. London 1: the City of London* (1997) p. 376.

60. Leases and counterpart leases Laboratory Stock 5 September 1786, Navy Stock 22 December 1786, GL Ms 8271. Notes on leases held by United Stock, 5 September, 22 December 1786, AHA.

61. CM 14 March 1792, 19 June, 16 October, 5 November 1793.

62. GL Ms 8234.
63. CM 10 May 1787. Plans of Paved Alley by Treeld (1787) and James Peacock, assistant Clerk of the Works for the City (1788), AHA. The Society exchanged premises on the south side of Paved Alley with Messrs North & Co.
64. For property transactions see CM 17 December 1771, 28 January 1772, 27 August 1777, 19 June 1783, 16 March 1784, 16 March, 10 April, 3 May 1785, 23 October 1801, 26 July 1822, 29 October 1841. GL Mss 8263, 8265, 8269. Deeds of four houses in Water Lane opposite the Hall (1751–89), and Paved Alley (1788); acquisition of Fleur de Luce Court (1794–95); freehold and leasehold estate records (1654–1789); Henry Field's extracts from Court Minutes, Hall and Estates, early nineteenth century; particulars of premises occupied by the United Stock 1846, AHA. The Times, *The site of the office of The Times* (1956).
65. CM 22 December 1813, 30 March 1814, 29 June 1815.
66. 10 June 1823, GL Ms 8223 vol i. The north wall of the courtyard was rebuilt at a cost of £692 in 1871, CM 22 December 1871.
67. The site of the Great Laboratory was leasehold until 1894 when the Society purchased the freehold from Lord Tredegar for £2,500, CM 20 June, 22 August 1893. Conveyance and plans re purchase of premises from trustees of Lord Tredegar (1893–94), AHA. GL Ms 8232 vol ii. CM 22 December 1813, 1 January 1814, 29 June 1815.
68. Conveyance to J. Walter (1848), AHA. 6 June 1846, 4 December 1847, 4 March 1848, GL Ms 8223 vol ii. Mills, Peter, "The Battle of London 1066" in *London Archaeologist* vol 8 no 3 (1996) pp.59–62.
69. Plan by J. Johnson (1882), correspondence and draft lease to Miller and Richard, AHA.
70. Plans of proposed examination halls by N.W. Robinson, October 1892, AHA. The plans were executed in 1893 at a cost of over £2,000. Conveyance with plan of dwellings Fleur de Luce Court, April 1896, AHA.
71. Gardiner, Stephen, "The Black Friars giant" in *The Sunday Observer* 26 June 1981.
72. CM 16 June, 8 December 1914, 18 May, 15 June 1915.
73. *The Electrical Times* 30 September 1915.
74. CM 14 July 1914, 10 October, 5 December 1916, 6 February 1917.
75. *Ibid* 8 February, 11 October 1921. Report and plan (1920–21), AHA. Proposals for Nestor House (1927–29), AHA. During demolition prior to rebuilding a layer of human bones was discovered, thought at the time to have indicated the cemetery of the Priory – since disproved.
76. Air-raid damage CM 1 July 1919. *Ibid* 14 February 1928. Hall restoration (1927–29), AHA.
77. The mantelpiece came from West Harling House, Norfolk, built in 1726, since demolished. The date of the hearth and grate was given as *circa* 1730, CM 19 December 1939.
78. *Ibid* 29 October 1940.
79. *Ibid* 17 December 1940, 13 May 1941.
80. *Ibid* 10 January, 11 February 1941.
81. Correspondence re meeting Sir Hugh Linstead and Professor Sir Charles Dodds in 1946 (1983–84), AHA. CM 9 August 1944.
82. Oswald, Arthur, "The Hall of the Worshipful Society of Apothecaries" in *Country Life* 10 October 1947 pp.726–29.
83. "The Worshipful Society of Apothecaries of London. Redevelopment Scheme 1980–87" – An album presented by Professor J.A. Dudgeon, Master (1985–86), AHA.

Gibson, Sir Ronald, "New developments at the Society of Apothecaries" in *BMJ* 21–31 December 1983. Files and boxes: Future Plans (1979–81), Minutes of Redevelopment Committee Meetings (1981–87), Architect's Instructions 1982–85, Miscellaneous papers re building (1982–84), Miscellaneous papers and correspondence (1987–90), and CM 1980s, AHA. I am indebted to Major C. O'Leary for information relating to the redevelopment.

84. Gardiner, Stephen, "The Black Friars giant" in *The Sunday Observer* 26 June 1981.

85. Palmer, C.F.R., "Burials at the Priories of the Black Friars" in *Antiquary* vol xxiii (1891) pp. 122–26, vol xxiv (1891) pp. 28–30, 76–79, 117–19. Fabrizi, Maria, "Finds Appraisal. Report for Apothecaries' Hall" August 1990. Museum of London Archaeological Archive APO 85. The conventual church was the burial place of Hubert de Burgh, the Earl of Worcester, Margaret daughter of the King of Scotland and the heart of Queen Eleanor, Queen of Edward I, was interred there.

Notes to chapter 5, pages 113–52.

1. CM 19, 29 August, 13 October 1631.
2. *Ibid* 1 September, 8, 15 November 1664.
3. *Ibid* 29 January 1673.
4. *Ibid* 22 July 1673.
5. *Ibid* 18 August, 8 October, 12 November, 15 December 1674, 1 January 1675. Clisbie was the carpenter at Apothecaries' Hall (1668–70), see chapter 4, pages 84–85.
6. The original Articles of Agreement of 14 July 1673 were seen by Cecil Wall and T.D. Whittet but are now missing, see Wall, Cecil, "The story of the Society's state barge 1673–1817" Ms *circa* 1935, and his typescript of the Society's history, AHA. Whittet, T.D., "The Barges of the Society of Apothecaries" in *Pharmaceutical Historian* vol 10 no 1 April 1980. For details of the Mercers' barge see Imray, Jean, *Mercers' Hall* (1991) p.331. Payments and disbursements on the barge and barge-house, £164 4s 2d, WA 1673–74. The Accounts give the names of the craftsmen: Sanders, the herald painter, Cleere could be either William or Richard, both joiners employed at Wren's City churches in the 1670s and 1680s.
7. A livery company's colours usually echoed those on the shield of the coat of arms, hence blue and yellow/gold have been accepted as the Society's colours. The streamers and banners for the Society's barge, however, were predominantly blue and crimson (1761).
8. CM 13 October 1715, 28 October 1717.
9. *Ibid* 21 September 1727, 14 March 1728. GL Ms 8289.
10. *Ibid* 28 August, 1 September 1761.
11. *Ibid* 29 November 1764, 14 March 1765. Cownden's payment seems to have been increased to £660, CM 24 October 1765. Painting and gilding was by Priest and Catton. Cownden built a barge for the Fishmongers' Company in 1773.
12. New set of colours ordered from Mr Sharp, CM 18 August 1797. *Ibid* 24 August, 13 October 1786, 19 June 1787, 18 August 1797, 3 August 1802.
13. *Ibid* 28 June 1811.
14. *Ibid* 19 August 1812, 21 January, 4 February, 4, 25 March 1817, 3 November 1818. Lease to Lyall 25 August 1818, GL Ms 8268. Repairs to barge-house, leases, nineteenth century, AHA. GCM 3 July 1869.
15. Philip Hardwick designed Goldsmiths' Hall (1829–35). The Goldsmiths bore the cost of alterations to the Chelsea barge-house, CM 4, 25 October 1836. Report on

Garden and barge-houses by Henry Dawson, GCM 6 March 1877.
16. CM 3 November 1818.
17. Seven Masters have been Fellows of the Royal Society: Chandler, Colebrook, Lane, W.T. Brande, Ward, Dodds, Ashton. The latter is added to the list of six given by Whittet, T.D., in "Some Masters of the Worshipful Society of Apothecaries" in *Pharmaceutical Historian* vol 12 no 3, December 1982 p.10. For the Oxford apothecaries' association with founders of the Royal Society see Whittet, T.D., "Apothecaries and their Lodgers; their part in the development of the sciences and of medicine" in *Journal of the Royal Society of Medicine* supplement no 2, vol 76 (1983).
18. Information about the Temple Coffee-house Club has been gleaned from the correspondence of its members, see Pasti, George, "Consul Sherard: amateur botanist and patron of learning 1659–1728" PhD University of Illinois 1950. There were three Temple Coffee-houses, see Lillywhite, Bryant, *London Coffee Houses* (1963) p.568.
19. D.E. Allen has identified the Apothecary members of Martyn's Society as William Withers, Isaac Rand, Samuel Latham, John Payne, Joseph Forsitt, John Wilmer, John Chandler, and the Harris brothers (apprentices), see Allen, D.E., "John Martyn's Botanical Society" in *Proceedings of the Botanical Society of the British Isles* vol vi May 1967 pp. 305–24.
20. CM 14 August 1678.
21. *Ibid* 29 June 1673. Henry Field (1755–1837), Apothecary to Christ's Hospital (1807–37), Master of the Society (1825–26) and author of *Memoirs of the Botanic Garden at Chelsea* (1820, 1878) was of the opinion that the Society owned a physic garden prior to the one at Chelsea, see Field, H., "An Introductory Address" (1835), AHA. His book (above) was dedicated to the Master, Wardens, Assistants and members of the Society of Apothecaries. His portrait hangs in the Court Room.
22. Faulkner, Thomas, *An Historical and Topographical Description of Chelsea* vol ii (1829) pp.175–76 (note from Earl Cadogan's records, since lost). Inventory of leasehold estates belonging to the Society, GL Ms 8233.
23. Gape's benefaction, CM 9 October 1673. Proposal to build wall, CM 21 January 1675. L. Sowersby was the surveyor and Edmund Pierce was the carpenter employed at the Garden. Total amount raised for the wall was £412 5s (1676–77), GL Ms 8204. CM 19 March, 26 June 1679. For Young's work at the Hall see chapter 4, page 85.
24. CM 1, 13 June 1676, 7 November 1677, 24 April 1678.
25. Morgan had accompanied Thomas Johnson on his herbarizing to North Wales (1639). He died *circa* 1677, see Gunther, R.T., *Early British Botanists and their Gardens* (1922). CM 7 November, 18 December 1677.
26. CM 15 November 1677, 29 January 1678. Spencer Piggot was the son of Baptist Piggot of Ashford, see Scott, Kenneth, "New York Doctors and London Medicines 1677" in *Medical History* vol xi (1967) pp. 389–98.
27. CM 28 October 1678.
28. *Ibid* 20 March, 4 May 1680. Phelps became Master in January 1680 on the death of his predecessor. A shed was built for lumber in 1681; stoves were installed during the winter 1683–84, *ibid* 16 August 1681, 14 February 1684.
29. *Ibid* 21 January 1680. Watts had been apprenticed to Henry Sykes (Master 1693–94). As well as being a keen botanist Watts was a wealthy merchant: some said he was known as a cheat, see Burnby, J.G.L., "The Career of John Watts Apothecary" in *Pharmaceutical Historian* vol 21 no 1, March 1991 pp.4–5.
30. CM 19 March, 1679, 23 August 1683, 25 June 1685. There is no confirmation that the queen did visit.
31. *Ibid* 6 August 1771. 1853 seems to be the most reliable date for the demise of the

third cedar, see note 75 below.

32. De Beer, E.S. (ed), *The Diary of John Evelyn* vol iv (1955) p.462, 6 August 1685.

33. Articles of Agreement between the Society and Watts 1685, Chelsea Physic Garden.

34. CM 25 June 1685, 3 March 1688.

35. Sloane Ms 3332 f.7v, BL Ms. Rev Dr Hamilton was Vice President of the Society of Antiquaries. His report was published in *Archaeologia* vol xii (1691) see Field, H., and Semple, R.H., *Memoirs of the Botanic Garden at Chelsea* (1878) p.16.

36. King, William, *A Journey to London* (1698) pp. 26–27.

37. Sloane Ms 3370 ff.14–19, BL Ms.

38. CM 2 August 1692, 29 June 1693, 30 April 1695, 2 July 1696, 19 August 1701, 26 March 1707.

39. *Ibid* 27 November 1706. 17 March 1708, GL Ms 8268.

40. Von Uffenbach, Zacharias Conrad, *London in 1710* edited and translated by Quarrell, W.H., and Mare, Margaret, (1934) pp.126, 160–61. Von Uffenbach's comments were disparaging generally. I am grateful to David V. Field of the Royal Botanic Gardens, Kew, for his comments on the "cucumber tree". Isaac Rand's *Index Plantarum . . . in Horto Chelseiano* (1730) lists a cork tree. There is no evidence that either *Magnolia accuminata* or *Dendrosicyos socotrana* were grown at the Physic Garden in the early eighteenth century. There may have been a mistranslation here.

41. For Sloane's friends and correspondents in the Society see chapter 6, note 22. Sloane Mss 4042 ff. 295, 305; 4052 f.15; 4040 f.378, BL Ms. Petiver's intention in 1711 had been to leave his collection to Sloane but by a later will it went to his sister, from whom Sloane purchased it.

42. CM 27 February 1679, 22 May 1696, 25 August 1698, 11 March, 23 April 1707.

43. CM 8 February 1722. Sloane's conveyance to the Society of Apothecaries 20 February 1722, Chelsea Physic Garden. Society's aims in establishing Garden, miscellaneous orders, accounts (1722–1812), GL Ms 8287. Improvements and new buildings including the greenhouse (1732 33) cost over £2,000 whereof £1,500 was raised "among their own body", augmented by contributions from the Royal College of Physicians, the Royal Society, noble Lords, Physicians and worthy gentlemen, Sloane Ms 4026, f.396, BL Ms.

44. CM 13 November 1747, 21 March 1748.

45. The previous Gardener, Charles Gardiner, was discharged in favour of Miller and given £12 10s (one quarter's wages) in compensation, CM 6 March, 22 June 1722. *DNB*. Rougetel, Hazel le, *The Chelsea Gardener. Philip Miller 1691–1771* (1990). Pulteney, Richard, *Historical and Biographical Sketches of the Progress of Botany in England* 2 vols (1790).

46. Rules and orders, 21 August 1722, GL Ms 8287. CM 25 February 1724. Engraving by Sutton Nicholls dedicated to Sloane (1725), AHA.

47. Gordon, Maurice B., *Aesculapius comes to the Colonies* (1949). Photocopy of a plan, "The Trustees' Garden in the Colony of Georgia [at Savannah] in America" made from contemporary (1743) descriptions, AHA.

48. Plans and elevations by Oakley (1732) engraved by Cole, Kings Maps xxviii 4g, BL Map Library. Also Chelsea Reference Library Local Studies Collection D229 and 230C. For Oakley see Colvin, H.M., *Biographical Dictionary of British Architects 1600–1840* (1978) p.599. The builder was Mr Lambert, carpenter Hillyard. Oakley was succeeded as architect/surveyor by Mr Horn. CM 9 June, 6 October 1732, 15 March, 18 October, 18 December 1733. Sloane Ms 4026 f.396, BL Ms.

49. CM 23 August 1733, 14 March 1734. Rysbrack had recently completed the monument to Sir Isaac Newton in Westminster Abbey. His statue of Sloane was

commissioned by the Society at a cost of £280.

50. James Gibbs advised on the erection of the statue, GCM 24 March 1735. It was completed and inscribed in 1737. Edward Anderson moved it to "the bottom of the walk facing the greenhouse", CM 11 July 1748, 28 June 1751, 14 May 1752.

51. GCM 19 May 1739. Dale was an apothecary and medical practitioner, geologist, topographer and author of *Pharmacographia* (1693), see Morris, A.D., "Samuel Dale 1659–1739" in *Proceedings of the Royal Society of Medicine* vol 67 February 1974 pp.120–24. One of his topographical works, dedicated to Sloane, is in the Library at the Hall. His portrait hangs in the Court Room.

52. Gibbs's and Dance's report dated 24 August 1741, CM 27 August 1741, GCM 3 September 1741. Hillyard was appointed the Society's carpenter in 1707, CM 26 June 1707.

53. Subscribers to Garden 1721–53, GL Ms 8304. A carpenter of Chelsea, Mr White, carried out repairs costing £185 16s, GCM 9 May 1745. CM 13 November, 7 December 1747, 18 January, 21 March, 2 August 1748.

54. Haynes's Survey, ref D231, Chelsea Reference Library Local Studies Collection. Coloured version, AHA.

55. Kalm, Pehr, *Account of his Visit to England on the Way to America in 1748* translated by Lucas, Joseph, (1892) p.111.

56. The Humble Memorial of Philip Miller Gardener, CM 20 August 1767.

57. *Ibid* 20 August 1767.

58. *Ibid* 15 June 1770. Meynell, Guy, "Philip Miller's resignation from the Chelsea Physic Garden" in *Archives of Natural History* 14 part 2 (1987) pp.77–84. For the Apothecary John Channing see Savage-Smith, Emilie, "John Channing: Eighteenth Century Apothecary and Arabist" in *Pharmacy in History* vol 30 no 2 (1988) pp.63–80. Burnby, J.G.L., "John Channing. Arabist and Apothecary" in *Pharmaceutical Historian* vol 18 no 4, December 1985 pp.4–6.

59. Rules and orders (1771), GL Ms 8236.

60. For Forsyth's subsequent career see Webber, Ronald, *The Early Horticulturalists* (1962).

61. A carpenter called Campbell paid £25 for the two cedars, 14 February 1772, GL Ms 8236. GCM 10 May, 7, 21 June 1771. CM 19 March, 6 August 1771. Alchorne's catalogue, "Index Horti Chelseiani" (1772), Chelsea Physic Garden.

62. CM 13 October 1748, 4 March, 1 July 1777.

63. GCM 25 October 1771, 16 September, 18 November 1772. 20 July 1771, GL Ms 8236. The lava was not from the volcano Hekla, as had previously been supposed, see Meynell, Guy, and Pulvertaft, Christopher, "The Hekla lava myth" in *Geographical Magazine* vol 53 no 7 (1981) pp. 433–36. It has been suggested that material used as ballast (shells, tuff, coral) on Banks's voyage of 1768–70 to Tahiti, New Zealand and Australia was incorporated into the rockery at the Physic Garden.

64. Banks's letter to the Society 15 December 1814, CM 7 March 1815. His mother lived in Paradise Row and Joseph had known the Physic Garden since boyhood. Banks purchased Philip Miller's herbarium after the latter's death, 1774. See O'Brian, Patrick, *Joseph Banks. A Life* (1987). CM 26 July 1824.

65. GCM 22 March 1773. 21 March 1773, GL Ms 8236.

66. CM 23 August 1816.

67. Field, Henry and Semple, R.H., *Memoirs of the Botanic Garden at Chelsea* (1878) pp.128–64. The description of Wheeler was contributed by Semple; they were related by marriage. Thomas Wheeler's portrait is in the Court Room. The *DNB* entry for T. Wheeler is misleading, see Wheeler, J.M., *Fowke alias Wheeler* (1969) and South, J.F.,

Memorials of John Flint South (1884). James L. Wheeler appointed in his father's place as Demonstrator, CM 27 March 1821. A copy of J.L Wheeler's *Catalogus Rationalis Plantarum Medicinalium in horto Societatis Pharmaceuticae Londinensis apud vicum Chelsea cultarum* (1830) is in the Library at Apothecaries' Hall.

68. Dinner at the King of Bohemia's Head, 20 July 1781, GL Ms 8257 no 8. Herbarizing dinner bills (1806–26), GL Ms 8262.

69. CM 28 May, 12 August 1784, 23 June 1785. The bricklayer, Britton, was paid £34 11s, Sanderson £23 2s 4d, GL Mss 8287, 8203 vol i. In 1797 the Society obtained a slip of land on the west side of the Garden from Tutton a maltster.

70. Faulkner, Thomas, *An Historical and Topographical Description of Chelsea* vol ii (1829) pp.174–87, superseding the first edition of 1810. Faulkner lived near the Physic Garden and obtained permission from the Court to interview Fairbairn, the Gardener, CM 21 December 1809.

71. Banks's letter of recommendation was copied into the Court Minutes 7 March 1815. Lindley's reports CM 20 December 1836, 31 March 1837. GCM 20 January 1837, 29 May 1838. Anecdotes on gardeners and artists at the Physic Garden from Ewan, Joseph, and MacPhail, I. (comps), *Hortus Botannicus. The Botanic Garden and The Book* (1972). Anderson's papers, family tree, etc. (1846–48), AHA.

72. GCM 27 May 1847, 31 May 1848.

73. There were occasional general herbarizings in the mid-nineteenth century, one to Epping Forest in 1902 (photograph, AHA) and most recently, one was held during the Mastership of Dr James Fisher in 1988. Allen, D.E., *The Botanists. A History of the Botanical Society of the British Isles* (1986).

74. GCM 3 May 1853. CM 29 October 1852, 27 June, 4 August, 28 October 1853. In the period 1816 to 1824 expenses on the Garden ranged from £413 to £512 p.a., see *Report and Accounts relating to the work and income of the Society's examinations department 1816–25* (1825), AHA. A new hothouse and greenhouse were erected in 1847, CM 6 October 1847.

75. GCM 1854. Stungo, Ruth, "Historic cedars" in *The Garden* July 1993 pp.289–91. Bryan, George, *Chelsea in the Olden and Present Times* (1869) pp.177–79. Bryan, who lived in Chelsea, is one of the few authorities to date the destruction of the third cedar to 1853 (I am grateful to Ruth Stungo for pointing this out). An illustration in *The Builder* 8 April 1854 p.187 shows just one remaining cedar. Nevertheless, an account in *The Illustrated London News* 19 April 1873 p.377 refers to "two noble cedars". Blunt, Reginald, *Paradise Row* (1906) gives 1875 as the date the third tree was cut down, and this is repeated in *The Survey of London. The Parish of Chelsea* part 1 (1929). Other sources quote 1878. The archives of the Society contain a photograph of the Garden before the construction of the Embankment (1871) showing only one cedar.

76. Notes re relinquishing Chelsea Garden (1861–62), AHA. GCM 8 November 1862, 7, 14 February, 29 May 1863, 25 March 1865, Report of Master and Wardens 1863, AHA. Provisional list of medicinal plants 1863, AHA.

77. GCM 1862–70. Chelsea Garden Accounts 1863–65, AHA. The builder was Gray, to designs by John Griffith (1865–70). Griffith's plan of July 1871 shows these improvements, AHA. Nathaniel Bagshaw Ward was an Examiner in botany to the Society (1836–54) and arranged for the transfer of the herbaria of Rand, Dale and Ray to the British Museum, see *DNB*.

78. Henry Dawson's proposals and account (1877–78), AHA. Chelsea Embankment, Society and Board of Works, 1870s, AHA. The credit value of the additional land was estimated at £1,000, see G.H. Makins's Notebook, AHA. GCM 1862–91. Barry gave his opinion of Dawson's plans for which he was paid 20 guineas, April 1878, Clerk's

Letter Book, AHA. The contractor was Macey and Sons for £2,800. Conveyance and drawings by Geoffrey Pownall, the arbitrator, (1877) GL Ms 8270.
79. CM 6 April 1875. GCM 14 May 1875, 1 January 1878, 28 May 1880, 11 August 1896. Chelsea Garden Accounts 1877–78, AHA.
80. Field and Semple *op cit* pp.239–72.
81. *Pall Mall Gazette* 18 July 1890.
82. CM 21 February 1893. Papers re relinquishing Garden and Minutes of Special Meeting of Garden Committee 1 November 1898, AHA. GCM 1891–98. 83. Charity Commission deed 21 February 1899, AHA. See also Belcher, Victor, *The City Parochial Foundation 1891–1991* (1991).
84. Reports of the Committee of Management (1899, 1905), AHA.
85. Minutes of the Committee of Management, 27 November, 13 May 1902, GL Ms 10,899.
86. Minutes of Committee of Management 20 November 1902, GL Ms 10,899.
87. *Ibid* 18 November 1903.
88. *Ibid* 1921–36.
89. Belcher, Victor, *op cit*.
90. I am grateful to the Curator, Sue Minter, for supplying up-to-date information, and to Ruth Stungo, historical researcher at the Physic Garden for advice.

Notes to chapter 6, pages 153–91.

1. CM 20 May 1623.
2. [Brande, W.T.], *The Origin, Progress and Present State of the Various Establishments for Conducting Chemical Processes and Other Medicinal Preparations at Apothecaries' Hall* (1823).
3. CM 12 October 1641.
4. *Ibid* 21 February, 2 May 1654.
5. Thomas, Sir Henry, "The Society of Chemical Physicians" in Underwood, E.A. (ed), *Science, Medicine and History* vol ii (1953) pp.56–71.
6. CM 8 September 1671, 4, 29 January 1672. Litlar left a silver tankard to the Society, 1675. Orders for the government of the Laboratory Stock 4 January 1672, GL Ms 8204.
7. CM 29 January 1672.
8. London County Council, *Survey of London. The Parish of St Margaret Westminster* vol xiii part 2 (1930) plate 1.
9. Details of the trading activities of the Apothecaries of the 1630s can be gleaned from GL Ms 8286. Appleby, John H., "Ivan the Terrible to Peter the Great: British formative influence on Russia's medico-apothecary system" in *Medical History* vol xxvii (1983) pp.289–304.
10. CM 29 January, 19 September 1672, 28 April 1674.
11. *Ibid* 29 January 1673.
12. *Ibid* 18 March 1673. Stringer was a Liveryman from 1773 and Assistant in 1687. He may have been related to Moses Stringer, a successful empiric, iatrochemist and mineral-master who supplied chemical medicines for the expedition to the West Indies in 1701.
13. *Ibid* 19 September 1672, 14, 29 January 1673 (one of the few references to the Society's property at Bromley, Kent), cf. GL Ms 8303.
14. *Ibid* 10 October 1672, 14 March 1675, 14 August 1678.
15. *Ibid* 23 May 1676.

16. *Ibid* 4, 18 December 1677. Sulphur was used in several preparations, sulphur balsam being a popular remedy for sore eyes, see Staphorst, N., *Officina Chymica Londinensis* (1685).
17. *Ibid* 6 March 1677. There is no record that the proposed visit took place. King Charles II was preoccupied at this time with foreign policy and under pressure from the Commons to wage war on France.
18. *Ibid* 6 October 1681, 24 October 1682.
19. *Ibid* 15 April 1673.
20. Gunther, R.T., *Early Science in Oxford* vol i (1923) pp.14–15, 22, 24.
21. CM 14 April 1673, 20 April 1674. Whittet, T.D., in *Clerks, Bedels and Chemical Operators of the Society of Apothecaries* (1977) presumed that Mr "Hall" (Stall/Stahl) was Hull's labourer. Whittet later realized that he had misread the Court Minutes and that the name "Hall" was Stall or Stahl, see Whittet, T.D., "Apothecaries and their Lodgers: their part in the development of the sciences and of medicine" in *Journal of the Royal Society of Medicine* supplement no 2, vol 76 (1983).
22. Birch, Thomas, "Memoirs relating to the Life of Sir Hans Sloane" Add Ms 4241, BL Ms. Sloane's earliest acquisition for his library was a work on chemistry bought from its author, Staphorst, for 2s 6d (1682), see MacGregor, Arthur, (ed), *Sir Hans Sloane. Collector, Scientist, Antiquary* (1994). Sloane's circle of friends and correspondents included the Apothecaries Petiver, Bernard, Dale, Doody, Miller, Rand, St Amand, Meres, Massey. Isaac Rand and St Amand were Apothecaries to some of Sloane's patients, Sloane Ms 4060 ff.150,152, BL Ms. Scott, E.J.L., *Index to Sloane Manuscripts* (1904).
23. CM 18 November 1683, 3 February, 10 April 1684. Staphorst also wrote "Index Metallorum et Mineralium et Animallium Preparationes", appended to some copies of *Officina Chymica Londinensis* (1685).
24. Poynter, F.N.L. (ed), *The Journal of James Yonge, Plymouth Surgeon 1647–1721* (1963) p.195. William Clarke's chest can be seen at the Hall.
25. Erndtel, C., *The Relation of a Journey into England and Holland 1706–7* (1711) p.42.
26. Godfrey, Ambrose, "Chemical and Pharmaceutical Formulary" (early eighteenth century?), Western Ms 2533, Wellcome Institute for the History of Medicine Library. Maddison, R.E.W., "Notes on some members of the Hanckwitz family in England" in *Annals of Science* vol ii no 1, March 1955 pp.64–73, and "Studies in the life of Robert Boyle" in *Notes and Records of the Royal Society* vol 11 no 1, January 1954 pp.159–65, and *The Life of the Hon Robert Boyle* (1969). Ambrose Godfrey Hanckwitz took a building lease on land formerly part of the site of Bedford House, Covent Garden, in December 1706 where his laboratory called The Golden Phoenix was built. The family business became Godfrey and Cooke in 1797 and was acquired by Savory and Moore in 1916. The Golden Phoenix was demolished in 1893 and the site is now occupied by the R.C. Church of Corpus Christi, see Greater London Council, *Survey of London. Parish of St Paul Covent Garden* vol xxxvi (1970) pp. 215–18. *Notes and Queries* 7th series vol viii (1889) pp. 257–58. Ince, Joseph, "Ambrose Godfrey Hanckwitz" in *Pharmaceutical Journal* vol xviii (1858–59) pp. 126–30, 157–62, 215–17, claims that Hanckwitz left a great mass of papers, diaries, pamphlets and receipts, as yet untraced.
27. Von Uffenbach, Zacharias Conrad, *London in 1710* edited and translated by Quarrell, W.H., and Mare, Margaret, (1934) p.110.
28. The Operators and staff of the Laboratory are listed by Whittet, T.D., *Clerks, Bedels and Chemical Operators of the Society of Apothecaries* (1977). James L. Wheeler should be added to the list of Chemical Operators, see Wheeler, J.M., *Fowke alias Wheeler* (1969). He titled himself "in Chemica et materia medica Praefectore" and took over Brande's

responsibilities in 1867, Minutes of Court of Proprietors and General Committee 7 March 1867, AHA. GL Ms 8223 vol i. Contrary to the dates given by Whittet, Griffin was still the Society's Chemical Operator in 1791, see *Catalogus Medicamentorum Chymicorum* (1791), AHA.

29. *State Papers Domestic* 1661–62 p.252, 1665–66 p.311.

30. *Ibid* 18 December 1665 pp. 65–66. Matthews, Leslie G., *The Royal Apothecaries* (1967) pp.108–12.

31. CM 4 March 1673.

32. *Ibid* 11 February 1692. *Calendar of Treasury Papers 1556–1696* pp.217–18, 412; 1697–1702, xliii,74.

33. Tanner J.R. (ed), *Private Correspondence and Miscellaneous Papers of Samuel Pepys 1679–1703* vol i (1926) p.124.

34. Cook, Harold J., "Practical Medicine and the British Armed Forces after the Glorious Revolution" in *Medical History* vol xxxiv (1990) pp.1–26.

35. CM 18 February, 15 March, 9 May 1702. Rules and Orders for the Laboratory Stock, 9 May 1702, AHA.

36. Minutes of Sick and Wounded Board 1702–04, ADM/99/2, PRO.

37. CM 15 June 1704, 3 October 1708.

38. 17 August 1702, ADM 99/2, PRO. The Surgeons were not an independent Company until 1745 but were referred to thus.

39. *State Papers Domestic* 1702–03 pp.334–35.

40. CM 5 January 1703. Charles Bernard had a large surgical practice in London and was Master of the Barber-Surgeons' Company in 1703.

41. CM 18 February, 1, 13, 20 July, 1703.

42. 16 February, 30 June 1703, ADM/E/1, NMML.

43. 3 August 1703, GL Ms 8213. Lease of three houses, south side of courtyard (1704), inventory of leases, GL Ms 8233. Navy Stock deeds 1703, 1766, 1767, 1777, AHA. Records of the Laboratory Stock and the Navy Stock are by no means complete.

44. Smith, Alan, "Steam and the City" in *Newcomen Society Transactions* vol 49 (1977–78). Rolt, L.T.C., and Allen J.S., *The Steam Engine of Thomas Newcomen* (1977). The *DNB* entry for Newcomen refers to Meres's role in the undertaking but confuses John Meres F.R.S., Clerk to the Apothecaries, with Sir John Meres F.R.S. Meres the Clerk left £200 to the Society to augment the salary of the Botanical Demonstrator, £50 for silver candlesticks, and his botanical books to the Chelsea Physic Garden. He had negotiated with Sloane for the conveyance of the Physic Garden and two letters from Meres to Sloane surive, Sloane Mss 4049 f.53, 4059 f.339, BL Ms.

45. 21 January, 4 November 1704, ADM/E/2, NMML. A repository of supplies from Apothecaries' Hall was established at Lisbon (1708).

46. e.g. Haslar: 29 April 1756, ADM 99/29. Gosport and Jamaica: 13 October 1742, ADM 98/1. Lisbon and Gibraltar: 18 November 1704, ADM 99/3. Greenwich: 1 April 1730 ADM 67/7, PRO. Keevil vol iii p.53.

47. *Calendar of Treasury Papers 1708–14* cv 60, p.257.

48. CM 6 January 1706, 15 September 1712. Report for Counsel's opinion (1767), AHA. Accounts for the Navy Stock survive for 1730–72, GL Ms 8225. Wall, Cecil, "The Stocks" Ts n.d., AHA.

49. Robinson, C.N., *The British Fleet* (1894). Keevil vol ii pp.395–96. Merriman, R.D., *Queen Anne's Navy* (1961) pp.239–40. CM 18 May 1709. ADM 7/169, PRO.

50. CM 1 January 1706. Articles of Copartnership (1774), AHA. GL Ms 8271.

51. GL Ms 8214. CM 14 March 1734. The Society insured the premises with the Sun Life Office (policy 64344, 19 July 1734) which provides a description of the buildings,

GL Ms 11,936 vol 41. Photograph of document, AHA.
52. GL Mss 8220, 8221 vols i-iii.
53. Quincy, J., *A Complete English Dispensatory* (1742) p.xii.
54. CM 20 August 1741, 22 May 1745, 18 August, 13 October, 13 November 1748, 7, 23 February 1749.
55. *Ibid* 8, 18, 23 December 1746, 23 January 1747. GL Ms 8284. *Chemist and Druggist* 31 July 1926 pp.198–99.
56. 13 October 1742, ADM 98/1; 3 June 1704, ADM 99/3, PRO. Petition of Henry Halstead, May 1707, includes an inventory of his shop, ADM/E/3, NMML. Appendix E in Keevil vol iii pp. 376–79 lists medicines for the navy, 1742.
57. The Navy Stock had a warehouse at Plymouth, see 2 March 1756, ADM/E/15, NMML. 12 March 1756, ADM/98/5, PRO. The Apothecaries' petition to regain the contract for Greenwich Hospital was rejected (1730), ADM 69/7 f.256, PRO. Cookworthy's bills for medicines and drugs were paid by the Sick and Wounded Board from 1756, 19 January 1756, ADM 99/29, PRO. Cookworthy, "chemist, scientist, inventor and philosopher" discovered china clay in Cornwall and produced the first true English hard-paste porcelain, see Selleck, A. Douglas, "William Cookworthy, an 18th century polymath" in *Pharmaceutical Historian* vol 9 no 3, December 1979 pp.8–12, and Madge, A.G.M., "Cookworthy – Chemist and Potter" in *Pharmaceutical Historian* vol 23 no 2, June 1993 pp.3–4.
58. 23 June 1742, ADM/3529, PRO. Cripps, Ernest C., *Plough Court. The story of a notable pharmacy 1715–1927* (1927). Tweedale, Geoffrey, *At the Sign of the Plough. Allen and Hanburys and the British Pharmaceutical Industry 1715–1990* (1990). Richard Phillips F.R.S., who was associated with the Apothecaries' Laboratory *circa* 1817 was trained at the Plough Court Pharmacy.
59. Anon, *The Apothecary Displayed* (1748) p.13.
60. The Apothecary George Haughton was supplying medicine chests for the East India Company *circa* 1634, see EAU p.276 and for Haughton's difficulties with the College of Physicians, chapter 2, page 50. It may be that the Apothecary and Assay Master of the Mint, Stanesby Alchorne, had a hand in negotiations with the East India Company in 1766 as he was paid £50 by the Directors, Minutes of the Court of Directors, 8 April, 29 October 1766, B/82 pp.238–39, Oriental and India Office Library. CM 12 December 1787.
61. CM 29 March 1811. 30 November 1819, copy letter to Comptrollers of Army Accounts, AHA.
62. GL Ms 8261. Laboratory Stock/United Stock Audit Books, AHA. As late as 1903 the Society was approached by the India Office with a proposal to manage a drug factory at Nassik for the supply of the army and civil dispensaries in India. The proposal was not pursued after the death of the General Manager and Superintendent of the trade, William Chattaway in 1904. Correspondence 1903–04, Minutes of Trade Management Committee 1902–04, AHA.
63. CM 21 March 1777.
64. Navy Stock Articles of Agreement/Copartnership 16 December 1766, Articles for regulating Navy Stock (1778) and Proprietors' covenants (1778–1822), AHA. Clerk's memorandum CM 3 February 1767.
65. CM 28 February 1811. This compared with the average annual bill of £21,582 for drugs and medicines supplied to the East India Company over the same five years.
66. Matthews, Leslie G., "Lambeth's Link with Pharmacy" in *Chemist and Druggist* vol 207 19 February 1977 pp.226–29. Edwards, Rhoda, "The Apothecaries' Windmill, Lambeth" in *The Pharmaceutical Journal* vol 212, 16 March 1974 pp.219–20. Short,

Michael, "The Lambeth Drug Mill" in *London Archaeologist* vol i no 12, autumn 1971 pp.267–71.
67. Lease 3 August 1808, GL Ms 8269. Laboratory Stock/United Stock Audit Book (1803–57), AHA.
68. Seven houses, Fleur de Luce Court (1794–95), tenement formerly The Queen's Head and premises, Glasshouse Yard (1801), GL Ms 8269. Rebuilding warehouses Playhouse Yard (1813–15), CM 22 December 1813, 1 March, 1814, 29 June 1815. New prescription room CM 24 November 1818. Purchase of lease of foundry and dwelling Glasshouse Yard September 1822, CM 26 July, 20 August 1822. GL Ms 8265. Extension of retail trade premises, CM 14 June 1823. Purchases and buildings of Laboratory Stock in Laboratory Stock/United Stock Audit Book (1803–57), AHA. Particulars of premises of United Stock (1846), AHA.
69. CM 2 December 1819, 5 May 1821. The dynasty of Garniers was established by Isaac Garnier, admitted to the Society in 1692, later on the Court of Assistants, Apothecary General and Apothecary to the Royal Hospital, Chelsea. He was one of many (including Charles Angibaud, Master 1728–29) French Protestants taking refuge in this country at the time of the Revocation of the Edict of Nantes (1685). Isaac Garnier's descendants were also Apothecaries to Chelsea Hospital and Apothecaries General. George Garnier senior made a fortune from supplying H.M. forces in the West Indies and America. His son held onto the monopoly, see *Calendar of Treasury Books and Papers 1739–41*. Garnier, A.E., *The Chronicles of the Garniers of Hampshire* (1900). Matthews, Leslie G., "London's Immigrant Apothecaries 1600–1800" in *Medical History* xviii (1974) pp. 262–274.
70. 2 December 1819, correspondence on supply of drugs to the army (1819–21), AHA.
71. For names of individual Apothecaries serving with the British Army in the Peninsular War, Crimea, etc., see Peterkin, Alfred, and Johnston, William, (comps), *Commissioned Officers in the Medical Services* vol i 1660–1898 (1968). Laboratory Stock/United Stock Audit Book (1803–57), AHA.
72. Russell, W.H., *The British Expedition to the Crimea* (1858). Nightingale, Florence, *Notes on matters affecting the health, efficacy and hospital administration of the British Army* (1858). Smith, Cecil Woodham, *Florence Nightingale* (1980).
73. 2 January 1872, Minutes of Court of Proprietors and General Committee, United Stock (1867–80), AHA. In 1823 the purchasing authority for navy medical supplies became the Victualling Board which began to purchase exclusively from private firms offering low prices. United Stock Audit Book (1858–80), AHA. 1, 7 April 1891, Minutes Managing Committee (1887–93), AHA. 6 September 1823, Minutes of Court of Proprietors and General Committee United Stock (1823–66), GL Ms 8223 vol i.
74. Black, R.C., *The younger John Winthrop* (1966), see chapter 2, note 14. Packard, F.R., *The History of Medicine in the United States* vol i (1931) p.17. Blanton, Wyndham M., *Medicine in Virginia in the seventeenth century* (1930).
75. Scott, Kenneth, "New York Doctors and London Medicines 1677" in *Medical History* vol xi (1967) pp. 389–98.
76. Burnby, J.G.L., "An Examined and Free Apothecary" in Nutton, Vivian, and Porter, Roy, (eds), *The History of Medical Education in Britain* (1995) pp.16–37.
77. Beaglehole, J.C. (ed), *The Journals of Captain Cook* vol i (1968) p.628. *Historical Records of New South Wales* vols i-iii (1892–93).
78. Beaglehole, J.C. *op cit* vol iii pp.1484, 1491. The rob of oranges and lemons for the *Endeavour* (1768) had been prepared at Haslar Royal Naval Hospital, see Watt, Sir James, "Medical Aspects and Consequences of Cook's voyages" in Fisher, Robin, and

Johnston, Hugh, (eds), *Captain Cook and His Times* (1979) pp.129–157.
79. A Thomas Arundell/Arndell was an apothecary with the British army in 1760. Gillen, M., *The Founders of Australia. A Biographical Dictionary* (1989). Simpson, Rob L., "Mortality on Convict Voyages 1787–1820: Whose responsibility?" in *New Perspectives in the History of Medicine* (1990) pp.85–92. HRNSW vol i pt 2. The cost of "Drugs etc" for the First Fleet was £1,178 17s 6d, see HRNSW vol iii p.388.
80. Chisholm, Alec H. (ed), *John White. Journal of a voyage to New South Wales, 1790* (1962). HRNSW vol iii p.317. Haines, Gregory, *The Grains and Threepenn'orth of Pharmacy* (1976) p.5. Collins, David, *An Account of the English Colony in New South Wales* (1804) pp.93–98.
81. Haslam, John, *Convict-ships. A narrative of a voyage to New South Wales in the year 1816* (1819) p.7. Minutes of Act of Parliament Committee, 5 June 1832, GL Ms 8211 vol i.
82. The cost of medicines per ship with 300 convicts was £14 7s 6d (1836–38), GL Ms 8224 vol i.
83. Johnson, F. Hansford, *A History of Medicine in Western Australia 1829–1870* vol vii (1993).
84. Information from G. Miller and Woomera Heritage Centre. Photographs of the pioneer's medicine chest from Arcoona from G. Miller, c/o the Clerk. *The Inquirer* 21 May 1879, see F. Hansford Johnson *op cit*.
85. CM 26 March, 29 October 1822. Copartnership deed, 9 November 1822, GL Mss 8217, 8275.
86. CM 25 July, 20 August 1822. Assignment of leasehold premises 3 September 1822, GL Ms 8265. Purchases and buildings belonging to Laboratory Stock, Laboratory Stock/United Stock Audit Book (1803–57), AHA. Particulars of Premises of United Stock (1846), AHA. For details of leases of the Foundry/Great Laboratory site see the Society's purchase of the freehold from Lord Tredegar's trustees (1893–94), AHA.
87. [Brande, W.T.], *The Origin, Progress and Present State of the Various Establishments for Conducting Chemical Processes and Other Medicinal Preparations at Apothecaries' Hall* (1823). Gray, Samuel, *The Operative Chemist* (1828) p.75. A simplified version of the plan in the above booklet has recently been reproduced by O'Leary, Charles, "The Elaboratory and Stocks of the Society of Apothecaries" in *Pharmaceutical Historian* vol 27 no 2, June 1997 pp.14–20.
88. 6, 30 September, 21 October, 11 November 1823, GL MS 8223 vol i. W.T. Brande's booklet, *op cit*. John Field put together an "Abridgement of the Proceedings of the Society 1617–1795", AHA.
89. 13 March 1824, 6 March 1830, GL Ms 8223 vol i.
90. *Ibid* 1 September 1838, 6 December 1845.
91. *DNB*. Haigh, Elizabeth, "William Brande and the chemical education of medical students" in French, Roger, and Wear, Andrew, (eds), *British Medicine in an Age of Reform* (1991) pp.186–202. Spiers, C.H., "William Thomas Brande, Leather Expert" in *Annals of Science* vol 25 no 3, September 1969 pp.179–201. Borman, Morris, *Social Change and Scientific Organization* (1978) pp.130–34. CM 2 March, 25 June, 29 October 1813.
92. Hennell had been apprenticed to John Hunter (Master 1831–32) and was made free in 1821, CM 1 May 1821. 16 July 1842, GL Ms 8223 vol ii. *John Bull* 4 June 1842.
93. The United Stock/Admiralty Office Account (1841) records medicines for the Niger Expedition (48 out of 145 Europeans died of disease on this unsuccessful sortie), and medicines and three medicine chests for troops in China, GL Ms 8224 vol ii. The Chemical Superintendent was entitled to "emoluments arising from the refractions of saltpetre for the East India Company", 6 March 1830, GL Ms 8223 vol i.
94. Wickham, Helen, "The Warington family" (1997), AHA.
95. Dickens, Charles (comp), *Household Words* 16 August 1856 pp.108–15. Dickens

conducted/edited the periodical and wrote a good proportion of it. Henry Morley, a member of the Society who was to be Senior Warden in 1893, was a regular contributor, usually on educational matters.

96. G.H. Makins's Notebook, AHA.
97. 2 March 1867, 2 January 1872, 7 June 1879, 24 March 1891, Minutes of Committee of Management; Minutes of Court of Proprietors and General Committee (1867–80), AHA.
98. 2 January 1872, Minutes of Committee of Management, AHA.
99. Report of special meeting of Proprietors, 2 April 1880. Minutes of Court of Proprietors and General Committee (1867–80), AHA. CM 3 August, 16 November 1880, 28 June 1881.
100. CM 28 June 1881. Revised rules for the wholesale and laboratory department, January 1887; Minutes of Court of Proprietors and General Committee (1867–80), AHA.
101. 31 January 1887, Clerk's Letter Book, AHA.
102. 7 October 1884, Minutes of Committee of Management; Correspondence about toothpaste (1898), AHA.
103. Trade Ledger (1912–21), AHA.
104. Report of Trade Committee (1903); Minutes of Committee of Management (1911–14), AHA.
105. Correspondence re Society's application for a licence to carry out experiments on living animals at the Hall (1908); Minutes of Committee of Management (1908–11), AHA.
106. CM 10 December 1918, 29 April 1919, 19 July 1920.
107. *Ibid* 7 February 1922. Apothecaries' Hall Dublin had sold its wholesale and manufacturing business in 1919.
108. Receipted Accounts (1922), AHA. Randall and Wilson were in business at 146 High Street, Southampton, until the Second World War. The area was destroyed by bombing in 1940, and as there is no trace of the firm in post-war directories, it seems that the Society's process book perished with the firm. I am grateful for information from Southampton Archives Service.

Notes to chapter 7, pages 193–226.

Dr E.A. Underwood's research notes for the proposed second volume of *A History of the Worshipful Society of Apothecaries of London* are a main source for this chapter. Dr Underwood died in 1980 before completing the project and his notes (chiefly on medical reform in the nineteenth century) were deposited with the Wellcome Institute for the History of Medicine Library, ref: PP/EAU F1–8 and F39–46.

1. Smith, Adam, *An Inquiry into the Nature and causes of the Wealth of Nations* 1776 (1910) vol i p.100.
2. Campbell, R., *The London Tradesman* 1747 (1969) p.63.
3. Holmes, Geoffrey, *Augustan England. Professions, State and Society 1680–1730* (1982) p.212.
4. Friendly Medical Society Minute Books (1725–1922), GL Ms 8278. Speech at centenary dinner, July 1825, GL Ms 8280. Framed copy of speech with observations and notes on eminent members, presented by G.J. Amsden (1886), and photograph album, AHA. Wall, Cecil, "Friendly Medical Society" Ts n.d., AHA.

5. Good, J.M., *The History of Medicine so far as it relates to the Profession of the Apothecary* (1795).
6. CM 6 September 1810.
7. Bellers, J., *An Essay towards the Improvement of Physic* (1714) p.10. *The London Medical and Physical Journal* vol 29 no 16, January 1813 p.3. Kerrison, R.M., *An Inquiry into the Present State of the Medical Profession in England* (1814) p.xii.
8. The petition to the Court of Assistants urged the Court to communicate with the Royal College of Physicians in this matter; it is undated but evidently early 1813, AHA. Kerrison, R.M., *An Inquiry into the Present State of the Medical Profession in England* (1814). Kerrison seems to have based his figures on the calculation that of 368 members of the Society, 148 were practitioners in London, of whom 110 concurred with Burrows's London Committee, see *A Letter to Sir Francis Milman, President the Royal College of Physicians, on the subject of Reform* (1813), AHA. Papers relating to the Associated Apothecaries, GL Ms 8299.
9. Proceedings of the Committee for Obtaining an Act of Parliament for better regulating the practice of Apothecaries throughout England and Wales, GL Ms 8211 vol i.
10. Act of Parliament Committee report 14 July 1815, GL Ms 8211 vol i.
11. In order of quotation: Poynter, F.N.L., (ed), *The Evolution of Medical Practice in Britain* (1961). Gelfand, Toby, "The History of the Medical Profession" in Bynum, W.F., and Porter, Roy, (eds), *Encyclopaedia of the History of Medicine* vol ii (1993) pp.1119–50. Holloway, S.W.F., "The Apothecaries' Act of 1815. A Reinterpretation" in *Medical History* vol x (1966) pp.107–29, 221–36. Newman, Charles, *The Evolution of Medical Education in the Nineteenth Century* (1957). Peterson, M.J., *The Medical Profession in Mid-Victorian London* (1878) p.22. Holloway, S.W.F., *The Royal Pharmaceutical Society of Great Britain 1841–1991* (1991) p.85. See also Loudon, Irvine, *Medical Care and the General Practitioner 1750–1850* (1986) and Holloway, S.W.F., "The Significance of the Apothecaries' Act 1815" in *Pharmaceutical Historian* vol 1 no 5, June 1970 pp.6–9.
12. Cope, Sir Zachary, "Influence of the Society of Apothecaries upon Medical Education" in *BMJ* January 1956 pp.4957–62. Peterson, M.J., *The Medical Profession in Mid-Victorian London* (1978) p.21.
13. CME 24 July 1815. Loudon, Irvine, *Medical Care and the General Practitioner 1750–1850* (1986).
14. CME 10 August 1815. Rules and Regulations of the Court of Examiners of the Society of Apothecaries (1815), AHA.
15. Burrows was the first Fellow of the Royal College of Physicians to have been a member of the Society of Apothecaries and the Royal College of Surgeons (his son Sir George Burrows Bt was President of the Royal College of Physicians). G.M. Burrows's special interest was insanity but his reputation was damaged when he ordered the detention of a young man without seeing him, see Loudon, Irvine, *op cit*. *DNB*. Burrows, G.M., *A Statement of Circumstances connected with the Apothecaries' Act and its administration* (1817). This was reviewed in *The London Medical and Physical Journal* vol 37 no 2, 20 June 1817 pp.488–96, which had published his letter of 2 October 1816 in vol 37 no 2, 15 January 1817 p.78. Burrows's portrait hangs in the Court Room.
16. CME 24 July–31 August 1815, 21 March, 13 June, 25 July 1816. GL Ms 8241 vol i. An analysis of the Society's registration books between 1815 and 1819 shows that 9 per cent of candidates passed the examination without complying strictly with the prescribed course work, hospital experience or apprenticeship, see Lawrence, Susan E., "Private enterprise and public interests; medical education and the Apothecaries' Act 1780–1825" in French, Roger, and Wear, Andrew (eds), *British Medicine in an Age of*

Reform (1991) pp.45–73.
17. CM 4 August 1846, 31 July 1860.
18. CME 25 July 1816. GL Ms 8241 vol i. Hewlitt, Dorothy, *A Life of John Keats* (1970) p.44. Gittings, Robert, *John Keats* (1968) p.72. Smith, Hillas, *Keats and Medicine* (1995). Rollins, Hyder E. (ed), *The Keats Circle* vol ii (1948) p.211. Clarke, Cowden Charles, *Recollections of Writers* (1878) pp.131–32. The Keats Memorial Lecture, arranged by the Society, Guy's Hospital and the Royal College of Surgeons, was inaugurated in 1969.
19. CME vol iv. CM 26 October 1827. Rules and Regulations of the Court of Examiners of the Society of Apothecaries (1815), Examination Regulations (1827), Examination Regulations (1841–1900), AHA. Regulations of Court of Examiners (1858–93), GL Ms 8250.
20. *Lancet* 1, 8 November 1828, pp.146–49, 178–79, 190. *Ibid* 17, 31 January, 28 February 1829 pp.511, 554–56, 684. The last recorded visitation of Apothecaries' shops by Censors of the Royal College and the Wardens of the Society was in 1858. Wakley's calculations failed to take into account the expenses of the Society's examinations: according to a return to the House of Commons (1833) the Society had received £39,974 for licences granted since 1815. With the expense of Examiners' fees etc. deducted, the balance in favour of the Society stood at £2,360 by 1833. This and other statistics are given in *House of Commons Report of the Select Committee on Medical Education* (1834) part iii.
21. *House of Commons Report* (1834) *op cit*.
22. CM 29 July 1834, 15 March, 25 October 1836, 3 January, 11 July 1837, 6 October 1841.
23. *Ibid* 3 August 1837, 24 December 1838, 19 February, 30 June 1841. Brande's letter to the Clerk, 24 December 1838, AHA.
24. This followed the resolution of the Court of Examiners 31 May 1860 "that the Professional Examinations be conducted forthwith partly in writing and partly viva voce – time for writing 1½ hours", Court of Examiners' Regulations (1858–95), GL Ms 8250. CM 30 July 1861, 28 October 1870.
25. CME 13 March, 1 May 1851, 23 July 1857, 20 May 1858, 28 June, 26 July 1860. CM 31 July 1860, 8 October 1861.
26. *BMJ* 18 May 1861 pp.529–30. CM 28 June 1861.
27. Bell, E. Moberly, *Storming the Citadel* (1953). *The Times* 18 December 1917. 25 April 1862, GL Ms 10,981 vol i. CME 31 March 1864, 28 September 1865, 14 February 1867. GL Ms 8241 vol xxi. Elizabeth Garrett had applied to be a candidate for matriculation at London University (1862), unsuccessfully, and to be examined for the licence of the Royal College of Physicians in April 1864, and again her application was rejected. A female disguised as a male, James Barry, had graduated in medicine from Edinburgh in 1812.
28. CM 22 March, 26 June, 1867. CME 28 February 1867, 22 March 1888. GL Ms 10,981 vol i. 18 August 1887, 22 March, 19 April 1888, GL Ms 8239 vol xi. Letter Isabel Thorne to Clerk, May 1887, Admission of women (1860s, 1880s), AHA. Women were admitted to the exams of the Conjoint Board from 1909.
29. CM 2 August 1843 gives a summary of the Court of Examiners' requirements in midwifery to that date, "the department of midwifery being undoubtedly one of the most important and responsible branches of the general practice of the Apothecary", as submitted by the Chairman, T.L. Wheeler. *Ibid* 9 December 1866, 9 October, 18 December 1867. Proposed Diploma in Public Health (1887–89), AHA.
30. *City Press* 4 June 1864, Misc. cuttings, AHA.
31. CM 14 December 1870, 1 March 1871.

32. *Ibid* 9 January 1872.
33. *Ibid* 23 October, 25 November 1884, 2 November 1886, 23 May 1887. Correspondence and Clerk's statement relating to the Medical Act, 1886 (1886–87), AHA. Correspondence and papers on the introduction of the surgery exam (1881–86), AHA. Elizabeth Garrett Anderson was one of many licentiates supporting the Society's defence of its position under the 1886 Medical Act (she took the opportunity to question the Clerk as to the Society's future policy with regard to the admission of women to medical exams).
34. R. Brudenell Carter, opthalmic surgeon at St George's Hospital (1810–93), wrote on hysteria and diseases of the nervous system. He took part in the foundation of several eye hospitals, and wrote for the *Lancet* and *The Times* where he was renowned for being the first to use a typewriter and for wearing two pairs of spectactles simultaneously. He was a licentiate and Liveryman of the Society (1898) and its representative on the G.M.C. (1887–1900) when Sir Hugh Beevor Bt succeeded him (1900–10). Brudenell Carter's action in the case of Hunter v. Clare led to his disfranchisement, CM 27 March 1900.
35. Copy letter 15 November, CM 30 November 1886. Clerk's Letter Book 22 November 1886, 5 February, 25 November, 1887, AHA. Minutes of Act of Parliament Committee (1883–88), GL Ms 14,472.
36. CM 20 December 1887, 21 March, 22 June 1893. CME 15 June 1887. Minutes and Reports, Examiners in Arts (1882–95), GL Mss 10,983 and 10,984. 37. Lectures in botany as part of the medical curriculum were no longer required after 1886, and botany as a subject of examination was discontinued by a resolution of the Court of Assistants, 13 February 1894. CM 9 June 1891, 17 February 1892, 13 February 1894, 11 February 1896. CME 6 December 1892, 22 June 1893, 30 May, 22 October 1895, 1 October 1896.
38. Barrett, C.R.B., *The History of the Society of Apothecaries of London* (1905) pp.262–66.
39. Visitors' Reports on Examinations April, May 1901, AHA.
40. *DNB. The Gentleman's Magazine* vol lxxxi (1811) p.81.
41. Case of Handey v. Henson, judgement of Lord Tenterden. Handey claimed payment for fifteen visits to the patient's family, see *Lancet* 16 January 1830 pp.538–40.
42. Moore, T.S., and Philip, J.C., *The Chemical Society 1841–1941* (1847). Warington was co-editor with Theophilus Redwood of the *British Pharmacopoeia* (1867). Wickham, Helen, "The Warington Family" (1997), AHA.
43. CM 22 December 1841.
44. *The Albion* 30 August 1841, unlicensed practitioners, AHA. Holloway, S.W.F., *Royal Pharmaceutical Society of Great Britain 1841–1991* (1991).
45. Fraudulent impersonation of an examination candidate (1819, 1875), bribery to steal examination papers (1870–71), AHA. CM 4 April 1871.
46. Burrows, G.M., *A Statement of Circumstances connected with the Apothecaries' Act and its administration* (1817).
47. *Accounts relating to the Apothecaries' Society* (1825), Petition to House of Commons (1825), AHA. Upton, R.B., *Observations by the Society of Apothecaries on the administration of the Apothecaries' Act viewed in connection with some proposed features in Sir James Graham's proposed measure of medical reform* (1844). CM 26 June 1846.
48. GL Ms 8238 vols i, ii.
49. *House of Commons Report of the Select Committee on Medical Education* (1834) part iii. Evidence from the Royal College of Physicians is in vol i, Royal College of Surgeons vol ii, Society of Apothecaries vol iii. Nussey, Burrows, Bacot, Ridout, Field and Watson gave evidence for the Society.

50. *Lancet* 17 October 1846 pp.434–36.
51. Clerk's Report 28 May 1847, GL Ms 8212 vol ii.
52. Holloway, S.W.F. *op cit* p.259. Cases of unqualified practice (1876–77), AHA. Introduction of power to strike off licentiates for infamous conduct (1870–76), AHA.
53. Orlando Millar, faith-healer, and John C. Purdue, medical botanist (1914), AHA.
54. The House of Lords imposed an expiry date of August 1826 on the Act in the expectation that further investigations would take place, CM 29 July 1825. Letter from Robert Peel, 27 April 1826, GL Ms 8212a. Petition to House of Commons (1825), AHA.
55. 3 April 1826, GL Ms 8212a. Wall, Cecil, "Apothecaries of London and the Study and Practice of Midwifery 1813–53", Ts n.d., AHA. CME 23 December 1852, 28 July 1853.
56. Dickens, Charles, *Martin Chuzzlewit* (1844) pp.20, 327. It has been calculated from a random selection of 2,000 medical men in London in 1847 that 680 were general practitioners holding the M.R.C.S. and L.S.A., 155 were Physicians, 165 Surgeons, see Loudon, Irvine, "Two Thousand Medical Men in 1847" in *The Society for Social History of Medicine Bulletin* no 33, December 1983. 25 February 1842, GL Ms 8212. CM 18 April 1845. College of General Practitioners (1951–58) includes a brief history, AHA.
57. *The Provincial Medical and Surgical Journal* vol viii 1844 p.578. *Lancet* 19 September 1846 pp.326–28.
58. *House of Commons Report* (1834) *op cit*. The requirements of the Court of Examiners in midwifery and the diseases of women, CM 2 August 1843. Nussey, John T.M., "Walker and Nussey – Royal Apothecaries 1784–1860" in *Medical History* vol xiv (1970) pp.81–89. Nussey memorabilia, including the handkerchief held by King George IV on his deathbed, AHA. For a brief life of Bacot and description of Apothecaries' Hall, see *The Medical Circular* vol i (1852) p.130.
59. Upton, R.B., *Observations by the Society of Apothecaries on the subject of their administration of the Apothecaries' Act viewed in connection with some supposed features in Sir James Graham's proposed measures of Medical Reform* (1844). Minutes of the Act of Parliament Committee concerned with the proposed legislation affecting the medical profession (1840–50), GL Ms 8212.
60. *Lancet* 12 September, 31 October 1846 pp.300, 485. CM 26 June 1846.
61. CME 25 June, 2 July 1829.
62. *Ibid* 4 November 1852.
63. *House of Commons Report* (1834) *op cit*.
64. McWalker, James C., *A History of the Worshipful Company of Apothecaries of the City of Dublin* (1916) and information from Dr M. Powell. *BMJ* 19, 28 February 1887 pp.403, 465.
65. Representatives of the Society gave evidence to the Parliamentary Committee on Anatomy, 1828.
66. 5 June 1832, GL Ms 8211 vol i. 28 March 1837, GL Ms 8211 vol ii.
67. 10 April 1883 to 23 May 1886, GL Ms 14,472. CM 4 May 1883, 28 October 1884, 23 May 1887.

Notes to chapter 8, pages 227–62.

1. *The Times* 18 April, 28 July 1916. CM 22 February 1916. Whittet, T.D., *Clerks, Bedels and Chemical Operators of the Society of Apothecaries* (1977) pp.20–21.
2. CM 12 June 1900, 7 April 1901, 10 October, 12 December 1905. 12 September, 3 October 1905, GL Ms 14,472. EAU notes for proposed chapter ten. Apothecaries' Act

(1907), petition, memorandum, Articles of Association of Physicians and Surgeons of the Society (1902–07), AHA. Dr A. Rivers Willson of Oxford (L.S.A. 1889) was also President of the Incorporated Medical Practitioners' Association.

3. CM 8 October 1901, 22 June 1943. Applications to use Royal in the Society's title 1897, 1901, 1922–25, AHA. I am grateful for the Bedel's notes on Crosby, taken from the Court Minutes. Crosby's Diploma, 6 May 1852, AHA. *Plarr's Lives of the Fellows of the Royal College of Surgeons of England* vol i (1930) pp.300–01.

4. Cowen, David L., "Notes on hospital pharmacy in the Royal Navy in the 18th century" in American Society of Hospital Pharmacists, *The Bulletin* vol 13 November-December 1956 pp.568–75. Burnby, J.G.L., "An Examined and Free Apothecary" in Nutton, Vivian, and Porter, Roy, (eds), *The History of Medical Education in Britain* (1995) pp.16–37.

5. *House of Commons Report of the Select Committee on Medical Education* (1834), evidence given by J.Ridout. Assistants' Register (1850–1900), GL Ms 10,988.

6. *Chemist and Druggist* 18 August 1917 p.719 and miscellaneous advertisements. The minimum age of candidates was seventeen in 1900, later raised to eighteen and nineteen, Apothecaries' Assistants' examination regulations and syllabuses (1900–78), AHA.

7. 14 March 1905, 27 March 1906, GL Ms 14,472.

8. CM 26 June 1911. 26 June, 10 October 1911, 23 January, 5 November 1912, GL Ms 14,472.

9. 19 November 1912, GL Ms 14,472.

10. CM 1 April 1913. Society's proposed Bill in Parliament (1913, 1919), AHA.

11. Admission without examination of Society's Assistants to Pharmaceutical Society registers of chemists and druggists, papers and correspondence (1907–19), AHA.

12. CM 11 March 1913, 3 February 1914, 8 May, 9 October 1917. Disdavantaged Assistants (1907–1919), AHA.

13. CM 7 August 1917, 4 June 1918, 4, 11 March, 13 May, 1 July 1919.

14. CM 1 July 1919.

15. CM 3 December 1918. Grievances of Dispensers (1920–24), AHA. Holloway, S.W.F., *Royal Pharmaceutical Society of Great Britain 1841–1991* (1991) p.356. The queen granted the title Royal to the Pharmaceutical Society of Great Britian in 1988.

16. Assistants' Register (1901–54), GL Ms 14,473. Agatha Christie (Dame Agatha from 1971) worked as a dispenser at University College Hospital during the Second World War, see Bardell, Eunice B., "Dame Agatha's Dispensary" in *Pharmacy in History* vol 26 (1984) no 1 pp.12–19. Gerald, Michael C., "Agatha Christie's helpful and harmful health providers: writings on Physicians and Pharmacists" in *Pharmacy in History* vol 33 no 1 (1991) pp.31–39. Gwilt, Peter R., and Gwilt, John R., "Dame Agatha's poisonous pharmacopoeia" in *Pharmaceutical Journal* 221 no 6002, 23, 30 December 1978 pp.572–73.

17. Clerk's Report on the position of Dispensers, April 1923, and list of public hospitals, institutions where Apothecaries' Assistants were employed, February 1921, AHA.

18. Registration and Position of Society's Dispensing Assistants (1923). Grievances of the Association of Certified Dispensers and Master's statement (1923), AHA.

19. *Report of the Royal Commission on National Health Insurance* vol xiv (1926) pp.585–86. Society's memorandum to the Commissioners, correspondence (1924–25), AHA.

20. Table of Assistants' Examinations 1931–58 (1959), AHA.

21. Regulations, examination and syllabus for Dispensing Assistants, June 1960, AHA.

22. Memorandum by T.D. Whittet (1964), AHA.

23. CM 4 April 1973, 6 February 1974.
24. CME 1900–09, AHA.
25. Table of twenty-five licensing bodies taken from the G.M.C. Minutes for 1937, AHA.
26. Dearman, E.J., "Firewatchers' Report relating to 10–11 May 1941", June 1941, AHA. See chapter 4, page 88 for the Society's fire brigade.
27. CM 14 March, 9 August 1944. Report of the Interdepartmental Committee on Medical Schools (1941–44), AHA.
28. 21 March 1911, GL Ms 14,472. Clerk's Letter Book 24 January 1911, AHA.
29. See chapter 7, pages 211, 221.
30. CME 24 February 1927, 13 June 1928. CM 17 May 1927, 16 October, 11 December 1928. Mastery of Midwifery (1925–28), Regulations *circa* 1930–32, Drawings for Mastery of Midwifery gowns and one blue gown, AHA. Shaw, Sir William Fletcher, *Twenty-Five Years. The Story of the Royal College of Obstetricians and Gynaecologists 1929–1954* (1954).
31. Examinations Committee Minute 20 October 1960. M.M.S.A. to be discontinued, 1961, AHA.
32. Minutes of the Bio-Physical Assistants' Committee (1929–33), GL Ms 10,990. Register (1929) and Memorandum (1945), AHA.
33. CM 10 July 1945.
34. Industrial Health Examination Committee Minutes (1950–63), AHA. The Faculty of Occupational Medicine papers and reports (1945–49), AHA. Nield, F.G., "The Apothecaries' Diploma of Industrial Health and its contribution to Occupational Medicine" in *Journal of the Society of Occupational Medicine* vol 37 (1987) pp.34–35.
35. Printed details of each of the Society's present Diplomas, syllabus, examination dates, fees, etc. from the Registrar, Apothecaries' Hall.
36. CM 14 March, 9 August 1944. Report of the Goodenough Committee summarized in "The Training of Doctors" in *BMJ* 22 July 1944 p.121.
37. Sir Charles Dodds F.R.S was elected President of the Royal College of Physicians in 1962. He was a founder member of the Faculty, served two terms as Master of the Society (1947–49) and twenty-five years as custodian of the cellar at the Hall. He presented the candelabrum in the Parlour (1971) and when he died in 1973 he left the Society £500.
38. CM 19 August 1944, 27 March 1945.
39. Lectures on modern therapeutics, Future Activities Committee Minutes 25 March, 13 November 1947, and 1947–59, AHA.
40. Published as "Influence of the Society upon medical education" in *BMJ* 7 January 1956 pp.4,957–62.
41. Minutes of meeting of sub-committee on Medical History, 27 January 1959, Faculty papers, AHA.
42. Dr Copeman was consistently generous to the Society, presenting a bust of King Charles I, returning his lecturing fees and entertaining the executive of the Faculty at the Athenaeum. Postcard August 1959 and correspondence, AHA.
43. The subject of Roberts's research was refined to the history of importation of drugs into this country in the seventeenth century. He wrote articles on "The Personnel and Practice of Medicine in Tudor and Stuart England" in *Medical History* vol vi (1962) and vol viii (1964), "The Early History of the Import of Drugs into Britain" in Poynter, F.N.L. (ed), *The Evolution of Pharmacy in Britain* (1965), and a doctoral thesis "The London Apothecaries and Medical Practice in Tudor and Stuart England" London University 1964.

44. The development of the Faculty can be traced in the Annual Reports 1959–60 to 1996–97 (not published between 1975/6 and 1978/9), AHA.
45. Copeman, W.S.C., *The Worshipful Society of Apothecaries of London. A History 1617–1967* (1967) p.71.
46. Annual Report of the Faculty of the History of Medicine (1970–71), AHA.
47. The current lecture programme is available from Apothecaries' Hall. An additional lecture, the Macdonald Critchley, alternates with the Sloane lecture but is not under the aegis of the Faculty.
48. I am grateful for information on the origin of the Diploma in the Philosophy of Medicine from the Dean of Rochester.
49. CM 19 February, 5 June 1973. Minutes of Executive Committee of the Faculty, 18 October, 13 November 1976, 14 February, 27 June 1977. Revised constitution 1976, Faculty papers, AHA
50. CM 6 July 1972, 19 February 1973. Minutes of Executive Committee of the Faculty (1977–78), AHA.
51. Memorandum on "The Place of the History of Medicine in Medical Education" (1965), AHA.
52. G.M.C., *Tomorrow's Doctors* (1993).
53. CM 10 January 1634. WA 1628–29, 1630–31, 1633–35. The smith was paid 5s 6d for work on the poor box (1630–31), presumably kept at Painter-Stainers' Hall at this date. 20 shillings voted to a poor brother of the Company, CM 17 October 1631. Evidence supplied to the Charity Commissioners 2 April 1860, *House of Commons, Report of the Livery Companies Commission* vol v (1884) p.1.
54. CM 6, 19 November 1701, 6 January, 18 February 1702, 4 July 1706.
55. CM 22 March, 25 June 1711. Peter Gelsthorp's portrait hangs in the Great Hall.
56. The names of benefactors to the Widow's and Distressed Members' Funds (1711–1905) were inscribed on panels in the Great Hall, removed 1910. A photographic record was made, *Widows and Distressed Members' Fund* (1910), AHA. See also Barrett, C.R.B., *The History of the Society of Apothecaries of London* (1905) pp.294–98. Report to Charity Commissioners, 2 April 1860, *House of Commons Report* (1884) op cit. Benefactions Book, GL Ms 8231. John Allen's portrait is in the Court Room.
57. E.A. Brande's Declaration of Trust 3 January 1854, Widows' Fund, AHA. *House of Commons Report* (1884) op cit.
58. Register of recipients of widows' pensions (1817–81), AHA.
59. Circular January 1863, letter J. Bacot to R.B. Upton, 5 February 1863, Distressed Members' Fund papers to Charity Commissioners 1925, AHA. The names of contributors (1863–1905), taken from panels in the Hall, *Widows' and Distressed Members' Fund* (1910), AHA.
60. CM 27 October 1812, 19 August, 30 September 1825. Petition from thirteen apprentices *circa* 1810–13, AHA.
61. Lists of prizewinners and copy examination paper for botany prize, 11 August 1858 in Report to Charity Commissioners 2 April 1860, *House of Commons Report* (1884) op cit. Botany prizes (1830–95) and for women (1878), AHA. Desmond, Adrian, *Huxley: The Devil's Disciple* (1994).
62. Letter W.T. Brande to R.B. Upton, 24 December 1838, AHA.
63. Letter Clerk to President Royal College of Physicians, 25 November 1840, AHA. Wyon was paid £189 15s, CM 3 January 1843.
64. *House of Commons Report* (1884) op cit. G.H. Makins's Notebook, AHA. The Physic Garden opened to female students for the first time in 1876. Botany prizes for women and reports, (1878), AHA.

65. Prizes and exam papers (1893–95), AHA. A botany prize book awarded in 1873, Sir Thomas Watson's *Lectures on the Principles and Practice of Physic* 2 vols (1871), was donated to the Library at the Hall by Dr John Price in 1982.
66. Surgical and Medical Scholarships, regulations (1882–83); Examinations Committee Minute 16 January 1883, AHA.
67. CM 14 August 1900, 6 March 1901. Copy of Gillson's will 19 April 1899 (he died in June 1900), correspondence, regulations, AHA.
68. Copy of Dr Rogers' will 26 November 1886, AHA. He was a licentiate (1841), M.R.C.S (1842).
69. Strickland Goodall Lecture and Medal, including biographical notes by Professor John Hay, AHA.
70. Galen Medal (1925–27), AHA.
71. Award of Galen Medal to Professor J.J. Abel (1928), AHA.
72. Honorary Diploma, H.R.H. Prince of Wales (1926), AHA. *The Times* 2 January 1926.
73. CM 19 December 1633, 8 September 1659. Honorary Freedom to Sir Ronald Ross (1915), AHA. Ross, Sir Ronald, *Memoirs* (1923) pp.37–38. The Society's records show that Ross failed in midwifery and was deficient in other subjects, Register of Failed Candidates (1868–81), AHA.
74. Letter from Master to past and present Court members and officials, January 1941, AHA.
75. Report of the Interdepartmental Committee on Medical Schools (1941–44) and interview with representatives of the Society, 6 January 1943, AHA. Evidence presented to the Ministry of Health Interdepartmental Committee, October 1942, AHA. L.V. Cargill left the Society a substantial bequest, CM 1, 20 October 1971.
76. CM 19 April, 9 August 1944.
77. Letter from Basil L. Steele and Russell Steele, 22 February 1943 and Master's reply, 26 February 1943, AHA.
78. CM 12 April 1946.
79. House of Commons, *Reports from Commissioners on Municipal Corporations* (1834) p.266.
80. CM 10, 17 December 1946, 25 March, 17, 24 June 1947. Enid Houghton, née Cyriax, was the first woman to be admitted to the membership.
81. G.M.C. Inspectors' Reports (1954–57), AHA.
82. CM 16 December 1975. Correspondence of Dr Pierre A. Gaulin with the Society (1975–76), AHA. Another case was that of Enibiene Ijona of Lagos who forged the L.M.S.S.A. Diploma (1961–62), AHA.
83. U.E.B., *Regulations* November 1995. U.E.B., *Annual Report and Accounts* (1995–96).
84. Examinations Committee Minute 20 March 1973. The first test was held in Edinburgh, June 1975, CM 12 August 1975. Between June 1975 and February 1976 1,019 candidates from overseas took the tests (the largest proportion coming from India), and 352 passed: see G.M.C., *Annual Report* (1975) pp.8–15. I am grateful for information from the Registrar.
85. The significance of 20 August remains obscure, unless it is related to the Assumption of the Blessed Virgin Mary on 15 August. According to the *Oxford Dictionary of Saints*, St Nicholas is the patron saint of apothecaries (also children, sailors, unmarried girls, merchants, pawnbrokers and perfumers). His feast day is 6 December. The Society attended St Ann Black Friars from 1633 until the church was destroyed in the Great Fire. St Ann's was not rebuilt and the parish was united with St Andrew-by-the-Wardrobe, one of the last City churches rebuilt under the direction of Wren

NOTES

(1694). St Andrew's was gutted by bombing 29 December 1941. Until it was restored the Society attended services at St James Garlickhythe and St Mary Aldermanbury, returning to St Andrew following its re-consecration in 1961.

86. Master's Day 1780, GL MS 8257. C.R.B. Barrett, *The History of the Society of Apothecaries of London* pp.140–41.

87. Brochure for the procession on Lord Mayor's Day, 9 November 1911, AHA.

Sources and Bibliography

Primary sources
The Society's archives are divided between the Department of Manuscripts at Guildhall Library, Aldermanbury, London EC2P 2EJ, and Apothecaries' Hall, Black Friars Lane, London EC4 6EJ, where a hitherto unknown and extensive collection of material has recently been discovered and surveyed by the newly appointed Archivist to the Society. References in the Notes indicate the location of items by either the abbreviation GL Ms (Guildhall Library Department of Manuscripts) or AHA (Apothecaries' Hall Archive, which is in the process of being set up together with a comprehensive list of holdings). The location of other documentary sources is given in the Abbreviations and Notes on page 263.

Bibliography
The selected bibliography gives works of general interest, followed by those relevant to a particular chapter. More specific references are given in the Notes (pages 263–95).

General
Barrett, C.R.B., *The History of the Society of Apothecaries of London* (1905)
Burnby, J.G.L., *The changing role of the Apothecary* (1991)
Clark, George N., and Cooke, A.M., *A History of the Royal College of Physicians* 3 vols (1964–72)
Colvin, H.M., *A Biographical Dictionary of British Architects 1600–1840* (1978, 1995)
Copeman, W.S.C., *The Worshipful Society of Apothecaries of London. A History 1617–1967* (1967)
Corfe, Gerald, *The Apothecary Ancient and Modern* (1887)
Field, Ian, *The Worshipful Society of Apothecaries. A guide to the Society and Apothecaries' Hall* (1992)
Matthews, Leslie G., *History of Pharmacy in Britain* (1962)
Munk, William, *The Roll of the Royal College of Physicians* 8 vols (1878–1989)
Nutton, Vivian and Porter, Roy (eds), *The History of Medical Education in Britain* (1995)
Porter, Roy, *Disease, medicine and society in England 1550–1860* (1995), *The Cambridge Illustrated History of Medicine* (1996), *The Greatest Benefit to Mankind. A Medical History* (1997)
Poynter, F.N.L., *The Evolution of Medical Education in Britain* (1966)
Sharpe, R.R., *London and the Kingdom* 3 vols (1894–95)
Underwood, E.A., Cameron, H.C., and Wall, Cecil, *A History of the Worshipful Society of Apothecaries of London* vol i 1617–1815 (1963)
Walters, Dai, *A Catalogue of selected Portraits and Pictures at Apothecaries' Hall* (1997)
Whittet, T.D., *Clerks, Bedels and Chemical Operators of the Society of Apothecaries* (1977) and "Some Masters of the Worshipful Society of Apothecaries" in *Pharmaceutical Historian* vol 12 no 3, December 1982

Chapter 1
Getz, F.M. (ed), *Healing and Society in Medieval England* (1991)
Jackson, Ralph, *Doctors and Diseases in the Roman Empire* (1988)
Matthews, Leslie G., *The Royal Apothecaries* (1967), *The Pepperers, Spicers and Apothecaries of London during the Thirteenth and Fourteenth Centuries* (1980)
Nightingale, Pamela, *A Medieval Mercantile Community. The Grocers' Company and the*

Politics and Trade of London 1000–1485 (1995)
Nunn, John F., *Ancient Egyptian Medicine* (1996)
Rubin, Stanley, *Medieval English Medicine* (1974)
Thrupp, Sylvia, *The merchant class of medieval London 1300–1500* (1948)
Whittet, T.D., "Pepperers, Spicers and Grocers. Forerunners of the Apothecaries" in *Proceedings of the Royal Society of Medicine* vol 61 August 1968 pp.801–06.

Chapter 2
Berlin, Michael, *The Worshipful Company of Distillers* (1996)
Cook, Harold J., *The Decline of the Old Medical Regime in Stuart London* (1986)
Debus, Allen (ed), *Medicine in Seventeenth Century England* (1974)
Larkin, James F., and Hughes, Paul L. (eds), *Stuart Royal Proclamations 1603–25* vol i (1973)
Matthews, Leslie G., "London's Immigrant Apothecaries 1600–1800" in *Medical History* vol xviii (1974)
Roberts, R.S., "The Personnel and Practice of Medicine in Tudor and Stuart England" part 2 in *Medical History* vol viii (1964)
Whittet, T.D., "The Charter members of the Society of Apothecaries" in *Proceedings of the Royal Society of Medicine* vol 64 October 1971

Chapter 3
Bell, Walter, *The Great Fire of London in 1666* (1923) and *The Great Plague in London in 1665* (1951)
Burch, B., "Parish of St Anne's Black Friars London to 1665" in *The Guildhall Miscellany* vol ii no 1 October 1969
Burnby, J.G.L., *A Study of the English Apothecary 1660–1760* (1983)
Milne, Gustav, *The Great Fire of London* (1965)
Pearl, Valerie, *London and the Outbreak of the Puritan Revolution* (1961)
Porter, Stephen (ed), *London and the Civil War* (1996) and *The Great Fire of London* (1996)
Whittet, T.D., *The Apothecaries in the Great Plague of London 1665* (1965)

Chapter 4
The Builder 7 December 1917
Fisher, James F., "The Buildings and Treasures of the Society of Apothecaries" in *Transactions of the Ancient Monuments Society* vol 33 (1989)
Fraser, Antonia, *The Six Wives of Henry VIII* (1992)
Hunting, Penelope, *Ludgate* (1993)
Kelly H.A., *The Matrimonial Trials of Henry VIII* (1976)
Oswald, Arthur, "The Hall of the Worshipful Society of Apothecaries" in *Country Life* 10 October 1947
Royal Commission on Historical Monuments, *An Inventory of the Historical Monuments in London* vol iv The City (1929)
Schofield, John, *The Building of London from the Conquest to the Great Fire* (1984)

Chapter 5
Bowack, John, *Antiquities of Middlesex* (1705)
Desmond, Ray, *Dictionary of British and Irish Botanists and Horticulturalists* (1977)
Drewitt, F. Dawtrey, *The Romance of the Apothecaries' Garden at Chelsea* (1924)
Field, Henry, and Semple, R.H., *Memoirs of the Botanic Garden at Chelsea* (1878)
Godfrey, Walter, *Survey of London, The Parish of Chelsea* part i (1909)

Gunther, R.T., *Early British Botanists* (1922)
Hill, Arthur W., *The history and function of Botanic Gardens* (1915)
MacGregor, Arthur (ed), *Sir Hans Sloane. Collector, Scientist, Antiquary* (1994)
Palmer, K. Nicholls, *Ceremonial Barges on the River Thames* (1997)
Rougetel, Hazel le, *The Chelsea Gardener, Philip Miller 1691–1771* (1990)
Royal Society, *The Record of the Royal Society of London* (1940)
Whittet, T.D., "The Barges of the Society of Apothecaries" in *Pharmaceutical Historian* vol 10 no 1 April 1980

Chapter 6
Bateson, C., *The Convict Ships 1787–1868* (1969)
Beaglehole, J.C. (ed), *The Journals of Captain James Cook on his voyages of discovery* 4 vols (1955–74)
Colonial Society of Massachusetts, *Medicine in Colonial Massachusetts 1620–1820* (1980)
Gordon, Maurice B., *Aesculapius comes to the Colonies* (1949)
Haines, Gregory, *Pharmacy in Australia* (1988)
Hall, Marie Boas, "Apothecaries and chemists in the seventeenth century" in *Pharmaceutical Journal* 28 October 1967
Keevil, J.J., *Medicine and the Navy 1200–1900* 4 vols (1957–63)

Chapter 7
Cartwright, F.F., *A Social History of Medicine* (1977)
Holloway, S.W.F., "Medical Education in England 1830–58. A Sociological Analysis" in *History* vol 49 1964
Kerrison, R.M., *An Inquiry into the present state of the medical profession in England* (1814)
Newman, Charles, *The Evolution of Medical Education in the Nineteenth Century* (1957)
Poynter, F.N.L. (ed), *The Evolution of Medical Practice in Britain* (1961)

Chapter 8
Doolittle, I.G., *The City of London and its Livery Companies* (1982)
Holloway, S.W.F., *Royal Pharmaceutical Society of Great Britain 1841–1991* (1991)
James, Robert Rhodes, *Henry Wellcome* (1994)
Shryock, Richard Harrison, *The Development of Modern Medicine* (1979)
Stevens, Rosemary, *Medical Practice in Modern England* (1966)

List of Masters of the Society 1617–1998

The starred names were original or charter members of December 1617. Two or three names in one year indicate the death of the Master while in office, whereupon a successor was chosen. Titles, Fellowship of the Royal Society, Membership of Parliament and Mayoralty achieved after the year as Master are cited (LM indicates a Lord Mayor).

Date	Master
1617–21	* Edmond Phillipps
1621–22	* Stephen Higgins
1622–23	* John Wolfgang Rumler
1623–24	* Richard Bacon
1624–26	* Thomas Fones
1626–27	* Adrian Barton
1627–28	* Josias Harris
1628–29	* Gideon de Laune
1629–30	* Israel Wolfe
1630–31	* Thomas Christie
1631–32	* William Clapham
1632–34	* Richard Edwards
1634–35	* Thomas Hicks
1635–36	* Josias Harris
1636–37	* John Wolfgang Rumler
1637–38	* Gideon de Laune
1638–39	* Stephen Higgins
1639–41	* Edward Cooke
1641–42	* William Bell
1642–43	* Ralph Yardley
1643–44	* Abraham Webb
1644–45	* William Shambrook
1645–46	* Richard Glover
1646–47	John Sotherton
1647–48	John Lawrence
1648–49	Oliver Reynolds
1649–50	* James Walsham
1650–51	* Samuel Harrison
1651–52	Samuel Skelton
1652–53	Richard Holland
1653–54	Thomas Smith
1654–55	John Lorrimer
1655–56	James James
1656–57	Leonard Buckner
	James Martin
1657–58	John Thomas
1658–59	Caleb Stephens
1659–60	Michael Markland
1660–61	John Shelburie
1661–62	Lt Col William Rosewell
1662–63	Jeremiah Richardson
1663–64	Benjamin Banister
1664–66	John Chase
1666–67	Michael North
1667–68	Edward Darnelly
1668–69	Richard Litlar
1669–70	Symon Williams
1670–71	Arthur Hollingsworth
1671–72	Walter Pelling
1672–73	William Gape
1673–74	George Johnson
1674–75	John Battersby
1675–76	Anthony Hinton
1676–77	Edward Pilkington
1677–78	William Butler
1678 79	Thomas Warner
1679–80	Thomas Mitchell
1680–81	Stephen Skynner
	Robert Phelps
1681–82	William Standen
1682–83	William Clerke
1683–84	Peter Sambrooke
1684–85	Thomas Barrow
1685–86	Edward Herne
	Benjamin Donne
1686–87	William Pott
1687–88	James St Amand MP
1688–89	James Chase MP
1689–90	Thomas Warren
1690–91	James Gover
1691–92	William Bradford
1692–93	Thomas Hall
	Thomas Soaper
1693–94	Henry Sykes
1694–95	Sir John Clarke
1695–96	John Danson
1696–97	Thomas Fige

1697–98	William Phillipps	1745–46	John de Raffen
1698–99	Spencer Piggot	1746–47	William Lake
	Thomas Elton	1747–48	John Pocklington
1699–1700	Thomas Elton	1748–49	Nathaniel Green
1700–01	Thomas Dalton	1749–50	Reuben Melmoth
1701–02	Peter Gelsthorp	1750–51	William Elderton
1702–03	Thomas Gardiner	1751–52	John Addis
1703–04	Peter Gelsthorp	1752–53	Thomas Northey
1704–05	Arthur Reeves		Robert Gamon
1705–06	William Rouse	1753–54	John Chase
1706–07	Thomas Bromfield	1754–55	John Markham
1707–08	Richard Malther	1755–56	Samuel Berkley
1708–10	Francis Dandridge	1756–57	William Massa
1710–11	Walter Drewry		Nathaniel Greene
1711–12	Joseph Biscoe		Sir Benjamin Rawling
1712–13	Jonathan Lee	1757–58	Daniel Peters
1713–14	Thomas Compere	1758–59	Andrew Lillie
1714–15	Samuel Birch		William Tyson
1715–16	John Jay	1759–60	William Gataker
1716–17	Simon Andrews	1760–61	Benjamin Charlewood
1717–18	Henry Smith	1761–62	Daniel Hanchett
1718–19	Thomas Shaller	1762–63	John Springett
1719–20	Colonel Robert Gower	1763–64	Josiah Higden
1720–21	James Siddall	1764–65	Sir Thomas Harris
1721–22	Joseph Nicholson	1765–66	Benjamin Charlewood
1722–23	Joseph Nicholson		Edmund Mills
	Henry Smith	1766–67	John Peck
1723–24	James Pitson	1767–68	Marmaduke Westwood
1724–25	Oliver Gaynes		John Chandler FRS
1725–26	Simon Andrews	1768–69	Samuel Latham
1726–27	Colonel Robert Gower	1769–70	Jeremiah Armiger
1727–28	John Smith	1770–71	John Lisle
1728–29	Charles Angibaud	1771–72	John Channing
1729–30	John Biscoe	1772–73	John Pearce
1730–31	Josiah Cruttenden	1773–74	James Kettilby
1731–32	William Withers	1774–75	Josiah Colebrooke FRS
1732–33	Ralph Forster		Thomas Basden
1733–34	John Warren	1775–76	William Prowting
1734–35	James Albin	1776–77	George Clarke
1735–36	Zechariah Allen	1777–78	William Lane
	Robert Hume	1778–79	Thomas Roberts
1736–37	Sir Benjamin Rawling	1779–80	Richard Elliott
1737–38	Robert Harris	1780–81	Joseph Partington
1738–39	Joseph Miller	1781–82	Isaac Mather
1739–40	John Salter	1782–83	Thomas Hawes
1740–41	Robert Nicholls	1783–84	Edward Thomas Nealson
1741–42	Benjamin Morris	1784–85	John Devall
1742–43	Joseph Richards	1785–86	John Field
1743–44	John Lyde	1786–87	Matthew Yatman
1744–45	Robert Gamon	1787–88	James Bromfield

1788–89	Peter Girod	1838–39	David Clapton
1789–90	Thomas Cater	1839–40	James Seaton
1790–91	Paul Julliott		Allen Williams
1791–92	Herbert Lawrence	1840–41	Allen Williams
1792–93	William Heckford	1841–42	Henry Robinson
1793–94	John Wiley	1842–43	Charles Edward Clarke
1794–95	John William Benson	1843–44	William Bagster
1795–96	John Devaynes	1844–45	Edward Wallace
1796–97	William Fowle	1845–46	John Bacot
1797–98	John Bradney	1846–47	John Ridout
1798–99	Isaac Bouquet	1847–48	Edward Bean
1799–1800	Thomas Watson	1848–49	John Callander
1800–01	John Collier	1849–50	John Brown Eyles
1801–02	Timothy Lane FRS	1850–51	Michael Lambton Este
1802–03	Richard Haworth	1851–52	WilliamThomas Brande FRS
1803–04	Uriah Bristow	1852–53	Richard Strong Eyles
1804–05	Augustine Towson	1853–54	John Parrott
1805–06	Adam Moore	1854–55	Nathaniel Bagshaw
1806–07	Robert Sherson		Ward FRS
1807–08	Hugh French	1855–56	Richard Clewin Griffith
1808–09	Elias de Gruchy Fassett	1856–57	John Francis De Grave
1809–10	William Henry Higden	1857–58	Jeronimo Simoens
1810–11	Charles Nevinson	1858–59	James Saner
1811–12	Richard Griffith	1859–60	Frederick Richard Gower
1812–13	Philip Nicholas	1860–61	John Hunter
1813–14	John Stephen Bacot	1861–62	William Buchanan
1814–15	John Newsom	1862–63	Charles West Wheeler
1815–16	Thomas Hardwick	1863–64	Henry Combe
1816–17	William Simons	1864–65	James Lowe Wheeler
1817–18	William Box	1865–66	Charles Higham
1818–19	Miles Partington	1866–68	George Cooper
1819–20	Samuel Lawford	1868–69	Tobias Browne
1820–21	Joseph Jackson	1869–70	Joseph Smith
1821–22	George Cabbell	1870–71	Henry Morley
1822–23	John Baker	1871–72	George Kelson
1823–24	Thomas Wheeler	1872–73	Thomas Hunt
1824–25	Edward Browne	1873–74	William Dickinson
1825–26	Henry Field	1874–75	Richard Stocker
1826–27	Joseph Littlefear	1875–76	Allin Foord Price
1827–28	Julian Mariner	1876–77	Edward Bradford
1828–29	Andrew Ewbank	1877–78	Willington Clark
1829–30	Joseph Hurlock	1878–79	Thomas George
1830–31	William R. Macdonald		Slaughter
1831–32	John Hunter	1879–80	John Hainworth
1832–33	James Hill	1880–81	Thomas Spry Byass
1833–34	John Nussey	1881–82	Hugh Worthington Statham
1834–35	James Upton	1882–83	James Saner
1835–36	William King	1883–84	Thomas Wakefield
1836–37	John Hingeston	1884–85	George Corfe
1837–38	George Johnson	1885–86	Edward Furley

1886–87	William Shillito	1933–34	John Oglethorpe Wakelin Barratt
1887–88	George John Amsden		
1888–89	Thomas Skeel	1934–35	Sir George Seaton Buchanan
1889–90	George Hogarth Makins		
1890–91	Edwin Chabot	1935–36	Sir William Henry Willcox
1891–92	John Wadham Robinson	1936–37	Arthur Philip Gibbons
1892–93	Charles Taylor	1937–38	Sir Hugh Lett Bt
1893–94	John Rees Withecombe	1938–39	Reginald Hewlett Hayes
1894–95	Thomas James Austin	1939–40	Lionel Vernon Cargill
1895–96	Francis Richard Gibbes	1940–41	Thomas Bramley Layton
1896–97	Edward Tegart	1941–44	Sir Stanley Woodwark
1897–98	Samuel Clewin Griffith	1944–45	John Prescott Hedley
1898–99	Joseph Stewart Burton	1945–46	Hugh Falkenburg Powell
1899–1900	John Sherwood Stocker	1946–47	Christopher Thackray Parsons
1900–01	Charles Browne		
1901–02	Thomas Edwin Burton Brown	1947–49	Sir Edward Charles Dodds Bt FRS
1902–03	William Parson	1949–50	Duncan Campbell Lloyd Fitzwilliams
1903–04	Clarence Cooper		
1904–05	Albert Bryan Day	1950–51	Frank Dutch Howitt
1905–06	James Henry Jeffcoat	1951–52	Gerald Roche Lynch
1906–07	Edward Parker Young	1952–53	Sir Wilson Jameson
1907–08	George Wilks	1953–54	Henry Seaward Morley
1908–09	Frederick Gordon Brown	1954–55	Sir Cecil Pembrey Grey Wakeley Bt
1909–10	Reginald Bligh Wall		
1910–11	Arthur Trehern Norton	1955–56	Neville Samuel Finzi
1911–12	Sir Thomas Boor Crosby LM Arthur Long (Deputy)	1956–57	Macdonald Critchley
		1957–58	Reginald Fisher
1912–13	William Bramley Taylor	1958–59	William Sydney Charles Copeman
1913–14	Martindale Ward		
1914–15	Meredith Townsend	1959–60	Richard Robertson Trail
1915–16	George Amsden	1960–61	Charles Francis White
1916–17	Arthur Henry Williams Ayling	1961–62	Archie Murrell Acheson Moore
1917–18	Charles Sangster	1962–63	Thomas Keith Selfe Lyle
1918–19	Benjamin Bloomfield Connolly	1963–64	Redvers Nowell Ironside
		1964–65	Sir Arthur Porritt Bt
1919–20	Samuel Osborn	1965–66	Richard Alan Brews
1920–21	Sir Shirley Murphy		Sir Arthur Porritt Bt
1921–22	William Frederick Richardson Burgess	1966–67	Harold Clifford Edwards
		1967–68	Hugh Macdonald Sinclair
1922–23	William Budd Slaughter	1968–69	Henry Reynolds Thompson
1923–24	Thomas Wakefield	1969–70	Peter Maxwell Farrow Bishop
1924–25	Algernon Dutton Brenchley		
1925–26	Thomas Vincent Dickinson	1970–71	Geoffrey Thomas Willoughby Cashell
1926–27	Alfred Hepburn		
1927–28	Reginald Whiteside Statham	1971–72	Sir John Samuel Richardson Bt
1928–31	Charles Thomas Samman		
1931–32	Ernest Carrick Freeman	1972–73	Sir Brian Wellingham Windeyer
1932–33	Reginald Cecil Bligh Wall		

LIST OF MASTERS OF THE SOCIETY

1973–74	Gordon Barrett Mitchell-Heggs	1987–88	James Frederick Fisher
1974–75	Sir Ronald Bodley Scott	1988–89	Frederic Guy Neild
1975–76	Elston Grey Grey-Turner	1989–90	Malcolm Paul Weston Godfrey
1976–77	Robert Donald Teare	1990–91	Douglas George Arnott Eadie
1977–78	Ian McGilchrist Jackson		
1978–79	Phillip Henry Almroth Willcox	1991–92	Tony William Alphonse Glenister
1979–80	Sir Gordon Wolstenholme	1992–93	David Treharne Dillon Hughes
1980–81	Guy Blackburn		
1981–82	Sir Ronald Gibson	1993–94	Michael Phelps Ward
1982–83	Thomas Douglas Whittet	1994–95	Sir John Chalstrey LM
1983–84	Sir Peter Tizard	1995–96	Barrie Samuel Jay
1984–85	Norman Henry Ashton FRS	1996–97	Frederick Brian Gibberd
1985–86	John Alastair Dudgeon	1997–98	Michael Arthur Pugh
1986–87	William Frederick Walter Southwood		

Index

abuses, 24, 25
accoucheurs, 220
Adam Brothers, 96
Adams, Dr Joseph, 195, 211
Alchorne, Stanesby, 130, 135, 136, 137, 195
Allen, John, 246
Allen & Hanbury, 172
Alsop, Thomas, 19–20
America, 177–83
Anatomy Act, 225
Anderson, Elizabeth Garrett, 207–10
Anderson, James, 165
Anderson, William, 141
Angibaud, Charles, 60, 165
animals, and drug testing, 190
Anne, Queen, 167
apothecaries:
    abuses by, 24, 25
    at court and in convent, 18–22
    emergence, 11–27
    equipment, ancient, 11
    fees, 216
    and grocers, 22–4
    inspections, 23–4, 38, 45, 50, 154
    legal sanction for the practice of medicine, 55, 153
    name, 16
    role in 16th century, 24–7
    see also Society of Apothecaries
Apothecaries Act 1815, 171, 193, 196–8, 217–18, 229, 230
Apothecaries Amendment Act 1874, 224
apothecaries' assistants (dispensers), 229–35
    examination, 210, 233
Apothecaries' Hall, 40
    Brande Block, 101–2
    Cobham House, Black Friars, 43, 45, 75, 79–81
    Cobham House (new), 102, 108–9, 110
    destroyed in Great Fire, 51, 67, 69
    eighteenth century, 88–97
    fire-fighting equipment, 88, 160
    garden, 119
    laboratory, 69, 86, 97, 99, 119, 154–60
    library, 77, 110, 130
    Mill House, 102
    more space, 86
    museum and strong room, 97
    new acquisition of land, 97–9
    new hall, 74–111
    nineteenth century and after, 101–11
    other stained glass, 105
    rebuilding, 69, 83–8
    redevelopment, 105–11
    tenements, 86
    war damage, 103–4, 232
    well, 99
    windows, Great Hall, 104
Apothecaries' Mill, Lambeth, 175
Apothecaries of Dublin, 224–5
apothecary-brokers, 17
apprentices, 45–7, 171, 194, 198, 224
    see also education
armaments, 186
armed forces, medical supplies for, 164–7, 176, 186, 187, 188
Arundell (Arndell), Thomas, 181
Ashton, Prof. N.H., 110
Association of Physicians and Surgeons, 227, 229
Atkins, Dr Henry, 29, 31, 32, 34, 37
Aubrey, John, 22
Australia, medical supplies to, 180–3

Bacon, Francis, 29, 31, 32, 35
Bacon, Richard, 154
Bacot, John, 206, 221, 247
Badger, John, 52
Baldwin, Charles, 101
Bambridge, Dr, 190
Banks, Sir Thomas, 136, 142, 196
Barber-Surgeons, 25, 113, 164, 170
barge-house, Chelsea, 114, 116
barges, 41, 69, 112–16
    banners, 105, 115, 116
Barlow, Edward, 90, 92
Barrett, C.R.B., 215–16
Barton, Adrian, 37
Baskett, Robert, 167
Battersby, John, 63, 64, 67, 122, 158, 159
Bedel, first, 34, 37
Bell, Jacob, 217
Bell, William, 34, 61
Benyon, Robert, 158
Bernard, Charles, 167
Bernard, Dr Francis, 65, 70
Besse, William, 30
Best, Henry, 63
Bevan, Sylvanus, and Timothy, 172, 193
Black Friars, *see* London
Blackwell, Elizabeth, 132
Blizard, Sir William, 223
Bobart, Jacob, 124
Boghurst, William, 57, 65–6
Botanical Demonstrator, 41
Botanical Society of London, 119, 142

botany, study of, 41
    see also herbarizings
Bott, Graham, 233–4
Bowack, John, 119
Bowman, George, 115
Boyle, Robert, 158, 160, 161, 163
Brande, Everard A., 203, 246
Brande, Prof. W.T., 101, 163, 184, 206, 211, 217, 248
Brembre, Sir Nicholas, 22
Bristow, Uriah, 136
British Medical Association, 221
Broad, William, 41, 42, 43
Browne, Edward, 195
Buchanan, Sir George, 233
Buckner, Leonard, 42
Buggs, John, 41, 42, 49, 50
Bullein, William, 26, 41
Burchett, Samuel, 92, 93
Burges, Robert, 85
Burrows, George Man, 195, 196, 200–2, 217
Burton, John, 159
Burton, William, 19
Busby, Ernest, 236

Cadogan, George Henry, Earl Cadogan, 148
Campbell, R., 193
Cargill, Lionel V., 254
Carter, Robert Brudenell, 214, 226
Cawarden, Sir Thomas, 79
Chalstrey, Sir John, 261 2
Chamberlen, Peter, 29, 60
Chandler, John, 134, 136
Channing, John, 134
Charing Cross Hospital, 223
Charitable Company, 247
charity, 245–7
Charles II, 69, 156, 158
Chartered Society of Physiotherapy, 239
Chase, James, 70–1, 72, 165
Chase, John, 51, 52–3, 70
Chase, Stephen, 43, 63
Chattaway, William, 188, 227
Chaucer, Geoffrey, 21
Chelsea Physic Garden, see Physic Garden
Chelsea porcelain, 134
Chemical Operators, see Operators
Chemical Physician, 156
Chemical Society, 216–17
chemistry, see laboratory
chemists and druggists, relations with apothecaries, 193, 196, 217
Cheyne, William, Viscount Newhaven, 120, 125
Chichele, John, 22
cholera, 225

Christie, Agatha, 233
City Parochial Foundation, and Physic Garden, 148, 151
Civil War, and the Society, 57–62
Clarges, Sir Thomas, 59–60
Clarke, Sir John, 70(2)
Clarke, Michael, 163
Clarke, William, 161
clinical pharmacology, 240
Clisbie, George, 84, 85, 114
Cobham, George Brooke, 9th Lord, 77, 79
Cobham, Henry Brooke, 11th Lord, 79–80
Cobham House, London, see Apothecaries' Hall
Cockburn, Dr, 171, 172
Condy (Condee), Francis, 161
Conjoint Examining Board, 225, 227
Considen, Dennis, 181
control and discipline, 23–4, 34
Conyers, John, 66
Cook, Captain James, 180
Cooke, Edward, 34, 43, 50, 60, 86, 154, 158, 178
Cooks' Hall, 67, 83
Cookworthy, William, 172
Cooper, George, 222
Cope, Sir Zachary, 241
Copeman, Dr W.S.C., 105, 241–3, 244
Corn Money, 40
Council of India, 187, 188
Court of Assistants, 38
Court of Examiners, 200, 202, 210, 213
Counden, Charles, 115
Critchley, Dr Macdonald, 240
Cromwell, Oliver, 60–1
Crosby, Sir Thomas Boor, 228–9, 261, 262
Crosse, Thomas, 42, 59
Culpeper, Nicholas, 43, 45, 60
Curtis, William, 136, 138

Dale, Samuel, 130
Dance, George, senior, 130
Dandridge, Francis, 167
Danforth, Samuel, 180
Dangerous Drugs Acts 1920, 1922, 233
Darnelly, Daniel, 37
Darwin, Francis, 150
Davenant, Sir William, 80–1
Davies, Robert P., 188
Davis, Roger, 85
Dawson, Henry, 146
De Hart, Dr Daniell, 180
de Laune, see Laune
Dennison, Reginald, 170, 174
Derkyn, Richard, 16
Dickens, Charles, 221
diplomas, 235–41
dispensaries, and teaching, 223

dispensaries for poor, 51–2, 54
dispensers of medicines, 229–35
distillers, 36
Dodds, Prof. Sir Charles, Bt, 105, 241
Doody, Samuel, 124
drugs, *see* medicines
Dryden, John, poem, 54
Dutch, Cornelius, 168–9

Eason, Michael, 32, 33
East India Company, 170, 173–4, 187
ecclesiastical households, apothecaries to, 20
education, 194, 198
  examinations, 198, 200–16
  see also apprentices
Edward, Prince of Wales (later Edward VIII), 252
Edwards, Carl, 105
Edwards, Richard, 42, 158
Egypt, ancient, apothecaries, 11
Ehret, G.D., 132, 134
electro-therapeutics, 239
Evans, John, 34
Evelyn, John, 123

Faculty of Occupational Medicine, 240
Faculty of the History of Medicine and Pharmacy, 241–5
Fage, Valentine, 63
Fairfax, General Sir Thomas, 60, 61
Farmer, Prof. J.B., 149–50
Faulkner, Thomas, 140–1
fees, for medical advice, 216
Field, Henry, 146, 175, 196
Field, John, 175, 184
Field, Thomas, 163
Fisher, Dr James, 259
Fisher, William Hayes, Baron Downham, 148, 149
Fitzwilliams, Duncan C.L., 247
Fleetwood, Edward, 70
Fones (Fownes), Thomas, 30, 33, 37, 154, 179
Forsyth, William, 135–6
Fortune, Robert, 142
Fowler, Ludwig, 63
Fraternity of St Anthony, 14, 15, 17
Friendly Medical Society (F.M.S.), 194–5, 259

Galen Medal, 250, 251–2
Gape, William, 120
Gardener, Thomas, 167
gardens, 116–17, 119
  see also Physic Garden
Garnier, George, 176
Garnier, Isaac, 165

Garrett, James, 41
Garth, Sir Samuel, poem, 54
Gelsthorp, Peter, 165, 246
General Medical Council (G.M.C.), 206–7, 214, 215, 222, 226, 255
General Phamaceutical Association of Great Britain, 196
general practitioners, 197, 221
genito-urinary medicine, 240
George, Prince (Queen Anne's husband), 167–8, 172
Gerard, John, 41, 43, 117
Gibbons, Revd, 252
Gibbs, James, 130
Gibson, Richard, 165–6
Gilbertus Anglicus, 13
Gillson, Dr William, 249–50
glass, tax on, 196
Glover, Ralph, 34
Goddard, Dr Jonathan, 156
Godfrey, Ambrose (Hanckwitz), 161–3
Godfrey & Cooke, 161, 163
Golden Phoenix, the, 163
Good, John M., 196
Goodenough, Sir William, 254
Gouge, William, 60, 252
Gover, James, 115
Gower, Robert, 165
Graham, Sir James, 222
Gray, Thomas, 41
Great Fire of London 1666, 51, 67–9, 83
Great Plague, *see* plagues
Great Windmill School, 223, 224
Greece, ancient, apothecaries, 11
Green, Lloyd and Adams, 107–8, 109, 110, 111
greenhouses, heated, at the Physic Garden, 120, 122, 123, 128–30
Grey, Sir George, Bt, 222
Grice, John, 19
Griffin, Stephen, 163
Grocers' Company, 14, 15, 17
  and the apothecaries, 22–4, 29–36, 47
  and the new Society, 35
Gwynn, Roger, 30, 35

Hakedy, Richard, 19
Hales, William, 149
Hall, John, 115
Halstead, Henry, 167, 172
Hanckwitz, Ambrose Godfrey, *see* Godfrey, Ambrose
Handey, James, 216
Harle, Edward, 165
Harrison, Dr Edward, 196
Harvey, Dr William, 50, 59
Hatton, Edward, 87–8
Haughton, George, 50, 158

INDEX

Hennell, Henry, 99, 184, 186
Hepburn, Alfred, 238
herbals, 43
herbarizings, 40, 41–3, 117, 134, 138–9, 142, 259
Hermann, Dr Paul, 122, 125
Hexham, John 23
Hicks, Thomas, 34, 41, 43, 50, 158
Higgins, Stephen, 32, 33, 37, 154
Hinton, Anthony, 177–8
Hodges, Nathaniel, 62
Holland, Richard, 50, 158
Holliday, Dr Jonathan, 20
Hong Kong, examinations held, 255
Honorary Diplomas, 252
Honorary Freemen, 252–3
hospitals, medieval, 21
Houghton, John, 64, 118
Hudson, William, 135
Hull, Samuel, 160
Hunter, H.K., 227
Hunter, William, 224
Huxley, Thomas, 248

India, medical supplies to, 173–4, 187
industrial medicine, 239–40
infirmarers, 20
inspections, 23–4, 38, 45, 47, 50, 154
Ireland, apothecaries of, 224–5

Jackson, John Hughlings, 225
James I, 28, 29, 35, 45, 47, 48
    portrait, 28, 85
James II, 70, 71–2
James, James, 65
Jamison, Dr David, 151
Jenner, Sir William, Bt, 225, 248
Jerman, Edward, 83–4
John Keats Memorial Lecture, 259
Johnson, George, 122
Johnson, John, 101
Johnson, Thomas, 41, 42–3, 49, 59, 63, 130
Johnson, William, 156
Jones, Dr John, 70, 85
Joseph the Spicer, 16
Jupp, William, 99

Keats, John, 202–4
Kent, HRH Prince Edward, the Duke of, 109
Kerrison, R.M., 196, 197
Kew, Royal Botanic Gardens, 142
King's College, London, 223–4
King's Spicers, 16–17

laboratory, *see* Apothecaries' Hall
Laboratory Stock, 153, 157, 158, 166, 170, 174

Lambkin, Thomas, and family, 114
Lane, Timothy, 211, 259
Latham, Dr John, 196, 197
Latin, need for, 203, 205
de Laune, Gideon, 29, 30, 31, 33, 37, 38, 45, 80, 81, 154, 158
    bust, 85
    portrait, 44, 67
    death, 60
de Laune, Paul, 60
Lawrence, Richard, 166–7
Layton, Thomas B., 254
Le Fèvre, Nicholas, 155–6, 158
Le Mire, Lewis, 34, 154
lectures, 258–9
Lee, Jonathan, 165
Leiden botanical garden, 122, 125
Licence of the Society of Apothecaries (L.S.A.), 198, 221, 223
Licentiate in Medicine and Surgery of the Society of Apothecaries (L.M.S.S.A.), 227, 236
Lightfoot, Dr Robert, 70–1
Linacre, Thomas, 25
Lindley, John, 141
Linnaeus, Carl, 132
Linnean Society, 119
Lisle, John, 135
Litlar, Richard, 157, 158
livery, *see* Society of Apothecaries
livery companies, scrutiny by Royal Commission 1880–84, 214
Lloyd, Sam, 107
Lobel, Paul, 34
Lock, Thomas, 84, 93
London:
    Black Friars, 43, 45, 75–81; plan, 74
    Black Friars Bridge, 90
    Bucklersbury, 16
    Cobham House, *see* Apothecaries' Hall
    Queen Victoria Street, 92–3
    Water Lane, name change to Black Friars Lane, 104
    Westcheap, 16
    see also Apothecaries' Hall
London Hospital, 223
London School of Medicine for Women (L.S.M.W.), 210
Lord Mayors, *see* Chalstrey, Sir John, *and* Crosby, Sir Thomas Boor
Lorkin, Robert, 42, 43
Lorrimer, John, 61, 62, 82
Lownes, Joliffe, 31, 32
Lynch, Dr Roche, 239

Maccabean Prize, 243
Macdonald, Isabella, 210
Macdonald Critchley Lecture, 259

Magnesia House, 109
Makins, George Hogarth, 187, 248, 249
Manchester, first medical school in the provinces, 223
Martyn, John, 119, 132
Masters of the Society, list, 301–5
Mastery of Midwifery (M.M.S.A.), 239
Mayerne, Dr Theodore, 29, 30, 31, 32, 37, 50, 155
Mead, Dr Richard, 171, 193
Medical Act 1858, 218, 222
Medical Act 1886, 214, 238
Medical Act 1950, 254
Medical Act Amendment Act 1883, 225
medical care of catastrophes, 240
Medical Defence Association, 218–19
medical ethics, 244
medical jurisprudence, 240
Medical Registration Act 1858, 216
medical scholarship, 249
medical schools, 223
Medical Society of London, 194–5
medicine, sixteenth century, 24–5
medicine, right to practice, 55, 153
medicines, schedule, 37
Melmoth, Reuben, 73
Meres, John, 70, 73, 159
Meres, John, junior, 125, 168–9
Merrett, Dr Christopher, 51, 62, 156, 252
Metcalf, Adrian and Francis, 58
Metcalfe, Robert, 37
midwifery, 220, 238–9
Midwives Act 1902, 238
Milk of Sulphur (*lac sulphuris*), 50
Miller, Philip, 126, 127–35, 152
Miller, Robert, 60, 127
Miller & Richard, typefounders, 101
Millington, Sir Thomas, 167
Mills, Peter, 77, 82, 83
Milman, Sir Francis, 197
monasteries, apothecaries to, 20–1
Monkhouse, William, 180–1
de Montpellier family, 16–17
Moore, Francis, 163
Moore, Leslie T., 105
Moore, Thomas, 142, 145
Morer, Robert, 30
Morgan, Edward, 120
Morgan, Hugh, 20, 24, 41
Morris, William, 165
Munden, Thomas, 120
musculoskeletal medicine, 240
Mylne, Robert, 90, 135

National Association of General Practitioners, 221, 222
National Health Insurance Act 1911, 230–1, 234, 254
National Health Service, and the Society, 254
Navy, and medical supplies to, 164–8, 176, 180, 184, 229–30
Navy Stock, 97, 99, 153, 158, 167, 168–72, 173, 174
Neild, Col. F.G., 108
Nestor House, 103, 111
Newcomen, Thomas, 168
Norris, Richard, 93, 95, 97
Nussey, John, 184, 218, 221, 222

Oakley, Edward, 128, 129, 130
Obstetrical Society, 220
Odling, Edward, 60
Operators, Chemical, of Laboratory, 157, 158–9, 160–3
Overbury, Sir Thomas, death, 32

Packe, Christopher, 158
Painter-Stainers' Hall, 37, 38, 75
Paracelsus, 154
Parkinson, John, 34, 37, 41, 42, 43
Pelling, John, 86
Pelling, Walter, 63, 86, 158, 159, 161
Pepperers' Guild, 14–15, 260
Pepys, Samuel, 63, 164, 166
Pereira, Jonathan, 217, 223
Petiver, Jacques, 123, 124–5
Pharmaceutical Society, 105, 216, 217, 219, 231, 232, 234
  School of Pharmacy, 230
Pharmacy Technician, 234
Pharmacopoeia Londinensis, 24, 34, 48–9, 155
Phelps, Robert, 120
Phillipps, Edmond, 30, 33, 34, 37, 154
Phillips, Henry, 85
philosophy of medicine, 245
Physic Garden, Chelsea, 41, 69, 116–52, 159
  catalogue of plants, 124
  charitable status, 148–52
  library, 150
  present situation, 151–2
Physicians, College of, 24, 25, 31, 165, 166, 171
  and Society of Apothecaries, 34–5, 38, 47
  disputes, 47–55
  and Great Plague, 62
  laboratory, 156
  eighteenth and nineteenth centuries, 193, 196, 197–8, 207, 212, 225
physiotherapy, 239
Piggot, Spencer, 120
plagues, 22–3, 51, 57
  Great Plague 1665, 62–6
Plukenet, Dr Leonard, 122–3

INDEX

Poisons and Pharmacy Act 1908, 230
Poisons Amendment Act, 233
Pott, Dr John, 179
Poynter, Dr F.N.L., 242, 243–4
Pratt, Richard, 120, 122
prizes and awards, 248–53
Professional and Linguistic Assessments Board (P.L.A.B.), 256
Prowting, William, 259

Quacks' Charter 1542/43, 25
Quick, William, 30, 32, 33, 34, 41
Quincy, John, 132, 170
Quo Warranto writ against Society, 52, 57, 69–70

Ramadge, Dr, 205–6
Rand, Isaac, 126, 134, 180
Randolph, William, 163
Rawling, Sir Benjamin, 89
Ray, John, 123, 161
Reeve, John, 49
regulatory toxicology, 240
Riche, John, 41
Ridout, John G., 206, 221, 223
Rivers, E.G., 149–50
Roberts, bargewright, 116
Robinson, N.W., 101
Robinson, Thomas, 167
Rogers, Dr Joseph, 250
Rogers Prize, 250–1
Rome, ancient, apothecaries, 11
Roscoe, Professor, 211
Rose, William, 55
Rosewell, Lt-Col William, 51, 59, 114, 119, 158
Ross, Sir Ronald, 252–3
Rowe, William, 218
Rowe & Maw, 109, 110
Rowlandson, Thomas, 194
Royal, title sought for Society, 229
Royal Apothecaries, 20, 22, 33–4
Royal Botanic Gardens, Kew, 142
Royal Botanic Society of London, 143
Royal College of Chemistry, 217
Royal College of General Practitioners, 221, 259
Royal College of Surgeons, 220, 221, 224
Royal Horticultural Society, 143–4
Royal Society, 113, 117–18, 125, 160
Rumler, J.W., 32, 33–4, 58–9, 71, 154
Rusden, Moses, 180
Ryder, Richard, 83

St Amand, James, 52, 53, 70, 71, 167
St Ann's Church, Black Friars, 45, 81
St Bartholomew's Hospital, 223
St Thomas' and Guy's Hospitals, 223

Sambrooke, Peter, 69, 83
Saunders, Martin, 102
Savery, Thomas, 168
Saward, Fanny, 210
Scriveners' Hall, 75
searches, *see* apothecaries: inspections
Selling, John de, 17
Selwyn, Prof. Sydney, 244–5
Semple, Dr R.H., 146
Severn, John, 135
Shakespeare, William, quoted, 26
Shaw, Sir William Fletcher, 238
Shelley, Frederick Farey, 188, 191
Sherard, James, 167, 169, 172
Shiers, George, 34
Ship Money, 57–8
Shirley, William, 180
Shotter, Revd Edward, 244
Sick and Wounded Board, Commissioners, 168, 172
Simons, William, 200–1, 221
simpling days, *see* herbarizings
Sloane, Sir Hans, 118, 122, 124–5, 126, 128, 130, 131–2, 161
 statue, 130
Smith, Adam, 193
Smith, Henry, 125
Smyth, George, 202
Snow, John, 225
Society of Apothecaries, 17–18
 charities, 245–7
 Charter 1617, 33–4
 Charter surrendered, 69–70
 Charter 1685, 70
 coat of arms, 36, 43
 control and discipline, 23–4, 34
 control of the medical profession, 197–8
 conversaziones, 211
 Court of Assistants, 38
 finances, 38
 herbarizings, 40, 41–3, 117, 134, 138–9, 142, 259
 livery, 38, 40, 41, 43
 livery dinners, 259
 Masters, list of, 301–5
 membership, 259
 the profession and the City, 254–62
 reform, 220–9
 services, 45
 treasures, 37–8, 61, 69, 105
Society of Chemical Physicians, 156–7
de Soda, Anthony, 30
Solander, Dr, 136
Solby, George, 164
Sotherton, John, 41
Sowersby, Leonard, 84–5
Spectacle Makers' Company, 259
Spicer, Bartholomew, 16

311

spicers, 13–14, 15
sports medicine, 240
Stahl, Peter, 160
Staphorst, Nicholas, 119, 161
Star Chamber, 36, 49, 50
steam engines, 168–9
stock companies, 93, 153, 174
   see also Navy Stock; United Stock
Strickland Goodall, Dr Joseph, 251
Stringer, Samuel, 158–9
Strype, John, 88
surgeon-apothecaries, 195–6, 197
surgery, and apothecaries, 21
surgical scholarship, 249

Talbor (Tabor), apothecary, 52
Tallow Chandlers' Company, 114
Taylor, Enid, 255
Teale, Isaac, 60, 165
Temple Coffee-house Club, 118
theatre, in Black Friars, 80–1
Thompson, Anthony Todd, 196
Thorne, Isabel, 210
trade:
   expansion of, 174–6
   dwindling, 188–91
Tradescant family, 41, 117
tropical medicine, 238
Turner, Dr William, 41
Turners' Company, 259

von Uffenbach, German traveller, 124, 163
United Examining Board, 256
United Stock, 101, 103, 183–7, 188, 227
University Dispensary (College Hospital), 223
unlicensed practitioners, 216–19
Upton, Archer Mowbray, 227
Upton, J.R., 196, 227
Upton, Nathaniel, 64
Upton, R.B., 218, 221

Wakley, Thomas, 205, 218, 221, 222
de Walden, Thomas, 17

Wallis, Thomas, 42
Walter, John, 101
Warburton Committee 1834, 206, 220, 221–2
Ward, Nathaniel Bagshaw, 142, 145, 186
Wardian cases, 142
Warington, Robert, 186, 217
Warner, Richard, 132, 134
Warren, Thomas, 54
Watson, Sir William, 195
Watts, John, 122, 123
Weale, Job, 41, 42, 50, 158
Webb, Abraham, 61
Wells, Sir William, 103, 104
Weston, William, 21
Wharton, Dr Thomas, 252
Wheatley, Nicholas, 114
Wheeler, Charles L., 145
Wheeler, Thomas, and family, 101, 138, 140
White, Surgeon John, 181
Whittet, T.D., 234–5
Whittle, Richard, 60, 165
Wilford, Thomas, 163
William the Spicer, 16
William III, 72–3
Williamson, Henry, 180
Willson, Dr A. Rivers, 227
Winthrop, John, 178–9
Wolstenholme, Sir Gordon, 244
women:
   first doctors, 207–10
   Freemen, 254–5
Wood, Frederick, 225
Woodwark, Sir Stanley, 104, 254
Wren, Sir Christopher, 67, 69, 83
Wyatt, George, 96, 135
Wyncke, Tobias, 34, 37
Wyon, William, 248

Yardley, Ralph, 34
Yonge, James, 161
Young, John, 82, 85, 86, 90
Young, Roger, 41

This Indenture

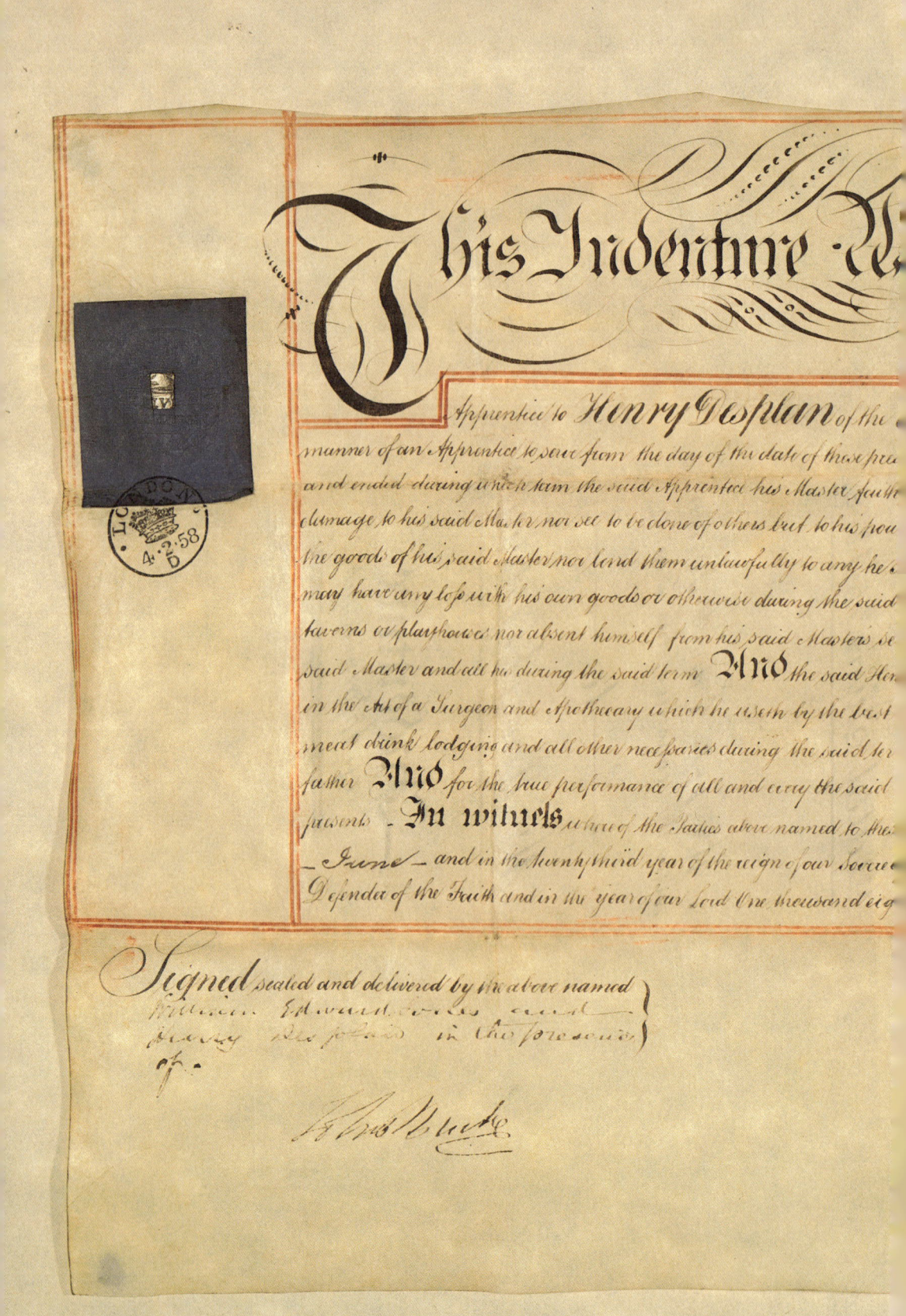

Apprentice to Henry Desplan of the
manner of an Apprentice to serve from the day of the date of these pres[ents]
and ended during which term the said Apprentice his Master faithf[ully]
damage to his said Master nor see to be done of others but to his pow[er]
the goods of his said Master nor lend them unlawfully to any he
may have any loss with his own goods or otherwise during the said
taverns or playhouses nor absent himself from his said Masters se[rvice]
said Master and all he during the said term **And** the said Hen[ry]
in the Art of a Surgeon and Apothecary which he useth by the best
meat drink lodging and all other necessaries during the said ter[m]
father **And** for the true performance of all and every the said
presents **In witness** whereof the Parties above named to thes[e]
— June — and in the twenty third year of the reign of our Sovere[ign]
Defender of the Faith and in the year of our Lord One thousand eig[ht]

Signed sealed and delivered by the above named
William Edward ____ and
Henry Desplan in the presence
of:—